CW00346803

EMPOWER

SECOND EDITION

TEACHER'S BOOK
WITH DIGITAL PACK

A2
ELEMENTARY

Tim Foster with Ruth Gairns, Stuart Redman, Wayne Rimmer, Lynda Edwards and Julian Oakley

Shaftesbury Road, Cambridge CB2 8EA, United Kingdom

One Liberty Plaza, 20th Floor, New York, NY 10006, USA

477 Williamstown Road, Port Melbourne, VIC 3207, Australia

314–321, 3rd Floor, Plot 3, Splendor Forum, Jasola District Centre, New Delhi – 110025, India

103 Penang Road, #05–06/07, Visioncrest Commercial, Singapore 238467

Cambridge University Press & Assessment is a department of the University of Cambridge.

We share the University's mission to contribute to society through the pursuit of education, learning and research at the highest international levels of excellence.

www.cambridge.org
Information on this title: www.cambridge.org/9781108962049

© Cambridge University Press & Assessment 2022

This publication is in copyright. Subject to statutory exception and to the provisions of relevant collective licensing agreements, no reproduction of any part may take place without the written permission of Cambridge University Press & Assessment.

First published 2022

20 19 18 17 16 15 14 13 12 11 10 9 8 7 6 5 4

Printed in Poland by Opolgraf

A catalogue record for this publication is available from the British Library

ISBN 978-1-108-96526-2 Elementary Student's Book with eBook
ISBN 978-1-108-96199-8 Elementary Student's Book with Digital Pack
ISBN 978-1-108-96202-5 Elementary Workbook with Answers
ISBN 978-1-108-96203-2 Elementary Workbook without Answers
ISBN 978-1-108-96200-1 Elementary Combo A with Digital Pack
ISBN 978-1-108-96201-8 Elementary Combo B with Digital Pack
ISBN 978-1-108-96204-9 Elementary Teacher's Book with Digital Pack
ISBN 978-1-108-96527-9 Elementary Presentation Plus
ISBN 978-1-109-11876-7 Elementary Student's Book with Digital Pack, Academic Skills and Reading Plus

Additional resources for this publication at www.cambridge.org/empower

Cambridge University Press & Assessment has no responsibility for the persistence or accuracy of URLs for external or third-party internet websites referred to in this publication and does not guarantee that any content on such websites is, or will remain, accurate or appropriate. Information regarding prices, travel timetables, and other factual information given in this work is correct at the time of first printing but Cambridge University Press & Assessment does not guarantee the accuracy of such information thereafter.

Contents

Teaching Notes

CAMBRIDGE

EMPOWER SECOND EDITION is a six-level general English course for adult and young adult learners, taking students from beginner to advanced level (CEFR A1 to C1). *Empower* combines course content from Cambridge University Press with validated assessment from the experts at Cambridge Assessment English.

Empower's unique mix of engaging classroom materials and reliable assessment enables learners to make consistent and measurable progress.

Content you love.
Assessment you
can trust.

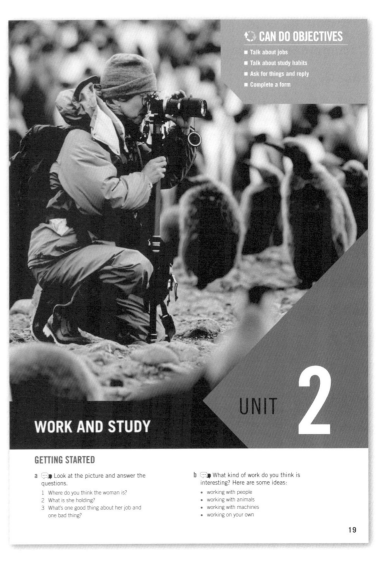

Better Learning with *Empower*

Better Learning is our simple approach where **insights** we've gained from research have helped shape **content** that drives **results**.

Learner engagement

1 Content that informs and motivates

Insights
Sustained motivation is key to successful language learning and skills development.

Content
Clear learning goals, thought-provoking images, texts and speaking activities, plus video content to arouse curiosity.

Results
Content that surprises, entertains and provokes an emotional response, helping teachers to deliver motivating and memorable lessons.

Textbook spread showing Unit 2A "SHE LOVES HER JOB" with reading about Gabby Scampone, "GATOR GIRL", vocabulary on jobs, grammar on present simple positive and negative, and speaking activities.

2 Personalised and relevant

Insights
Language learners benefit from frequent opportunities to personalise their responses.

Content
Personalisation tasks in every unit make the target language more meaningful to the individual learner.

Results
Personal responses make learning more memorable and inclusive, with all students participating in spontaneous spoken interaction.

> *There are so many adjectives to describe such a wonderful series, but in my opinion it's very reliable, practical, and modern.*
>
> **Zenaide Brianez, Director of Studies, Instituto da Língua Inglesa, Brazil**

Measurable progress

1 Assessment you can trust

Insights
Tests developed and validated by Cambridge Assessment English, the world leaders in language assessment, to ensure they are accurate and meaningful.

Content
End-of-unit tests, mid- and end-of-course competency tests and personalised CEFR test report forms provide reliable information on progress with language skills.

Results
Teachers can see learners' progress at a glance, and learners can see measurable progress, which leads to greater motivation.

Results of an impact study showing % improvement of Reading levels, based on global *Empower* students' scores over one year.

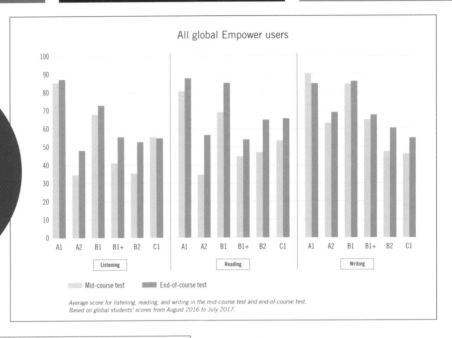

Average score for listening, reading, and writing in the mid-course test and end-of-course test.
Based on global students' scores from August 2016 to July 2017.

We started using the tests provided with Empower *and our students started showing better results from this point until now.*

Kristina Ivanova, Director of Foreign Language Training Centre, ITMO University, Saint Petersburg, Russia

2 Evidence of impact

Insights
Schools and universities need to show that they are evaluating the effectiveness of their language programmes.

Content
Empower (British English) impact studies have been carried out in various countries, including Russia, Brazil, Turkey and the UK, to provide evidence of positive impact and progress.

Results
Colleges and universities have demonstrated a significant improvement in language level between the mid- and end-of-course tests, as well as a high level of teacher satisfaction with *Empower*.

Manageable learning

1 Mobile friendly

Insights
Learners expect online content to be mobile friendly but also flexible and easy to use on any digital device.

Content
Empower provides easy access to Digital Workbook content that works on any device and includes practice activities with audio.

Results
Digital Workbook content is easy to access anywhere, and produces meaningful and actionable data so teachers can track their students' progress and adapt their lesson accordingly.

> *I had been studying English for ten years before university, and I didn't succeed. But now with* Empower *I know my level of English has changed.*

Nikita, *Empower* Student, ITMO University, Saint Petersburg, Russia

2 Corpus-informed

Insights
Corpora can provide valuable information about the language items learners are able to learn successfully at each CEFR level.

Content
Two powerful resources – Cambridge Corpus and English Profile – informed the development of the *Empower* course syllabus and the writing of the materials.

Results
Learners are presented with the target language they are able to incorporate and use at the right point in their learning journey. They are not overwhelmed with unrealistic learning expectations.

Rich in practice

1 Language in use

Insights
It is essential that learners are offered frequent and manageable opportunities to practise the language they have been focusing on.

Content
Throughout the *Empower* Student's Book, learners are offered a wide variety of practice activities, plenty of controlled practice and frequent opportunities for communicative spoken practice.

Results
Meaningful practice makes new language more memorable and leads to more efficient progress in language acquisition.

2 Beyond the classroom

> *There are plenty of opportunities for personalisation.*
>
> Elena Pro,
> Teacher, EOI
> de San Fernando
> de Henares,
> Spain

Insights
Progress with language learning often requires work outside of the classroom, and different teaching models require different approaches.

Content
Empower is available with a print workbook, online practice, documentary-style videos that expose learners to real-world English, plus additional resources with extra ideas and fun activities.

Results
This choice of additional resources helps teachers to find the most effective ways to motivate their students both inside and outside the classroom.

Unit overview

Unit Opener

Getting started page – Clear learning objectives to give an immediate sense of purpose.

↓

Lessons A and B

Grammar and Vocabulary – Input and practice of core grammar and vocabulary, plus a mix of skills.

— **Digital Workbook (online, mobile):** Grammar and Vocabulary

↓

Lesson C

Everyday English – Functional language in common, everyday situations.

— **Digital Workbook (online, mobile):** Listening and Speaking

↓

Unit Progress Test

↓

Lesson D

Integrated Skills – Practice of all four skills, with a special emphasis on writing.

— **Digital Workbook (online, mobile):** Reading and Writing

↓

Review

Extra practice of grammar, vocabulary and pronunciation. Also a 'Review your progress' section for students to reflect on the unit.

↓

Mid- / End-of-course test

↓

Additional practice

Further practice is available for outside of the class with these components.

Digital Workbook (online, mobile)

Workbook (printed)

Components

Resources – Available on cambridgeone.org

- Audio
- Video
- Unit Progress Tests (print)
- Unit Progress Tests (online)

- Mid- and end-of-course assessment (print)
- Mid- and end-of-course assessment (online)

- Digital Workbook (online)
- Photocopiable Grammar, Vocabulary and Pronunciation worksheets

Getting Started

Striking and unusual images arouse curiosity.

Clear learning objectives give an immediate sense of purpose.

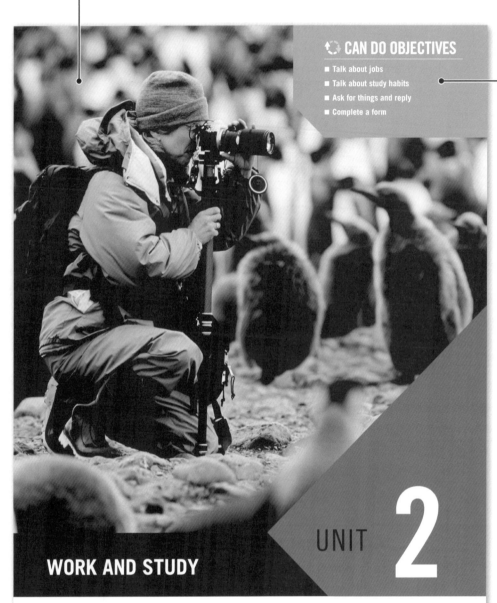

✪ CAN DO OBJECTIVES

- Talk about jobs
- Talk about study habits
- Ask for things and reply
- Complete a form

WORK AND STUDY

UNIT **2**

GETTING STARTED

a 💬 Look at the picture and answer the questions.
1 Where do you think the woman is?
2 What is she holding?
3 What's one good thing about her job and one bad thing?

b 💬 What kind of work do you think is interesting? Here are some ideas:
- working with people
- working with animals
- working with machines
- working on your own

19

Activities promote emotional engagement and a personal response.

Lessons A and B
Grammar and Vocabulary and a mix of skills

'Teach off the page'
A straightforward approach and clear lesson flow help to minimise preparation time.

Clear goals
Each lesson starts with a clear, practical, and achievable learning goal, creating an immediate sense of purpose.

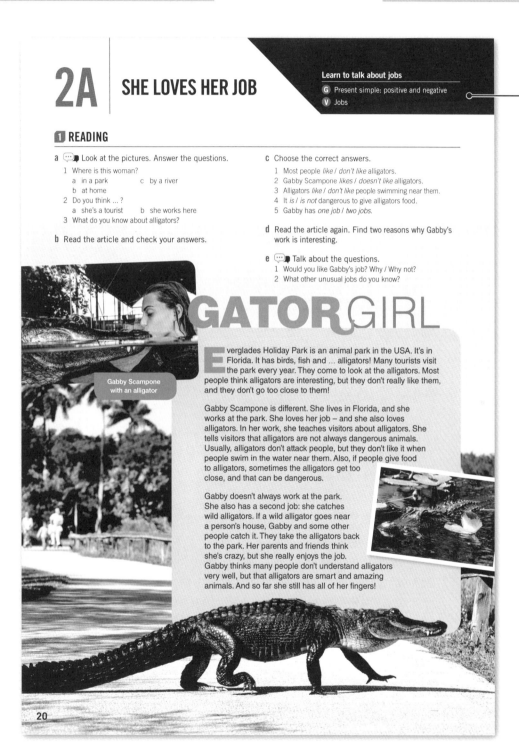

2A | SHE LOVES HER JOB

Learn to talk about jobs
G Present simple: positive and negative
V Jobs

1 READING

a Look at the pictures. Answer the questions.
1 Where is this woman?
  a in a park   c by a river
  b at home
2 Do you think ... ?
  a she's a tourist   b she works here
3 What do you know about alligators?

b Read the article and check your answers.

c Choose the correct answers.
1 Most people *like / don't like* alligators.
2 Gabby Scampone *likes / doesn't like* alligators.
3 Alligators *like / don't like* people swimming near them.
4 It *is / is not* dangerous to give alligators food.
5 Gabby has *one job / two jobs*.

d Read the article again. Find two reasons why Gabby's work is interesting.

e Talk about the questions.
1 Would you like Gabby's job? Why / Why not?
2 What other unusual jobs do you know?

GATOR GIRL

Everglades Holiday Park is an animal park in the USA. It's in Florida. It has birds, fish and ... alligators! Many tourists visit the park every year. They come to look at the alligators. Most people think alligators are interesting, but they don't really like them, and they don't go too close to them!

Gabby Scampone is different. She lives in Florida, and she works at the park. She loves her job – and she also loves alligators. In her work, she teaches visitors about alligators. She tells visitors that alligators are not always dangerous animals. Usually, alligators don't attack people, but they don't like it when people swim in the water near them. Also, if people give food to alligators, sometimes the alligators get too close, and that can be dangerous.

Gabby doesn't always work at the park. She also has a second job: she catches wild alligators. If a wild alligator goes near a person's house, Gabby and some other people catch it. They take the alligators back to the park. Her parents and friends think she's crazy, but she really enjoys the job. Gabby thinks many people don't understand alligators very well, but that alligators are smart and amazing animals. And so far she still has all of her fingers!

Gabby Scampone with an alligator

20

Manageable learning

The syllabus is informed by English Profile and the Cambridge English Corpus. Students will learn the most relevant and useful language at the most appropriate point in their learning journey. The target language is benchmarked to the CEFR.

2 VOCABULARY Jobs

a Match words 1–9 with pictures a–i.

1 ☐ nurse   4 ☐ dentist   7 ☐ cleaner
2 ☐ shop assistant   5 ☐ pilot   8 ☐ photographer
3 ☐ police officer   6 ☐ engineer   9 ☐ taxi driver

b ▶ 02.01 **Pronunciation** Listen to the words and underline the stressed syllable.

police officer   engineer   photographer   dentist

c 🗨 Complete the sentences with jobs from 2a. Talk about your answers.

1 A(n) _____ has a dangerous job.
2 A(n) _____ has an easy job.
3 A(n) _____ has an exciting job.
4 The pay for a(n) _____ isn't very good.

d ≫ Now go to Vocabulary Focus 2A on p. 163 for more jobs vocabulary.

Rich in practice

Clear signposts to **Grammar Focus** and **Vocabulary Focus** sections offer extra support and practice.

3 GRAMMAR
Present simple: positive and negative

a ▶ 02.03 Look at the sentences from 1b and complete them with the verbs from the box. Listen and check.

catches come doesn't don't (x2) go attack think work works

	I / we / you / they	he / she / it
+	Tourists _____ to look at the alligators. Her parents _____ she's crazy.	She _____ at Everglades Holiday Park. She _____ wild alligators.
–	They _____ too close to them. Alligators _____ _____ people.	Gabby _____ always _____ at the park.

b Underline more present simple verbs in the text in 1b. Make two lists: positive and negative forms.

c ≫ Now go to Grammar Focus 2A on p. 140.

d Underline the verbs in sentences 1–2.

1 She loves her job.
2 She catches wild alligators.

e ▶ 02.05 **Pronunciation** Which verb in 3d has an extra syllable when we add the letter -s? Listen and check.

f Underline the correct answers.

1 After the sounds /z/, /s/, /dʒ/ (spelled j), /ʃ/ (spelled sh) and /tʃ/ (spelled ch), we *add / don't add* an extra syllable.
2 We *add / don't add* an extra syllable after other sounds.

g ▶ 02.06 Listen to these verbs. Tick (✓) the verbs that have an extra syllable.

☐ works   ☐ eats   ☐ teaches
☐ finishes   ☐ listens   ☐ stops
☐ drives   ☐ uses   ☐ watches

h ≫ **Communication 2A** Student A: Go to p. 130. Student B: Go to p. 133.

4 SPEAKING

a Think about your job or the job of someone you know. Write four sentences about the job: two positive (+) and two negative (–). Use the verbs in the box.

work drive have like study
speak go start leave know

+ I start work at 7:00 in the morning.
– I don't drive to work.

b 🗨 Tell your partner your sentences. Can they guess the job?

c Tell other students about your partner's job. Can they guess it?

She starts work at …

Regular speaking activities

Frequent speaking stages get students talking throughout the lesson.

Learner engagement
Engaging images and texts motivate students to respond personally. This makes learning more memorable and gives learners ownership of the language.

2B | DO YOU WORRY ABOUT EXAMS?

Learn to talk about study habits
G Present simple: questions and short answers
V Studying; Time

1 READING

a Ask and answer the questions.
1 Are you good at exams?
2 Do you worry about exams and tests?
3 Do you study a lot for an exam or test?

b Read comments 1–3 in the online chat and match them with pictures a–c.

c Read the comments again and answer the questions with a partner.
1 Which study habits are ... ?
• useful • funny
2 Put the study habits in the order you want to try them from 1 (really want to try) to 3 (don't want to try).

2 VOCABULARY Studying

a Look at the underlined words in questions 1–7. Match them with pictures d–j below.
1 Do you have a break in the middle of your English lesson?
2 Do you have a timetable for your study routine?
3 Do you take notes when you read something in English?
4 Do you get good marks in English tests?
5 How many weeks is a term at your school?
6 Do you have an exam at the end of the year?
7 Do you and your friends enjoy your studies?

b Match the words in the box with 1–4. You can use some of the words more than once.

get	good	pass	bad	take	fail

1 an exam   3 notes
2 marks   4 a test

c Ask and answer the questions in 2a.

CHAT Home Forums Articles Archives

Exam stress!
Hi guys! I have a big exam on Friday. It's really hard to study. I read my study notes for an hour and then I watch really bad TV programmes! What about you? Do you worry about exams? What are your study habits? MIMI23

1 Yeah, I hate tests. They're really difficult and I can't always remember everything. I need to study every day and take a lot of notes. It's not easy, but it helps to listen to R&B music – really loud! It helps me think.
SOUL BOY2 REPLY

2 I agree – exams and tests are really, really hard. In my study breaks I play with my pet cat. Some people say that animals stop stress and relax people. I think it's true, well, for me it is! Everybody needs a cat to help them study!
CAT LOVER5 REPLY

3 I think it helps to have a good study routine. I make a study timetable and that helps me to pass my exams. I always plan a lot of breaks and have a cup of tea and something small to eat. I don't want to get tired when I study! But the breaks are only short – about five or ten minutes. Then I go back to studying hard for one or two hours. Good marks come from a lot of hard work!
BOOKWORM8 REPLY

22

UNIT 2

Tania and Jack

3 LISTENING

a ▶02.07 Jack talks to Tania about her study habits. Listen and tick (✓) the things they talk about.
1 ☐ places to study   3 ☐ exams
2 ☐ hours of study   4 ☐ free time

b ▶02.07 Listen again. Complete the information about Tania's studies.
• Part-time or full-time student?   • When?
• Hours a week?   • Where?

4 VOCABULARY Time

a Match the times that Tania talks about with the clocks.
1 Usually at **half past eight** ...
2 ... last night at a **quarter past eleven**.

 a
 b

b Complete the sentences with the words in the box.

to	past	o'clock	half

1 four _____   3 (a) quarter _____ four
2 _____ past four   4 (a) quarter _____ five

c Now go to Vocabulary Focus 2B on p. 164 for more practice with time vocabulary.

5 GRAMMAR Present simple: questions

a ▶02.09 Look at the questions. Which is correct? Listen and check.
1 You study full-time or part-time?
2 Do you study full-time or part-time?
3 Study you full-time or part-time?

b Complete the questions with one word.
_____ ... you study engineering?
_____ ... they like tests?

c ▶02.10 Jack asks Tania about her daughter, Ellie. Listen and complete the information about Ellie's studies.
• Hours a week?
• When?
• Where?

d Read the question Jack asks Tania.
Does she study more before an exam?
Look at the questions in 5b. How are they different? Why?

e Now go to Grammar Focus 2B on p. 140.

f ▶02.12 Put the questions in the correct order. Listen and check.
1 a week / do you study / hours / how many ?
2 study grammar / or vocabulary / do you ?
3 you / when / study / do ?
4 study / do / where / you ?

g ▶02.12 Pronunciation Notice the pronunciation of *do you* in each question. Can you hear both words clearly?

6 SPEAKING

a Look at the questions in 5f. Write another question about studying.

b Ask and answer your question in 6a.

c Do you have any new ideas about studying now?

Natalia studies very early in the morning because she isn't very tired. I think it's a good idea, but I prefer to sleep!

Spoken outcome
Each A and B lesson ends with a practical spoken outcome, so learners can use language immediately.

23

Lesson C
Effective real-world spoken communication

Comprehensive approach to speaking skills
A unique combination of language input, pronunciation, and speaking strategies offers a comprehensive approach to speaking skills.

Everyday English
Thorough coverage of functional language for common everyday situations helps learners to communicate effectively in the real world.

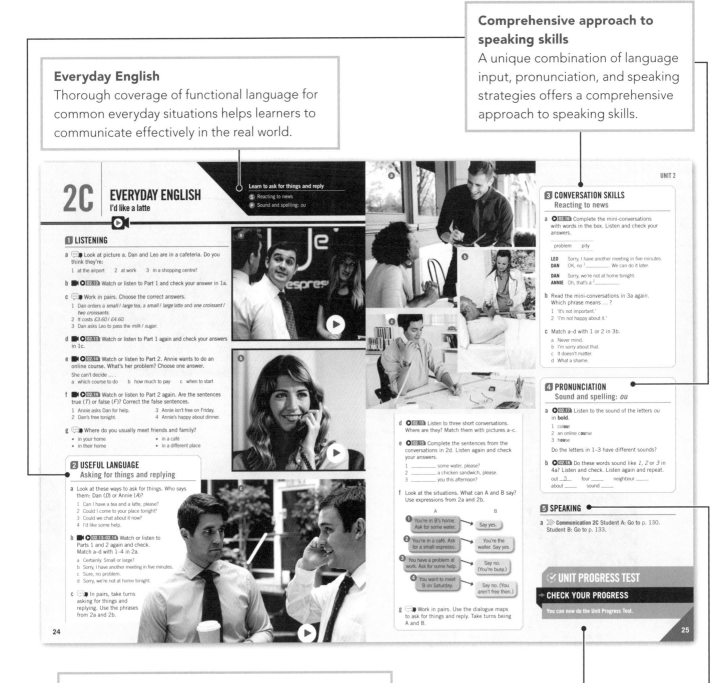

Everyday English video
Language is showcased through high-quality video, which shows language clearly and in context.

Unit Progress Test
Learners are now ready to do the Unit Progress Test, developed by Cambridge Assessment English.

Spoken outcome
Each C lesson ends with a practical spoken outcome.

Lesson D
Integrated skills with a special focus on writing

Skills for writing
The D lessons are highly communicative and cover all four skills, with a special focus on writing. They also recycle and consolidate the core language from the A, B and C lessons.

Personal response
Clear model texts on which students can base their own writing are provided.

2D SKILLS FOR WRITING
I need English for my job

Learn to complete a form
W Spelling

1 SPEAKING AND LISTENING

a 💬 Why do you want to study English?
- to get a good job
- to meet new friends
- for travel and tourism
- to study something in English
- a different reason

b ▶ 02.19 Listen to three International College students talk about where they're from and their reasons for studying English. Underline the correct answers.

I'm from *Acapulco / Mexico City* and I need English for my *job / studies*. ❶

Daniela

I'm from *Riyadh / Jeddah* and I need English for my *job / studies*. ❷

Said

I'm from *Krakow / Warsaw* and I need English for my *job / studies*. ❸

Justyna

c ▶ 02.19 Listen again and complete the table with the words in the box.

grammar   the lessons   the teacher
reading and writing   listening   the timetable

	Likes at the college	Needs to improve
Daniela		
Said		
Justyna		

d 💬 Talk about the questions with other students.
1 What do you need to improve in English?
2 Why is this important for you?

e ▶ 02.20 Listen to Kate talk about a competition at International College. What can you win?

f ▶ 02.20 Listen again. Answer the questions.
1 Can students who don't go to International College enter the competition?
2 Is it OK to use a computer for the entry form?
3 Where can students get entry forms?

26

2 READING

a Look at the information about Daniela. Complete Part 1 of the form. Can you remember her nationality?

✉ 📝 ☆ 🏳   ⊗

From: EIC Student Care
To: danielar@supermail.com

Dear Daniela

We're looking forward to welcoming you to International College on 6th July.

You will be in class P1 and your teacher will be Kate Marks. We hope …

🌐 INTERNATIONAL COLLEGE COMPETITION ENTRY FORM

Part 1
First name:
Last name: Romero
Gender: ☐ female ☐ male
Nationality:
Mobile (UK): 074822 294576
Email address:
Your class:
Course start date:

Part 2
Why is English important for you?

I work as a(n) ¹_____ in Mexico City. I love my job except for the ²_____! Every day they speak to me and ask me for information. I can't understand them and it is difficult for me to answer. English is important for me because it helps me do my ³_____ well.

What do you want to improve in your English?

I think my speaking in English is OK for my level. But ⁴_____ and understanding is still very difficult for me. I really want to stay an extra month at your school and improve my listening.

b Read Part 2 of Daniela's form. Complete it.

c ▶ 02.21 Listen to Daniela again and check your answers.

Receptive skills development
Clearly staged tasks practise and develop listening and reading skills while supporting learners' understanding of texts.

Comprehensive approach to writing skills
A clear focus on key aspects of writing helps develop effective real-world writing skills.

Staged for success
Careful staging and scaffolding generate successful outcomes.

3 WRITING SKILLS Spelling

a Read Daniela's first draft of her entry form. Cover p. 26. Look at the example spelling problem. Find eight more spelling problems.

b Tick (✓) when it's important to have correct spelling.
1 ☐ a first draft of a text
2 ☐ a final draft of a text
3 ☐ a text other people read
4 ☐ a text only you read

c Find and correct a spelling mistake in each sentence.
1 I really love swimming in the see.
2 Can you please right your name on the form?
3 I don't no the answer to this question.
4 Can you speak up? I can't here you.
5 Where can I bye bread?

d In what way are the incorrect and correct words in 3c the same?

4 WRITING

a Complete the form with your information.

b Use your ideas in 1d to write answers to the questions in Part 2.

c Swap forms with another student. Are your ideas in Part 2 the same?

INTERNATIONAL COLLEGE COMPETITION ENTRY FORM

Part 2

Why is English important for you?

I work as a trafic traffic police offiser in Mexico City. I love my job except for the toorists! Every day they speak to me and ask me for informashion. I can't understand them and it is dificult for me to anser. English is important for me becos it helps me do my job well.

What do you want to improve in your English?

I think my speaking in English is OK for my level. I also find reading and writing quite easy. But listning and understanding is still very hard for me. I really want to stay an extra month at your scool and improve my listening.

INTERNATIONAL COLLEGE COMPETITION ENTRY FORM

Part 1

First name: _____
Last name: _____
Gender: ☐ female ☐ male
Nationality: _____
Mobile (UK): _____
Email address: _____
Your class now: _____
Course start date: _____

Part 2

Why is English important for you?
_____

What do you want to improve in your English?
_____

27

Written outcome
Each D lesson ends with a practical written outcome, so learners can put new language into practice right away.

Personal response
Frequent opportunities for personal response make learning more memorable.

Review and Extension
Extra practice of grammar and
vocabulary is provided.

UNIT 2
Review and extension

1 GRAMMAR

a Complete the text with the correct form of the verb in brackets.

I'm a university student, but I ¹_____ (work) in a clothes shop every weekend. On Saturday I ²_____ (start) work at 9:00 am, but on Sunday I ³_____ (not start) until 11:00 am. My sister's a nurse, so she ⁴_____ (not have) a normal timetable. She sometimes ⁵_____ (work) all night, but she ⁶_____ (not like) it. My parents are both teachers, so they ⁷_____ (work) from Monday to Friday.

b Write possible questions for the answers.

1 **A** What _____? **B** I'm a receptionist.
2 **A** Do _____? **B** No, I don't. I work in a hospital.
3 **A** Do _____? **B** Yes, I do. It's great.
4 **A** When _____? **B** I start at 9 o'clock in the morning.
5 **A** Does _____? **B** Yes, he does. My husband is a teacher.
6 **A** Where _____? **B** He works in a local school.
7 **A** Does _____? **B** Yes, he does. He loves it.

c 💬 Practise the conversation in 1b with a partner. Then answer about your own life.

2 VOCABULARY

a Put the letters in brackets in the correct order to complete the job.

1 n _____ e (s r u)
2 d _____ t (t e i s n)
3 p _____ t (l o i)
4 e _____ r (n n i e g e)
5 c _____ r (e e n a l)
6 p _____ r (o o h e h p r a t g)

b Write the times in words.

10:15 – (a) quarter past ten *or* ten fifteen
1 11:30   3 6:00   5 2:40
2 12:45   4 8:15   6 5:20

c Match 1–5 with a–e to complete the sentences.

1 Read the text and take
2 I'm not worried because I usually get good
3 I hope we have
4 He is worried because he often fails
5 I need to study for the end-of-

a a break soon because I'm tired.
b important exams.
c notes on a piece of paper.
d term test next week.
e marks in tests.

3 WORDPOWER work

a Match sentences 1–3 with pictures a–c.
1 I **work in** a hospital.
2 I **work for** Larkin Computers.
3 I **work as** a receptionist.

b Look at the phrases in **bold** in 3a. Match them with 1–3.
1 the job I do
2 the place of work
3 the company

c Is *work* a verb or a noun in sentences 1–5?
1 I start **work** at 8:00 am each day.
2 She leaves **work** at about 6:00 pm.
3 I can't talk to you now – I'm at **work**.
4 I'm an actor, but I'm out of **work** at the moment.
5 They go to **work** very early in the morning.

d Which *work* phrase in 3c do we use when … ?
a we don't have a job
b we are at the place we work

e Put the word in brackets in the correct place in the sentence.
1 He works a nurse at night. (as)
2 We all work at 6:00 pm. (start)
3 She'd like a job because now she's of work. (out)
4 She's a photographer and works *The Times*. (for)
5 When I'm work, I have no free time. (at)
6 We both work a large office in the city centre. (in)

f Write four sentences about people you know. Use *work* in different ways.
My brother works in a shoe shop in the city centre.

↻ REVIEW YOUR PROGRESS

How well did you do in this unit? Write 3, 2 or 1 for each objective.
3 = very well   2 = well   1 = not so well

I CAN ...	
talk about jobs	☐
talk about study habits	☐
ask for things and reply	☐
complete a form.	☐

Wordpower
Vocabulary
extension recycles
the vocabulary.

Documentary video
Engaging video
documentaries
provide students
with further
opportunities to
explore the themes
of the unit.

Review Your Progress
helps students reflect on
their success.

28

Each unit links to additional sections at the back of the book
for more grammar, vocabulary, and speaking practice.

Grammar Focus

Provides an explanation of the grammar presented in the unit,
along with exercises for students to practise.

Vocabulary Focus

Extends and consolidates the vocabulary.

Communication Plus

Provides a series of communication activities
for each unit, providing additional opportunities
for students to practise their speaking.

Empower Methodology

A Learner-Centred Approach

Empower, with its unique mix of learning and assessment, places students and their needs at the centre of the learning process. This learner-centred approach also applies to the course methodology – the Student's Book and the additional resources provide a range of classroom materials that motivate learners, address their language needs, and facilitate the development of their skills. This wide range of materials also means different learning preferences are catered to in each unit of the course. It provides teachers with flexibility with different learner groups.

Meeting the Needs of Learners at Different Levels

Supporting the Teacher

Empower also supports the teacher with classroom methodology that is familiar and easy to use, and at the same time is flexible and creative. A number of key methodological principles underpin the course, enhancing the interface between learners and their learning, and between students and teachers. *Empower*:

1 encourages learner engagement
2 delivers manageable learning
3 is rich in practice
4 provides a comprehensive approach to productive skills.

Measurable Progress

Empower includes a uniquely reliable assessment package developed by test experts at Cambridge Assessment English. This allows teachers and learners to measure progress and determine learners' strengths and needs. Not only do learners feel more motivated when they can see they are making progress, but they are then able to target and address specific learning needs.

Key Methodological Principles

1 Learner engagement

Getting Started

Each unit begins with a Getting Started page, designed to engage students from the very start of the unit – leading to greater motivation and more successful learning. It does this in the following ways:

- Striking images take an unusual perspective on the theme – this raises curiosity, prompts ideas and questions in the mind of the learner, and stimulates them to want to communicate.
- Speaking activities prompt a personal response – exploring beyond the surface of the image – while providing a cognitive and linguistic challenge for the student and a diagnostic opportunity for the teacher.

Remarkable texts, audio and video

Throughout the course, learners encounter a range of **reading texts**, along with **audio and video**. The texts have been carefully selected to appeal to learners from a variety of cultural backgrounds. The topics will inform, amuse, surprise, entertain, raise questions, arouse curiosity and empathy and provoke an emotional response. The texts, audio and video in *Empower* provide learners with new insights and perspectives on a variety of topics. By using a varied range of spoken and written contexts, students are consistently motivated to engage with the target grammar and vocabulary.

Frequent opportunities for personal and critical response

There are frequent opportunities to contribute personal views, experiences and knowledge when discussing each lesson's themes. Every lesson includes regular activities that encourage learners to respond personally to the content of the texts and images. These include **personalisation** tasks which make the target language in every unit meaningful to the individual learner. Many activities also involve some kind of critical response to the content of texts. This helps develop students' critical thinking skills as well as gives them further speaking practice.

Independent learning

In order to make progress, learners must build their language knowledge and their ability to use this knowledge in an active way. Reading and listening widely in English will help students to progress faster, as will the development of good study skills. In *Empower*, **Learning Tips** support learners both in and outside the classroom. These features accompany the texts and audio and encourage learners to notice and systematically note useful language. The Teacher's Notes for each lesson include **Homework activities** which encourage students to put the Learning Tips into practice in their independent learning and motivate further reading and listening outside the classroom.

2 Manageable learning

A second core principle that informs *Empower* is a recognition of the importance of manageable learning. This offers students (and their teachers) reassurance that the material is suitable for the level being taught: the language syllabus avoids overly complex language at any given level, and the reading, listening and video materials are carefully chosen to be accessible while consistently acknowledging learners' linguistic competencies and challenging them. *Empower* classroom materials reflect the concept of manageable learning in the following ways:

1 Syllabus planning and the selection of language

A key element in making learning material appropriate is the selection of target language. In *Empower*, two powerful Cambridge English resources – the Cambridge Corpus and English Profile – have been used to inform the development of the course syllabus and the writing of the material. This means that learners using *Empower* are presented with target language that includes:

Grammar
- a logically sequenced progression of grammar items and activities that focus clearly on both meaning and form
- systematic recycling of grammar within units and across each level
- a fresh approach to familiar language – accompanied by Cambridge Corpus–informed Tips, with notes on usage and typical errors – helps learners improve usage and tackle habitual mistakes

Vocabulary
- lexical sets that make vocabulary memorable and easier to learn
- an appropriate lexical load for each lesson so learners are not overwhelmed by too many vocabulary items
- activities that clarify different meanings of vocabulary
- Wordpower activities that aim to develop learners' vocabulary range.

Each level is carefully designed to offer measurable progress through the core syllabus while students develop toward each level's competency as independent individual learners.

2 Lesson flow

Teaching and learning are also made manageable through the careful staging and sequencing of activities, ensuring that each individual learner will be challenged and engaged while working together as a class. Every lesson is comprised of several sections, each with a clear focus on language and/or skills. Each section builds on the next, and activities within sections do likewise. Every section of language input ends in an output task, offering learners the opportunity to personalise the target language. At the end of each lesson, there is a substantial, freer speaking and/or writing activity that motivates learners to use new language in context.

3 Task and activity design

Tasks and activities have been designed to give students an appropriate balance between freedom and support. As an overall principle, the methodology throughout *Empower* anticipates and mitigates potential problems that learners might encounter with language and tasks. While this clearly supports students, it also supports teachers because there are likely to be fewer unexpected challenges during the course of a lesson, which means that necessary preparation time is reduced to a minimum. Students at all levels need to increase their language knowledge and their ability to use spoken and written language in a variety of situations. However, learners' needs can vary according to level. For example, at lower levels, students often need more encouragement to use language in an active way so they can put their language knowledge into immediate use. Conversely, at higher levels, learners need to be more accurate in the way they use language in order to refine their message and convey their ideas with more complexity and subtlety. *Empower* responds to these varying needs in the following ways as the course progresses from level A1 to C1:

- **Topics, tasks, and texts with an appropriate level of cognitive and linguistic challenge at each level** motivate learners by providing new challenges.
- **Multiple communicative opportunities** in every lesson either encourage fluency or allow students to refine their message using a wider range of language.
- **Varied and stimulating texts** motivate learners to develop their reading and listening skills so that a wider range of texts becomes accessible as the course progresses.
- **Listening and video materials** expose students to a wide variety of voices and natural, colloquial speech, while giving a strong focus on the language that students need to produce themselves.
- **Learning Tips** support learners in developing a broad vocabulary both in and outside the classroom.

3 Rich in practice

It is essential that learners be offered frequent opportunities to practise the language they have been focusing on – they need to activate the language they have studied in a meaningful way within an appropriate context. *Empower* is rich in practice activities and provides students and teachers with a wide variety of tasks that help learners to become confident users of new language.

Student's Book

Throughout each *Empower* Student's Book, learners are presented with a wide variety of practice activities, appropriate to the stage of the lesson and real-world use of the language.

- There are frequent opportunities for spoken and written practice. Activities are clearly contextualized and carefully staged and scaffolded. Extended spoken and written practice is provided in the final activity in each lesson.
- Grammar Focus and Vocabulary Focus pages at the back of the Student's Book offer more opportunities for practicing the grammar and vocabulary, helping to consolidate learning.
- Review and Extension activities at the end of each unit provide more opportunities for both written and spoken practice of the target language.

Teacher's Book

- Many learners find practice activities that involve an element of fun to be particularly motivating. Such activities – seven per unit – are provided in the photocopiable activities in Cambridge One, providing fun, communicative practice of grammar, vocabulary, and pronunciation.
- The main teacher's notes also provide ideas for extra activities at various stages of the lesson.

Other components

- The Workbook provides practice of the target input in each A, B and C lesson.
- The Digital Workbook component offers practice activities that can be completed on a mobile device or computer.
- Through Cambridge One, *Empower* provides an extensive range of practice activities that learners can use to review and consolidate their learning outside the classroom.

4 A comprehensive approach to productive skills

Most learners study English because they want to use the language in some way. This means that speaking and writing – the productive skills – are more often a priority for learners. *Empower* is systematic and comprehensive in its approach to developing both speaking and writing skills.

Speaking

The **C lesson** in each unit – Everyday English – takes a comprehensive approach to speaking skills, and particularly in helping learners to become effective users of spoken language for social and professional purposes. The target language is clearly contextualised by means of engaging video and audio that will be relevant and familiar to adult learners.

These Everyday English lessons focus on three key elements of spoken language:

- Useful language – focusing on functional language that is most relevant to learners' needs
- Pronunciation – focusing on intelligibility and the characteristics of natural speech, from individual sounds to extended utterances, developing learners' ability to express meaning by varying intonation and stress
- Conversation skills – speaking strategies and sub-skills that help learners to become more effective communicators

This comprehensive approach ensures that speaking skills are actively and appropriately developed, not just practised.

Writing

In the *Empower* Student's Book, learners receive guidance and practice in writing a wide range of text types. Writing lessons are not 'heads-down.' Instead, and in keeping with the overall course methodology, they are highly communicative, mixed-skills lessons with a special focus on writing. In *Empower*, writing is dealt with in the following ways:

- **Writing is fully integrated into listening, reading, and speaking** – as it is in real life – and is not practised in isolation.
- **There is an explicit focus on key linguistic features of written language** that encourage students to express themselves with greater clarity and accuracy.
- **A process writing methodology** is embedded in the instructions for writing activities, and learners are often encouraged to self-correct and seek peer feedback.
- **Communicative outcomes** – writing lessons lead to a final, communicative task, ensuring that learners are always writing for a purpose.

Assessment

Learning Oriented Assessment
What is Learning Oriented Assessment (LOA)?
Teachers are naturally interested in their students' progress. Every time they step into the classroom, teachers note if a learner is struggling with a language concept, is unable to read at a natural rate, or can understand a new grammar point but still can't produce it in a practice activity. This is often an intuitive and spontaneous process. By the end of a course or a cycle of learning, the teacher will know far more about a learner's ability than an end-of-course test alone can show.

An LOA approach to teaching and learning brings together this ongoing informal evaluation with a more formal or structured assessment, such as end-of-unit or end-of-course tests. LOA is an approach that allows the teacher to pull together all this information and knowledge in order to understand learners' achievements and progress and to identify and address their needs in a targeted and informed way. A range of insights into students and their progress feeds into total assessment of the learner. It also allows the teacher to use all of this information not just to produce a report on a learner's level of competence, but to plan and inform future learning.

How does *Empower* support LOA?
Empower supports LOA both informally and formally, and both in and outside the classroom:

1 Assessment that informs teaching and learning
- Reliable tests for both formative and summative assessment (Unit Progress Tests and skills-based Competency Tests)
- A clear record of learner performance through Cambridge One

2 LOA classroom support
- Clear learning objectives and activities that build toward those objectives
- Activities that offer opportunities for learner reflection and peer feedback
- A range of tips for teachers on how to incorporate LOA techniques, including informal assessment, into their lessons as part of normal classroom practice

1 Assessment that informs teaching and learning
Empower offers two types of tests written and developed by teams of Cambridge Assessment English exam writers. The tests in the course have been piloted, involving thousands of candidates across all tests and levels, to ensure that test items are appropriate to the level. Cambridge Assessment English tests are underpinned by research and evaluation and by continuous monitoring and statistical analysis of performance of test questions. *Empower* tests are designed around the following essential principles:
- **Validity** – tests of real-world English and the language covered in the Student's Book
- **Reliability** – tasks are consistent and fair
- **Impact** – tests have a positive effect on teaching and learning, in and outside the classroom
- **Practicality** – tests are user-friendly and practical for teachers and students.

Unit Progress Tests
The course provides an online Unit Progress Test at the end of every unit that tests the target grammar, vocabulary, and functional language from the unit. The teacher and learner are provided with a score for each language area that has been tested, identifying the areas of mastery and where the learner has encountered difficulties and needs more support. Paper-based versions of the tests are also available.

Competency Tests

Empower offers mid-course and end-of-course Competency Tests. These skills-based tests cover Reading, Writing, and Listening and Speaking and are calibrated to the Common European Framework of Reference (CEFR). They provide teachers and students with a digital record of achievement which indicates the students' performance in all language skills within the relevant course level.

Cambridge One provides teachers and students with a clear and comprehensive record of each learner's progress during the course, helping teachers and learners to recognise achievement and identify further learning needs. Cambridge One helps teachers to systematically collect and record evidence of learning and performance, and in doing so demonstrates to teachers and students how much progress has been made over time. Paper-based versions of the tests are also available.

2 LOA classroom support

Clear objectives

An LOA approach encourages learners to reflect and self-assess. In order to do this, learning objectives must be clear. In *Empower*, each unit begins with a set of 'can do' objectives so that learners feel an immediate sense of purpose. Each lesson starts with a clear 'Learn to ...' goal, and the activities all contribute toward that, leading to a significant practical outcome at the close of the lesson. At the end of each unit, there is a Review Your Progress feature that encourages learners to reflect on their success, relative to the 'can do' objectives at the start of the unit. Within the lessons, there are also opportunities for reflection, collaborative learning and peer feedback.

LOA classroom tips for teachers

In a typical lesson, teachers are likely to use some or perhaps all of the following teaching techniques:

- **monitor** learners during learner-centred stages of the lesson
- **elicit** information and language
- **concept check** new language
- **drill** new vocabulary or grammar
- encourage learners to **review and reflect** after they've worked on a task.

The chart below summarizes core and LOA-specific aims for each of the above techniques. All of these familiar teaching techniques are a natural fit for the kind of methodology that informally supports LOA. An LOA approach will emphasise those parts of a teacher's thinking that involve forming evaluations or judgments about learners' performance (and therefore what to do next to better assist the learner). The 'LOA teacher' is constantly thinking things like:

- *Have they understood that word?*
- *How well are they pronouncing that phrase?*
- *Were they able to use that language in a freer activity?*
- *How many answers did they get right?*
- *How well did they understand that listening text?*
- *How many errors did I hear?*
- *What does that mean for the next step in the learning process?*

The *Empower* Teacher's Book provides tips on how to use a number of these techniques within each lesson. This will help teachers to consider their learners with more of an evaluative eye. Of course, it also helps learners if teachers share their assessment with them and ensure they get plenty of feedback. It's important that teachers make sure feedback is well balanced so that learners know what they are doing well in and what needs a little more work.

	Teaching techniques				
	monitoring	**eliciting**	**concept checking**	**drilling**	**providing feedback**
Core aims	• checking learners are on task • checking learners' progress • making yourself available to learners who are having problems	• checking what learners know about a topic in order to generate interest	• checking that learners understand the use and meaning of new language	• providing highly controlled practice of new language	• finding out what ideas learners generated when working on a task • praising learners' performance of a task • indicating where improvement can be made
LOA aims	• listening to learners' oral language, and checking learners' written language, in order to: » diagnose potential needs » check if they can use new language correctly in context	• finding out if learners already know a vocabulary or grammar item • adapting the lesson to take into account students' individual starting points and interests	• checking what could be a potential problem with the use and meaning of new language for your learners • anticipating and preparing for challenges in understanding new language, both for the whole class and for individuals	• checking that learners have consolidated the form of new language • checking intelligible pronunciation of new language	• asking learners how well they feel they performed a task • giving feedback to learners on specific language strengths and needs • fostering 'learning how to learn' skills

LOA and learner motivation

The teaching and learning materials in *Empower* ensure learners maintain motivation throughout the course. In addition, teachers can further amplify learner motivation by adopting LOA approaches in their lessons. Here are some core LOA motivation ideas:

- **Make learning aims explicit to learners** – teachers should point out the 'can do' objectives and tell students how they will help their language development.
- **Modify learning objectives** on the basis of learner feedback – after learners complete an activity, teachers can get feedback on how they thought it went and respond to their suggestions (for example, learners may wish to repeat the activity because they feel they could do it better the second time).
- **Judge when to give feedback on learner language** – different learner groups and different activities require different types of feedback. Sometimes a teacher can give language feedback as learners are speaking, and sometimes it's better to wait until they have finished the activity; teachers should consider the most appropriate approach for each activity.
- **Balance developmental feedback with praise** – it's important to acknowledge what learners do well and praise their efforts, so teachers should give balanced feedback, but they should also make sure praise is targeted and not too general, otherwise it may sound insincere.

LOA and capturing learner language

One of the biggest challenges for teachers during the course of a lesson is being able to tune into learner language. This is particularly difficult with larger classes, when students are all speaking at the same time in pair or group work. If teachers want to adopt an LOA approach and capture language samples from a range of learners, they can consider some of the following techniques:

- **Listen only for the target language** that has just been taught and whether students are using it accurately – don't worry about the other mistakes learners might make.
- **Target specific learners for each activity** – sometimes it's not possible to listen to all learners for every activity, so if there are three speaking activities during the course of the lesson, the teacher can aim to tune into a different third of the class for each activity. By the end of the lesson, the teacher will have listened to all of the learners.
- **Ask learners to complete the speaking activities** located in each unit of the Digital Workbook – they can record their responses using a smartphone and submit the recordings in Cambridge One. The teacher can then give written feedback – it's not very different from giving feedback on written work that students have submitted.

Documentary videos

Expose your students to English via authentic, real-world contexts.

These high-interest supplementary Empower videos are thematically linked to the topics and language of each unit.

Each video comes with a downloadable and printable video worksheet.

Teachers can use the video and worksheet at any point in a unit.

Available on cambridgeone.org

eBooks

The *Empower* eBook includes all of the content from the print Student's Book, and can also be used to:

Listen to audio

Highlight text

Make notes

The eBook is ideal for iPads and Android tablets.

Empower and the CEFR, English Profile

The CEFR and English Vocabulary Profile

The *Empower* course syllabus is informed by English Profile and the Cambridge English Corpus and is carefully benchmarked to the Common European Framework of Reference (CEFR). This ensures that students encounter the most relevant and useful language at the right point in their learning.

The Cambridge English Corpus is a multi-billion word collection of texts taken from a huge variety of sources, including newspapers, the Internet, books, magazines, radio, schools, universities, the workplace and even everyday conversation – and is constantly being updated.

Our language research features in most of our materials. In particular, we use it to:

- ensure that the language taught in our courses is natural, accurate and up-to-date
- select the most useful, common words and phrases for a topic or level
- focus on certain groups of learners and see what they find easy or hard
- analyze spoken language so that we can teach effective speaking and listening strategies.

English Vocabulary Profile offers reliable information about which words (and which meanings of those words) and phrases are known and used by learners at each level of the CEFR.

For more information on English Profile and the Cambridge English Corpus, please use these links:

http://www.englishprofile.org
https://languageresearch.cambridge.org/cambridge-english-corpus

The CEFR is a standard guideline to recognise a learner's level of language fluency. Each level of *Empower* is carefully mapped to the appropriate CEFR level in accordance with English Vocabulary Profile, guaranteeing that students encounter the right language at the right level.

Empower	CEFR Level
Starter	A1
Elementary	A2
Pre-Intermediate	B1
Intermediate	B1+
Upper Intermediate	B2
Advanced	C1

Resources – How to access

To access the online resources, go to cambridgeone.org and register.

Resource	For Teachers	For Students	
	Teacher's Book with Digital Pack	Student's Book with eBook	Student's Book with Digital Pack
Class Audio	cambridgeone.org	cambridgeone.org	cambridgeone.org
Class Video	cambridgeone.org	cambridgeone.org	cambridgeone.org
Video Activity Sheets	cambridgeone.org	cambridgeone.org	cambridgeone.org
Video Teaching Notes / Answer Keys	cambridgeone.org		
Digital Workbook	cambridgeone.org		cambridgeone.org
End-of-unit assessment (Online version)	A Unit Progress Test for every unit (automatically marked) covers grammar, vocabulary, and functional language. cambridgeone.org		A Unit Progress Test for every unit (automatically marked) covers grammar, vocabulary, and functional language. cambridgeone.org
Mid- and end-of-course assessment (Online version)	Mid-course and end-of-course competency tests cover all four skills and generate a CEFR report which reliably benchmarks learners to the target level. cambridgeone.org		Mid-course and end-of-course competency tests cover all four skills and generate a CEFR report, which reliably benchmarks learners to the target level. cambridgeone.org
End-of-unit assessment (Print version)	Unit Progress Tests with Teacher's answer key for every unit which covers grammar, vocabulary, and functional language. cambridgeone.org	Please ask your teacher for further information.	Please ask your teacher for further information.
Mid- and end-of-course assessment (Print version)	Mid-course and end-of-course competency Tests with Teacher's answer key for every unit which covers grammar, vocabulary, and functional language. cambridgeone.org	Please ask your teacher for further information.	Please ask your teacher for further information.
Workbook audio	cambridgeone.org	cambridgeone.org	cambridgeone.org
Workbook answers	In Workbook with Answers or cambridgeone.org		
Photocopiables	cambridgeone.org		
Presentation Plus	Displays all Student's Book material, plays all Class Audio and Video, shows answer keys and more. For access, contact your local Cambridge representative.		
Teaching with *Empower*	An introduction to the *Empower* online assessment and practice materials, via a short teacher training course. For access, contact your local Cambridge representative.		

Empower components

The following *Empower* components are available for 6 levels (A1–C1):

- Student's Book with eBook
- Student's Book with Digital Pack
- Workbook with Answers
- Workbook without Answers
- Combo A with Digital Pack
- Combo B with Digital Pack

- Student's Book with Digital Pack, Academic Skills and Reading Plus (levels A2, B1, B1+, B2)
- Teacher's Book with Digital Pack
- Presentation Plus

Find out more:
cambridge.org/empower

Introduction to the Cambridge Life Competencies Framework (CLCF)

How can teachers prepare their students to succeed in a world that is rapidly changing? They need to help students develop transferable skills, to work with people from around the world, to think creatively, to analyze sources critically and communicate their views effectively. How can they teach these skills alongside language? In response to these questions, Cambridge University Press has developed the Cambridge Life Competencies Framework. The Life Competencies are explored throughout the *Empower* course.

The Cambridge Life Competency Framework

The Framework outlines core areas of competency that are important for development: creative thinking, critical thinking, learning to learn, communication, collaboration, social responsibilities.

Creative Thinking	Preparing for creativity	Generating ideas	Implementing ideas and solving problems	
Critical Thinking	Understanding and analysing ideas and arguments	Evaluating ideas and arguments	Solving problems and making decisions	
Learning to Learn	Developing skills and strategies for learning	Taking control of own learning	Reflecting on and evaluating own learning	
Communication	Using appropriate language and register for context	Facilitating interactions	Participating with appropriate confidence and clarity	
Collaboration	Taking personal responsibility for own contribution to a group task	Encouraging effective group interaction	Managing the sharing of tasks in a group activity	Working towards task completion
Social Responsibilities	Understanding personal responsibilities as part of a social group	Showing intercultural awareness	Understanding global issues	
Emotional Development	Identifying and understanding emotions	Managing own emotions	Empathy and relationship skills	

For more information about *Empower* and the CLCF, scan the QR code.
Or visit cambridge.org/empower/clcf

Listening	Reading	Speaking	Writing
Five conversations		Saying hello and introducing people	Names and addresses
A conversation about where you're from		Where you're from	Sentences about you
A conversation about people you know	Social media posts about people you know	People you know	Notes about people you know
At the gym reception		Asking for and giving information; Checking understanding	Unit Progress Test
First day of an English class	Online profiles	Using social media	An online profile; Capital letters and punctuation
	An article about Gabby Scampone	Jobs	Sentences about jobs
A survey about study habits	An online forum about study habits	Studying; Study habits	Questions about study habits
Ordering in a café; Asking for help		Asking for things and replying; Reacting to news	Unit Progress Test
Three monologues about studying English; A teacher addressing her class	A competition entry form	Studying English	A form; Spelling
A conversation about family routines	An article about an unusual workplace	Daily routines; Spending time with your family; Routines you share with others	A dialogue; Notes about routines you share with other people
Three conversations about gadgets	An interview about using the Internet	Technology in your life	Sentences about gadgets you've got; Questions about gadgets you've got
Making arrangements to go out		Making arrangements; Thinking about what you want to say	Unit Progress Test
A monologue about someone's family	Two informal emails	Plan a party	An informal email invitation; Inviting and replying
A conversation about buying food	An article about world markets	Buying food; The food you like and don't like	
A conversation about cooking	A factfile about Albert Adrià; Two personal emails	Cooking programmes; Cooking; The food you eat	Questions about food
At a restaurant		Arriving at a restaurant; Ordering a meal in a restaurant; Changing what you say	Unit Progress Test
Four monologues about cooking	A cooking blog	Cooking; A good cook you know; Cooking for others	A blog post about something you know how to do; Making the order clear
	An article about an unusual town	Places you like; Describing a picture of a town; What there is in a town	Questions and sentences about what there is in a town
A conversation about a new home	An advertisement	Your home and furniture	Sentences about your home
On the street		Giving and following directions; Checking what other people say	Unit Progress Test
Three monologues about neighbourhoods	A website about neighbourhoods around the world	What makes a good neighbourhood; Your neighbourhood	A description of your neighbourhood; Linking ideas with *and*, *but* and *so*
A conversation about a family tree		Your family	Notes about your family
A conversation about childhood hobbies	An article about Steve Jobs	Steve Jobs; What you did at different times; A childhood hobby	Notes about a childhood hobby
On the phone		Leaving a voicemail message; Asking for someone on the phone; Asking someone to wait	Unit Progress Test
A monologue about someone's life story	A life story	Important years in your life	A life story about someone in your family; Linking ideas in the past

Listening	Reading	Speaking	Writing
A conversation about travelling	Three stories about holidays	A trip around your country	Notes about a trip around your country
A conversation about transport in Moscow	A webpage about city transport around the world; Four reviews of transport systems	Metros and express buses you know; Disagreeing about transport; Transport you use	Notes about transport
On the train		Saying excuse me and I'm sorry; Showing interest	Unit Progress Test
A conversation about choosing a homestay family	Two online profiles; An email from Ahmed	Homestay families; English-speaking countries you'd like to visit	An email about yourself; Linking ideas with after, when and while
A podcast about training for a marathon	An article about Paralympian Jonnie Peacock	Famous sporting events and people; Running and exercise; Present and past abilities	Sentences about present and past abilities
Two monologues about exercise	An article about High Intensity Interval Training	Getting fit; The things people have to do; Yoga; Parts of the body	Sentences and notes about what people have to do
At the gym		Health and how you feel; Expressing sympathy	Unit Progress Test
A conversation about a free-time activity	An email about a company blog; A blog article about a free-time activity	Free-time activities in your country; Your free-time activities	An article; Linking ideas with however; Adverbs of manner
Four phone conversations about meeting		Meeting friends in town; Saying where you are and what you're doing	Sentences about what you are doing
Two phone conversations about what people are wearing	Two posts about living abroad; Text messages about what people are doing	Shopping; Festivals in your country; Clothes	Notes about what someone you know is wearing
Shopping for clothes		Choosing clothes; Paying for clothes; Saying something nice	Unit Progress Test
Four monologues about giving presents	Two thank-you emails	The presents you like to get; Giving presents and thanking people for them	A thank-you email; Writing formal and informal emails
A conversation about phones	An online discussion about headphones and earbuds	Headphones and earbuds; Phones; Comparing two similar things	Notes about two similar things
A radio programme about languages	A blog about languages	Languages; Blogs and language websites; High numbers	
Asking for help		Asking for help; Checking instructions	Unit Progress Test
Three monologues about text messages	Four text messages; Six posts on an online discussion board	Sending messages; Social media posts	A post expressing an opinion; Linking ideas with also, too and as well
A conversation about a magazine quiz	Three fact files about actors; A magazine quiz about actors; An article about actors	Popular films, TV programmes and books	Questions about films, TV programmes and books
A conversation about music in Budapest	An article about Budapest	Budapest; Kinds of music; Entertainment events in your town or city	Notes about entertainment events in your town or city
A night out		Going out in the evening; Asking for and expressing opinions; Responding to an opinion	Unit Progress Test
A conversation about a film	Three film reviews	Films	A film review; Structuring a review
Two conversations about holidays	A web page about holidays	Natural places; Important things when on holiday; Holiday plans	
Two monologues about things people like when travelling	An article about living in a different country	Living in a different country; Travelling and holidays; Giving advice about travelling	
A prize holiday		Checking in at a hotel; Asking for tourist information; Showing surprise	Unit Progress Test
A conversation about a planned holiday	An email with travel advice; An email asking for travel advice	Planning holidays; Porto	An email with travel advice; Paragraph writing

WELCOME!

⟲ UNIT OBJECTIVES

At the end of this unit, students will be able to:

- understand and take part in conversations in which people introduce themselves and others
- recognise and use numbers and the alphabet
- exchange information about themselves, including their names and addresses
- talk about things in the classroom and ask basic classroom questions

UNIT CONTENTS

G GRAMMAR
- Possessive adjectives
- *a/an*
- Regular plural forms: *-s, -ies, -es*
- Question words: *What, When, Where, Who, How*

V VOCABULARY
- Numbers
- The alphabet
- Colours: *black, blue, brown, green, grey, orange, pink, red, white, yellow*
- Classroom objects: *answer, cupboard, desk, dictionary, notebook, pen, projector, question, textbook, whiteboard*
- Classroom instructions: *ask, close, look at, open, read, turn to, work, write*

P PRONUNCIATION
- The alphabet: letters with /iː/, /eɪ/ and /e/ sounds
- Word stress in classroom objects

C COMMUNICATION SKILLS
- Saying hello and introducing people
- Exchanging names and addresses and spelling them correctly
- Asking and answering classroom questions: *What's '…' in English?, How do you spell '…'?, What's a '…'?, How do you say this word?*

♡ OPTIONAL LEAD-IN

Books closed. Point to yourself and say: *Hello. I'm (your name).*

Look at a student, point to yourself again and repeat: *Hello. I'm (your name).* Then, gesture to the student and show an open palm to elicit: *Hello I'm (student's name).* Smile, say *Hello* again, and then gesture to another student to elicit his/her name. Choose students at random rather than working your way around the classroom systematically, as this will prevent students feeling stressed as they see their turn approaching.

Continue until you have elicited all the students' names. If you have a student list, show students how you are ticking off their names as you work your way around the class. If you have two students with the same first name (i.e., given name), clarify their surname by using a simple rising intonation and emphasis on the last name: *Andrea? Andrea Hein? Andrea López?*

1 FIRST CONVERSATIONS

a ▶ 00.02–00.06 Students listen to the conversations for general meaning and match them with the pictures. Check answers as a class.

Answers
1 b
2 e
3 c
4 d
5 a

Audioscript

CONVERSATION 1 (Track 00.02)
A Hello. I'm Tony, and this is my wife, Joanna.
B Hello. Nice to meet you. I'm Pierre.
C Hello, Pierre. Nice to meet you.

CONVERSATION 2 (Track 00.03)
A Hi, Nick. How are you?
B I'm fine, thanks. And you?
A I'm OK, thanks.

CONVERSATION 3 (Track 00.04)
A Hi. Can we pay, please?
B Yeah, sure. That's 13 euros, please.
A 30 euros? For coffee and ice cream?
B No, 13 euros. Six for the coffees and seven for the ice cream.

A Ah, OK. … There you are. 15. Keep the change.
B Oh, thank you.

CONVERSATION 4 (Track 00.05)
A What's your name and address?
B It's Mike Kato, K-A-T-O.
A Kato, OK …
B 10 Kings Road, Ashley
A OK … 10 Kings Road …
B Ashley.
A How do you spell that?
B A-S-H-L-E-Y.
A Right, OK.

CONVERSATION 5 (Track 00.06)
A Ah, this is a nice photo. This is my wife and her brother.
B Oh, yes. Is that your flat?
A Yes, that's our flat in London.
B Mm, it's very nice.

b ▶ 00.02–00.06 Students listen to the conversations again for specific phrases and find out who says the sentences. Students compare their answers in pairs. Then, check answers as a class. When checking answers, ask students: *Who says (Nice to meet you.)?* and get them to point to the specific person who says each sentence.

Answers
2 e
3 d
4 d
5 c
6 a

2 SAYING HELLO

a ▶ **00.02** Point to yourself and say your name, then point to two or three more students at random and elicit their names. Next, point to the man in the blue shirt in picture b and say *Tony*. Then, point to the woman and elicit *Joanna*. Finally, point to the man in the suit jacket and elicit *Pierre*. Say *Conversation 1* and hold up one finger. Individually, students put the sentences in the correct order. Play the recording for students to listen and check. Check answers as a class.

> **Answers**
> 1 Hello. I'm Tony, and this is my wife, Joanna.
> 2 Hello. Nice to meet you. I'm Pierre.
> 3 Hello, Pierre. Nice to meet you.

b 💬🗩 If you have real beginners, they may need some extra support to complete 2b and 2c. If so, consider writing model conversations on the board to guide students. As they are practising, you can remove random words from the board so that ultimately they are relying on their memories.

Model the conversation by addressing a student: *Hello. I'm (your name)*. Elicit the response: *Hello. I'm (student's name)*. Do the same with another student and respond with: *Hello. Nice to meet you. I'm (your name)*. Drill the phrase *Nice to meet you*. Repeat these conversations with one or two more students until the class seems confident. If space allows, then gesture for students to stand up and mill around and say hello to their classmates. If there isn't enough space, get students to work in pairs.

c 💬🗩 Demonstrate the activity with three students. Say: *Hello. I'm (your name), and this is (Student A's name)*. Elicit a response from one of the other students: *Hello. Nice to meet you. I'm (Student B's name), and this is (Student C's name)*. In groups, students practise saying their names and introducing their partners. Monitor and praise students with a smile or a nod when they use the language for saying hello correctly.

d ▶ **00.03** Point to picture e and say *Conversation 2* and hold up two fingers. In pairs, students complete the conversation. Play the recording for students to listen and check. Drill the conversation.

> **Answers**
> 1 How
> 2 fine
> 3 thanks

e 💬🗩 If space allows, gesture for students to stand up and have conversations in small groups. If there isn't enough space, get students to work sitting down in groups of three or four. Monitor, but don't interrupt fluency unless students make mistakes with the phrases for saying hello.

3 NUMBERS

a ▶ **00.04** Students may need some extra work on numbers before they continue. Be prepared to teach/revise numbers 1–100. If you model the teen numbers in sequence, be careful that you don't inadvertently move the stress to the first syllable, i.e., *thir<u>teen</u>, four<u>teen</u>, fif<u>teen</u>*, etc., NOT *<u>thir</u>teen, <u>four</u>teen, <u>fif</u>teen*, etc. Point to picture c and say *Conversation 3* and hold up three fingers. Say: *Numbers*. Point to the bill and play the recording for students to complete it. Students compare their answers in pairs. Then, check answers as a class. When checking answers, write the numbers on the board to make sure students have understood them.

> **Answers (For audioscript, see Conversation 3 p. 2)**
> 2 coffees   €6
> 2 ice creams   €7
> TOTAL   €13
> They pay €15.

b ▶ **00.07** Play the recording for students to listen and circle the numbers. They then check in pairs. Check answers as a class.

> **Answers**
> 30
> 15
> 60
> 70
> 12

⟳ LOA TIP DRILLING

- Check that students can hear the difference between the pairs of numbers (*thirteen/thirty, fourteen/forty*, etc.) by beating the rhythm with your hand and showing where the stress falls.

c In pairs, students look at the options and choose the correct answers. After checking answers as a class, write some more numbers in numerals on the board and elicit from the class how to say and write them.

> **Answers**
> 25 = twenty-five
> 61 = sixty-one
> 110 = a hundred and ten

d Students read the first sequence and continue it as a class. They then work in pairs, continuing the sequences.

> **Answers**
> 5, 6, 7
> 40, 50, 60
> 45, 55, 65
> 37, 39, 41
> 200, 250, 300

♀ FAST FINISHERS

Ask fast finishers to invent new sequences like those in 3d to test their partner.

4 THE ALPHABET

a ▶ **00.08** Books closed. Say: *I'm (your name).* Write your name on the board slowly, spelling the letters out as you go. Spell it again clearly, pointing to the letters. Then say: *The alphabet.* Students open their books. Play the recording or model the alphabet yourself for students to listen and repeat.

b **Pronunciation** Read the questions with the students. Model clearly the long 'ee' sound, the word *see* and the letter *B.* Elicit another letter with the same sound by modelling *A* and shaking your head. Model *C,* nod your head and indicate students should write it. Individually, students complete the three groups. When checking answers, write the groups of letters on the board and drill them.

> **Answers**
> 1 B, C, D, E, G, P, T, V   2 A, J, K   3 F, L, M, N, S, X, Z

c 💬 Demonstrate the activity by pointing at two or three letters and eliciting them from the class. In pairs, students test each other on the letters. Monitor and correct students' pronunciation as appropriate.

> 💡 **EXTRA ACTIVITY**
>
> In pairs, students practise spelling their own names. They tell their partner their name: *I'm (student's name).* Then, they spell it out, pointing to the letters in 4a. Monitor and correct students' pronunciation as appropriate.

d The question *How do you spell '…'?* isn't formally practised until 7c on Student's Book (SB) p. 8. In 4d and 4e, don't distract students by using this question form, but elicit spelling 'silently' by showing an open palm, pointing at letters or standing with your pen positioned to write on the board as students call out the letters to you. Point to the red blot and elicit the word *red.* Write it on the board slowly, spelling the letters out as you go. Then say: *Colours.* Give students one minute to look at the colours and write down the ones they think they know. In pairs, students then practise saying and spelling the words. When checking answers, elicit the spelling from the class and write the colours on the board.

> **Answers**
> (from left to right) top: red, grey, blue, green, black
> bottom: pink, brown, orange, yellow, white

e 💬 Demonstrate the activity by saying two words to the class, e.g., *answer* and *number,* and eliciting the spelling. Students then write down another two words. Monitor and check their spelling or allow them to check the words in their dictionaries. In pairs, students practise spelling their partner's words.

f ▶ **00.05** Point to picture d and say *Conversation 4* and hold up four fingers. Point to the man in picture d and elicit *Mike.* Show students Mike's details in the Student's Book, pointing to the first line and saying *name* and the second and third lines and saying *address.* Play the recording for students to complete the name and address. Check answers as a class.

> **Answers**
> Mike <u>Kato</u>
> <u>10</u> Kings Road
> <u>Ashley</u>

g 💬 Elicit the question *How do you spell your first name?* by writing *M-I-K-E* on the board and writing a question mark above it. In pairs, students say their names and addresses and ask each other to spell them. Students can, if they prefer, invent an address. Monitor, but don't interrupt fluency unless students make mistakes with the alphabet.

5 POSSESSIVE ADJECTIVES

a ▶ **00.06** Tell students to close their books. Write on the board: *I'm Tony, and this is … wife, Joanna.* Point to the gap. Elicit the missing word (*my*) and write it in the sentence. Leave the sentence on the board. Students open their books. Point to picture a, say *Conversation 5* and hold up five fingers. Play the recording for students to read and listen and underline the correct answers. Check answers as a class.

> **Answers**
> **A** … This is <u>my</u> wife and <u>her</u> brother.
> **B** Oh, yes. Is that <u>your</u> flat?
> **A** Yes, that's <u>our</u> flat in London …

b In the sentence on the board *I'm Tony, and this is my wife, Joanna,* circle the words *I* and *my.* Draw a line to link the two words and repeat them clearly for students. Point to the table and read through the example sentences with *I/my* and *you/your.* Individually, students complete the table. Check answers as a class.

> **Answers**
>
> | He lives here. | This is <u>his</u> flat. |
> | --- | --- |
> | She lives here. | This is <u>her</u> flat. |
> | We live here. | This is <u>our</u> flat. |
> | They live here. | This is <u>their</u> flat. |

c Individually, students complete the sentences. They then check in pairs. Check answers as a class.

> **Answers**
> 1 His   2 their   3 your   4 our   5 her

> 🔄 **LOA TIP** REVIEW AND REFLECT
>
> • Draw a thumbs-up symbol in a box on the left of the board and a thumbs-down symbol in a box on the right of the board. Then stand in the centre, point to the thumbs up and nod and look confident. Point to the thumbs down and shake your head and look worried. Ask students: *Possessive adjectives?* Elicit an indication of their confidence level.

> 💡 **EXTRA ACTIVITY**
>
> Students are usually very interested to learn something about their new teacher. Show students some photos of your family and/or friends and tell them something about the people, recycling simple language from the Welcome! unit and possessive adjectives, e.g., *This is my wife. Her name's Sarah. Mark is an old friend and that's his daughter.*
>
> If students have pictures of family and/or friends on their mobile phones, allow them to show each other some photos of their family and/or friends and make simple sentences.

6 CLASSROOM OBJECTS

a Books closed. Pre-teach some of the vocabulary by pointing to the classroom objects that you have in your classroom. Don't allow students to write anything down. Repeat the words several times and then 'test' individual students by saying their name and pointing to an object. When you're confident that students can remember most of the vocabulary, elicit *dictionary* from a student and ask: *How do you spell that?* Students then open their books, look at the spelling of the vocabulary and match objects 1–10 with a–j in the picture. Check answers as a class.

> **Answers**
> 1 g   2 h   3 a   4 c   5 f   6 d   7 j   8 b   9 e   10 i

b ▶ 00.09 **Pronunciation** Play the recording and highlight the pronunciation for students. Individually or in pairs, students practise saying the words.

c Draw a large question mark on the board. Read the words in 6a quickly, placing extra emphasis on the article *a*. When you reach *an answer*, place extra emphasis on the article *an* and then point to the question mark on the board. Repeat if necessary and then read the question in the Student's Book and elicit the answer as a class.

> **Answer**
> a before *a, e, i, o, u*

d Individually, students write *a* or *an* next to the words. They then check in pairs. Check answers as a class.

> **Answers**
> 1 a book
> 2 an apple
> 3 a camera
> 4 a glass
> 5 an egg
> 6 a baby
> 7 a box
> 8 an ice cream

> ## 💡 FAST FINISHERS
> Ask fast finishers to write a list of any 'international English' words that they know, e.g., *orchestra*, *pizza*, *taxi*, and decide if they use *a* or *an*.

e Demonstrate the activity by thinking of one of the words yourself and eliciting questions from the class. Students then work in small groups and ask questions to guess each other's words. Monitor and help with vocabulary if necessary.

f Books closed. Pick up a pen, show the class and say: *One pen.* Pick up another pen and say: *Two …* to elicit the plural, *pens.* Point to three desks and say: *Three …* to elicit *desks.* Students open their books and complete the rules. Check answers as a class. Elicit an indication of their confidence level for the indefinite article and regular plural forms.

> **Answers**
> Most words add *-s* in the plural.
> Change a final *-y* to *-i* and add *-es*.
> If a word ends in *-s, -x, -sh* or *-ch*, we add *-es*.

7 CLASSROOM INSTRUCTIONS

a ▶ 00.10 Play the recording, pausing after each item for students to follow the instructions. Elicit the actions for instructions 1 and 2. Repeat the recording, again pausing after each item, for students to identify which verbs they hear.

> **Answers**
> 1 open, turn to, read (The first word of the text on SB p. 83 is *so*.)
> 2 turn to, look at (The place in the picture on SB p. 77 is Dubai.)
> 3 close, look at
> 4 write
> 5 work, ask

> **Audioscript**
> 1 Open your books and turn to page 83. Read the first word of the text. What is it?
> 2 Turn to page 77 and look at the picture. What place is it?
> 3 Close your books and look at the board.
> 4 Write a question on a piece of paper.
> 5 Work in pairs. Ask your question to your partner.

b ▶ 00.11 Individually, students underline the correct question words. Play the recording for students to listen and check. Check answers as a class.

> **Answers**
> 1 What's   3 How   5 When's
> 2 Where's   4 Who's

> ## 🔄 LOA TIP CONCEPT CHECKING
>
> Check that students understand the meaning of each question: for Question 1, point to the picture of the apple in 6d, ask the question and elicit the answer: *It's an apple.* For Question 2, ask the question and elicit the answer: *Japan.* For Question 3, point to the word *dictionary* in 6a and elicit the pronunciation. For Question 4, ask the question and elicit the name of the president in the country where you are teaching or another country that has a president. For Question 5, ask the question and elicit the day(s) of your English lessons with the class.

c Students read the questions and match them with the answers. Check answers as a class. Drill the questions, substituting other words for *amigo*, *night* and *ferry*.

> **Answers**
> 1 c   2 d   3 a   4 b

d Give students a few minutes to prepare their questions. Monitor and help as necessary. Students then work in small groups, asking and answering each other's questions.

> ## 💡 EXTRA ACTIVITY
> Students prepare an end-of-section test for a partner. They write ten questions about the content of the unit using the question words in 7b and 7c, e.g., *How do you spell 'whiteboard'?* or *How do you say 'gelato' in English?* Monitor and help as necessary. Point out errors for students to self-correct.
>
> In pairs, students ask and answer each other's questions. They then give their partner a score out of ten. Monitor the tests and give feedback to the class.

≫ Photocopiable activities: Pronunciation Welcome!

UNIT **1** PEOPLE

⟳ UNIT OBJECTIVES

At the end of this unit, students will be able to:
- understand information, texts and conversations about people and places, countries and nationalities and people's personalities
- ask for and give information about themselves and other people, including their nationality and personality
- use simple phrases to check understanding
- introduce themselves in an online profile with correct capital letters and punctuation

UNIT CONTENTS

G GRAMMAR
- *be*: positive and negative
- *be*: questions and short answers

V VOCABULARY
- Countries: *Australia, Brazil, France, Japan, Mexico, Spain*, etc.
- Nationalities: *Australian, Brazilian, French, Japanese, Mexican, Spanish*, etc.
- Adjectives: *cool, fantastic, friendly, great, kind, nice, pleasant, popular, quiet, warm, well-known, amazing, awful, modern, old, poor, rich, terrible, wonderful*
- Wordpower: *from* to talk about times, a starting place, our country or city, how far away something is

P PRONUNCIATION
- Word stress in nationalities
- Sound and spelling: /k/
- Rising and falling intonation
- Consonant clusters

C COMMUNICATION SKILLS
- Talking about where you are from
- Using adjectives for description
- Asking for and giving information
- Checking understanding using *So that's …* and *Excuse me?*
- Discussing social networking and online profiles
- Writing an online profile about yourself

GETTING STARTED

⊚ OPTIONAL LEAD-IN

Books closed. Revise the alphabet by writing it on the board one letter at a time, saying each letter clearly and asking the class to repeat it after you. When you have the complete alphabet on the board, point to letters at random to elicit them from the class. Repeat any letters that are problematic.

Say the word *alphabet* and then gesture for students to write it down as you spell it out: *A-L-P-H-A-B-E-T*. Check spelling by writing the word on the board. Repeat with *question, pink, textbook, address* and *camera,* or choose words covered in the Welcome! unit containing letters that your students find difficult. Finish by asking students to spell the word *people*. Check meaning by gesturing to several students and saying *people*.

a 💬📢 Give students one minute to think about their answers to the questions and check that students understand the vocabulary in Questions 2 and 3. Discuss the answers as a class.

> **Possible answers**
> 1 Brazil, Germany, Italy, Spain, the USA

⊚ EXTRA ACTIVITY

Write the country names from the picture on the board. Tell students to put the names of the countries in alphabetical order. They then compare their answers with a partner. Check answers as a class. (See the suggested answers above for the correct alphabetical order.)

b 💬📢 Read the question and the ideas with the students and check that they understand the vocabulary. Ask them when they usually meet people from other countries and ask students to share any other ideas they have. Help with vocabulary and pronunciation, but don't interrupt fluency.

⊚ EXTRA ACTIVITY

Write *a music concert* on the board, point to yourself and say: *I feel excited.* Write *watch sport* on the board, point to yourself and say: *I feel bored.* Students then work in pairs and use the adjectives in Exercise a to say how they feel about the activities in Exercise b. Monitor and help as necessary.

Exercises a and b can be prepared as homework before this lesson to give students time to look up unfamiliar vocabulary. Ask students to look at the picture and to prepare their answers to the questions as homework to talk about in the next lesson.

1A | I'M FROM FRANCE

At the end of this lesson, students will be able to:

- understand a conversation about people's countries and nationalities
- use a lexical set of countries and nationalities correctly
- use present simple positive and negative forms of *be*
- ask for and give simple personal information about other people

♀ OPTIONAL LEAD-IN

Books closed. Draw a world map on the board and elicit the name in English of the country where you are teaching by pointing to it and writing the first letter on the board. When you have elicited the name of the country, ask: *How do you spell that?* Elicit the spelling from the class, writing it on the board as the class calls out the letters to you.

If you're from a different country, point to it and say the name of the country in English. Elicit the question *How do you spell that?* from the class before spelling the country for them. With multi-nationality classes, you could also ask some students to point to their country and see if they know how to say it in English. Don't worry if students don't know the names of the countries or how to spell them correctly at this point.

Leave the map on the board for 1a and 1b.

1 LISTENING AND READING

a 💬 Give students one minute to think about their answers to the questions before talking about the pictures as a class. Don't check answers at this point.

b ▶ 01.01 Play the recording for students to listen and check. Check answers as a class. Play the recording again, or model the countries yourself for students to listen and repeat.

Answers
1 football
2 1 a 2 e 3 c 4 d 5 f 6 b

♀ EXTRA ACTIVITY

Quickly revise the question *Where's (city)?* from the Welcome! unit by asking students about a city in the country where you are teaching. Then ask them about six other cities, one from each country in 1a, e.g., *Where's Sydney?* (Australia), *Where's Guadalajara?* (Mexico). If you used the optional lead-in, use the drawing of the world map on the board again and ask students to locate the cities using the question *Where's (city)?*

c ▶ 01.02 Ask students: *What's the World Cup?* Elicit possible answers, e.g., *It's a football championship for the world.* Remember that students will have very limited language at this point, so praise students who are able to express the basic idea, however simply. You may wish to pre-teach the word *team* (a group of people who play a sport or game together). Students listen to the conversation for general meaning and check the things Thomas and Lena talk about. Check answers as a class.

Answers
1 football ✓
2 countries ✓
4 a city ✓

d ▶ 01.02 Students listen to the recording again for specific words and complete the conversation. They compare in

pairs. Check answers as a class. When checking answers, ask students: *How do you spell (word)?* Write the correct answers on the board.

Answers
1 name
2 from
3 where
4 France
5 great

e Play the recording again, or allow students to read the conversation at their own pace, and decide if the sentences are true or false. Check answers as a class.

Answers
1 F (Thomas and Lena meet at the World Cup.)
2 T
3 T
4 F (Lena says the French team's really good.)

♀ FAST FINISHERS

Ask fast finishers to look at the pictures and identify all the colours, using the vocabulary from the Welcome! unit.

f Individually, students underline the two nationalities in the conversation. Check answers as a class.

Answers
Russian, French

2 VOCABULARY Countries and nationalities

a ▶ 01.03 Read Thomas's sentence with the class. Read the countries and nationalities in the box and elicit another example of a country/nationality pair. Students work in pairs, matching the words. Play the recording for students to listen and check. Check answers as a class.

Answers and audioscript
She's from Russia. She's Russian.
They're from Brazil. They're Brazilian.
They're from Spain. They're Spanish.
They're from Germany. They're German.
They're from Japan. They're Japanese.

b ▶ 01.03 **Pronunciation** By counting on your fingers and breaking the words into chunks, show students how *Brazil* has two syllables but *Brazilian* has four. Point out the dividing line between syllables in the Student's Book. Students read the other words in the box and count how many syllables there are in each. Play the recording again for students to underline the stressed syllable in each word. Check answers as a class.

Answers
Russia, Brazilian, Spanish, Japan, Russian, Germany, Japanese, German, Brazil, Spain

c ▶ 01.03 Play the recording again for students to listen and repeat.

🔄 **LOA TIP DRILLING**

- Check that students are aware that the stress shifts from the second syllable in *Ja | pan* to the third syllable in *Ja | pa | nese*.
- Highlight the changing vowel sound in *Spain* /speɪn/ and *Spanish* /ˈspænɪʃ/.

d Complete the first sentence as a class and elicit another example using picture a. Students work individually, writing sentences about the people in the pictures. They then check in pairs. Check answers as a class.

Answers
1 Russia
2 a Brazilian, Brazil   d Japanese, Japan
  b French, France   e Spanish, Spain
  c German, Germany   f Russian, Russia

e 💬📖 Individually, students complete the question. Before they work in pairs, quickly check that they have completed the question correctly (*Where*). Monitor and give students other nationalities if they are from countries other than those in 2a. If your students are from various different countries, ask each student: *Where are you from?*

f ≫ ▶ 01.04–01.05 Students complete the exercises in Vocabulary Focus 1A on SB p. 162. Play the recordings as necessary, monitor Exercises b and h and check other answers as a class. Tell students to go back to SB p. 11.

Answers (Vocabulary Focus 1A SB p. 162)
a1 the USA   6 Poland   11 Colombia   16 Ireland
  2 Mexico   7 Saudi Arabia   12 South Africa   17 Italy
  3 Turkey   8 Argentina   13 Canada   18 Pakistan
  4 the UK / Britain   9 Australia   14 New Zealand   19 Thailand
  5 China   10 Iran   15 Nigeria   20 Russia
c 1 a 2 c 3 d 4 e 5 b 6 f
d 1 China – in Asia   3 Russia – speak Russian
  2 Brazil – in South America   4 Spain – in Europe
e 1 A 2 C 3 B 4 B 5 D 6 F
f Brit̲ish, Chi̲nese, Tur̲kish, Me̲xican, Japa̲nese, Bra̲zilian, Aus̲tralian, Pakis̲tani, I̲talian
g 1 A Chinese C Pakistani 2 different (Me̲xican, Japa̲nese, Bra̲zilian)

3 GRAMMAR *be*: positive and negative

a ▶ 01.06 Play the next part of the conversation for students to answer the question. Check the answer as a class.

Answer
b the town where Thomas is from

Audioscript

LENA So where are you from? From Paris?

THOMAS No, I'm not from Paris. I'm from a town called Rouen.

L Hmm ... Where's that?

T Oh, it's a town near Paris. It's not very big.

L Oh, right.

T So are you here with friends?

L Yes, we're a big group. We're all from St Petersburg.

T But they aren't here.

L No, they're all in the hotel. They say they're tired!

T Oh, right. ... Well, look, it's only 8:00, the match isn't on yet. So how about a coffee?

L Hmm, yeah OK. Good idea! ...

b ▶ 01.06 Students underline the correct answers. Play the recording again for students to listen and check. Check answers as a class.

Answers
1 isn't
2 are
3 aren't
4 It isn't

c Read the sentences with the students and give them one minute to think about how to complete the rule before they work in pairs. Check the answer as a class.

Answer
1 not

🌍 **CAREFUL!**

There are several common student mistakes with *be* positive and negative. Common errors include: They miss *be* altogether, particularly before adjectives, e.g., *Brazil very big* (Correct form = *Brazil **is** very big*) and also in the second clause of a sentence, e.g., *This is a small town and the people very friendly* (Correct form = *This is a small town and the people **are** very friendly*). They confuse the forms *am/are/is*, e.g., *Here is the answers ...* (Correct form = *Here **are** the answers to the homework*). They confuse colours because students often try to include the word *colour* and may leave out *be*, e.g., *It a blue colour* (Correct form = *It's blue*). Students may also have problems with word order, e.g., *They all are from Germany* (Correct form = *They **are** all from Germany*). They confuse capitals and apostrophes in the contracted forms, e.g., *Hes Spanish and i'm Brazilian* (Correct form = *He's Spanish and **I'm** Brazilian*). They may also use *have* instead of *be*, e.g., *She has 20 ...* (Correct form = *She **is** 20 years old*).

d Individually, students complete the table. They then check in pairs. Check answers as a class. Show students three fingers: point to the first finger and say *I*; point to the second and say *am*; and point to the third and say *not*. Then, close up the space between the first and second fingers to show how *I* and *am* are contracted as *I'm*. Repeat the process with *She isn't*: close up the second and third fingers to show how *is* and *not* are contracted as *isn't*. Say *She is not*, point to your three fingers and gesture to indicate for the class to show you which fingers should be closed up to represent the contraction *She isn't* (i.e., second and third fingers). Repeat with *They are not*. Use this same strategy to show the alternative contraction that joins the form of *be* with *not*: *'s not* and *'re not*. Explain there are two possible answers, but the first contractions (*He isn't, She isn't, They aren't*) are more common in British English.

Answers

Positive (+)	Negative (–)
I'm from St Petersburg.	I'm not French.
He's a really good player.	She isn't from Moscow.
They say they're tired.	They aren't at the match.

e 🔊 ▶ **01.07** Students read the information in the Grammar Focus 1A on SB p. 138. Draw their attention to the different options for contractions that are possible. Play the recording where indicated and ask students to listen and repeat. Students then complete the exercises. Check answers as a class, making sure students are using contractions correctly. Tell students to go back to SB p. 11.

> **Answers (Grammar Focus 1A SB p. 139)**
> **a** 2 is 3 are 4 are 5 am / 'm 6 is / 's 7 is 8 are
> **b** 2 It's a beautiful city. It isn't a beautiful city.
>   3 We're from Ankara. We aren't from Ankara.
>   4 They're at a party. They aren't at a party.
>   5 I'm tired. I'm not tired.
>   6 You're right. You aren't right.
> **c** 3 'm 4 isn't 5 's 6 aren't 7 's 8 's 9 aren't 10 're
> **d** 2 He isn't a doctor. He's a student.
>   3 They aren't my brothers. They're my friends.
>   4 We aren't from London. We're from Bangkok.
>   5 I'm not a good cook. I'm a very bad cook.

f Complete the first sentence as an example with the class. Students work individually, adding the correct form of *be* to the sentences. Point out errors for students to self-correct. Check answers as a class.

> **Answers**
> 1 My brother <u>is</u> at university in Madrid.
> 2 My mother and father <u>are</u> not here.
> 3 Russia <u>is</u> not very hot in April.
> 4 My friends <u>are</u> really interesting and fun.

> 💡 **EXTRA ACTIVITY**
>
> Demonstrate 3g and 3h before students start to write their own sentences, two positive and two negative. Write *True or False?* on the board and then tell students four sentences about yourself using the verb *be*, e.g., *My mother and father are from Italy. I'm from Toronto.* Two of these should be true and two false. Students listen and try to identify the false sentences. Check answers as a class and correct the false sentences, e.g., *I'm not from Toronto. I'm from Ottawa.*

g Individually, students write four sentences about themselves. Monitor and help with vocabulary and give students ideas if necessary.

h 💬 In pairs, students decide if their partner's sentences are true or false. To make this a class activity, get each student to then read one or two of their sentences for the class to guess if they're true or false.

4 SPEAKING

a 🔊 Divide the class into pairs and assign A and B roles. Student As read about Robert on SB p. 130 and Student Bs read about Lora on SB p. 133. Monitor for any problems and clarify these before students start on the pairwork stage. Put students into A/B pairs for them to ask and answer the questions about Roberto and Lora. As you monitor, don't interrupt fluency, but note any mistakes with *be*. After the activity, write these on the board and ask students to correct them. Tell students to go back to SB p. 11.

b 💬 Put students into small groups to tell each other their names, countries, nationalities and home towns.

> 💡 **FAST FINISHERS**
>
> Ask fast finishers to show each other pictures of their friends and families on their mobile phones. They tell the group their names, countries, nationalities and home towns using the third person. Alternatively, ask fast finishers to continue talking about the other people in their group and practise giving information about each other using the third person.

> ⊕ **ADDITIONAL MATERIAL**
>
> Workbook 1A
>
> Photocopiable activities: Grammar 1A, Vocabulary 1A, Pronunciation 1A

1B | SHE'S A LOVELY PERSON

At the end of this lesson, students will be able to:

- read and understand short texts about pictures
- use a lexical set of personality adjectives correctly
- understand a conversation about people's nationalities and personalities
- use the present simple question form of *be*
- talk about people they know from other countries

⚲ OPTIONAL LEAD-IN

Books closed. Draw the following puzzle on the board:

```
1
 — — — — — C — —
  2
   — — — — O — — — — —
     3
      — — — U — — — — — — —
4
 — — — — — — N — — —
        5
         — — — T — — —
      6
       — — — R — — —
       7
        — — — I — — —
        8
         — — — E — — —
     9
      — — — — S — —
```

Point to the first line of the puzzle and say: *1 She's Mexican. She's from …* . Elicit *Mexico* as an example. Ask students to spell out the answer and fill it in. Students then work individually as you read clues 2–9 to the class:

2 He's Colombian. He's from Bogotá in … . (Colombia);
3 They aren't British. They're Australian. They're from … . (Australia);
4 He's Polish. He's from … . (Poland);
5 They're Italian. They're from Rome in … . (Italy);
6 She isn't French. She's Turkish. She's from … . (Turkey);
7 They're Chinese. They're from … . (China);
8 She's Irish. She's from Dublin in … . (Ireland);
9 He isn't Pakistani. He's Russian. He's from … . (Russia).

Students check in pairs. Then, check answers as a class. When checking answers, ask students to spell out the countries to you as you write them in the puzzle.

1 READING

a 💬▶ Discuss the question as a class and write students' ideas on the board.

b Students read the texts quickly and match them with the pictures. Check answers as a class and find out if students' guesses in 1a were correct. You may wish to help students with words in the Vocabulary Support box.

> **Answers**
> Suzi c
> James d
> Alex a
> Saddah b

📖 VOCABULARY SUPPORT

colleague (A2) – a person you work with at your job
cousin (A2) – the son/daughter of your father's/mother's brother/sister

c Read the first sentence with the class and elicit who students think says it. Read the sentence aloud to justify the answer: *We're teachers and we work together in a school.* Individually, students decide who said the other sentences. They then check in pairs. When checking answers, elicit which words or sentences in the texts helped students decide.

> **Suggested answers**
> 1 Saddah   3 James
> 2 Alex   4 Suzi

d 💬▶ In pairs, students talk about who they would like to meet and why. Ask students to share their answers to find out who the most popular person to meet is.

2 VOCABULARY Adjectives

a Point to picture c and read the sentence with the class. Read the adjectives again and elicit that the sentence is about Claudia.

> **Answer**
> Claudia

b Students work individually to find the other adjectives. You can tell them that there are two or three adjectives in each text. Check that students have found the correct words before they start to put them into the correct gaps. Students check in pairs. Then, check answers as a class.

> **Answers**
> 1 brilliant, great, fantastic
> 2 kind, nice, lovely
> 3 well-known
> 4 quiet
> 5 popular

c **Pronunciation** Model the pronunciation of the three words from the text and highlight the /k/ sounds for students. Look at one or two words together as a class before students work individually, underlining the /k/ sounds and identifying the two words that don't have /k/. When checking answers, model and drill all the words for students to listen and repeat.

> **Answers**
> cold, car, kitchen, like, coffee, quick, back, key, come, make, school, cat
> *Cheap* and *know* don't have /k/.

⚲ FAST FINISHERS

Ask fast finishers to look at the countries in Vocabulary Focus 1A on SB p. 162 and identify the seven countries that have the /k/ sound (Canada, Colombia, Mexico, Pakistan, South Africa, Turkey, the UK).

d 💬 Read the examples with the class. Students work in pairs or small groups, talking about people they know. If they wish, they can show pictures of the people they are talking about on their mobile phones if they have them. Monitor, but don't interrupt fluency unless students make mistakes with the adjectives.

e ⟫ ▶01.08–01.11 Students complete the exercises in Vocabulary Focus 1B on SB p. 163. Play the recordings as necessary and monitor students as they speak. Check answers as a class, making sure students are pronouncing the words correctly. Tell students to go back to SB p. 13.

> **Answers (Vocabulary Focus 1B SB p. 163)**
> **a** 1 not very good 2 very good 3 very good 4 not very good
> **b** old – modern; poor – rich

> 💡 **EXTRA ACTIVITY**
>
> Ask students to give an example for each adjective, e.g., *a rich celebrity, an awful national dish*. Remember that they still have limited vocabulary, so praise them for making the correct connections between the meaning of the adjectives and other words.

3 LISTENING

a ▶01.12 Point to the man in the first picture and say: *This is Roman.* Then ask: *What's his nationality?* Play the first part of the recording for students to listen and complete the nationality on the profile. Check the answer as a class. Then repeat the process with Diego and Mia and Laura. Make sure students understand that they should give the nationality, not the country, in each case. You may wish to pre-teach the word *married* (when you have a husband/wife).

> **Answers**
> 1 Polish 2 Mexican 3 Spanish

> **Audioscript**
>
> **1**
> **A** This is my good friend Roman. He's really friendly.
> **B** Is he from Poland?
> **A** Yes, he is.
>
> **2**
> **A** These are my friends Mia and Diego. They're really great.
> **B** Are they married?
> **A** Yes, they are.
> **B** Are they Spanish?
> **A** No, they aren't. They're from Mexico.
>
> **3**
> **A** This is my friend Laura. She's really cool.
> **B** Is she Italian?
> **A** No, she isn't. She's from Spain.

b ▶01.12 Play the recording again without stopping for students to listen for the specific adjectives and complete the profiles. They compare in pairs. Then, check answers as a class. When checking answers, ask students: *How do you spell (word)?* Write the correct answers on the board.

> **Answers**
> 4 friendly 5 great 6 cool

4 GRAMMAR

be: questions and short answers

a ▶01.13 Look at picture c and text 1 on SB p. 12 again. Books closed. Write: *Claudia / Spanish (+)* on the board and elicit the positive sentence: *Claudia is Spanish.* Then write: *Claudia / French (–)* on the board and elicit the negative sentence: *Claudia isn't French.* Finally, write *Claudia / Spanish (?)* on the board and see if students can form the question *Is Claudia Spanish?* Students open their books. Then, read the questions in 4a with the class. Individually, students complete the short answers. Play the recording for students to listen and check. Check answers as a class.

> **Answers**
> 1 isn't 2 is 3 are 4 're not

b Individually, students complete the table. Remind them that there are two possible alternatives for the negative form of *he/she* and *they*. They then check in pairs. Check answers by copying the table onto the board and asking individual students to come up and complete the gaps.

> **Answers**
>
> | Questions (?) | Short answers | |
> |---|---|---|
> | <u>Are</u> you Australian? | Yes, I am. | No, I'm not. |
> | <u>Are</u> you Brazilian? | Yes, we are. | No, we aren't. |
> | <u>Is</u> he/she Turkish? | Yes, he/she <u>is</u>. | No, he/she <u>isn't</u>. |
> | <u>Are</u> they Russian? | Yes, they <u>are</u>. | No, they <u>aren't</u>. |

> 🔄 **LOA TIP CONCEPT CHECKING**
>
> • Write example questions on the board to check that students are assimilating correct word order. Point to each question one by one and ask students: *Is this correct?* Ask them to correct the questions as necessary, e.g., *She is Italian?* (No), *He French is?* (No), *From the USA is he?* (No), *Are they Pakistani?* (Yes), *They're Canadian?* (No).
>
> • Check that students understand that they also need to think about the verb forms. Write example questions with correct word order but with incorrect verb forms and ask students to correct them, e.g., *Is they from Japan?* (Are they from Japan?), *Am Laura Spanish?* (Is Laura Spanish?), *Be you Chinese?* (Are you Chinese?).

> 👁 **CAREFUL!**
>
> The most common student mistake with *be* questions and short answers is for students to use *it* instead of *that* in Yes/No questions that ask if something is OK, e.g., ~~Is it OK?~~ (Correct form = Is *that* OK?), or ~~Is it good for you?~~ (Correct form = Is *that* good for you?). Students may also have problems with the inversion required to form questions, possibly because there is no change in the word order for questions in their own language, e.g., ~~Claudia is Spanish?~~ (Correct form = **Is Claudia** Spanish?).

c ⏩ ▶️**01.14** Students read the information in Grammar Focus 1B on SB p. 138. Play the recording where indicated and ask students to listen and repeat. Students then complete the exercises. Check answers as a class, making sure students are using correct word order and contractions where possible. Tell students to go back to SB p. 13.

Answers (Grammar Focus 1B SB p. 139)
a 2 Where are you from?   6 Are you friends?
   3 Are you American?   7 Is it very cold?
   4 Is she popular?   8 Is he from France?
   5 What are your names?
b 2 f   3 b   4 g   5 c   6 a   7 e
c 1 'm; are; 'm   2 's; 's; 's; 's   3 are; 're; 're
   4 's; is; Are; aren't; 're; 're; are

💡 **FAST FINISHERS**

Ask fast finishers to write simple conversations of their own, using the conversations in Grammar Focus Exercise c as a model.

d ▶️**01.15** Individually, students complete the conversations. They then check in pairs. Play the recording for students to listen and check. Check answers as a class. Then, elicit an indication of their confidence level for *be*: positive, negative, questions and short answers.

Answers
2 's   6 're
3 Is   7 Are
4 is   8 aren't
5 are   9 're

💡 **EXTRA ACTIVITY**

Drill the questions *Is he from London?* and *Are they married?* and then tell students about some of your friends, using the conversations in 4d as a model. If possible, show students pictures of the people as you're talking about them. Elicit questions about your friends from individual students, e.g.:

Teacher   *My friend Fiona's Australian. She's very friendly.*

Student   *Is she from Sydney?*

Teacher   *No, she isn't. She's from Melbourne.*

5 SPEAKING

a Give students a few minutes to prepare and write notes about the people they know. Monitor and help as necessary.

b 💬 Students work in small groups, telling each other about the people they know and asking and answering each other's questions. Monitor and listen for correct usage of the target language from this lesson. You may ask each student to tell the class about one of the people they know and, if possible, show a picture.

⊕ **ADDITIONAL MATERIAL**

Workbook 1B

Photocopiable activities: Grammar 1B, Vocabulary 1B, Pronunciation 1B

Documentary video Unit 1 *People*

Video worksheet Unit 1 *People*

1C

EVERYDAY ENGLISH
What's your surname?

At the end of this lesson, students will be able to:

- understand an informal conversation about registering for an exercise class
- use appropriate phrases for asking for and giving information
- use appropriate phrases for checking understanding
- identify how many sounds groups of letters have and pronounce them correctly
- maintain a conversation in which they register for a course

💡 **OPTIONAL LEAD-IN**

Write the adjectives from Lesson 1B on the board in random order: *amazing, brilliant, cool, fantastic, friendly, great, kind, lovely, modern, nice, old, rich, poor, popular, quiet, terrible, warm, well-known, wonderful.*
Say a variety of people/places/things that your students will know about and elicit adjectives to describe them, e.g. *Ariana Grande, New York, the weather in England.* As this is very subjective, students will very probably disagree on which adjectives are appropriate, but accept all suggestions and clarify meaning as you go along.

1 LISTENING

a 💬 Point to the pictures of Leo and Dan at the top of the page. Students then work in pairs to choose personality adjectives to describe them. If you didn't use

the Optional lead-in, students refer back to SB p. 12 as necessary. Monitor and allow time for class feedback.

💡 **FAST FINISHERS**

Ask fast finishers to look at the pictures of the people on earlier pages of the Student's Book and describe the people with personality adjectives.

b ▶️**01.16** Play Part 1 of the video or the audio recording for students to choose the correct answers. Check answers as a class.

Answers

1 a
2 b
3 b

Video/Audioscript (Part 1)

LEO OK, all finished. Time to go.

DAN I want to finish this. You go. See you tomorrow.

L All this sitting. I need to do some exercise.

D Off to the gym?

L Yeah.

D Say hello to Martina when you see her.

L Sure! … Bye!

D Bye, Leo.

c ▶ **01.17** Point to the picture at the bottom of the page and ask students: *Where is Leo now?* (at the gym). Play Part 2 of the video or the audio recording for students to listen to the conversation for general meaning and answer the question. Check the answer as a class.

Answer

b book a fitness class

Video/Audioscript (Part 2)

SONIA Hi. How can I help?

LEO I'd like to do a fitness class.

S Your card, please?

L Sorry – it's at home.

S OK. No problem. … What's your name?

L Leo.

S Sorry, what's your surname?

L Seymour.

S Can you spell that, please?

L S-E-Y-M-O-U-R.

S Seymour – yes, here you are. And what's your address?

L 18 New Street.

S 18 New Street.

L Yes, that's right.

S So a fitness class?

L Yes, what time's the next one?

S It's at twenty past seven.

L Sorry?

S 7:20.

L And … is it a big group?

S No, only ten people.

L Great. Can I book a place?

S Of course. … There you go.

L And where's the class?

S It's in Studio 1.

L So that's 7:20 in Studio 1?

S That's right.

L Thanks for your help.

S You're welcome.

d ▶ **01.17** Students watch or listen again for specific details. Play Part 2 of the video or the audio recording again for students to decide if the sentences are true or false and correct the false sentences. To help students who may still need some extra support with telling the time, the receptionist uses two ways of telling the time: *twenty past seven* and *seven twenty*. Times using *past/to* and *quarter/half*, etc. are covered in detail in Lesson 2B, so avoid spending time in class teaching/revising telling the time at this point.

Answers

1 T
2 T
3 F (The class is in Studio 1.)

💡 **EXTRA ACTIVITY**

Ask students the following questions about Part 2 of the video: *1 Where's Leo's card?   2 How do you spell his surname?   3 What's his address?*
Play Part 2 of the video or the audio recording again, repeating the relevant sections as necessary. Check answers as a class (*1 at home   2 S-E-Y-M-O-U-R   3 18 New Street*).

2 USEFUL LANGUAGE
Asking for and giving information

a Individually, students decide who they think says each sentence. They then compare their ideas in pairs. Don't check answers at this point.

b ▶ **01.18** Students match the pairs of sentences. Play the recording for students to listen and check. Check answers as a class. Drill the key phrases from the conversation for correct intonation.

Answers

1 (V) d (R)
2 (R) g (V)
3 (R) f (V)
4 (V) b (R)
5 (R) c (V)
6 (V) e (R)
7 (R) a (V)

Video/Audioscript (Part 2)

SONIA How can I help?

LEO I'd like to do a fitness class.

S What's your surname?

L Seymour.

S Can you spell that, please?

L S-E-Y-M-O-U-R.

S Seymour – yes, here you are. And what's your address?

L 18 New Street. What time's the next class?

S It's at twenty past seven.

L And where's the class?

S It's in Studio 1.

L Thanks for your help.

S You're welcome.

c Students underline the correct answers. Check answers as a class and point out that we use *in* with a place and *at* with a time.

Answers

1 Room 6
2 eight o'clock

d ▶ **01.19** Individually, students complete the conversation. They then check in pairs. Play the recording for students to listen and check. Check answers as a class.

Answers

1 help
2 like
3 where's
4 What's
5 spell

e 💬 Practise the conversation in 2d as a choral drill, with you taking the role of the receptionist and the class the role of the person who wants information. When students are confident of the role of the person who wants information, change roles so that they also practise the role of receptionist. In pairs, students practise the conversation, using their own surname. Monitor and correct students' pronunciation as appropriate.

💡 **FAST FINISHERS**

Ask fast finishers to change the additional information, e.g., *an (art) course, it's on (Friday) at (six) o'clock, in Room (3),* and practise the conversation again.

3 LISTENING

a ▶ **01.20** Students watch or listen to Part 3 for specific details. Play the video or the audio recording for students to answer the questions. Check answers as a class.

> **Answers**
> 1 She's Dan's wife.
> 2 b He's a bit lazy.

> **Video/Audioscript (Part 3)**
> **MARTINA** Leo!
> **LEO** Martina – hi!
> **M** Good to see you here.
> **L** All day at the computer – I need to do something.
> **M** Yes, well, tell my husband that.
> **L** Dan's very busy.
> **M** And a bit lazy! See you later.
> **L** See you later.

b 💬🗪 Discuss the question as a class. Encourage students to justify their ideas as far as possible, e.g., *before work – it is quiet before work* or *never – I'm lazy!*

4 CONVERSATION SKILLS
Checking understanding

a In pairs, students look at the mini-conversations and try to complete them. Check answers as a class.

> **Answers**
> 1 Sorry
> 2 So that's

b Give students a moment to think about the meaning of each expression individually before discussing them as a class.

> **Answers**
> 1 So that's
> 2 Sorry

c ▶ **01.21** **Pronunciation** Play the recording or model the sentences yourself and highlight the intonation for students. Drill the sentences, making sure students are using a rising intonation.

> **Answer**
> The intonation goes up.

d 💬🗪 Read through the dialogue map with students before they start. Remind students to make sure the intonation goes up on the expressions for checking understanding. In pairs, students practise conversations using their surnames.

5 PRONUNCIATION Consonant clusters

a ▶ **01.22** Play the recording or model the example yourself and highlight the consonant groups for students.

> 🌣 **CAREFUL!**
>
> Many students have problems with the complex consonant clusters found in English because they are very different from the sound combinations that exist in their own language. These consonant clusters can have up to four consonant sounds grouped together, but to start off simply, the examples in this section all contain just one or two sounds. When drilling, it may help students if you break consonant clusters down into their individual parts before putting them together for students, e.g. /k/ ➤ /l/ ➤ /kl/ and /θ/ ➤ /r/ ➤ /θr/. You may also wish to point out that in English, the number of letters in a written word frequently doesn't match the number of sounds.

b ▶ **01.23** Individually, students listen to the words and count how many consonant sounds the letters in bold have. They check in pairs. Then check answers as a class. Model the pronunciation for students to listen and repeat.

> **Answers**
> **thr**ee – thr = two sounds: /θr/
> si**x** – x = two sounds: /ks/
> ei**ght**y – ght = one sound: /t/

c ▶ **01.24** Play the recording or model the times yourself for students to listen and repeat. Test students by writing further times on the board in numerals and eliciting the times from the class.

6 SPEAKING

a ⋙ Divide the class into pairs and assign A and B roles. Student As read the first card on SB p. 131 and Student Bs read the first card on SB p. 133. Students then role play the conversation. Monitor, but don't interrupt fluency unless students make mistakes with the content of this lesson. Students then read the second card and role play the second situation.

> 🔄 **LOA TIP** MONITORING
>
> - Listen to see if students are using the expressions for checking understanding at appropriate points. Praise students with a smile or a nod when they use this language correctly.
>
> - Monitor and identify students who use the language for asking for and giving information well. Ask these pairs to perform their conversations for the class.

> ⊕ **ADDITIONAL MATERIAL**
>
> Workbook 1C
>
> Unit Progress Test

1D SKILLS FOR WRITING
I'm Carla and I'm from Italy

- understand a conversation in which people introduce themselves
- understand written personal profiles
- use capital letters and punctuation correctly
- write a short personal profile introducing themselves

💡 OPTIONAL LEAD-IN

Write *social media site* on the board. Ask students: *What's a social media site?* Elicit possible answers, e.g., *a website where people or friends share information and photos on the Internet.* In monolingual classes, you may wish to ask students: *What's a 'social media site' in (students' L1)?*

Draw a line running out from the words *social media site* on the board and start writing the name of a social media site which will be familiar to your students, e.g., *Instagram, Twitter.* Elicit the name of the site and then continue to draw lines from the words and elicit other social media sites your students know. You may also give students information from the Culture Notes below.

🌍 CULTURE NOTES

Social media sites change dramatically in popularity and can go in and out of fashion at great speed. At time of publication, some of the most important social networks around the world include the following:

Facebook (the first social network to have over a billion users around the world), Instagram (a picture-based social network, designed for use on smartphones and other mobile devices), LinkedIn (a business networking tool) and Twitter (a social network where users write short, public messages, called tweets, of up to 140 characters).

1 SPEAKING AND LISTENING

a 💬🔊 Read the questions with the students and then give them one minute to think about their answers. Discuss the questions as a class and find out which social media sites are most popular with your students.

b Check that students know the difference between *Lives in* (the place where they live now) and *From* (the place where they were born or grew up) in Kate's and Carla's profiles. Tell students to complete the table, using the information in the two profiles. Check answers by copying the table onto the board and asking students to complete the missing information. After students complete each item in the table, point to it and ask the class: *Is it correct?* Elicit the general opinion before confirming if it's the correct answer or not.

Answers

She's …	20 years old	from London	Italian	a teacher	a student
Kate	DK	DK	DK	✓	✗
Carla	✓	✗	✓	✗	✓

c ▶️ 01.25 Play the recording for students to listen for general meaning and answer the questions. Check answers as a class.

Answers
1 the first day
2 London

Audioscript

KATE Welcome to the class, very nice to see you all. I'm Kate, as you know, and this is Mike. We're your two teachers, and we're both from London. So, first, can we all say our names and where we're from? OK? Carla, you start …

CARLA Yes, of course. Hello, I'm Carla, and I'm from Italy. I'm a student in Milan. It's my first time in London, so it's great to be here.

MASATO OK. Well, I'm Masato, and I live in Kyoto, Japan. I work in a restaurant in Kyoto, so English is really important to me.

CARMEN Yes, I'm Carmen. I'm from Barcelona in Spain. I'm also a student. I study IT. It's not my first time in England. I know London quite well but it's nice to be here again.

ORHAN I'm Orhan and I'm from Turkey. I live in London now with my family. I work for a bank here.

MARISA I'm Marisa and I'm a student in Recife, Brazil. It's my first time in London, too, but I have a brother here, so I can stay with him and his family.

K OK, great, thank you. Well, er, to start off then, I think I'll just explain what the…

💡 EXTRA ACTIVITY

Before students listen again, give them one minute to work in pairs and see what, if anything, they remember from the first listening. Ask them to look at the picture in the Student's Book, or project the picture on the board and ask students to close their books. Students say what they remember about the people, e.g., *Kate and Mike – teachers, from London; Carmen – Spanish, from Barcelona.* Students share ideas as a class. Don't check answers at this point. This extra 'scaffolding' will help students complete the task in 1d better.

d ▶️ 01.25 Students listen to the recording again for specific details and complete the chart. Make sure students understand that they should give the country, not the nationality, in each case. They compare in pairs. Then, check answers as a class.

Answers

Name	Country	One other thing we know
Kate and Mike	UK	They're <u>teachers</u>.
Carla	Italy	She's a <u>student in Milan</u>.
Masato	<u>Japan</u>	English is <u>important</u> for his work.
Carmen	<u>Spain</u>	She's a <u>student</u> of IT.
Orhan	<u>Turkey</u>	His <u>family</u> is in London.
Marisa	<u>Brazil</u>	Her <u>brother</u> is in London.

e 💬🔊 Put students into small groups, nominating the strongest student in each group, Student A, to be the 'teacher'. Students then work together, introducing themselves to their group. Monitor, but don't interrupt fluency.

⟳ **LOA TIP ELICITING**

- Elicit some example sentences from the class before students work in groups in 1e. Say *I'm …* and then point to a person in the picture to elicit the person's name, e.g., *Marisa*. Then say: *I'm from …* to elicit *I'm from Recife / Brazil / Recife in Brazil*. Continue with *I'm a …* to elicit *student*.

- Bear in mind that although the language in the recording is A2 level, it does include items that have not yet been studied in this course. How much of this language you choose to use at this point will depend on the confidence level of your students.

⏻ EXTRA ACTIVITY

Do the task in 1e 'for real', i.e., with you introducing yourself to the class as if it were the first day of class and then asking each student to say who they are along with one more thing about themselves. Explain the task clearly first and give students one minute to prepare what they are going to say. Monitor and help with vocabulary and give students ideas if necessary. Then work as a class, with you welcoming the students and then inviting them to introduce themselves one after another. Choose students at random rather than working your way around the classroom systematically, as this will prevent students feeling stressed as they see their turn approaching.

❷ READING

a Write *New information?* on the board and point to the text about Kate. Start reading and pause at her last name, and then point to the question on the board and ask: *Is it new information?* (No). Continue reading and pause after *Wigan*. Again, point to the question on the board and ask: *Is it new information?* (Yes). Indicate students should underline this. Individually, students continue reading the two texts and underline the new information. Check answers as a class.

> **Answers**
> Kate – It's a small town near Manchester in England; I'm married and I have two small children: a boy and a girl; I like languages, music and films.
> Carla – I study marketing; I like running, swimming and yoga.

❸ WRITING SKILLS
Capital letters and punctuation

a Write *capital letters* on the board, then erase it and write *CAPITAL LETTERS*. Ask students: *What are capital letters?* and elicit possible answers, e.g., *big letters*. Complete the first one or two items in the list as examples before students work individually, ticking the words that have capital letters. Check answers as a class.

> **Answers**
> 1 ✓
> 2 ✓
> 3 ✓
> 4 ✓
> 6 ✓
> 8 ✓
> 9 ✓

⏻ FAST FINISHERS

Ask fast finishers to look back through the Welcome! unit and Unit 1 and find more examples of all the areas in 3a, e.g., *1 Pierre – SB p. 6; 5 football, 6 St Petersburg – SB p. 10*.

b Students write the full forms of the words. Check answers by asking individual students to come up and write them on the board.

> **Answers**
> 1 it is
> 2 she is
> 3 you are
> 4 is not
> 5 are not

c Circle the words *it is* on the board from the previous exercise. Next to it, write *it's* and circle the apostrophe. Students then add apostrophes to the words in the book. Check answers as a class.

> **Answers**
> 1 I'm   4 he's
> 2 aren't   5 we're
> 3 isn't   6 they're

d Discuss the questions as a class and ask students to find examples of both commas and full stops in Kate's and Carla's online profiles.

> **Answers**
> a full stops
> b commas

e Students read the sentences and rewrite them with capital letters and the correct punctuation. They compare their answers in pairs. Check answers as a class by asking individual students to come up and write the sentences on the board.

> **Answers**
> 1 I'm from Shanghai. It's a big city in China.
> 2 I like basketball, old cars and jazz.
> 3 I'm a French teacher in Australia.
> 4 This isn't my first time in London.
> 5 Are all the teachers from Britain?

❹ WRITING

a Individually, students write their profiles. Remind students to be careful with the use of capital letters and punctuation. Monitor and help with vocabulary and give students ideas if necessary. If you're short of time, this exercise can be completed for homework. Students could then bring their profiles to the next lesson.

b In pairs, students swap profiles and check their partner's work. They then give each other feedback. If they've made any mistakes with capital letters and/or punctuation, they prepare a second draft of their profile and correct their mistakes. Finally, elicit an indication of students' confidence level for using capital letters and punctuation correctly.

⊕ ADDITIONAL MATERIAL

Workbook 1D

UNIT 1
Review and extension

1 VOCABULARY

a Individually, students complete the sentences. Check answers and spelling as a class by asking students to write the correct answers on the board.

> **Answers**
> 1 Brazilian   3 German   5 French
> 2 Spanish   4 Australian 6 Japanese

b Students complete the text, working individually. They check in pairs. Check answers as a class.

> **Answers**
> 1 fantastic   3 kind   5 brilliant   7 friendly
> 2 warm   4 nice   6 quiet

> **💡 FAST FINISHERS**
>
> Ask fast finishers to write sentences or a complete paragraph about their families, using the text in 1b as a model.

2 GRAMMAR

a Students complete the text with the correct form of the verb *be*. They check in pairs. Check answers as a class.

> **Answers**
> 1 'm 2 'm 3 'm 4 'm 5 's 6 's 7 's 8 're 9 are 10 're

b Complete the first question as an example with the class. Individually, students write the questions. Monitor and help as necessary. Point out errors for students to self-correct.

> **Answers**
> 1 Are you (French/Portuguese/Spanish, etc.)?
> 2 Is she kind?
> 3 Are they from (France/Portugal/Spain, etc.)?
> 4 What's your name?
> 5 Where are you from?

c Students write the questions and short answers. Remind them that there are two possible negative answers in some cases. Check answers as a class and drill the questions and short answers.

> **Answers**
> 1 Are you Turkish? Yes, I am.
> 2 Is she your sister? No, she isn't.
> 3 Are they friendly? Yes, they are.
> 4 Are you both from the USA? No, we aren't.
> 5 Is he well known? No, he isn't.

d Check that students understand that contractions count as one word. Individually, students complete the conversation. Check answers as a class.

> **Answers**
> 1 your   3 I'm   5 isn't   7 She's
> 2 Are   4 she   6 where's

e 💬 In pairs, students practise the conversation, using their own personal information. As you monitor, don't interrupt fluency, but note down mistakes with the verb *be*. After the activity, write them on the board and ask students to correct them.

3 WORDPOWER *from*

a Tell students to close their books. Write the four sentences from 3a on the board, leaving a gap in place of *from*. Point to the four gaps and ask students: *What's this word?* Elicit *from* and write it in a circle above the sentences. Students open their books, look at the sentences with *from* and match them with the pictures. Check answers as a class.

> **Answers**
> 1 c 2 a 3 d 4 b

b Students read the rules and match them with the sentences with *from* in 3a. They then check in pairs. Check answers as a class.

> **Answers**
> a 3 b 1 c 2 d 4

c Students read the sentences and match them with the rules in 3b. Check answers as a class.

> **Answers**
> 1 a 2 d 3 b 4 c

d Write *I'm the UK* on the board and ask students: *Is this correct?* (No). Elicit the correct answer (*I'm from the UK.*). Students then work individually, adding *from* to the sentences. Check answers by asking individual students to come up and write the sentences on the board.

> **Answers**
> 1 This postcard is <u>from</u> New Zealand.
> 2 Breakfast is <u>from</u> seven o'clock to ten o'clock every morning.
> 3 The bank's only 200 metres <u>from</u> here.

e Write *the plane / this is / from Rome* on the board and use arrows to show how the phrases need to be put in order to make a sentence (*This is the plane from Rome.*). Students order the phrases to make sentences. Check answers as a class.

> **Answers**
> 1 I'm from Denmark.
> 2 The supermarket's open from 7:30 am to 9:30 pm.
> 3 My place is two kilometres from school.

f As an example, make the sentences in 3e true for yourself, e.g., *I'm from the UK.* Students then change the sentences to make them true for themselves. Monitor and point out errors for students to self-correct.

> **💡 EXTRA ACTIVITY**
>
> Tell students four sentences about yourself, each including an example of *from*, e.g., *I'm from Chiang Mai.*; *My place is five kilometres from the school.*; *The shops are only 100 metres from my house.*; *My day at school is from nine o'clock to seven thirty.* Make some true and some false, and ask students to identify which are true and which are false.

>>> Photocopiable activities: Wordpower 1

> **🔄 LOA REVIEW YOUR PROGRESS**
>
> Students look back through the unit, think about what they've studied and decide how well they did. Students work on weak areas by using the appropriate sections of the Workbook and the Photocopiable activities.

WORK AND STUDY

At the end of this unit, students will be able to:

- understand information, texts and conversations about work, jobs and studying
- ask for and give information about themselves and other people, including their jobs and study habits
- tell the time
- use simple phrases to react to news
- identify and correct spelling mistakes in their written work
- complete a form explaining why English is important for them and why they want to improve their English

UNIT CONTENTS

G GRAMMAR
- Present simple: positive and negative
- Present simple: questions and short answers

V VOCABULARY
- Jobs: *actor, businessman, businesswoman, chef, cleaner, dentist, engineer, farmer, manager, mechanic, nurse, photographer, pilot, police officer, receptionist, secretary, shop assistant, taxi driver, tour guide*
- Studying: *break, exam, get good/bad marks, make notes, pass/fail an exam, pass/fail a test, schedule, term, studies*
- Time: *o'clock, five past, ten past, (a) quarter past, thirty, (a) quarter to,* etc.
- Wordpower: *work* as a verb with *in* + place, *for* + company, *as* + job; *work* as a noun: *be at work, be out of work, go to work, leave work, start work,* etc.

P PRONUNCIATION
- Word stress in jobs
- Third person -*s*
- Present simple questions: *Do you*
- Sound and spelling: *ou*

C COMMUNICATION SKILLS
- Talking about jobs
- Talking about study habits
- Asking for things and replying
- Reacting to news using *That's a pity* and *No problem*
- Writing a competition entry about learning English

GETTING STARTED

♀ OPTIONAL LEAD-IN

Books closed. Write *jobs* on the board. Elicit the names of jobs students know and write them on the board, e.g., *banker, doctor, teacher.* If necessary, ask students: *How do you spell that?* In monolingual classes, you may ask: *What's '(doctor)' in (students' L1)?* Students then listen to you give four simple clues using the present simple, e.g., *This person is very smart. / He or she knows about medicine. / You go to this person when you are sick.* Students then try to identify the job (*a doctor*). Unless students thought of the word *scientist* in the initial brainstorm, delete all the jobs from the board before reading out the following four clues: *This person works outside or in a laboratory. / This person is usually good with numbers. / This person is very clever.* Elicit the answer from the class or ask students to open their books and look at the photo. Write *scientist* on the board.

a 💬 Give students one minute to think about their answers to the questions before talking about the picture as a class.

b 💬 Read the ideas with the students and check that they understand *machines*. Discuss which kinds of work they think are interesting and ask students to share any other ideas they have.

♀ EXTRA ACTIVITY

If your students work, ask them to write down one good thing and one bad thing about their job, e.g., *It's an easy job, but it's very boring.* Ask students to say their sentences to the class, and ask the rest of the class: *Is it the same for you?* Don't let students tell each other exactly what their jobs are at this point, and tell them that they'll find out this information at the end of Lesson 2A. Then ask students to write down one good thing and one bad thing about being a student and to share their sentences with the class.

Exercises a and b can be prepared as homework before this lesson to give students time to look up unfamiliar vocabulary. Ask students to look at the picture and to prepare their answers to the questions as homework to talk about in the next lesson.

2A | SHE LOVES HER JOB

At the end of this lesson, students will be able to:
- read and understand a text about a dangerous job
- use a lexical set of jobs correctly
- use the positive and negative forms of the present simple
- talk about their jobs or the jobs of people they know

OPTIONAL LEAD-IN

Books closed. Ask students: *What's a 'gator girl'?* Tell them: *It's a job!* Write it on the board. Under *gator*, write *alligator* and help students to locate *gator* in the word by covering up *alli* with your hand. Help them understand that *gator* is a shortened version of the word 'alligator'. In a monolingual class, you could ask: *What's 'alligator' in (students' L1)?* Alternatively, to help students connect the pictures with the job title and understand the job, point at the pictures and say: *This is an alligator. This is a girl.*

1 READING

a Individually, students look at the pictures and answer the questions. Ask some students to tell the class their ideas, but don't check answers at this point.

b Students read the text quickly and check their answers to 1a. Check answers as a class. You may wish to help students with words in the Vocabulary Support box.

> **Answers**
> 1 a 2 b

VOCABULARY SUPPORT

wild (B2) – describing an animal that lives away from people in natural conditions

smart (B1) – intelligent, clever

c Read the sentences with students. Then, tell students to read the text again in detail and choose the correct answers. Check answers as a class.

> **Answers**
> 1 don't like
> 2 likes
> 3 don't like
> 4 is
> 5 two jobs

d Make sure students understand that the information could be anywhere in the text, not necessarily in the section about Gabby. They then check in pairs. Check answers as a class.

> **Answers**
> Students' own answers

FAST FINISHERS

Ask fast finishers to look at the text again, find words that are new for them and write them down in their notebooks, either with a definition, an example or a translation.

e Students talk about the questions in pairs, small groups or as a class. Encourage students to justify their ideas as much as possible, e.g., *I think Gabby's job is awful. It's very dangerous!*

2 VOCABULARY Jobs

a Ask students to cover the words and see how many of the jobs in the pictures they already know. Individually, students then match the words with the pictures. Monitor for any problems and clarify these as you check answers as a class.

> **Answers**
> 1 i   4 f   7 g
> 2 d   5 e   8 h
> 3 c   6 b   9 a

FAST FINISHERS

Ask fast finishers to write down all the other jobs they can think of. After they complete Vocabulary Focus 2A on p. 163, they can see how many jobs they had already thought of.

b ▶ 02.01 **Pronunciation** Look at the example with the class and make sure students understand how the underlining relates to word stress by over-stressing the underlined syllable, i.e., *poLICE officer*. Play the recording for students to underline the stressed syllable. Check answers as a class.

> **Answers**
> engi<u>neer</u>
> pho<u>tog</u>rapher
> <u>den</u>tist

c Read the sentences with the students and then give them one minute to think about their answers. Check that students understand that there are no correct answers in this case. They then compare their ideas in pairs. Invite pairs to share their answers with the class.

> **Answers**
> Students' own answers

d ▶ 02.02 Students complete the exercises in Vocabulary Focus 2A on SB p. 163. Play the recording for students to check their answers to Exercise a, monitor Exercise c and check other answers as a class. Tell students to go back to SB p. 21.

> **Answers (Vocabulary Focus 2A SB p. 163)**
> **a** 1 farmer   6 actor
>   2 chef   7 secretary
>   3 businessman / businesswoman   8 mechanic
>   4 receptionist   9 tour guide
>   5 manager
> **b** a nurse   e chef   i receptionist
>   b tour guide   f dentist   j farmer
>   c actor   g mechanic
>   d taxi driver   h pilot

3 GRAMMAR
Present simple: positive and negative

a ▶ **02.03** Write the following three jumbled sentences about the text on SB p. 20 on the board and ask students to put them in order: *1 is / in Florida / Everglades Holiday Park* (Everglades Holiday Park is in Florida.) *2 animal park / It's / an* (It's an animal park.) *3 birds and alligators / It / has* (It has birds and alligators.) Say: *Sentence 3 is different.* Ask: *Why?* Elicit that it doesn't use the verb *be*. Students then look at the table and complete it with the present simple verbs. Play the recording for students to listen and check. Check answers as a class.

Answers

	I / we / you / they	he / she / it
+	Tourists <u>come</u> to look at the alligators. Her parents <u>think</u> she's crazy.	She <u>works</u> at Everglades Holiday Park. She <u>catches</u> wild alligators.
−	They <u>don't</u> go too close to them. Alligators <u>don't</u> <u>attack</u> people.	Gabby <u>doesn't</u> always <u>work</u> at the park.

b Elicit the first two or three examples with the class. Students then underline the present simple verbs and classify them as positive or negative. Check answers by drawing two columns on the board and asking individual students to come up and write their examples on the board.

Answers

Positive: has, visit, come, think, lives, works, loves, teaches, tells, swim, give, get, think, enjoys, thinks, has

Negative: don't like, don't go, don't attack, don't like, doesn't work, don't understand

---

⊙ CAREFUL!

When using the present simple, students often make mistakes with the negative forms, either using *haven't* instead of *don't have* before a main verb, e.g., *I haven't a dangerous job* (Correct form = *I **don't have** a dangerous job*), or *didn't* instead of *don't*. This second type of error may sometimes cause misunderstandings, e.g., *I didn't like alligators.* (Correct form = *I **don't like** alligators. Present simple* = it's not a usual action).

Another problem area is subject/verb agreement. Students may either omit the *-s* on the third person singular, e.g., *Lisa work in a ...* (Correct form = *Lisa work**s** in a hospital*), or use it where they shouldn't, e.g., *Our English classes finishes in June* (Correct form = *Our English classes **finish** in June*).

---

c ⟫ ▶ **02.04** Students read the information in Grammar Focus 2A SB p. 140. Play the recording where indicated and ask students to listen and repeat. Students then complete the exercises. Check answers as a class, making sure students are spelling the *-s* forms correctly and using *don't/doesn't* to form the negatives correctly. After students complete the Grammar Focus activities, ask them: *Is the present simple easy? Is it difficult?* Elicit an indication of their confidence level. Tell students to go back to SB p. 21.

Answers (Grammar Focus 2A SB p. 141)

a 2 finishes   4 buys   6 misses   8 teaches   10 watches
   3 relaxes   5 wants   7 says   9 worries

b 1 work; start   3 goes; leaves   5 get; makes   7 study; enjoy
   2 finishes; does   4 watches; tries 6 has; loves

c 2 don't drive   4 doesn't have   6 doesn't go
   3 don't cook   5 don't worry   7 don't do

d 2 ~~don't~~ doesn't   4 ~~haves~~ has   6 ~~am love~~ love
   3 ~~gos~~ goes   5 ~~no~~ don't

d Write the sentences on the board and ask the class to tell you which words to underline.

Answers

1 loves
2 catches

e ▶ **02.05** **Pronunciation** Play the recording for students to identify which verb has an extra syllable. Check answers as a class. If necessary, by counting on your fingers, show students how *love/loves* both have one syllable, how *catch* has one syllable, but the third person singular form *catches* has two.

Answer

Catches has an extra syllable.

f Give students one minute to read the rules and choose the correct answers. Check answers as a class.

Answers

1 add
2 don't add

g ▶ **02.06** You may wish to ask students to apply the rule from 3f to the verbs before they listen. Play the recording for students to check the verbs that have an extra syllable. Check answers as a class. Drill each pair of words, e.g., *work* (one syllable) − *works* (one syllable); *finish* (two syllables) − *finishes* (three syllables), to help students get a feel for when we add an extra syllable and when we don't.

Answers

✓ finishes   ✓ uses   ✓ teaches   ✓ watches

h ⟫ Divide the class into pairs and assign A and B roles. Student As read the sentences about a shop assistant on SB p. 130 and Student Bs read the sentences about a nurse on SB p. 133. They complete the sentences. Monitor for any problems and clarify these before the pairwork stage. Put students into A/B pairs for them to read out their sentences to each other and guess the jobs. Tell students to go back to SB p. 21.

↻ LOA TIP MONITORING

- Monitor the two stages of the pairwork activity closely. In the first step, check carefully that students are writing the verb forms with *-s* correctly and point out any errors in spelling for students to self-correct.

- During the speaking stage, listen carefully to check that students are pronouncing the verb forms correctly. When students make a mistake with the pronunciation, try to catch their eye discreetly so that they can correct their mistake.

- If students continue to pronounce the verb forms incorrectly, you may wish to check this again or ask them to do the activity in Workbook 2A.

💡 **FAST FINISHERS**

Ask fast finishers to choose another job from SB p. 21. They make their own sentences about it and read them out to their partner who tries to guess the job.

4 SPEAKING

a To help students, you may give them some example sentences about your own job, e.g., *I work in a really great place.* Make sure students understand that if they choose to write about someone they know, they will need to use the *-s* form of the verb. Monitor and help with vocabulary and suggest ideas if necessary.

b 💬🗨 Put students into pairs to tell their partner their sentences and try to guess the jobs.

c Students work in new pairs or small groups and tell each other what their partner told them. Point out that in this stage of the activity all students will need to use the *-s* form of the verb. As you monitor, don't interrupt fluency, but note any mistakes with the pronunciation of the *-s* forms of the verbs. After the activity, write any verbs that caused pronunciation problems on the board and drill them.

💡 **EXTRA ACTIVITY**

Write *Who am I?* on the board. Think of a famous person, real or fictional, who your students will know and tell them four sentences about the person using *I* as if you were the person, e.g., *1 I work on my own. 2 I go to interesting places. 3 I stop bad people. 4 I drive an Aston Martin.* (Answer: You're James Bond!) Students could then prepare their own *Who am I?* sentences about famous people to share in small groups.

⊕ **ADDITIONAL MATERIAL**

Workbook 2A

Photocopiable activities: Grammar 2A, Vocabulary 2A, Pronunciation 2A

Documentary video Unit 2 *Work and Study*

Video worksheet Unit 2 *Work and Study*

2B | DO YOU WORRY ABOUT EXAMS?

At the end of this lesson, students will be able to:

- read and understand a text about exam stress
- use vocabulary for talking about studying correctly
- understand an interview about study routines
- tell the time using *o'clock, (a) quarter past, half past,* etc.
- use the question form of the present simple
- ask and answer questions about studying

💡 **OPTIONAL LEAD-IN**

Books closed. Walk into class and give students a surprise test revising five items from the class so far to elicit the answers in brackets, e.g., *1 Where are you from?* (I'm from (students' country/city). / I'm (students' nationality).)
2 How do you spell 'wonderful'? (W-O-N-D-E-R-F-U-L)
3 A coffee is €3 and an ice cream is €3. Two coffees and one ice cream is … ? (€9)
4 What's a cupboard? (a thing with doors to put things in)
5 What's the next number? 1, 2, 4, 7, 11, 16, … (22).

After checking answers, ask students: *How do you feel?* Elicit their feelings, e.g., *Great!, Fantastic!, Stressed!, Worried!,* and then look at the questions in 1a.

1 READING

a 💬🗨 Give students one minute to think about their answers to the questions before talking about exams and tests as a class. You may wish to pre-teach the word *worry* (v.) (to think a lot about bad things).

b Students read the comments quickly and match them with the pictures. You may wish to pre-teach the words in the Vocabulary Support box. Check answers as a class.

Answers
1 c
2 b
3 a

📖 **VOCABULARY SUPPORT**

habit (B1) – a thing you do regularly

relax (B1) – to stop worrying about something and feel happy

routine (B1) – things you do regularly at the same time every day

stress (B1) – a feeling of worry at a difficult time

c 💬🗨 Tell students to read the comments again in detail. Students answer the questions in pairs. Then, check their ideas as a class. Check that students understand that there are no correct answers in this case.

💡 **EXTRA ACTIVITY**

Divide the class into small groups. Ask half of the groups to complete the sentence *Before exams, it's a good idea to …* in as many ways as possible, and the other half to complete the sentence *Before exams, it's a bad idea to …* , e.g., *… it's a good idea to have a lot of short breaks and relax*; *… it's a bad idea to worry.* Monitor and help with vocabulary and give students ideas if necessary. Regroup students and put them into pairs so that in each pair, one student has *It's a good idea …* sentences and the other has *It's a bad idea …* sentences. Students compare their ideas.

2 VOCABULARY Studying

a Individually, students read the sentences and match them with the pictures. They then check in pairs. Check answers as a class. Check pronunciation by pointing to each word and asking students: *How do you say this word?* Elicit the correct pronunciation. Ask the class: *Is that correct?* before modelling the pronunciation yourself if necessary.

Answers

1 j	5 g
2 h	6 d
3 e	7 i
4 f	

b Complete the first item as an example with the class. Students work individually, matching the words to make phrases. Check answers as a class.

Answers

1 pass/fail/take an exam
2 get good/bad marks
3 take notes
4 pass/fail/take a test

💡 **FAST FINISHERS**

Ask fast finishers to look back at the reading text and see how many of the words and phrases from 2a and 2b they can find there.

c 💬🔊 Before students start asking and answering the questions in 2a, drill them for correct pronunciation. Monitor, but don't interrupt fluency unless students make mistakes with the vocabulary for studying.

3 LISTENING

a ▶ 02.07 Play the recording for students to listen for general meaning and tick the things Jack and Tania talk about. Check answers as a class.

Answers

1 ✓
2 ✓
4 ✓

Audioscript

JACK Umm, excuse me. Hi. Look, can I ask you a few questions about your study routine?
TANIA Sorry?
J Your study routine.
T Umm … OK … but I've got to …
J Great! So, first question, do you study full-time or part-time?
T Part-time. I have a job – I'm a nurse and I have a family. I'm really busy.
J OK … and how many hours a week do you study?
T Well, at the university … about five hours.
J And at home?
T I don't know – maybe about ten hours.
J Do you study in the morning or afternoon?
T I usually study early in the morning or late at night.
J When do you start studying each day?
T Usually at half past eight or nine o'clock.
J Do you finish studying very late?
T Well, it changes every day.
J Well, last night, for example.
T Hmm … last night … at a quarter past eleven.
J That's quite late! And where do you study?
T Everywhere! On the bus, at work, at lunch time, in the kitchen, in the bedroom – everywhere!
J And in your free time?
T Free time?!
J What do you do in your free time?
T I don't have any free time!

b ▶ 02.07 Pre-teach the words *full-time* and *part-time* in the Vocabulary Support box. Students listen to the recording again for specific details and complete the information. They compare in pairs. Check answers as a class.

Answers

- part-time
- 15 hours a week
- early in the morning or late at night
- everywhere – on the bus, at work, at lunchtime, in the kitchen, in the bedroom

📖 **VOCABULARY SUPPORT**

full-time (B1) – all the time, for all the hours of the week that people normally work, e.g., *a full-time job* (= 40 hours a week)

part-time (B1) – only some of the time; you have time for other things, e.g., *a part-time student* (= not all day on every working day)

4 VOCABULARY Time

a Draw a question mark on the board and point to your watch to elicit the question: *What's the time?* or *What time is it?* Tell students what the time is using the simpler form they used in Lesson 1C, e.g., *It's ten twenty.*, *It's three twenty-five.*, etc. Look at the first clock in the Student's Book and say the time using this same system, i.e., *It's eleven fifteen.* Then, read the examples with the class for students to match them with what Tania said.

Answers

1 b
2 a

b Individually, students complete the sentences. Check answers as a class.

Answers

1 o'clock
2 half
3 past
4 to

c ⏵ `02.08` Students complete the exercises in Vocabulary Focus 2B on SB p. 164. Play the recording for students to check their answers to Exercise a and monitor Exercise b. Tell students to go back to SB p. 23.

Answers (Vocabulary Focus 2B SB p. 164)
a 1 c 2 e 3 g 4 d 5 h 6 a 7 f 8 i 9 b

5 GRAMMAR Present simple: questions

a ⏵ `02.09` Write the following three jumbled questions about Tania and Jack on the board and ask students to put them in order: *1 Tania / busy / is ? (1 Is Tania busy?) 2 a nurse / is / Jack ? (2 Is Jack a nurse?) 3 students / they / are ? (3 Are they students?)*. Ask students the questions and elicit the answers. (*1 Yes, she is. 2 No, he isn't. He's a student. 3 Yes, they are.*) Point to the questions on the board and say *Questions with 'be'*. Then, point students to the Student's Book and say: *Present simple questions.* Students then look at the questions and decide which one is correct. Play the recording for students to listen and check. Check the answer as a class.

Answer
Question 2 is correct.

b Read the two questions as a class and elicit the word.

Answer
Do

c ⏵ `02.10` Tell students to listen to the next part of Jack and Tania's conversation for specific details about Ellie (Tania's daughter) and to complete the information. They compare in pairs. Check answers as a class. You may then wish to teach the word *library* (a place with lots of books that you can use to read or study).

Answers
• about 40 hours a week
• at about nine o'clock
• mostly at the university library and sometimes at home

Audioscript

JACK Are you the only student at home?	**J** What time does she start each day?
TANIA No, my daughter Ellie is a student, too.	**T** I'm not sure. At about nine o'clock.
J Can I ask about her …?	**J** Where does she study?
T All right, but look, I really have to …	**T** Mostly at the university library and sometimes at home.
J Thank you so much. So, Ellie is it?	**J** Does she study more before an exam?
T Yes.	**T** Yes, I think so. Look, I really have no idea. I'm in a hurry … I must go. Goodbye!
J How many hours a week does she study?	**J** Please just one more question. Maybe not.
T She's a full-time student, so she studies about 40 hours a week.	

d Read the question as a class and refer students back to the questions in 5b. Elicit the difference.

Answer
Jack's question uses *Does*, not *Do*. It's a third person singular question form.

⟳ LOA TIP CONCEPT CHECKING

• Check that students understand the connection between the use of the auxiliary verb in present simple negative sentences and questions by writing *You study early in the morning.* After the sentence, write the plus sign (+) on the board. Directly underneath the (+), write (–) and elicit a negative sentence, e.g., *You don't study in the afternoon.* Under the (+) and the (–), write a question mark (?) and elicit a question, e.g., *Do you study early in the morning?* Circle the verb *study* in each sentence and the auxiliaries *don't* and *do*.

• Repeat the process with a third person singular form, e.g., *Ellie studies full-time.* (+); *Ellie doesn't study part-time.* (–); *Does Ellie study full-time?* (?). Circle the *-s* ending of the verb in the positive sentence and show students how this transfers to the auxiliary verb in the negative and in the question.

⊙ CAREFUL!

Students may have problems with the word order in present simple questions, particularly with the position of the auxiliary verb in relation to the subject and the main verb, e.g., ~~You do study at university~~ (Correct form = ***Do you study*** at university?), or they may omit the auxiliary verb completely, e.g., ~~Where you live?~~ (Correct form = *Where **do** you live?*).

Another common error is to use a full stop at the end of a question instead of a question mark or to omit the punctuation altogether, e.g., ~~What do you study~~ (Correct form = *What do you study?*). As students work through the Grammar Focus, make sure they are using correct word order and punctuation.

e ⟫ ⏵ `02.11` Students read the information in Grammar Focus 2B on SB p. 140. Play the recording where indicated and ask students to listen and repeat. Students then complete the exercises. Check answers as a class, making sure students are using *does/doesn't* for third person singular forms correctly. Tell students to go back to SB p. 23.

Answers (Grammar Focus 2B SB p. 141)
a 2 Do you go   5 What do they wear
  3 Does he want   6 What time do they have lunch
  4 Where do you play
b 2 Does 3 does 4 Do 5 don't 6 do 7 Does 8 doesn't
c 2 does she study   5 does the bus go
  3 does the shop open   6 do you go to the gym
  4 do you want   7 do they work

f ⏵ `02.12` Students order the phrases to make questions. Play the recording for students to listen and check. Check answers as a class.

Answers
1 How many hours a week do you study?
2 Do you study grammar or vocabulary?
3 When do you study?
4 Where do you study?

g ⏵ `02.12` **Pronunciation** Play the recording again and highlight the pronunciation of *Do you* for students. Check the answer as a class.

Answer
No, you can't.

💡 **EXTRA ACTIVITY**

Ask students questions about specific times and ask them to write down short answers in numerals in their notebooks, e.g., *1 What time does your English class start (on Tuesdays)? 2 What time do you go to bed on Mondays? 3 What time do you have dinner? 4 What time does your English class end today? 5 What's your favourite TV programme? What time does it start?* In pairs, students compare the times they wrote down and try to make sentences using the information, e.g., *My English class starts at 10:00 on Tuesdays; I go to bed at 10:30 on Mondays.* Ask some students to tell the class their sentences.

Ask students in pairs or small groups to reconstruct the questions you originally asked them. Write the questions on the board for students to check their own answers, paying particular attention to the use of *Does* in the third-person question forms.

💡 **FAST FINISHERS**

Ask fast finishers to write sentences to summarise their discussion, e.g., *Sonia studies English because she loves it!*

c 💬🎬 Discuss the question as a class. Praise students who are able to express their ideas, even if their English isn't perfect, and avoid correcting errors in front of the whole class.

⊕ **ADDITIONAL MATERIAL**

Workbook 2B

Photocopiable activities: Grammar 2B, Vocabulary 2B

6 SPEAKING

a Give students one minute to write another question about study. Point out errors for students to self-correct.

b 💬🎬 Students work in small groups, asking and answering the questions they wrote in 6a. Monitor, but don't interrupt fluency unless students make mistakes with the present simple forms.

2C | EVERYDAY ENGLISH
I'd like a latte

At the end of this lesson, students will be able to:

- understand informal conversations in which people make requests and respond
- use appropriate phrases for asking for things and replying
- use appropriate phrases for reacting to news
- relate the letters *ou* to the sounds /ə/, /ɔː/ and /aʊ/
- maintain informal conversations in which they make requests and respond

💡 **OPTIONAL LEAD-IN**

Point to picture c on SB p.24 or project it on the board. Ask: *Who are they?* and elicit *Leo* and *Dan*. Read sentences 1–5 to the students and ask them to decide if they are true or false. They could do this in pairs. Check answers as a class.

1 Martina is Leo's wife. (F – Martina is Dan's wife.)

2 Leo and Dan work together. (T)

3 Dan doesn't go to the gym. (T)

4 Leo works at a computer all day. (T)

5 Martina and Dan live at 18 New Street. (F – Leo lives at 18 New Street.)

answer as a class. Ask students: *Who do you think Annie is?*, but don't tell them at this point.

Answer

2 at work

1 LISTENING

a 💬🎬 If you didn't use the optional lead-in, ask students what they can remember about Leo and Dan from Lesson 1C. Look at picture a with the class and read through the question. Elicit students' ideas, but don't check the answer at this point.

b ▶️ 02.13 Play Part 1 of the video or the audio recording for students to check their answer to 1a. Check the

Video/Audioscript (Part 1)

DAN What do you want?

LEO Oh, thanks. I'd like a latte.

D Can I have a tea and a latte, please?

WAITRESS Certainly. Small or large?

D A small tea and … ?

L Large for me, please.

W So, a large latte and a small tea?

D Yes. And could I have a croissant as well, please? … So, we need to talk about the meeting on Wednesday.

L Oh yes. Is it here or at their office?

D At their office. Could we chat about it now?

L Sorry, I have another meeting in five minutes.

D OK, no problem. We can do it later. … How much is that?

W £3.60.

D Here you go.

W Thanks.

L So, this meeting on Wednesday …

D Yeah. Oh! Could you pass the milk? Thanks. Annie!

ANNIE Hi, Dan. Sorry to call you at work.

D That's OK. Don't worry.

c 🗨️ In pairs, students read the sentences and see if they remember the answers from the first listening. Don't check answers at this point.

d ▶️02.13 Students watch or listen again for specific details. Play Part 1 of the video or the audio recording again for students to check their answers to 1c.

> **Answers**
> 1 small (tea), large (latte), one croissant
> 2 £3.60
> 3 milk

e ▶️02.14 Point to picture b and tell students that it's Annie. Play Part 2 of the video or the audio recording for students to find out what her problem is. Check the answer as a class and then ask students: *Who's Annie?* (Dan's sister) and find out if they guessed correctly in 1b.

> **Answer**
> a which course to do

> **Video/Audioscript (Part 2)**
>
> **ANNIE** Hi, Dan. Sorry to call you at work.
> **DAN** That's OK. Don't worry.
> **A** But you see, I need … Well, I'd like some help.
> **D** Sure, no problem.
> **A** It's about this online course I want to do. I'm not sure which one … I mean, I can't decide.
> **D** So you want your big brother to help you …?
> **A** Yes, I do. Could I come to your place tonight?
> **D** Sorry, we're not at home tonight.
>
> **A** Oh, that's a pity.
> **D** But, look, come on Friday – for dinner.
> **A** Friday?
> **D** Yes.
> **A** For dinner?
> **D** Yes!
> **A** Lovely!
> **D** OK. See you then. Bye!
> **A** Bye!
> **D** My sister! Always asking me to do things for her. … ugh! Too much sugar!

f ▶️02.14 Students watch or listen again for specific details. Play Part 2 of the video or the audio recording again for students to decide if the sentences are true or false and correct the false sentences.

> **Answers**
> 1 T
> 2 F (Dan and Martina aren't at home tonight.)
> 3 F (Annie's free on Friday.)
> 4 T

> 💡 **EXTRA ACTIVITY**
>
> Write the following four jumbled sentences on the board (two from Part 1 and two from Part 2) and ask students to put them in order:
>
> 1 need / we / the meeting on Wednesday / to talk about (We need to talk about the meeting on Wednesday.)
>
> 2 is / at their office / it / here or ? (Is it here or at their office?)
>
> 3 I want to do / it's / online course / about this (It's about this online course I want to do.)
>
> 4 to help you / so you / your big brother / want (So you want your big brother to help you.).
>
> Check answers by playing both parts of the video or audio recording again and pausing when the characters say the sentences for students to check their answers.

g 🗨️ In pairs, students discuss where they usually meet friends. Ask any students who think of different places to share their ideas with the class.

> 💡 **FAST FINISHERS**
>
> Ask fast finishers to talk about what they usually do when they meet their friends, e.g., *play computer games, chat, do sport*.

2️⃣ USEFUL LANGUAGE
Asking for things and replying

a Individually, students decide who says each sentence. They then compare their ideas in pairs. Don't check answers at this point.

b ▶️02.13–02.14 Check answers by playing both parts of the video or audio recording again and pausing each time Dan and Annie ask for something. Elicit from the class which reply (a–d) they expect to hear before continuing to play the recording to find out if they were correct.

> **Answers**
> 1 D 2 A 3 D 4 A
> a 1 b 3 c 4 d 2

c 🗨️ Demonstrate the activity by asking one student: *Hello. Can I have a coffee, please?* and eliciting an appropriate response, e.g., *Certainly. Small or large?* Encourage students to play around with the phrases and use their own ideas. Monitor and praise students with a smile or a nod when they use the language from this section correctly.

d ▶️02.15 Point to each of the three photos on SB p. 25 in turn and ask: *Where is this?* Elicit *a a café, b a hospital, c an office*. Play the recording for students to listen and match the conversations with the pictures. Check answers as a class.

> **Answers**
> 1 b 2 a 3 c

> **Audioscript**
>
> **CONVERSATION 1**
> **A** Nurse!
> **B** Yes.
> **A** Could I have some water, please?
> **B** Sure, no problem. Here you are.
> **A** Thank you.
>
> **CONVERSATION 2**
> **A** Yes?
> **B** I'd like a chicken sandwich, please.
> **A** Sorry, we don't have chicken. We have cheese or egg.
> **B** Oh, OK. Hmm … a cheese sandwich, then.
>
> **CONVERSATION 3**
> **A** Can I phone you this afternoon? I'm very busy just now.
> **B** Sure, no problem. Call me at about two?
> **A** Yes, that's fine. Speak to you later.
> **B** OK, bye.

e ▶️02.15 Individually, students complete the sentences from the conversations. Play the recording again for students to listen and check. Check answers as a class.

> **Answers**
> 1 Could I have 2 I'd like 3 Can I phone

f Brainstorm phrases for each of the situations as a class and write these on the board for students to refer to in the next exercise, e.g. *Dimitri, can I have some water, please? – Sure, no problem.*; *Could I have a small espresso, please? – Certainly.*

g In pairs, students role play the four situations. Monitor and check that students are using appropriate ways to ask for things and, equally importantly, using appropriate ways to respond.

💡 FAST FINISHERS

Ask fast finishers to improvise more conversations of the same type, e.g., borrowing notes from the last English class, ordering a meal in a restaurant.

③ CONVERSATION SKILLS
Reacting to news

a ▶️ 02.16 In pairs, students look at the mini-conversations and try to complete them. Play the recording for students to listen and check. Check answers as a class.

> **Answers**
> 1 problem
> 2 pity

b Read the mini-conversations as a class and check what the phrases mean.

> **Answers**
> 1 OK, no problem.
> 2 Oh, that's a pity.

c Individually, students match the four phrases to the phrases in 3b with a similar meaning. Check answers as a class.

> **Answers**
> a 1
> b 2
> c 1
> d 2

🔄 LOA TIP DRILLING

- Drill *OK, no problem*, *Oh, that's a pity* and the four phrases in 3c before continuing. Try drilling the phrases backwards to add variety to the class, i.e., *problem – no problem – OK, no problem*.

- Pay particular attention to the intonation in these phrases. Exaggerate the 'musicality' as you drill them as many students tend to shy away from this. If the intonation on these phrases is too flat, then the listener could easily think there's a lack of sincerity on the speaker's part.

④ PRONUNCIATION
Sound and spelling: *ou*

a ▶️ 02.17 Play the recording and highlight the three possible sounds for the letters *ou* for students. Check the answer as a class.

> **Answer**
> Yes, they do.

📖 LANGUAGE NOTES

Sound and spelling relationships can cause native English speakers problems. This section introduces the three most frequent sounds which correspond to the letters *ou*: /ə/, /ɔː/ and /aʊ/ (whether or not you wish to introduce students to the phonemic symbols themselves at this point will depend on the level of your class). Don't ask students to look for other examples of words with *ou* themselves, as they may well find words which contain the letters *ou*, but are not pronounced with the three sounds being worked on.

b ▶️ 02.18 Students classify the words into three groups. Play the recording for students to listen and check. Check answers as a class. Then ask students to repeat the words after the recording and practise the pronunciation.

> **Answers**
> four 2   neighbour 1   about 3   sound 3

⑤ SPEAKING

a ⏩ Divide the class into pairs and assign A and B roles. Student As read the first card on SB p. 130 and Student Bs read the first card on SB p. 133. Students then role play the conversation. Monitor, but don't interrupt fluency unless students make mistakes with the content of this lesson. Students then read the second card and role play the second situation.

💡 EXTRA ACTIVITY

Students write a dialogue based on one of the conversations from 5a. They should use phrases for asking for things and replying from the lesson and pay particular attention to spelling the phrases correctly.

⊕ ADDITIONAL MATERIAL

Workbook 2C

Photocopiable activities: Pronunciation 2C

Unit Progress Test

SKILLS FOR WRITING

I need English for my job

At the end of this lesson, students will be able to:

- understand a conversation in which students talk about where they're from and why they're learning English
- understand personal information on a written form
- identify and correct spelling mistakes
- complete a form with their own personal information

💡 **OPTIONAL LEAD-IN**

Books closed. Tell students you have a list of common reasons for learning English (the reasons in 1a on SB p. 26). Give them a few minutes in pairs to try to guess the reasons on the list. Ask students to share their answers with the class, writing their ideas on the board. When a pair gives a reason that is in 1a, say: *Good job! That one is on the list.* If students have the same basic idea as one on the list but express it in different words, congratulate them too, e.g., *to go to university in the UK* (= *to study something in English*). Write all their ideas on the board. Then, ask them to open their books and look at the ideas in 1a.

1 SPEAKING AND LISTENING

a 💬 Discuss the question as a class and find out why each of your students wants to study English. If you didn't use the optional lead-in, be prepared to help with vocabulary where necessary.

b ▶ 02.19 Point to each of the three photos on SB p. 26 one by one and say: *This is Daniela / Said / Justyna.* Play the recording for students to listen for general meaning and underline the correct answers. Check answers as a class.

Answers
1 Mexico City; job   2 Riyadh; job   3 Warsaw; studies

Audioscript

DANIELA My name is Daniela, and I'm a police officer in Mexico City – but just traffic police. I need to speak English because sometimes tourists ask me questions in English. For example, they ask me for directions or some tourist information. I like studying at this college. The timetable works well – we have a two-hour break in the middle of the day. I want to improve my listening. I find listening quite hard and it's difficult to listen to something and make notes at the same time. So I need to do some extra listening practice.

SAID Hi. My name is Said, and I'm a dentist in Riyadh in Saudi Arabia. Sometimes English-speaking people come to my work, so I need to speak good English. This college is very good – the lessons are very interesting and we do lots of different things in class. I want to stay here for a term – until December. Listening and speaking is OK for me, but I need to work hard at reading and writing. I'd like to read books in English – maybe even some books about my work.

JUSTYNA Hello, my name's Justyna, and I'm a photographer for a newspaper in Warsaw in Poland. In the future, I'd like to study at a university in the UK, so I need better English to do that. Our teacher, Kate, is great. She's very friendly and she helps us a lot in class. Only one thing worries me a bit: the marks I get in tests. I think my progress is OK and I can speak better, but I'm not very good at tests and exams. But maybe I need to study grammar a bit more, too!

c ▶ 02.19 Students listen to the recording again for specific details and complete the table. They compare in pairs. Check answers as a class.

Answers

	Likes at the college	Needs to improve
Daniela	the timetable	listening
Said	the lessons	reading and writing
Justyna	the teacher	grammar

d 💬 Put students into small groups to talk about the questions together. Monitor, but don't interrupt fluency.

💡 **FAST FINISHERS**

Ask fast finishers to also talk about what they think is difficult to improve in English and why, e.g., *It's difficult to improve pronunciation because it's really irregular!*

e ▶ 02.20 Play the recording for students to find out what you can win in the competition. Check the answer as a class.

Answer
an extra month of English lessons for free

Audioscript

KATE Hi, everyone. Before we begin the lesson, I just want to tell you about this competition we're having here at school. It's really good because you can win an extra month of English lessons for free. That's right – an extra month for nothing. So all you need is … Well, you need to be a student at this school – and you all are – and you need to complete this entry form by hand – you know, you can't use a computer. But you also need to make sure that what you write on the entry form is correct – no mistakes! So if you want to enter, you can get an entry form from me or you can also get them from reception. It's a really good competition – one more month of study. So, are there any questions?

f ▶ 02.20 Before students listen again, give them one minute to work in pairs and see what, if anything, they remember from the first listening. Play the recording again for students to answer the questions. Check answers as a class.

Answers
1 No, they can't.
2 No, it isn't.
3 from Kate or from reception

2 READING

a Individually, students read the information about Daniela and complete the form, using their own ideas for Daniela's last name and phone number. Check answers by copying Part 1 of the form onto the board and asking students to complete the information.

Answers
First name: Daniela
Last name: Romero
Gender: female
Nationality: Mexican
Mobile phone (UK): 074822 294576
Email address: danielar@supermail.com
Your class now: P1
Class start date: 6th July

b In pairs, students discuss what words complete Part 2 of the form. Don't check answers at this point.

c ⏵ **02.21** Play the recording for students to listen to Daniela and check their answers. Check spelling by writing the words on the board.

> **Answers**
> 1 police officer
> 2 tourists
> 3 job
> 4 listening

3 WRITING SKILLS Spelling

a Write *Englesh speling* on the board. Students should realise that it is spelt incorrectly, so rub it out and ask: *How do you spell it?* and write the correct spelling on the board. Tell students to cover SB p. 26 and look at the first copy of Daniela's entry form on SB p. 27. Look at the example together and explain that there are eight more spelling problems. Ask students: *How many spelling problems are there in total?* Elicit the answer *nine* (the example plus eight more problems). Individually, students find and correct the spelling mistakes. Check answers as a class.

> **Answers**
> ~~offiser~~ officer
> ~~toorists~~ tourists
> ~~informashion~~ information
> ~~dificult~~ difficult
> ~~anser~~ answer
> ~~becos~~ because
> ~~listning~~ listening
> ~~scool~~ school

💡 FAST FINISHERS

Ask fast finishers to make a list of words they know they often have problems spelling. They write the incorrect form of each word, strike it through and put a cross after it, and then write the correct spelling next to it with a tick after it, e.g., *riting* ✗ *writing* ✓.

b As a class, discuss when it is important to use correct spelling.

> **Answers**
> 2 ✓
> 3 ✓

c Individually, students find and correct the spelling mistake in each sentence. Check answers by writing the sentences on the board and asking students to tell you where the mistake is. Strike the incorrect word through and ask them to spell the correct word to you all together as you write it on the board.

> **Answers**
> 1 ~~see~~ sea
> 2 ~~right~~ write
> 3 ~~no~~ know
> 4 ~~here~~ hear
> 5 ~~bye~~ buy

d Discuss as a class how the incorrect and correct words in 3c are the same. Then, elicit an indication of students' confidence level for English spelling.

> **Answer**
> They're pronounced the same.

📖 LANGUAGE NOTES

Homophones (words which have different spellings and meanings but are pronounced the same) may not exist in your students' own languages, so the idea may seem very strange to them. Many problems with English spelling stem from homophones, like those in 3c. Some native speakers have real problems with even basic differences, such as *your* and *you're* and *there*, *they're* and *their*. These problems have become even more noticeable in recent years with the advance of social media, where people are not as careful with their grammar and spelling.

💡 EXTRA ACTIVITY

Give students a spelling test with ten items from the course so far, e.g., *1 grey, 2 awful, 3 Australian, 4 amazing, 5 secretary, 6 Germany, 7 businesswoman, 8 brilliant, 9 photographer, 10 timetable.* Ideally, personalise the test for your group by choosing words which you know your students often have problems spelling. Check answers by getting students to write the words on the board, spelling them aloud as they go. Students award themselves one point for each word they spell correctly.

4 WRITING

a Individually, students complete the form with their information. If you're short of time, this exercise and 4b can be completed for homework. Students could then bring their forms to the next lesson.

b Students write their answers to the two questions for the competition. Remind them to use their ideas from the discussion in 1d. If you used the Fast Finishers activity after 1d, make sure you have corrected any errors you heard students make in their speaking before they start writing in order for them not to repeat them in written form here.

🔄 LOA TIP ELICITING

• Before students start writing, consider eliciting orally another example about yourself. Use the texts about Daniela in 2a as a guide. Students close their books. Point to yourself and say: *I work as …* (elicit: an English teacher) *in …* (elicit: the city). *I love my job, but not the …* (elicit suggestions). Continue eliciting ideas for what you might say about yourself in answer to the first question.

• After building up a paragraph about why the students' language is important to you, repeat the process with a second paragraph about what you want to improve in the students' language. This will also be valuable as it will help students understand that the problems they may be experiencing in learning English are relatively common and apply to people learning other languages, too.

c In pairs, students swap their forms and see if their ideas are the same. They can also check their partner's work for spelling mistakes. If students have made any spelling mistakes, or if their partner can offer any other ideas for improving their answers, they prepare a second draft of their answers before giving it to you for correction.

⊕ ADDITIONAL MATERIAL

Workbook 2D

UNIT 2
Review and extension

1 GRAMMAR

a Individually, students complete the text. Check answers as a class by asking individual students to write the correct answers on the board.

Answers

1 work	5 works
2 start	6 doesn't like
3 don't start	7 work
4 doesn't have	

b Students write possible questions for the answers. Monitor for any problems and clarify these before students start on the pairwork stage in 1c.

Possible answers
1 What do you do?
2 Do you work in an office?
3 Do you like your job?
4 When do you start work?
5 Does your husband work?
6 Where does he work?
7 Does he like his job?

c 💬🗩 In pairs, students ask and answer the questions, making any changes necessary, e.g., *husband – wife, he – she.*

2 VOCABULARY

a Students put the letters in order. Check answers by writing the words on the board one letter at a time, saying each letter clearly and asking the class to repeat it after you.

Answers

1 nurse	4 engineer
2 dentist	5 cleaner
3 pilot	6 photographer

b Students write the times in words. Check answers as a class.

Answers
1 half past eleven *or* eleven thirty
2 (a) quarter to one *or* twelve forty-five
3 six o'clock
4 quarter past eight *or* eight fifteen
5 twenty to three *or* two forty
6 twenty past five *or* five twenty

c Individually, students match the parts of the sentences. Check answers as a class.

Answers
1 c 2 e 3 a 4 b 5 d

> ♀ **FAST FINISHERS**
>
> Ask fast finishers to write sentences using some of the other words from the Vocabulary: Studying section on SB p. 22, e.g., *timetable, studies, pass a test.*

3 WORDPOWER *work*

a Tell students to close their books. Write the bold phrases from the three sentences in 3a on the board, i.e., *work in, work for* and *work as.* Point to yourself and say: *I work in a (language) school/university)*, then: *I work for (name of your school/university)* and finally: *I work as a teacher.* Students open their books, look at the sentences and match them with the pictures. Check answers as a class.

Answers
1 c 2 a 3 b

b Match the meanings with the marked phrases in 3a as a class.

Answers
1 work as   2 work in   3 work for

> ♀ **EXTRA ACTIVITY**
>
> If your students work, ask them to write sentences about themselves using the phrases in 3a. Ask each student in turn to tell the class their three sentences, and check they're using the words *in, for* and *as* correctly.

c Give students one minute to think about the sentences individually before discussing them as a class.

Answer
It's a noun in all five sentences.

d Elicit the *work* phrases that match the meanings from the class. Check that students understand that these are normally used with the verb *be.*

Answers
a (be) out of work
b (be) at work

e Individually, students put the words in brackets in the correct place in the sentences. They then check in pairs. Check answers as a class.

Answers
1 He works as a nurse at night.
2 We all start work at 6:00 pm.
3 She'd like a job because now she's out of work.
4 She's a photographer and works for *The Times.*
5 When I'm at work, I have no free time.
6 We both work in a large office in the centre of town.

f Give students one or two examples for someone you know using *work* as a verb and as a noun, e.g., *My best friend works as a doctor in a big hospital. She starts work at seven o'clock in the morning.* Monitor and listen for correct use of *work* as a verb and a noun. Point out errors for students to self-correct. If you wish, ask each student to tell the class about the person they wrote about.

⫸ Photocopiable activities: Wordpower 2

> ◐ **LOA REVIEW YOUR PROGRESS**
>
> Students look back through the unit, think about what they've studied and decide how well they did. Students work on weak areas by using the appropriate sections of the Workbook and the Photocopiable activities.

↻ UNIT OBJECTIVES

At the end of this unit, students will be able to:

■ understand information, texts and conversations and exchange information about daily life and routines and the role of the Internet and technology in people's lives

■ talk about and give simple descriptions of their own and other people's possessions

■ understand conversations in which people make arrangements and make arrangements themselves

■ use simple phrases to hesitate while thinking about what they want to say

■ write an informal invitation to an event and an appropriate reply

UNIT CONTENTS

G GRAMMAR

■ Position of adverbs of frequency: *always, usually, often, sometimes, never*
■ *have got*

V VOCABULARY

■ Time expressions: *every week/month/year, once a week/ month/year, twice a week/month/year, three times a week/ month/year*, etc.
■ Common verbs: *buy, cost, decide, find, help, meet, prefer, sell, stay, try*
■ Technology: *camera, computer, headphones, keyboard, laptop, printer, smartphone, smartwatch, speaker, tablet*
■ Wordpower: Prepositions of time: *at* + times / night / the weekend, *in* + months / parts of day / seasons, *on* + days

P PRONUNCIATION

■ Sentence stress on important words
■ Sound and spelling: /ʌ/, /oʊ/, and /u/
■ Word stress in technology words
■ Main stress in sentences and intonation
■ Pronunciation of *Hmm* when hesitating

C COMMUNICATION SKILLS

■ Talking about your daily routine and the routines of people you know well
■ Talking about the Internet and technology in your life
■ Talking about your own and other people's possessions
■ Making arrangements and responding appropriately
■ Using appropriate phrases while thinking about what you want to say
■ Writing an informal invitation to an event and writing a reply to an invitation you receive

GETTING STARTED

♀ OPTIONAL LEAD-IN

Divide the class into small groups. Ask half of the groups to brainstorm *jobs* and the other half to brainstorm *countries*. After two minutes, put students into pairs, one with a list of jobs and the other a list of countries. Students take turns thinking of jobs/ countries that aren't on their partner's list. When they say a new job/country, their partner asks them: *How do you spell that?* Students can check their partner's spelling in the Student's Book or a dictionary. Students win one point for every job/country not on their partner's list and an extra point for spelling it correctly. The student with the most points wins.

a 💬 Give students one minute to think about their answers before talking about the picture as a class. If you didn't use the optional lead-in, you could elicit a lot of possible countries and jobs for Questions 1 and 4 to give students some extra practice. You may also give students information from Culture Notes below.

🌍 CULTURE NOTES

The photo shows an underground train with a man dressed in a traditional Chinese opera costume. Chinese opera is one of the oldest dramatic art forms in the world. The costumes can be very expensive. For this reason, they are usually passed down from teacher to student.

b 💬 Read the questions and the ideas with the students and check that they understand the vocabulary. In pairs, they ask and answer the questions. Ask students to share their answers with the class and then ask additional questions using the present simple, e.g., *Juan — you buy a newspaper. What newspaper do you buy?; Max — you listen to music on the bus. What kind of music?*

♀ EXTRA ACTIVITY

In pairs or small groups, students brainstorm other things they do every day. A1-level items which students will probably know include: *brush your teeth, drink coffee/tea, have a bath/ shower, have breakfast/lunch/dinner, get up, go to work/school/ university, watch TV*. Ask students to share their ideas with the class and collate them on the board.

Exercises a and b can be prepared as homework before this lesson to give students time to look up unfamiliar vocabulary. Ask students to look at the picture and to prepare their answers to the questions as homework to talk about in the next lesson.

3A | SHE OFTEN GOES TO AN ENGLISH LESSON

At the end of this lesson, students will be able to:

- read and understand a text about the daily life and routine of a woman in Norway
- use adverbs of frequency correctly with *be* and other common verbs
- understand a conversation in which people give information about the routines of themselves and others
- use time expressions to talk about how often things happen
- talk about what they do with people they know well and how often

💡 OPTIONAL LEAD-IN

Write ten common 'daily routine' items on the board, e.g., *cook, get up, go home, go to bed, go to work/university, have breakfast, have dinner, have lunch, watch TV, work/study*. If you used the extra activity at the end of the Getting Started section, recycle some of the vocabulary students thought of then. In pairs, students decide what the usual 'daily routine order' is for people in their country and if there is anything important missing from the list on the board. Add to the list if necessary and then ask pairs to decide at what time people in their country do these things, e.g., *People have lunch at around two o'clock*. Get pairs to share their answers with the class and check that students are saying the times correctly. Notice if students are using adverbs of frequency. Don't correct any mistakes with these, but see if students are having problems positioning them in the sentences.

1 READING

a 💬🔊 Give students one minute to look at the pictures and think about their answers. Don't check answers at this point.

b Students read the text quickly and answer the questions. Check answers as a class.

Answers
1. Answers will depend on work routines in different companies. Nora's work day is nine hours, but she gets breaks during the day, which probably help make her work life easy.
2. She has an English or knitting lesson during work time. The company has pets she can play with in her break.

c Tell students to read the text again in detail. Individually, students decide if the sentences are true or false. When checking answers, ask students to correct the false sentences.

Answers
1. F (She has her breakfast at home.)
2. T
3. T
4. F (She goes to a knitting lesson or an English lesson.)
5. T
6. F (She often has dinner at the company restaurant and goes home at 7:30 pm)

💡 FAST FINISHERS

Ask fast finishers to use the information in the text and write more true sentences about Nora's daily routine.

d 💬🔊 In pairs, students talk about the good things in Nora's work life. Students share their answers with the class.

2 GRAMMAR
Position of adverbs of frequency

a Books closed. Write *She … arrives at work at about 8:15 am* on the board. Point to the gap and ask students if they can remember what the word was (*usually*). Underneath, write: *Nora … leaves the office before 5:30 pm* and elicit the missing word (*never*). Individually, students look at the text in the book and underline more adverbs of frequency. Check answers as a class.

Answers
… and the trains are <u>always</u> crowded. At about 10:15 or 10:30, Nora <u>usually</u> takes a break.
She <u>often</u> goes to an English lesson, but she <u>sometimes</u> has a knitting lesson …
It is <u>usually</u> a sandwich with fish or cheese.
In the middle of the afternoon, Nora <u>always</u> takes another break at about 3:00 pm.
Nora feeds the rabbits, and she <u>often</u> takes one of the dogs for a walk.
Nora <u>never</u> leaves the office before 5:30 pm.
She <u>often</u> has dinner with her colleagues at the company restaurant.

b Point to the two sentences on the board and show students that *never* is on the far left of the timeline. Elicit the correct position of *always* on the far right before students work individually, and put the other adverbs of frequency in the correct place. Check answers by drawing the timeline on the board and asking individual students to come up and write in the adverbs of frequency.

Answers

never	sometimes	often	usually	always
0%				100%

👁 CAREFUL!

The most common student mistakes with adverbs of frequency involve word order. Students may place the adverbs before the subject, e.g., ~~Always I get up~~ … (Correct form = *I always get up at 7 am*.) or after verbs other than be, e.g., ~~I have usually coffee~~ … (Correct form = I *usually have* coffee at breakfast). They may also place the adverbs before the verb be instead of after it, e.g., ~~I often am tired~~ … (Correct form = I *am often* tired after work).

At this level, other errors are usually connected with spelling, e.g., ~~She's allways …~~ / ~~She's alway …~~ (Correct form = She's *always* busy); ~~He usualy has …~~ (Correct form = He *usually* has a nap after lunch); ~~They sometime eat …~~ (Correct form = They *sometimes* eat together).

c ⟫ ▶**03.01** Students read the information in Grammar Focus 3A on SB p. 142. Play the recording where indicated, and ask students to listen and repeat. Students then complete the exercises on SB p. 143. Check answers as a class, making sure students position the adverbs of frequency correctly and use a positive verb with *never*. Tell students to go back to SB p. 30.

> **Answers (Grammar Focus 3A SB p. 143)**
> **a** 1 I <u>always</u> go and see them.
> 2 I'm <u>sometimes</u> late for work, but my boss <u>never</u> gets angry.
> 3 He <u>usually</u> comes here for a coffee at 10 o'clock – he's <u>never</u> late.
> 4 We <u>often</u> have lunch together and talk. It's <u>always</u> good to see him.
> 5 They're <u>never</u> away on holiday – they're <u>always</u> at home.
> **b** 2 My parents sometimes eat in a restaurant.
> 3 I often play tennis.
> 4 Natasha's never late for work.
> 5 We always watch TV in the evening.
> **c** 2 Do you usually walk to work?
> 3 Why are you always tired?
> 4 Where do you usually go at weekends?
> 5 How often do they play football?
> 6 Is he often late for work?
> 7 Why do you never write to me?

⟳ LOA TIP ELICITING

- After looking at the rules in Grammar Focus 3A on SB p. 142, write example positive and negative sentences and questions on the board to check that students are assimilating correct word order. Point to each sentence in turn and ask students: *Is this correct?* Ask them to correct them as necessary, e.g., *I get up usually at seven o'clock.* (I <u>usually</u> get up …); *She often doesn't get up late.* (She doesn't <u>often</u> get up …); *Do sometimes you watch TV in the evening?* (Do you <u>sometimes</u> watch TV …?).

- Also check that students understand that although *never* is negative in meaning, it is used with a positive verb. Write three sentences with *never* on the board, and ask students: *Which is correct?*, e.g., *1 He doesn't never eat with his family. 2 He never eats with his family. 3 He doesn't eat never with his family.* (Sentence 2 is correct.)

---

d 💬▣ Students work in pairs or small groups, talking about the things they do. Monitor, but don't interrupt fluency unless students make mistakes with the position of the adverbs of frequency.

💡 EXTRA ACTIVITY

Play a guessing game with students. Tell students five sentences about something you do and ask them to guess what it is, e.g., *1 I often do this in the morning and in the evening. 2 I sometimes do this at noon or after lunch. 3 I usually do this in the bathroom. 4 I never do this in class. 5 I always do this before I go to the dentist.* (The answer is *brush my teeth.*) Students then think of an activity themselves and write five clues using adverbs of frequency. In pairs or small groups, they then tell each other their sentences and try to guess the activity.

---

3 LISTENING

a 💬▣ Discuss the questions as a class.

b ▶**03.02** Play the recording for students to listen for general meaning and answer the questions. You may wish to pre-teach the phrase *in a hurry* (doing things more quickly than usual). Check answers as a class.

> **Answers**
> 1 They talk about their free time.
> 2 Martin wants the family to have dinner together once a week.

> **Audioscript**
>
> **MARTIN** Hey Katherine, I've got an idea.
>
> **KATHERINE** Oh yeah, what's that?
>
> **M** I'd like us to have a family dinner together once a week.
>
> **K** Oh really? … Why?
>
> **M** Well, our lives are so busy and we're always in a hurry. You, me and the kids, we never have dinner together these days. Spending some time together – just one night – it feels like a nice idea.
>
> **K** OK, why not? When do you want to do it?
>
> **M** When are you free?
>
> **K** Most nights, but I go to my Spanish lesson once a week. It's on Wednesdays, so that's no good.
>
> **M** OK, so not Wednesday. What about Liz and Pete?
>
> **K** Well, Liz goes to volleyball training.
>
> **M** Of course. How often does she go?
>
> **K** Twice a week – on Mondays and Thursdays.
>
> **M** And Pete goes to band practice a lot.
>
> **K** Yes, three times a week – on Mondays, Thursdays and Fridays.
>
> **M** OK. So that means … Tuesday! Yes, Tuesday night we can all have dinner together. Everyone's free then.
>
> **K** Ah. No, they're not.
>
> **M** What do you mean?
>
> **K** I work late every Tuesday.
>
> **M** Oh. But you said, 'Most nights are free.'
>
> **K** Yeah, *most* nights – not *all* nights. You know I work late on Tuesdays. I don't need to tell you that!
>
> **M** Sorry. Well, this is impossible!

c ▶**03.02** Students listen to the recording again for specific details and complete the schedule. They compare in pairs. Check answers as a class.

> **Answers**
> Katherine – Tuesday: work late; Wednesday: Spanish lesson
> Liz – Monday and Thursday: volleyball training
> Pete – Monday, Thursday and Friday: band practice

d 💬▣ Students work in pairs or small groups, answering the questions. Share answers to Question 1 as a class.

💡 EXTRA ACTIVITY

Give students time for a 'long turn' (a chance for the students to prepare what they're going to say on a topic and then talk to the whole class) at this point. This allows students to practise speaking under a little more pressure than normal and have the teacher's total attention for a few moments, both of which can be very beneficial. Ask students to think about their families' routines in more detail and to write notes, but not write complete sentences. Give students an example about yourself before they start, e.g., *In my family, we are always in a hurry! On Monday, my son goes to football practice, and my daughter …* Monitor and help as necessary as students write notes. Then, tell students not to look at their notes and to work with a partner, taking turns practising what they are going to say. Discreetly point out errors for students to self-correct. Finally, ask students to speak to the class in turn about their families' routines. Remind students not to look at their notes while they're speaking, and choose students at random. After each long turn, allow two or three students to ask the speaker questions based on the speaker's talk.

4 VOCABULARY Time expressions

a ▶ **03.03** Read the sentences with the students. Ask: *Who gives this information in the recording?* (Katherine). Individually, students complete the sentences with the words in the box. Play the recording for students to listen and check. Check answers as a class.

> **Answers**
> 1 once
> 2 twice
> 3 a
> 4 every

b Elicit the rule as a class.

> **Answer**
> at the end of a sentence

📖 LANGUAGE NOTES

Time expressions like these can also be placed at the beginning of sentences when the speaker wishes to put more emphasis on the expression, e.g., *Once a week, we have a vocabulary test.* This difference is too subtle for students at A2 level, so, as with adverbs of frequency, students are taught only a limited part of a more complex rule at this point.

c ▶ **03.04** **Pronunciation** Play the recording. Highlight the stressed words for students by beating the rhythm with your hand to show where the stresses fall.

d Answer the question as a class. Drill the sentences in 4c.

> **Answer**
> a Important words like time expressions and verbs

e ▶ **03.05** Check that students understand that the lines of the conversation are in the correct order but the words within each line are jumbled. Individually, students put the words in the correct order. Play the recording for students to listen and check.

> **Answers and audioscript**
>
> **A** How often do you and your family do things together?
> **B** About once a week.
> **A** What do you do?
> **B** We usually go for a picnic or to a restaurant.
> **A** Do you do that at the weekend?
> **B** Yes, every Sunday, but we sometimes go to the cinema.
> **A** Do you do anything else?
> **B** Well, about twice a year we go away for a weekend.
> **A** It sounds like you have a nice time with your family.

f ≫ ▶ **03.06–03.07** Students complete the exercises in Vocabulary Focus 3A on SB p. 165. Play the recording for students to check their answers to Exercise a and complete Exercise b as a class. Monitor Exercise c. Tell students to go back to SB p. 31.

> **Answers (Vocabulary Focus 3A SB p. 165)**
> **a** 1 b 2 f 3 e 4 g 5 a 6 d 7 c
> **b** 1 stay   2 long
> **c** Students' own answers

💡 FAST FINISHERS

Ask fast finishers to continue asking and answering questions with their partners after they have completed Exercise c, inventing their own questions using present simple verbs.

5 SPEAKING

a Give students a few minutes to prepare and write notes about the people they know well. Monitor and help as necessary.

b 💬🗨 Students work in pairs or small groups, telling each other about the people they know well and asking and answering each other's questions. As you monitor, don't interrupt fluency, but note down any mistakes with the position of adverbs of frequency and time expressions. After the activity, write them on the board and ask students to correct them.

⊕ ADDITIONAL MATERIALS

Workbook 3A

Photocopiable activities: Grammar 3A, Vocabulary 3A, Pronunciation 3A

Documentary video Unit 3 *Daily Life*

Video worksheet Unit 3 *Daily Life*

3B IMAGINE YOU HAVEN'T GOT THE INTERNET

At the end of this lesson, students will be able to:

- read and understand a text about using the Internet
- use a lexical set of technology words correctly
- understand conversations in which people talk about the technology they have and how they use it
- use the positive, negative and question forms of *have got*
- talk about and give simple descriptions of their own and other people's possessions

ⓦ OPTIONAL LEAD-IN

Before students arrive, write the incomplete text below on the board. If possible, show students a picture of yourself or other people in the 1990s to give context to the activity. Put students into pairs. If you have a class with a variety of ages, try to mix older and younger students together as it will give them more to talk about. Students look at the sentences and choose a word to complete each gap. Check that students understand that they need to use the present simple form of the verb.

It's the 1990s! We:

1 *usually … to the library to find information.*

2 *often … our friends at a café to talk.*

3 *sometimes … letters to family and friends.*

4 *often … games like Monopoly and Scrabble at home.*

5 *always … music from shops.*

Check answers (*1 go 2 meet 3 write 4 play 5 buy*).
Then ask: *Life is very different today. Why?* Elicit the answer *because we have the Internet.* Students might be surprised to know that the Internet only became available to the general public in the early 1990s, but most people didn't use it in their daily life.

1 READING

a Individually, students think about how they use the Internet and tick the things in the list.

b 💬▮ Students compare their ideas in small groups. Take feedback as a class, and ask them if there's anything they think is missing from the list in 1a.

c Tell students they should read only the first part of the text *This month on TechBlog*. They then work individually, answering the questions. Check answers as a class.

> **Answers**
> 1 b
> 2 They are offline / haven't got the Internet.

d Tell students to read the second part of the text *The Interview* and answer the questions. Pre-teach the words in the Vocabulary Support box. Students compare their answers in pairs. Check answers as a class.

> **Answers**
> 1 a, b, d
> 2 c, e, f

📖 VOCABULARY SUPPORT

upload (v.) (B1) – copy or move programs or information to a larger computer system or to the Internet

go online (v. + adv.) (A2) – access the Internet

chess (A2) – a popular game played on a square board

e 💬▮ Put students into small groups to talk about the questions together; if possible, mix older and younger students together. Monitor, but don't interrupt fluency.

ⓦ FAST FINISHERS

Ask fast finishers to also talk about how much time they spend on the things in 1a every week and which websites they use to do each of the things.

2 VOCABULARY Technology

◌ LOA TIP ELICITING

- Consider eliciting some of the vocabulary in 2a by bringing in as many of the objects shown in the pictures as possible to show to the class. Ask students to close their books, explain *technology* (*electronic objects for science or personal use*) and elicit the words for each object. Drill each word for correct pronunciation.

a Individually, students match the words with the pictures. Check answers as a class.

> **Answers**
> 1 smartwatch   6 computer
> 2 printer   7 headphones
> 3 laptop   8 tablet
> 4 smartphone   9 keyboard
> 5 camera   10 speaker

b ▶03.08 **Pronunciation** Play the recording for students to underline the stressed syllable. Check answers by writing the words on the board and asking individual students to come up and underline the stressed syllables on the board (see the underlining in the answers to 2a).

c Elicit possible answers to the first sentence from the class. Check that students understand that more than one answer may be possible for each sentence. Students decide what they think the people are talking about. Check answers as a class.

> **Possible answers**
> 1 smartwatch, laptop, smartphone, computer, tablet
> 2 laptop, smartphone, computer, tablet
> 3 headphones, speakers
> 4 printer
> 5 smartwatch, laptop, smartphone, tablet

ⓦ EXTRA ACTIVITY

Students write their own sentences about the technology items in 2a, using the sentences in 2c as a model. Monitor and help with vocabulary as necessary. In pairs or small groups, students read each other their sentences and try to guess what they are about.

3 LISTENING

a ▶03.09 Play the recording for students to listen to the answers and match the people with the questions. Check students understand that this isn't the complete recording, just a short sentence to identify the topic each person talks about. Check answers as a class.

Answers
1 Bella   2 Don   3 Chris

Audioscript

DON Yes, I've got my daughter's phone. She's got a new phone, so I've got her old one.

BELLA Yes of course, in fact I've got two, a PC and a laptop.

CHRIS Yes, I have. It takes really good photos, but I don't use it very often – just for special photos.

b ▶03.10 Play the complete recording for students to listen for specific details and complete the table. Check answers as a class.

Answers

	Gadgets	Do they often use them?
Don	1 smartphone	no: sometimes, but not very often
Bella	1 PC 2 laptop	yes: all the time
Chris	1 digital camera 2 smartphone	no: not very often yes, usually

📖 **VOCABULARY SUPPORT**

gadget (C1) – a small piece of technology that does a specific job

Audioscript

CONVERSATION 1

INTERVIEWER So tell me, Don, have you got a smartphone?

DON Yes, I've got my daughter's phone. She's got a new phone, so I've got her old one.

I Do you use it a lot?

D No, never. Well, sometimes, but not very often.

I Why not?

D I don't know really. If I'm at home, I use the house phone. Umm … If I go out, I don't want to chat to people or send texts. I just want to be quiet. So, no. In fact, I usually leave my phone at home. I don't want to lose it!

CONVERSATION 2

I So, Bella, have you got a computer?

BELLA Yes of course, in fact I've got two, a PC and a laptop.

I Do you use them both?

B Oh, yes, all the time. I use the PC for studying mainly and also for downloading films. And I use the laptop when I go to university or when I study in the library.

CONVERSATION 3

I Have you got a digital camera?

CHRIS Yes, I have. It takes really good photos, but I don't use it very often, just for special photos. I've also got a smartphone of course, and usually I take photos on that, like holiday photos or photos of friends – the photos are OK, but they're not fantastic.

c ▶03.10 Students listen again for specific details about exactly how Bella and Chris use each gadget. Check answers as a class. Ask students: *Which person is like you?* and discuss who they are most similar to.

Answers
Bella – the PC for studying and downloading films; the laptop when she goes to university or when she studies in the library
Chris – the digital camera for special photos; the smartphone for holiday photos or photos of friends

4 GRAMMAR *have got*

a Write *I've got my daughter's phone.* and *We've got friends in Japan and in the USA.* on the board. Point to the first sentence and ask: *Is this information in the Reading text or the Listening?* and elicit *Listening*. Point to the second sentence, ask the same question and elicit *Reading*. Individually, students do the exercise, then check answers in pairs. Check answers as a class.

Answers
1 L   2 R   3 L   4 R   5 R   6 L

b Individually, students underline the forms of *have got* in 4a and then decide what *I've got* means. Check the answer as a class.

Answer
b I have

c Students complete the table, working individually. They then check in pairs. Check answers as a class. Show students three fingers, point to the first and say: *I*, the second and say: *have* and the third and say: *got*. Then close up the gap between the first and second finger to show how *I* and *have* are contracted as: *I've*. Repeat the process with *I haven't got*, but using four fingers and closing up the second and third fingers to show how *have* and *not* are contracted as: *haven't*. Show students the three fingers for: *I have got* again and then use a gesture to show how we swap around the first two words to make the question: *Have I got?* Repeat the process with the positive, negative and question third person forms, but indicate that the class should tell you which fingers should be closed up or swapped around.

Answers

	I / We / You / They	He / She
+	've	's
–	haven't	hasn't
?	Have	Has

d ▶03.11 **Pronunciation** Play the recording for students to listen for the main stress.

e ▶03.12 Students listen to the sentences and underline the main stress in each sentence. Check answers as a class.

Answers
1 They've got a <u>computer</u>.
2 He's got a <u>smartphone</u>.
3 She's got a new <u>laptop</u>.

f ▶03.12 Play the recording again for students to listen for the intonation movement. Check the answer as a class.

Answer
The intonation goes down on the main stress.

CAREFUL!

When using *have got*, students often have problems with subject/verb agreement and so may use *have* instead of *has*, e.g., ~~He have got a ...~~ *(Correct form = He **has got** a new smartphone.).* They may also omit *have* altogether, e.g., ~~Filippo and Max got friends ...~~ *(Correct form = Filippo and Max **have got** friends in Australia.).*

Another very common error is to confuse *have got* and *got*, particularly when talking about being given presents, e.g., ~~I have got a smartwatch ...~~ *(Correct form = I **got** a smartwatch for my birthday.).*

g ≫ ►**03.13** Students read the information in Grammar Focus 3B on SB p. 142. Play the recording where indicated and ask students to listen and repeat. Students then complete the exercises. Check answers as a class, making sure students are using the correct form for the third person and are not using additional auxiliaries in their answers. After students complete the Grammar Focus activities, ask them: *Is 'have got' easy? Is it difficult? What is it important to remember with 'have got'?* (i.e., not to use the auxiliaries *do/does/doesn't*). Tell students to go back to SB p. 33.

Answers (Grammar Focus 3B SB p. 143)
a 2 ~~Do you have~~ Have you got 4G ...
   3 We ~~not~~ haven't got a ...
   4 They've got a TV ...
   5 My brother ~~haven't~~ hasn't got a ...
   6 My parents haven't got a ...
b 2 Have your grandparents got a digital camera? Yes, they have.
   3 Has your mum got a smartwatch? No, she hasn't.
   4 Has your teacher got blue eyes? No, he hasn't.
   5 Has your dad got a satnav? Yes, he has.
   6 Have you got a lot of homework? No, I haven't.
c 2 haven't 3 've got 4 haven't got 5 's got
   6 Have you got 7 have 8 's got 9 have your parents got
   10 haven't got 11 's got 12 Has he got 13 hasn't

h Individually, students write sentences that are true for them. Monitor and point out errors for students to self-correct.

Answers
Students' own answers

FAST FINISHERS

Ask fast finishers to write more sentences using the words and phrases in the box, but about their friends and family. Remind them to use the third person forms correctly.

i Students write three questions with *have got* and the words and phrases in 4h. Monitor and point out any errors for students to self-correct before students start on the pairwork stage in the next section.

5 SPEAKING

a Students put the words in the correct order to make questions. Check answers by asking individual students to come up and write them on the board.

Answers
1 How often do you use it?   4 How old is it?
2 Do you like it?   5 Where do they live?
3 What kind is it?   6 Would you like one?

b 💬🗨 Demonstrate the activity by asking one student: *Have you got a smartphone?* and then asking one or two follow-up questions from 5a, e.g., *What kind is it?, How old is it?* Students work in pairs, asking and answering their questions and asking additional questions from 5a. Monitor and listen for correct use of *have got* with *I* and *you*.

c 💬🗨 Regroup students and put them into new pairs. Read the example with the class and ask them: *What is this exercise practising?* (third person form of *have got*). Students work in pairs, telling each other what they learned about the other students in 5b.

EXTRA ACTIVITY

Invite students to ask questions with *Have you got ... ?* about what you've got in your bag. They can ask about things from the Student's Book, e.g., *Have you got a notebook/pen/dictionary/timetable/smartphone?* or use any other words they know. At A2 level, students may know *a key for your house, a purse/wallet, an identity card, a sandwich.* Answer clearly with *Yes, I have.* or *No, I haven't.* to reinforce the short answers. Concentrate on the correct use of *have got.* Don't worry if students try to use *some/any* and use them incorrectly as these will be covered in detail in Lesson 4A.

⊕ ADDITIONAL MATERIALS

Workbook 3B

Photocopiable activities: Grammar 3B, Vocabulary 3B

At the end of this lesson, students will be able to:

- understand informal conversations in which people make arrangements
- use appropriate phrases for making arrangements and responding appropriately
- identify the main stress in sentences
- use appropriate phrases to hesitate while thinking about what they want to say
- maintain informal conversations in which they make arrangements

♀ OPTIONAL LEAD-IN

Point to the pictures on SB p. 34 or project them on the board. Ask: *Who are they?* and elicit *Martina, Annie and Dan.* Write sentences 1–5 on the board for students to complete with the correct names. Allow students to refer back to Lessons 1C and 2C if necessary. Check answers as a class.

1 *Dan is …'s husband.* (Martina)
2 *Annie is …'s little sister.* (Dan)
3 *Dan works with his friend …* . (Leo)
4 *… doesn't do exercise, but … goes to the gym.* (Dan, Leo)
5 *… likes tea – with sugar!* (Dan).

1 LISTENING

a 💬▶ Read through the questions with the students and give them one minute to think about their answers before they work in pairs. Monitor and allow time for class feedback.

b ▶03.14 Tell students to look at the top picture and ask them what kind of magazine Annie and Martina have got (a TV guide). Play Part 1 of the video or the audio recording for students to answer the question. Check the answer as a class.

> **Answer**
> Yes, they do.

> **Video/Audioscript (Part 1)**
> **DAN** Here's your coffee, Annie …
> **ANNIE** Thanks, Dan!
> **D** Martina …
> **MARTINA** Thank you.
> **A** My favourite programme's on in five minutes.
> **M** The cooking one?
> **A** Yeah, I love it.
> **D** *Top Cook*?
> **A** That's it – *Top Cook*. Can we watch it?
> **M** Sure! We always watch it too.
> **A** Fantastic! Cooking, food, restaurants. I love all that.
> **M** So do we.

c ▶03.14 Students watch or listen again for specific details. Play Part 1 of the video or the audio recording again for students to decide if the sentences are true or false. When checking answers, ask students to correct the false sentences.

> **Answers**
> 1 F (The programme Annie wants to watch is *Top Cook*.)
> 2 F (They always watch it.)
> 3 T

d ▶03.15 Play Part 2 of the video or the audio recording for students to find out what they plan to do. Check the answer as a class.

> **Answer**
> They plan to go to a new restaurant for dinner.

> **Video/Audioscript (Part 2)**
> **ANNIE** Hey! I know this new restaurant – near my office. Why don't we try it?
> **MARTINA** Yeah! That'd be great. For dinner?
> **A** Yeah.
> **DAN** That's a good idea.
> **A** How about next Wednesday?
> **M** Mm, maybe. Let me see. I'm sorry I can't. I need to work late next Wednesday.
> **A** Are you free next Friday?
> **M** Mm, possibly. Friday's fine. Dan?
> **D** Friday? Sure, I'd love to.
> **A** Great!
> **D** Mm, can I bring Leo? You know, the guy I work with.
> **A** Leo? Yeah, great idea. Look! My programme!

e ▶03.15 Students watch or listen again for specific details. Play Part 2 of the video or the audio recording again for students to answer the questions. Check answers as a class.

> **Answers**
> 1 Martina works late on Wednesday.
> 2 They decide to go out on Friday.
> 3 Dan wants to ask Leo to dinner.
> 4 Annie thinks it's a great idea.

♀ EXTRA ACTIVITY

Ask students to answer questions 1–5 as a class. Play both parts of the video or the audio recording again.

1 *Who makes Annie and Martina's drinks?* (Dan)
2 *What do they drink?* (coffee)
3 *When does* Top Cook *start?* (in five minutes)
4 *Where is the new restaurant Annie talks about?* (near her office)
5 *Why do you think Dan wants to ask Leo to dinner?*
(Students' own answers)

2 USEFUL LANGUAGE Making arrangements

a Individually, students match the beginnings with the endings of the sentences. They then check in pairs. Check answers as a class.

> **Answers**
> 1 c 2 e 3 b 4 a 5 f 6 d

b Students classify the questions and sentences in 2a. Check answers as a class.

> **Answers**
> Make suggestions – *Why don't we try it?; How about next Wednesday?; Are you free next Friday?*
> Say *yes* to suggestions – *That'd be great.; That's a good idea.; I'd love to.*

c Read Martina's sentence to the class. Ask students which phrase means *no* (I'm sorry, I can't.). Tell students that in English, it's considered rude to say just *no* or *I can't*, so people usually use a phrase like *I'm sorry, I can't*, which includes an apology, and then also give an excuse (*I need to …*).

> **Answer**
> I'm sorry, I can't. I need to work late next Wednesday.

d ▶ **03.16** Tell students to work individually and order the sentences to make a conversation. Play the recording for students to listen and check. Check answers as a class.

> **Answers and audioscript**
> **A** Why don't we go to the cinema?   **B** I'm sorry, I can't. I'm away this
> **B** The cinema? That's a good idea.   weekend.
> **A** How about this Saturday?   **A** Are you free on Monday?
> **B** Yes, Monday's fine.

> **Answer**
> 4 1 6 3 5 2

e 💬📢 In pairs, students practise the conversation and then make similar conversations using their own ideas. Monitor and correct the phrases for making arrangements as appropriate.

> **♀ FAST FINISHERS**
> Ask fast finishers to close their books and practise the conversation and make similar conversations without looking at 2d to help them.

3 PRONUNCIATION Main stress

a ▶ **03.17** Play the recording and highlight the main stress for students.

b Individually, students choose the correct answer. Check the answer as a class.

> **Answer**
> a short and loud

c ▶ **03.18** Play the recording for students to underline the main stress. Check answers by writing the sentences on the board and asking individual students to come up and underline the main stress in each sentence.

> **Answers**
> 1 We'd <u>love</u> to.   3 That's a <u>lovely</u> idea.
> 2 That'd be <u>good</u>.   4 That'd be <u>fantastic</u>.

d 💬📢 Drill the sentences in 3c. Students then work in pairs, practising saying the examples. Monitor and correct students' pronunciation as appropriate.

4 CONVERSATION SKILLS
Thinking about what you want to say

a Ask students to read the conversation and think about why Martina uses the underlined phrases. Check the answer as a class.

> **Answer**
> b give her time to think

b ▶ **03.19** **Pronunciation** Play the recording for students to listen and notice the pronunciation of *Mm* for hesitation. Ask students: *What do you say in your language when you don't know what to say?*

> **⟲ LOA TIP DRILLING**
>
> • Drill Martina's responses in the conversation in 4a before continuing. Drill her first response, building it up word by word until the class can chorus it together with correct pronunciation. Then ask Annie's first question: *How about next Wednesday?* and elicit the response from the class as a chorus. Repeat with Martina's second response and then put the whole conversation together with you taking the parts of Annie and Dan and the class taking the part of Martina.
>
> • Pay particular attention to the intonation of the phrases for hesitation. Exaggerate the 'musicality' as you drill them and show students the up and down movements using hand gestures to give them a visual reference.

c 💬📢 Read through the questions with the students. Remind students to use the underlined phrases in 4a and give themselves time to think before they reply. Monitor and correct students' pronunciation if they make mistakes with the phrases for hesitation.

> **♀ FAST FINISHERS**
> Ask fast finishers to extend their conversations. If their partner says *no*, offer an alternative, just as Annie does in the conversation in 4a.

5 SPEAKING

a–b ⫸ Divide the class into pairs and assign A and B roles. Student As read the first card on SB p. 35 and Student Bs read the first card on SB p. 132. Students then role play the conversation. Monitor, but don't interrupt fluency unless students make mistakes with the content of this lesson. Students then read the second card and role play the second situation. Tell Student Bs to go back to 5c on SB p. 35.

c 💬📢 Students work in new pairs, or small groups, and tell each other about the arrangements they made in the two role plays.

> **♀ EXTRA ACTIVITY**
> Students work in small groups to plan a class party, using phrases from the Useful language section to make suggestions and say *yes* and *no*, and phrases from the Conversation skills section to give themselves time to think as necessary. Write the following ideas on the board to help students keep the conversation going: *When? (in the evening? / at the weekend? / a different time?) Where? (at the school? / in the park? / a different place?) Fun? (games? / music? / more ideas?) Food? (party food? / drinks? / other things?)*. Monitor and praise students who are able to express their ideas, even if their English isn't perfect.

> **⊕ ADDITIONAL MATERIALS**
>
> Workbook 3C
>
> Photocopiable activities: Pronunciation 3C
>
> Unit Progress Test

3D SKILLS FOR WRITING
Can you join us?

At the end of this lesson, students will be able to:
- understand a person talking about his family and how they stay in contact
- understand emails inviting people to a family party
- use expressions for inviting and replying correctly
- write an invitation to an event and a reply to an invitation they receive

💡 **OPTIONAL LEAD-IN**

Ask students how many letters there are in the English alphabet and elicit them from the class. If necessary, students refer back to SB p. 7. Put students into small groups and tell them they have three minutes to try to think of one country for each of the 26 letters. They aren't allowed to look at their books or their notes. When the three minutes are up, groups share their answers with the class. Ask students to spell the countries they've seen in the class so far, but don't test them on any other countries they have thought of (the countries in brackets). *Possible answers:* **A**rgentina, **B**ritain, **C**anada, **D**enmark, (**E**gypt), **F**rance, **G**ermany, (**H**ungary), **I**ran, **J**apan, (**K**enya), (**L**ibya), **M**exico, **N**igeria, (**O**man), **P**akistan, (**Q**atar), **R**ussia, **S**pain, **T**urkey, the **U**SA, (**V**ietnam), (**W**ales), (**X** – there isn't a country beginning with X), (**Y**emen), (**Z**ambia).

1 SPEAKING AND LISTENING

a 💬🔊 Read the questions with the students and then give them one minute to think about their answers. Discuss the questions as a class and find out who has family or friends in the most unusual places.

b ▶️ **03.20** Play the recording for students to listen for general meaning and put the countries in order. Check answers as a class.

Answers
1	Turkey	4	France
2	England	5	Sweden
3	Germany	6	Italy

Audioscript

I've got a large family and we all live in many different countries. I come from Izmir in Turkey, but I live in England now with my parents. I've got a brother and sister in Germany. My sister Ayda lives in Munich and my brother Mustafa lives in Berlin. Some of our family is still in Turkey, but I've also got an uncle in France – he lives in Lyon with his family – and another uncle in Sweden. And I've also got family in Italy; they live in Milan, but I don't know them very well.

We all stay in contact by Skype and email but we don't often see each other, unfortunately. But we always get together every five years and we spend a long weekend together, and it's always in Turkey because my grandmother is there and she's very old, she's over 80 and she can't travel. We stay with family and we have a big party. It's a great family occasion but we also invite friends, so there are usually about 50 people there. It's a very nice way to keep in contact, and we've always got lots to talk about!

c ▶️ **03.20** Students listen to the recording again for specific details and correct the mistakes in the summary text. They compare in pairs. Check answers as a class.

Answers
2 He's got a brother and a sister.
3 every five years …
4 Turkey

5 They stay with family and …
6 … have a big party.
7 This isn't only for people in the family …
8 … they also invite friends.

💡 **EXTRA ACTIVITY**

Play the recording again for students to answer Questions 1–5 about what Emrah says.
1 *Where does Emrah live? Who does he live with?* (He lives in England with his parents.)
2 *What is his sister's name and where does she live?* (Her name's Ayda and she lives in Munich.)
3 *Where does his uncle live in France?* (He lives in Lyon.)
4 *Where in Italy does he have family?* (in Milan)
5 *Why is the family party always in Turkey?* (His grandmother is there. She's over 80 and can't travel.)

2 READING

a Individually, students read the emails quickly and decide why Emrah emails his brother and sister. Check the answer as a class.

Answer
to invite them to the family party

b Tell students to read the emails again in detail and complete the information about the family party. They then check in pairs. Check answers as a class.

Answers
Place: Izmir (in Turkey)
Date: Friday 14th to Sunday 16th September
How many days: three days
Where to stay: Ayda with Melis, Mustafa with Mert (Melis and Mert are Emrah's friends from school)

💡 **FAST FINISHERS**

Ask students to read the two emails again and find out what new information they contain about Ayda and Mustafa. (*Ayda has got a new job; Mustafa has got a family.*)

3 WRITING SKILLS Inviting and replying

a Look at the email to Ayda with the class and check that students understand that they need to use the numbers 1–6 to complete this exercise. Elicit the answer to b as a class. Students then work individually, identifying the sentences. Check answers as a class.

Answers
b	1	e	5
c	6	f	3
d	2		

b Make sure students are clear about the task before they start. Check answers as a class.

Answers

Email to Mustafa	Email to Ayda
1 How are you?	How are things?
2 same	same
3 same	same
4 Would you like to come?	Can you join us?
5 Mert / he / his	Melis / she / her
6 Please let me know if you would like to join us.	Please let me know if you can come.

c Individually, students read the questions and decide which ones are used to invite people. When checking answers, make sure students understand that Questions 2, 4 and 5 aren't possible because they're grammatically incorrect.

Answers

1 ✓
3 ✓
6 ✓
7 ✓

d Students order the words to make statements and questions. Check answers as a class by asking individual students to write the correct answers on the board.

Answers

1 How are things?
2 It would be great to see you.
3 Hope you can make it.
4 I'd love to see you.
5 How are you?
6 I hope you can come.

e Students read the statements and questions in 3d again and decide which mean the same. Check answers as a class.

Answers

1 and 5; 2 and 4; 3 and 6

f Students read the emails from Mustafa and Ayda for general meaning to find out if they can come. Check the answer as a class.

Answer

Adya can't come, but Mustafa can.

g Individually, students look at the emails in 3f again and find sentences that match the meanings. They then check in pairs. Check answers as a class.

Answers

1 I'd love to come.
2 I'm afraid I can't.
3 Hope you all have a great time.

> **♀ FAST FINISHERS**
>
> Ask fast finishers to circle other useful phrases in the emails that they could use in their own emails, e.g., *I'm really looking forward to it, See you soon, Great to hear from you, Keep in touch.*

4 WRITING AND SPEAKING

a Students work individually to plan a party or other event. Monitor and help with vocabulary and give students ideas if necessary.

b 💬📢 Tell students that this activity is about communication – it's not about perfect English. In small groups, students talk about their plans and see if their classmates have any additional ideas for the event.

> **🔄 LOA TIP ELICITING**
>
> - Although students won't be using the phrases for inviting and replying in this discussion stage, they'll be using other vocabulary and grammar structures that they'll probably need to use in their written invitation. Monitor and try to preempt any problems students may have, such as using words that they're incorrectly transferring from their L1 or making common mistakes, like confusing *fun* and *funny*.
> - Note down problems individual students have so that you can correct those on a one-to-one basis before students work on their written invitations in 4c.

c Individually, students write an invitation to their event to another student. You could tell them who to write to so that everyone gets an invitation. If you're short of time, this exercise can be completed for homework. Students could then bring their invitations to the next lesson.

d Students swap invitations and check their partner has included the information in 4a.

e Students write a reply to the invitation they received, explaining why they can or can't go. Remind students that if they can't go, they shouldn't just say *no* but should use one of the phrases in Lessons 3C or 3D and give an excuse. Students give their reply back to the student who invited them. Invite students to share their answers with the class and find out how many accept the invitation and how many of them say *no*.

> **♀ EXTRA ACTIVITY**
>
> Write a short checklist on the board to help students when they check their invitations and replies in pairs: <u>Spelling</u>: check difficult words in the Student's Book, in a dictionary or on your phone. <u>be</u>: negatives use *'m not / aren't / isn't;* questions use *Am/Are/Is* + subject. <u>Present simple</u>: negatives use *don't/ doesn't*; questions use *Do/Does* + subject + verb. *have got*: negatives use *haven't/hasn't got*; questions use *Have/Has* + subject + *got* + noun. <u>Word order</u>: check adverbs of frequency / time expressions are in the right position. <u>Phrases</u>: include phrases for making plans / inviting and replying. If students have made mistakes in any of these areas, they prepare a second draft of their invitation and/or reply before you collect pairs of invitations and replies to give feedback on them both.

> **⊕ ADDITIONAL MATERIALS**
>
> Workbook 3D

UNIT 3
Review and extension

1 GRAMMAR

a Students work individually, inserting the adverb of frequency in the correct place in each sentence. Check answers as a class.

Answers
1 He <u>often</u> gets up at about 10 or 11.
2 He <u>never</u> goes to bed before 2:00 am.
3 He <u>sometimes</u> studies all night.
4 He <u>usually</u> has black coffee and toast for breakfast.
5 He is <u>often</u> away for a week or more.
6 His windows are <u>always</u> closed, even in summer.

b Individually, students complete the text. They then check in pairs. Check answers as a class.

Answers
1 have got
2 've got
3 has got
4 haven't got
5 haven't got
6 've got
7 've got

2 Have your neighbours got children?
3 Has your flat or house got a garden?
4 Have you got a TV in your bedroom?
5 Has someone in your family got a smartwatch?
6 Have you got a lot of free time?
   Short answers: Students' own answers

2 VOCABULARY

a Students rewrite the sentences with time expressions in the correct position. Check answers as a class.

Answers
2 three times a year
3 twice a year
4 three times a week
5 every morning and evening / twice a day
6 four times a week

b Individually, students look at the pictures and write the names of the objects. Check answers and spelling as a class.

Answers
1 printer   6 camera
2 computer   7 smartphone
3 tablet   8 smartwatch
4 speaker   9 keyboard
5 headphones 10 laptop

3 WORDPOWER Prepositions of time

a Tell students to close their books. Write the following three gapped sentences on the board: *I work … the morning.*, *I start work … 9 am.*, *I never work … Sunday.* Point to the three gaps and ask students about each missing word in turn. Write *in, at, on* on the board in each sentence. Students open their books, look at the

sentences and match them with the pictures. Check answers as a class.

Answers
1 c 2 b 3 a 4 e 5 d

b Individually, students answer the questions and find examples in 3a. Check answers as a class.

Answers
1 a at b on c in d in, at e in f at
2 a 3 (6 am, 1 pm)
   b 4 (weekdays, Sunday)
   c 5 (January)
   d 2 (the evening)
   e 1 (the winter)
   f 2 (the weekend, night)

c Students work individually, adding prepositions of time to the sentences. When checking answers, make sure students understand that this exercise is testing both the prepositions and their position. If students have used the wrong preposition but put it in the correct position, then their answer can be considered partially correct.

Answers
1 I always get up <u>at</u> 6:30 <u>in</u> the morning <u>on</u> weekdays.
2 It's usually cold here <u>in</u> the winter, and it often snows <u>in</u> January.
3 Are you free <u>at</u> the weekend? I have tickets for a concert <u>on</u> Saturday. It starts <u>at</u> 7:30 pm.

d As an example, make a sentence using *get up* which is true for yourself, e.g., *I get up at 7 am.* Students then write sentences that are true for themselves. Monitor and point out errors for students to self-correct.

Answers
Students' own answers

e 💬 Give students one or two example questions, using the things in 3d, e.g., *What time do you usually get up at weekends? What about on weekdays?* In pairs, students ask and answer questions. Monitor and listen for correct question formation and for correct use of the prepositions of time. Praise students with a smile or a nod when they use the language from this section correctly.

> ### ♀ EXTRA ACTIVITY
>
> Write jumbled questions a–d on the board. Ask students to put them in order and decide which things in 3d they are connected to: *a prefer / you / do / which ?* (Which do you prefer? 6); *b go / usually / where / you / do ?* (Where do you usually go? 4); *c what / have / you / do / usually ?* (What do you usually have? 3); *d things / kind / of / you / do / what / buy ?* (What kind of things do you buy? 5). Check answers as a class. Students can then use the questions to extend their conversations in 3d.

≫ Photocopiable activities: Wordpower 3

> ### ↻ LOA TIP ELICITING
>
> Students look back through the unit, think about what they've studied and decide how well they did. Students work on weak areas by using the appropriate sections of the Workbook and the Photocopiable activities.

UNIT 4

FOOD

↻ UNIT OBJECTIVES

At the end of this unit, students will be able to:

- understand information, texts and conversations and exchange information about places to buy food, cooking and TV cookery programmes and different recipes and dishes
- ask for and give information about the food they eat
- use appropriate phrases when arriving at a restaurant and ordering a meal
- write about something they know how to do and explain how to do it better

UNIT CONTENTS

G GRAMMAR
- Countable and uncountable nouns
- *a/an*, *some*, *any*
- Quantifiers: *much, many, a lot (of)*

V VOCABULARY
- Food: *beans, burger, carrots, cereal, chicken, cola, crisps, garlic, grapes, jam, lamb, lemons, melon, mushrooms, onions, pears, salad, steak, yoghurt*
- Cooking verbs: *bake, boil, fry, grill, roast*
- Cooking adjectives: *baked, boiled, fried, grilled, roast*
- Containers: *bag, bar, bottle, can, jar, packet*
- Sequencing words: *first, then, next, after that, finally*
- Wordpower: *like* to talk about wants (*I'd like …*), make invitations (*Would you like … ?*), express general likes (*I like …*), ask 'How is it?' (*What's it like … ?*), say 'the same as' (*He's like me*), give examples (*… fruit, like apples*) and say 'in that way' (*… live like that*).

P PRONUNCIATION
- Sound and spelling: *ea* (/iː/, /eə/, and /eɪ/)
- Sound and spelling: /k/
- Stress in phrases with containers
- Word groups, e.g., *For my starter*, || *I'd like raw fish.*

C COMMUNICATION SKILLS
- Talking about shopping for food, eating habits, markets and food likes and dislikes
- Discussing healthy and unhealthy food and describing ways of cooking
- Arriving at a restaurant and ordering a meal
- Changing what you say
- Asking and answering questions about cooking
- Writing a blog post

GETTING STARTED

♀ OPTIONAL LEAD-IN

Books closed. Draw three digital clocks on the board, one with 7:30, one with 1:15 and one with 7:00 or other appropriate times for mealtimes. Write the words *breakfast*, *lunch* and *dinner* on the board, but not connected in any way to the times. Say: *I usually have this at half past seven in the morning.* Elicit *breakfast*. Draw a line from the 7:30 clock to *breakfast*. Repeat the process with *lunch* and *dinner*. Then, ask some students: *What time do you usually have breakfast/lunch/dinner?* Elicit the times.

a 💬📢 If you didn't use the optional lead-in, check that students understand *breakfast*, *lunch* and *dinner*. Give students one minute to think about their answers to the questions before talking about the picture as a class.

b 💬📢 Read the questions with the students before they ask and answer them. Ask students to share vocabulary for what they usually have for breakfast, lunch and dinner, and what they talk about when they eat as a family. Help with vocabulary and pronunciation, but don't interrupt fluency. Monitor to see what food vocabulary students already know.

♀ EXTRA ACTIVITY

Review and consolidate A1-level food vocabulary by writing jumbled words on the board, e.g., *toatpo* (potato), *hicwands* (sandwich). Use either A1-level items that students will probably know (*bread, cake, cheese, coffee, biscuit, egg, fish, meat, milk, orange juice, tea, tomato, vegetables*) or consolidate the spelling of items you heard students use in Exercise b, or use a combination of both. Be careful, however, not to pre-empt the lexical set of food vocabulary in Lesson 4A.

Exercises a and b can be prepared as homework before this lesson to give students time to look up unfamiliar vocabulary. Ask students to look at the picture and to prepare their answers to the questions as homework to talk about in the next lesson.

4A | TRY SOME INTERESTING FOOD

At the end of this lesson, students will be able to:

- read and understand a text about places to buy food
- identify countable and uncountable nouns
- use a lexical set of foods correctly
- understand a conversation about planning what to cook
- use *a/an*, *some* and *any* correctly
- ask for food they need to cook dinner

♀ OPTIONAL LEAD-IN

Write on the board: *Where do you buy food?* and under it write the following prompts: *in small shops? at a supermarket? online? at a market?* Check that students understand *market*. Tell the class where you usually buy food, e.g., *I usually buy food online*. Ask each student to tell the class where they buy food. Tell students to listen to what their classmates say and elicit from the class where most people usually go shopping.

☐ VOCABULARY SUPPORT

amazing (A2) – very good

customer (A2) – a person who buys something in a shop or market

dish (A2) – food that is prepared and cooked for people to eat

historic (B1) – interesting because it is old

d 💬🗨 Students talk about the questions in pairs, small groups or as a class. Students share their answers as a class.

1 READING

a 💬🗨 Give students one minute to think about their answers to the questions before talking about the pictures as a class. Encourage students to justify their ideas as much as possible.

b Students read the texts quickly and match them with the pictures. Check answers as a class. You may also give students information from Culture Notes below.

> **Answers**
> 1 b
> 2 c
> 3 a

🌏 CULTURE NOTES

Union Square Greenmarket started in 1976 and has become more and more successful over the years. The market takes place year round. At peak times of the year, over 100 farmers may be selling their products in the heart of Manhattan, giving New Yorkers the opportunity to buy fresh, locally produced ingredients.

The Municipal Market opened in the centre of São Paulo in 1933 in a historic building that is known for its eclectic style and stained glass windows. It is filled with market stalls selling a huge variety of foods, including most of the exotic fruit that is native to Brazil.

Nishiki Market is the largest traditional food market in Kyoto. It is styled as a traditional *shōtengai* (shopping street) so visitors can get an idea of what this would have looked like. As well as market stalls selling the main ingredients of traditional Kyoto cuisine, there are some restaurants and food stands with takeaway food.

c Read the first sentence with the class and elicit where students think Sam is. Read out the end of the final sentence of text 3 to justify the answer: *At Nishiki Market, you can try local foods such as tofu, pickled vegetables, grilled fish and sweets.* Individually, students decide where Maisie and Sarah are. They then check in pairs. When checking answers, elicit which words or sentences in the texts helped students decide. You may wish to help students with words in the Vocabulary Support box.

> **Answers**
> Sam is at the Nishiki Market in Kyoto.
> Maisie is at the Municipal Market in São Paulo.
> Sarah is at the Union Square Greenmarket in New York.

2 GRAMMAR Countable and uncountable nouns

a Write the four nouns on the board and ask students which two words have plural endings. Circle the *-s* of *vegetables*, then cover the *-s* with your hand and say *one vegetable*. Next, uncover the *-s* and say *two vegetables*. Point to *tomatoes* and hold your pen up to the board for students to tell you to circle the *-es*. Again, cover the plural ending and say *one tomato*. Then, uncover it and say *two tomatoes*.

> **Answer**
> *Vegetables* and *tomatoes* have plural endings.

b Elicit the rule as a class.

> **Answer**
> never

☐ LANGUAGE NOTES

Note that in 2c, the words *cheese, chocolate* and *fish* are treated as uncountable. They can, however, be countable in certain circumstances, e.g., *Go to the shop and buy me a good cheese.* (= a complete cheese, not only a part), *Do you want a chocolate?* (= referring to a chocolate from a box of chocolates), *I have a pet fish called Nemo!* (= referring to the living creature).

Unless students ask about this, don't mention it at this point, but be prepared to explain if necessary. After students have studied *some/any* later in this lesson and the containers in Lesson 4B, you may like to give further explanation.

c Individually, students complete the table. Check answers by copying the table onto the board and asking students to add the words.

> **Answers**
> Countable nouns: potatoes, carrots, ingredients, mushrooms, tomatoes, spices, sandwiches, pastries, sweets
> Uncountable nouns: pasta, meat, cheese, bread, chocolate, tofu, fish

♀ FAST FINISHERS

Ask fast finishers to add the food words that they thought of in Exercise b of the Getting Started section to the table.

3 VOCABULARY Food

a Ask students to cover the words and see how many words for the food in the pictures they already know. Individually, students then match the words with the pictures. Monitor for any problems and clarify these as you check answers as a class.

Answers

1 chicken	4 lamb	7 carrots	9 lemons
2 pears	5 mushrooms	8 grapes	10 onions
3 steak	6 beans		

b Complete the first item as an example with the class. Students work individually, identifying the different word in the other groups. They then check in pairs. Check answers as a class.

Answers

1 carrot – It's not fruit. It's a vegetable.
2 lamb – It's not a vegetable. It's meat.
3 grape – It's not meat. It's fruit.

> 💡 **EXTRA ACTIVITY**
>
> Students classify the vocabulary from 3a as countable or uncountable and add it to the table in 2c. Check answers as a class. If you drew the table on the board in 2c, check answers by asking students to add the words to the table (Countable nouns – *beans, lemons, mushrooms, onions, pears, carrots, grapes*; Uncountable nouns* – *chicken, steak, lamb*).
>
> *See Language Notes on the previous page. Both *chicken* and *lamb*, like *fish*, can be countable when referring to the living creature. Note that we also use *a chicken* when buying the complete animal in a shop, and *a steak* when buying or ordering an individual steak.

c ▶ 04.01 **Pronunciation** Answer the first question as a class. Individually, students then match the pairs of words. Play the recording for students to listen and check.

Answers

1 All the words have *ea* in them.
2 green – bean; hair – pear; make – steak

d ▶ 04.02 Read the examples and check that students understand that the three phonemic symbols at the top of the table are the same as the ones in 3c. Students add the words to the sound groups. Play the recording for students to listen and check. Drill each word.

Answers and audioscript

Sound 1 /eɪ/	Sound 2 /iː/	Sound 3 /eə/
steak	bean	pear
eight	eat	where
rain	these	wear
day	green	fair

e 💬 In pairs, students talk about the food they like and don't like. Monitor, but don't interrupt fluency unless students add *-s* to uncountable nouns.

f ≫ ▶ 04.03–04.05 Students complete the exercises in Vocabulary Focus 4A on SB p. 166. Play the recording for students to check their answers to Exercise a and complete the Pronunciation activities. Monitor Exercises d and f and check other answers as a class. Tell students to go back to SB p. 41.

Answers (Vocabulary Focus 4A SB p. 166)

a 1 e 2 d 3 c 4 b 5 j 6 f 7 g 8 i 9 h 10 a
c 1 b 2 a 3 a 4 a
e 1 chicken; steak; lamb
  2 salad; onions; carrots; beans; mushrooms
  3 cereal; yoghurt; jam 4 pears; grapes; melon 5 chips; cola

4 LISTENING

a 💬 Discuss the questions as a class. Find out how many students like cooking.

b ▶ 04.06 Play the recording for students to listen for specific details and answer the questions. They compare in pairs. Check answers as a class.

Answers

1 No, she doesn't.	3 at the farmers' market
2 Milly	4 Tom

Audioscript

TOM We've got almost nothing to eat for dinner.
MILLY OK. We can order some pizza then.
T Not again.
M Well, it's the weekend – I don't really want to cook.
T All right, fine. I can cook.
M OK. If you want to.
T But you can come to the shops with me.
M Like I said – it's the weekend. I don't cook and I don't go to the supermarket.
T We can go to the farmers' market then. It's open today.
M OK, fine. What do we need?
T Well, we've got some potatoes, so we can have roast potatoes, maybe. But we haven't got any meat.
M Do you want to make that chicken and mushroom dish – you know, the one you like to make?
T Yeah – good idea. Have we got any mushrooms?
M No, I don't think so.
T OK, we can get some. And I need an onion and a chicken, of course.
M So, let's put that on the shopping list – a chicken, some mushrooms and an onion. Is that all?
T Yeah, I think so.
M Oh and Tom … I haven't got any money at the moment, so … .
T All right, Milly. I can pay.

c ▶ 04.06 Students listen to the recording again and tick the food that Tom and Milly need. Check answers as a class. If students tick *potatoes*, clarify that Tom says that they have potatoes, so they don't need to buy more.

Answers

✓ chicken ✓ an onion ✓ mushrooms

5 GRAMMAR *a / an, some, any*

a ▶ 04.07 Pick up two pens and say to the class: *I've got two pens.* Then, add another two pens and elicit from the class how many pens you've got: *I've got four pens.* Finally, add several other pens so that students can't see the exact number and say: *I've got [silence] pens.* Elicit/ Teach the word *some*. Look at the first sentence in the Student's Book and complete it as a class. Individually, students complete the other sentences. Check answers as a class.

Answers

1 some 2 any 3 an 4 any

b Show the students all the pens again and say: *I have.* Ask: *Positive or negative?* (positive), *countable or uncountable?* (countable), *singular or plural?* (plural). Then look at sentence 1 in 5a and ask the same questions. Show students how to complete the first space in the table with *some*. Students complete the table. Check answers by copying the table onto the board and asking individual students to come up and complete it.

Answers

	Countable	Uncountable
+	*some* potatoes	*some* fruit
– / ?	*an* onion *any* onions	*any* cheese

🔵 LOA TIP ELICITING

- Check that students fully understand when we use *a/an*, *some* and *any* by asking them further questions, e.g., *What word do we use with an uncountable noun in a question?* (any); *What word do we use with a singular countable noun in a positive sentence?* (a).

- Write sentences 1–3 on the board:
  1 *We need to buy … vegetables from the market.*
  2 *I'm hungry. Have you got … food?*
  3 *I don't want … burger, thank you.*
  Point to sentence 1 and ask students: *What's the noun?* (vegetables); *Is it countable or uncountable?* (countable); *Is it singular or plural?* (plural); *Is the sentence positive or negative, or is it a question?* (positive). Once students have answered all four questions correctly, ask them what word goes in the gap. Repeat with sentences 2 and 3 (Answers *1 some, 2 any, 3 a*).

👁 CAREFUL!

The most common student mistake with countable and uncountable nouns is adding a final *-s* to uncountable words like *fruit, furniture, hair, homework* and *money*.

Students may also have problems with the indefinite article and include it where it isn't needed, e.g., *I travel to school by a bus* (Correct form = *I travel to school **by bus***), or not include it where it is needed, e.g., *This smartphone has very good camera …* (Correct form = *This smartphone has **a** very good camera*). They may also confuse *the* and *a*, e.g., *There's the big market …* (Correct form = *There's **a** big market in my town*).

When using the determiners *some* and *any*, students may leave them out, e.g., *I want new shoes* (Correct form = *I want **some** new shoes*) or *Do you have money?* (Correct form = *Do you have **any** money?*). In some cases, students may use *a* instead of *some*, e.g., *I need a bread …* (Correct form = *I need **some** bread to make a sandwich*).

c ⏩ 🔊 **04.08** Students read the information in Grammar Focus 4A on SB p. 144. Play the recording where indicated and ask students to listen and repeat. Students then complete the exercises. Check answers as a class, making sure students are clear on the differences between countable and uncountable nouns. Tell students to go back to SB p. 41.

Answers (Grammar Focus 4A SB p. 145)
a 2 C 3 U 4 U 5 U 6 U 7 C 8 U 9 C 10 U
b 2 a 4 any 6 a 8 some 10 any
  3 some 5 an 7 any 9 any
c 2 ~~furnitures~~ any furniture 5 ~~a~~ some cheese 7 long ~~hairs~~ hair
  3 any ~~moneys~~ money 6 ~~some~~ any meat 8 ~~any~~ an apple
  4 ~~a~~ an onion

💡 FAST FINISHERS

Ask fast finishers to rewrite the conversation in Grammar Focus Exercise b using vegetables instead of fruit.

d 🔊 **04.09** Individually, students complete the conversation. They then check in pairs. Play the recording for students to listen and check.

Answers
1 a
2 an
3 some
4 any
5 any
6 some

6 SPEAKING

a ⏩ Divide the class into pairs and assign A and B roles. Student As read the instructions and look at the picture on SB p. 130, and Student Bs read the instructions and look at the words on SB p. 133. Students then role play the conversation. Monitor, but don't interrupt fluency unless students make mistakes with the content of this lesson. Students then role play the second conversation.

💡 EXTRA ACTIVITY

Play a 'listing game' (see p. 154) with students. Mime having a bag of shopping and say: *This is my shopping. I've got two melons.* Pass the 'bag of shopping' to a student, who has to repeat your sentence and add an item, e.g., *This is my shopping. I've got two melons and some chicken.* They pass it on to the next student, who repeats the sentence and adds an item, and so on until the list is too long to remember. Students can then play in small groups. Monitor and check students are using *a/an* and *some* correctly.

⊕ ADDITIONAL MATERIALS

Workbook 4A

Photocopiable activities: Grammar 4A, Vocabulary 4A, Pronunciation 4A

Documentary video Unit 4 *Food*

Video worksheet Unit 4 *Food*

4B | HOW MUCH CHOCOLATE?

At the end of this lesson, students will be able to:
- read and understand short friendly emails
- use a lexical set of verbs and adjectives about cooking correctly
- understand a conversation about recipes
- use the quantifiers *much*, *many* and *a lot (of)* correctly
- ask and answer questions about the food they eat

💡 **OPTIONAL LEAD-IN**

Write *My favourite meal is …* on the board. Tell the students what your favourite three-course meal is using vocabulary from the previous lesson, e.g., *My favourite meal is soup – either French onion soup or mushroom soup – then meat (I love lamb!) with some vegetables – carrots, beans and potatoes. To finish, I love ice cream – banana and chocolate ice cream. Delicious!* Students then think about their own favourite meal and share it with a small group or the class.

1 READING

a 💬🗨 Give students a few minutes to think about their answers to the questions and read the text about Albert Adrià before they discuss the questions in small groups. Ask students to share their ideas. You may give students information from Culture Notes below.

🌍 **CULTURE NOTES**

Albert Adrià is a world-famous Spanish chef. He is the younger brother of Ferran Adrià, also a well-known chef, with whom he has often collaborated. Previously, he was the head pastry chef of one of Spain's most famous restaurants, called *elBulli*, and he played an important role in making *elBulli* so successful during his 23 years there. After *elBulli* closed in 2011, Albert and his brother opened *Tickets*, a tapas bar in Barcelona. In 2018, *Tickets* was listed as number 25 of the world's best restaurants, and Albert was recognised as one of the 13 most influential people in the restaurant and food industry.

b Tell students they should only read the first email. They then work individually, answering the questions. Check answers as a class.

Answers
1 Josh lives in Barcelona.
2 He wants to go to *Tickets*.
3 It looks fun and his friend Pete says the food is good.

c Tell students to read the second email for general meaning and find out if Josh's dad wants to go to *Tickets*. Check the answer as a class.

Answer
No, he doesn't.

d Students read Josh's dad's email again in detail. Individually, students underline the correct answers. Encourage students to guess the meaning of any new words from the context. Check answers as a class.

Answers
1 different
2 normal
3 expensive for Josh

💡 **EXTRA ACTIVITY**

Ask students to read both emails again and also look at the information about Albert Adrià in 1a. Ask students to decide if the following sentences are true or false.

1 *Albert Adrià is famous because he has written two cookbooks.* (F – He is famous because he makes creative dishes.)
2 *Josh's dad wants to take Josh for dinner.* (F – Josh wants to take his dad for dinner.)
3 *Josh loves the grilled fish at* Tickets. (F – Josh's friend's mother loves the grilled fish at *Tickets*.)
4 *Josh's dad likes his wife's cooking.* (T)
5 *Josh's dad wants him to cook roast chicken and boiled potatoes.* (F – He wants to go to a normal restaurant or have a tin of soup at Josh's place.)

e 💬🗨 Discuss the questions as a class. Encourage students to justify their answers as much as possible.

2 VOCABULARY Cooking

a Individually, students read the cooking instructions and match them with the pictures. Check answers as a class. Drill each word.

Answers
1 c
2 e
3 a
4 d
5 b

b ▶04.10 Individually, students complete the table. Play the recording for students to listen and check. Check answers as a class.

Answers

Verb	Adjective
boil	boiled
fry	fried
grill	grilled
bake	baked
roast	roast

c Look at the example together and check that students understand that the base verb is *boil*, so *-ed* has been added to form the adjective. Students complete the examples, working individually. They then check in pairs. Check answers as a class.

> **Answers**
> - add *-ed*   boiled, grilled
> - add *-d*   baked
> - changes *-y* to *-ied*   fried
> - ends with the sound /t/   baked, roast

> 📖 **LANGUAGE NOTES**
>
> Students may confuse the words *roast* and *bake* or be unsure about the distinction, as they are both used for cooking in the oven. To help them understand, explain that *roast* is generally used for things that are cooked with oil, e.g., beef, chicken, potatoes, while *bake* is used for things that are made with flour, e.g., biscuits, bread and cakes.

d 💬🗩 Put students into pairs or small groups to talk about the questions. Pre-teach the words *healthy* (good for your body) and *unhealthy* (bad for your body). Monitor, but don't interrupt fluency unless students make mistakes with the vocabulary for cooking.

e ⟫ ▶ 04.11 Students complete the exercises in Vocabulary Focus 4B on SB p. 166. Play the recording as necessary and monitor students as they speak. Check answers as a class, making sure students pronounce and stress the phrases correctly. Tell students to go back to SB p. 43.

> **Answers (Vocabulary Focus 4B SB p. 166)**
> **a** 1 d 2 a 3 e 4 b 5 c 6 f
> **b** 1 the nouns
> **c** 2 a jar of jam   5 a can/tin of tuna
>   3 a packet of spaghetti   6 a bag of apples
>   4 a bar of chocolate

> 💡 **FAST FINISHERS**
>
> Ask fast finishers to think of other things that can collocate with the containers, e.g., *a bottle of oil*, *a packet of cereal*.

3 LISTENING

a ▶ 04.12 Pre-teach the word *recipe* (written information about how to make a dish). Students listen to the conversation for general meaning and check the two recipes Olivia and Harry talk about. Check answers as a class.

> **Answers**
> ✓ Ultimate mashed potato
> ✓ Coffee and chocolate sauce

> **Audioscript**
>
> **OLIVIA** I want to try this recipe.
> **HARRY** Which one?
> **o** Ultimate mashed potato.
> **H** Mashed potato? That's a bit boring.
> **o** But it says 'ultimate' – you know, really great.
> **H** What's so special about it?
> **o** Well, it says to use 300 grams of butter.
> **H** 300 grams? That's a lot of butter.
> **o** I know! That's why I want to try it. And then you boil the potatoes once, let them get cold and then boil them again.
> **H** Twice?
> **o** Yeah. I don't know why. But I'm going to make it today. Anyway, which recipe do you want to try?
> **H** Something sweet. Let's see … oh yes, this one, coffee and
>
> chocolate sauce. Sounds really good! I can put it on ice cream.
> **o** What's in it?
> **H** Well, some coffee beans, of course.
> **o** How many do you need?
> **H** It says you need 40.
> **o** Woah! That's a lot! And how much chocolate?
> **H** Only a little – 60 grams. But I need dark chocolate, not milk chocolate.
> **o** How many grams of butter?
> **H** None – no butter at all, just water and sugar. It looks really easy to make. I just boil everything together.
> **o** Once or twice?
> **H** Only once with this recipe. Now, no more talking. I'm hungry! Let's get cooking.

b ▶ 04.12 Play the recording again for students to underline the specific food words. They compare in pairs. Then check answers as a class.

> **Answers**
> 1 potatoes, butter
> 2 boil
> 3 sugar, coffee beans, dark chocolate
> 4 boil

c 💬🗩 Discuss the question as a class. If students are interested in learning more about Albert Adrià's recipes, more information and pictures are readily available by searching the Internet.

> 💡 **EXTRA ACTIVITY**
>
> Give the class some additional listening practice through a 'live listening'. Tell the group about a typical dish from your country, e.g., roast chicken, and explain how to make it using the food vocabulary from Lesson 4A and the cooking verbs and adjectives from this lesson, e.g., *This is my recipe for roast chicken with onions, lemon and garlic. Fry the onions and the garlic in a little oil. Put two lemons inside the chicken with the onion and garlic and roast it in the oven for around two hours.* Students write down the ingredients and the main steps of the recipe. They then check in pairs and ask you to clarify any steps they are not sure of, e.g., *Where do you put the lemons?*

4 GRAMMAR
Quantifiers: *much, many, a lot (of)*

a ▶ 04.13 Look at the first sentence in the Student's Book and complete it as a class. Individually, students complete the other sentences. Check answers as a class.

> **Answers**
> 1 a lot
> 2 much; a little
> 3 many

b Read the first mini-conversation as a class and make sure students understand that it's possible to use all four phrases. Ask them: *Is butter a countable or uncountable noun?* (uncountable). Repeat the process with the second mini-conversation: *Are beans countable or uncountable?* (countable). Repeat with the final sentence: *Are potatoes countable or uncountable?* (countable). Ask: *What about chocolate?* (uncountable). Check students understand that *a lot (of)* can be used with both countable and uncountable nouns. Also point out that *of* is only used when followed by a noun.

> **Answers**
> 1 uncountable nouns
> 2 countable nouns
> 3 both

⊙ CAREFUL!

At this level, students will probably use *How much* correctly, but may still make mistakes with *How many*, sometimes using it in place of *How much*, e.g., ~~How many cheese do~~ ... (Correct form = **How much** cheese do we need?). Another common error is using *much/many* in contexts where *a lot of* would sound more natural, e.g., ~~There are many people~~ ... (Correct form = *There are **a lot of** people at the restaurant*) or ~~We always have much fun~~ ... (Correct form = *We always have **a lot of** fun in class*). Students also often use *much* instead of *many*, e.g., ~~Albert hasn't got much restaurants~~ (Correct form = *Albert hasn't got **many** restaurants*), and may occasionally use *many* instead of *much*. They also sometimes spell *a lot* as one word or include *of* when *a lot* appears at the end of a sentence, e.g., ~~I like this dish alot / a lot of~~ (Correct form = *I like this dish **a lot***).

---

c ≫ ▶04.14–04.15 Students read the information in Grammar Focus 4B on SB p. 144. Play the recording where indicated and ask students to listen and repeat. Students then complete the exercises. Check answers as a class, making sure students are clear about which quantifiers are used with countable nouns and which are used with uncountable nouns. For Exercise a, tell students that they should choose from the quantifiers in the table on p. 144. Tell students to go back to SB p. 43.

> **Answers (Grammar Focus 4B SB p. 145)**
> **a** 2 little   3 a lot of   4 few   5 much   6 a lot of
> **b** 2 much   4 many   6 many   8 much
>   3 much   5 much   7 much
> **c** 1 much   3 many   5 much   7 much
>   2 much   4 a little   6 a lot of   8 a few

♀ FAST FINISHERS

Ask fast finishers to look at the picture of the market stall on SB p. 130 and write sentences about it using the quantifiers.

---

d ▶04.16 Individually, students complete the conversation and put it in order. Play the recording for students to listen and check. Check answers as a class.

> **Answers**
> **B** 2 A ¹_____lot_____ – about five or six pieces.
> **A** 5 Really? That's ²_____quite_____ a lot.
> **B** 4 About four or five.
> **A** 3 And what about drinks? How ³_____many_____ cups of coffee do you have a day?
> **A** 1 How ⁴_____much_____ fruit do you eat a day?

> **Audioscript**
> **A** How much fruit do you eat a day?
> **B** A lot – about five or six pieces.
> **A** And what about drinks? How many cups of coffee do you have a day?
> **B** About four or five.
> **A** Really? That's quite a lot.

⟳ LOA TIP ELICITING

- Draw a smiley face ☺ on the left of the board, a neutral face 😐 in the centre of the board and a sad face ☹ on the right of the board.
- Point to the smiley face and give a thumbs up, the neutral face and give a 'so-so' shaky-hand gesture, and the sad face and give a thumbs down. Ask students: *Countable and uncountable nouns?* Elicit an indication of their confidence level. Repeat with *Some and any?* and *Much, many and a lot of?*

---

e 💬 Discuss the question as a class. Encourage students to justify their answers as much as possible.

⑤ SPEAKING

a Students work individually, writing questions to ask their partner about the food they eat. Monitor and point out errors for students to self-correct.

b 💬 Put students into pairs to ask and answer their questions. Tell them to make a note of their partner's answers.

c 💬 Students read the information on SB p. 131 and then look at their notes from 5b. Ask volunteers to share their answers to find out who eats in a healthy way.

⊕ ADDITIONAL MATERIALS

Workbook 4B

Photocopiable activities: Grammar 4B, Vocabulary 4B

Documentary video Unit 4 *Food*

Video worksheet Unit 4 *Food*

EVERYDAY ENGLISH

Do we need a reservation?

At the end of this lesson, students will be able to:

- understand conversations in a restaurant in which people ask for a table and order food
- use appropriate phrases when arriving at a restaurant and ordering a meal
- identify word groups in sentences and the main stress in each group
- use appropriate phrases for changing what they want to say
- order food in a restaurant

♀ OPTIONAL LEAD-IN

Ask a student to write *American* on the board. Point to the board and ask the rest of the class: *Is that correct?* to confirm the student has spelt it correctly. Repeat the process with *British, Chinese, French, Greek, Indian, Italian, Japanese, Mexican, Russian.* Ask students: *What kind of restaurants are popular in your country?* and elicit their ideas. Finally, ask students: *What kind of restaurants do you think are popular in the UK?* (Food from many different countries is popular in the UK, but Chinese, Indian and Italian restaurants are especially popular.).

1 LISTENING

a ⫶💬 Pre-teach the phrase *eat out* (have a meal in a restaurant, not at home). Give students one minute to think about their answers to the questions before talking about restaurants and eating out as a class.

b ⫶💬 Look at picture a as a class and ask students what they can remember about Annie, Leo, Martina and Dan from Units 1–3. In pairs, students decide why the restaurant is empty. Elicit students' ideas, but don't check the answer at this point.

c ▶04.17 Play Part 1 of the video or the audio recording for students to check their answer to 1b. Check the answer as a class.

> **Answer**
> 3 It's very early.

Video/Audioscript (Part 1)

DAN Is this it?	**W** Certainly.
ANNIE This is it.	**A** Can we have a table by the window?
LEO Great.	
A It's empty.	**W** Yes. These two over here are both free.
MARTINA Maybe it isn't open.	
WAITER Good evening, good evening.	**D** What do you think? The one on the left?
A Hello. Are you open?	**M** Fine.
W Yes, of course. Do you have a reservation?	**L** Sure.
A No, we don't. Do we need a reservation?	**A** What about the one on the right?
W Erm, not really. It's very early …	**D** If you prefer …
A OK, then, we'd like a table for four.	**A** Maybe not. The one on the left is fine …
	W Of course. This way, please.

d ▶04.17 Students watch or listen again for specific details. Play Part 1 of the video or the audio recording again for students to decide if the sentences are true or false and correct the false sentences. Check answers as a class.

> **Answers**
> 1 F (They don't have a reservation.)
> 2 F (They want a table by the window.)
> 3 T

2 USEFUL LANGUAGE
Arriving at a restaurant

a Check students understand that the lines of the conversation aren't in the correct order, but that they don't have to put them in the order yet. They read for general meaning to identify which speaker is the waiter. Check the answer as a class.

> **Answer**
> The waiter is A.

b ▶04.18 Students read the sentences again in detail. Individually, students put them in order to make a conversation. Play the recording for students to listen and check. Check answers as a class.

Answers and audioscript

A	Good evening. Do you have a reservation?	**A**	No problem.
B	No, we don't. We'd like a table for four.	**B**	Can we have a table by the window?
		A	Yes, of course. This way, please.

c 💬 Drill the conversation before students work in pairs. Monitor and correct students' pronunciation as appropriate.

d 💬 Read through the sentences with the students and, if possible, put them into pairs with a new partner to practise the conversation with the new information.

♀ FAST FINISHERS

Ask fast finishers to invent their own conversations with different information, e.g., *Can we have a table in the corner? We have a reservation for three people at 8:30 pm. I'm sorry we're late. The name's Wilson.*

3 LISTENING

a Look at the menu with the students. Ask: *What do you eat first? A starter or a main course?* (a starter) and check the meaning of *smoked, mixed, fresh* and *pie* if necessary. Then look at picture b and read what the friends say. Individually, students predict what they choose for their main course. Don't check answers at this point.

b ▶04.19 Play Part 2 of the video or the audio recording for students to check their answers to 3a and find out who can't decide what to have. They check in pairs. Check answers as a class.

> **Answers**
> 1 Martina – lamb with roast potatoes; Annie – lamb with roast potatoes; Dan – lamb with roast potatoes; Leo – Thai chicken curry
> 2 Annie can't decide what she wants to have.

Video/Audioscript (Part 2)

WAITER Are you ready to order?

DAN Yes?

MARTINA I'm ready.

LEO Fine.

ANNIE I think so …

W What would you like for your starter?

M I'd like the mushroom soup, please.

W And for your main course?

M I'll have the lamb with roast potatoes.

W And for you, madam? What would you like to eat?

A Oh dear. It's hard to decide. OK, for a starter I'll have the fish. No, wait! I'll have chicken salad and then … yes … I'd like the spaghetti for my main course.

W Very good. And for your starter, sir?

D I'll have chicken salad.

W Chicken salad.

D Then lamb with roast potatoes.

A Oh, lamb – that sounds nice. Can I change my order?

W Of course.

A I'll have the same – lamb for my main.

W Certainly. And finally?

L I'd like the chicken curry.

W Would you like rice with that?

L Yes, please. And for my starter I'd like the fish.

A Fish. My first idea. Sorry, sorry … I'll have the same as Leo.

W So, that's the fish?

A Yes.

L Are you sure about that, Annie?

A What? I think so. Yes.

W And what would you like to drink?

A To drink? Umm …

W Would you like a moment to think about that?

� EXTRA ACTIVITY

Play both parts of the video or the audio recording again and ask students to answer questions 1 and 2: *1 What time of day is it?* (evening) *2 What do the friends choose for their starters?* (Martina – fresh mushroom soup; Annie – fried fish in lemon sauce; Dan – smoked chicken salad; Leo – fried fish in lemon sauce).

c 💬 Discuss the questions as a class. Encourage students to justify their answers as far as possible.

4 USEFUL LANGUAGE
Ordering a meal in a restaurant

a Individually, students complete the conversations. They then check in pairs. Check answers as a class.

> **Answers**
> 1 like
> 2 I'll
> 3 have
> 4 Then
> 5 with

� FAST FINISHERS

Ask fast finishers to invent more short conversations by changing words and phrases in the conversations in 4a.

b Refer students to the conversations in 4a and, as a class, elicit which two phrases we use to order food.

> **Answers**
> 2 ✓ I'd like
> 4 ✓ I'll have

c ▶04.20 Individually, students put the words in the correct order. Play the recording for students to listen and check. Check answers as a class. Drill the sentences.

> **Answers**
> 1 I'd like bean salad for my starter.
> 2 I'll have spaghetti for my main course.
> 3 I'd like chicken curry with rice.

5 PRONUNCIATION Word groups

a ▶04.21 Play the first sentence and highlight the break between the word groups for students. Then play the rest of the recording for students to listen and mark where the new word groups start. They check in pairs. Check answers as a class. You may wish to teach the word *raw* (not cooked).

> **Answers**
> 2 And I'll have vegetable pie || for my main course.
> 3 I'd like chicken salad || for my starter.

b ▶04.21 Point out the underlined words in the sentences in 5a. Play the recording again. Highlight the main stresses for students by beating the rhythm with your hand to show where the stresses fall.

c ▶04.22 Play the recording for students to listen and mark where the new word groups start. Check answers by copying the text onto the board and asking students to mark the word groups. Drill the text before students work in pairs in 5d.

> **Answers**
> For my starter || I'll have mushroom soup. || And then I'd like chicken curry || for my main course. || And I'll have some rice || with my curry.

d 💬 In pairs, students practise saying the text in 5c. Monitor and help as necessary.

6 CONVERSATION SKILLS
Changing what you say

a Ask students to read the sentences from the conversation and underline the phrases Annie uses to change what she wants to say. Check answers as a class.

> **Answers**
> 1 Maybe not.
> 2 No, wait.

b ▶04.23 Individually, students complete the sentences. Play the recording for students to listen and check. Check answers as a class.

> **Answers**
> 1 not
> 2 wait

7 SPEAKING

a 💬 Put students into small groups and tell them to decide together on one more starter and one more main course for the menu. Students may well add the word *steak* to the menu. If so, be prepared to feed in the question: *How would you like your steak?* and the answers: *rare*, *medium* and *well done*.

LOA TIP DRILLING

- Drill some of the key phrases students will need to complete the task in 7b before they start. Try focusing on the main stress in each phrase first, before filling in the other words, e.g., *table – Can we have a – Can we have a* <u>table</u> *– window – by the – by the* <u>window</u> */ Can we have a* <u>table</u> *by the* <u>window</u>?

- Once students are confident with the phrases, ask them to chorus them to you. Then give them a new word so that they have to repeat each phrase immediately with a slight change, e.g., Students: *Can we have a table by the window?* Teacher: *door*. Students: *Can we have a table by the door?* Other phrases that work well with this type of substitution drill include: *I'd like the fried fish, please.* (Teacher: *chicken salad*), *And I'll have the vegetable pie for my main course.* (Teacher: *spaghetti with tomato sauce*), *Would you like rice with that?* (Teacher: *potatoes*).

b 🗨 Read through the instructions with the students. Remind students to use the phrases in 6a when they change what they say. Monitor, but don't interrupt fluency unless students make mistakes with the content of this lesson.

⊕ ADDITIONAL MATERIALS

Workbook 4C

Photocopiable activities: Pronunciation 4C

Unit Progress Test

4D

SKILLS FOR WRITING

Next, decide on your menu

At the end of this lesson, students will be able to:

- understand people talking about cooking
- understand information on a blog about learning how to cook
- make the order of items in a written text clear
- write a blog post about something they know how to do and explain how to do it better

♀ OPTIONAL LEAD-IN

Ask students to look at pictures a–d. Write on the board: *cheese, chicken, chocolate, fish, pears, lemon, pasta, pie, sauce, tomatoes, vegetables*. Put students into pairs or small groups to decide what the ingredients of each of the four dishes are. Invite pairs or small groups to share their ideas with the class before students talk about the questions in 1a (*dish a: chocolate, pears, pie; dish b: cheese, pasta, sauce, tomatoes; dish c: cheese, vegetables; dish d: fish, lemon, tomatoes*).

1 SPEAKING AND LISTENING

a 🗨 Read the questions with students, then put them into pairs or small groups to ask and answer the questions together. Monitor and allow time for all students to share their ideas.

b ▶ 04.24 Play the recording for students to listen for general meaning and underline the correct answers. Students check in pairs. Check answers as a class. If you wish, elicit the names of the four dishes and write them on the board (*dish a: pear cake with chocolate sauce; dish b: spaghetti with tomato and mushroom sauce; dish c: vegetable moussaka; dish d: grilled fish with lemon*). You may wish to point out to students that Toby uses the word *cookies*, not *biscuits*, because he's American.

Answers

Name	Talks about		
Jake	himself	a bad cook	picture b
Rosie	her husband	a good cook	picture c
Johanna	herself	a good cook	picture d
Toby	his mother	a good cook	picture a

Audioscript

JAKE I'm really bad at cooking. I eat a lot of fast food and frozen meals. I'm OK at making pasta – usually spaghetti with sauce. The one sauce I make is tomato and mushroom. It's not very good, but I like it! So I eat a lot of pasta because it's easy to make.

ROSIE My husband's a great cook, and he does all the cooking at home. He can look in our fridge and find some vegetables and cheese and then make a dish from it that's wonderful to eat, like a vegetable moussaka. I don't know how he does it. But I'm lucky to have a husband like that!

JOHANNA My friends say I'm a good cook. I'm not sure, but I enjoy cooking and if you enjoy something, you're often good at it. I think it's fun to try new dishes, and I certainly like eating the things I make! Tonight, I want to try a new fish dish. First, you grill the fish. Then you make a lemon sauce. I think it'll go well with a bean salad I often make.

TOBY My mother is a fantastic cook. But isn't everyone's mother a fantastic cook?! I eat everything she makes, and I always want more. I really, really like the cakes and cookies she makes. My favourite is her pear cake – I love eating it warm with chocolate sauce.

c ▶ 04.24 Students listen to the recording again for specific details and answer the questions. They then compare in pairs. Check answers as a class.

Answers
1 Toby
2 Jake
3 Rosie
4 Johanna

d Individually, students think of someone they know who's a good cook and make notes. Monitor and help with vocabulary if necessary.

🔄 **LOA TIP ELICITING**

- Students close their books. In order to elicit similar questions to those in the speech bubbles in 1e and other questions which students might find useful in 1e, write sentences on the board about a person you know who's a good cook, e.g., *My brother is a good cook. He makes great fish tacos. He's a good cook because he always finds new and unusual recipes. He watches cookery programmes on TV every week.*

- Point to the sentences on the board and elicit possible questions from the class, e.g., *Who do you know who's a good cook? What does he/she make? Why is he/she a good cook? Does he/she watch cookery programmes?* Write these questions on the board. Students then open their books and refer to the questions on the board during 1e.

e 💬🗨 In pairs, students ask and answer questions about a good cook they know. Monitor, but don't interrupt fluency. Ask some students to tell the class about the person their partner talked about, and make sure they are using the third person -*s* form correctly.

💡 **FAST FINISHERS**

Ask fast finishers to write sentences about the people their partners told them about, e.g., *Ahmed's sister is a great cook. She makes fantastic cakes and biscuits.*

2 READING

a Point to the picture on SB p. 46 and say: *This is Jake.* Explain to students that this person is not the same Jake as in exercises 1b and 1c above. Tell students they should only read the text *Jake Cooks!* They then work individually, answering the question. Check the answer as a class.

Answer
b people who want to learn how to cook

b Tell students to read the second part of the text, *My food – shared!*, and answer the question. Check the answer as a class. Ask students: *What kind of text is this?* (a blog). Then ask: *Do you write a blog?* to find out if anyone in the class has their own blog.

Answer
b planning a dinner

c Students read *My food – shared!* again in detail. Individually, students decide if the sentences are true or false. When checking answers, ask students to correct the false sentences.

Answers
1 T
2 T
3 F (It's too hard to try new dishes.)
4 F (Call or text to invite your friends and agree on a night that's good for everyone.)
5 T

💡 **EXTRA ACTIVITY**

Ask students to read both texts again and answer Questions 1–5:
1 *Is Jake a good cook?* (No, he's not.)
2 *Who sometimes helps Jake?* (his family and friends)
3 *How many people does Jake usually invite?* (four)
4 *Does Jake always call his friends to invite them to dinner?* (No, he calls or texts them.)
5 *Why does Jake prefer Saturday or Sunday for cooking dinner?* (He has all day to prepare.)

d 💬🗨 Discuss the questions as a class. Encourage students to justify their answers as much as possible.

3 WRITING SKILLS
Making the order clear

a Books closed. Write on the board: *… , think about how many people you want to invite.* and *… , call or text to invite your friends.* Point to the gap in the first sentence and ask: *Do you remember this word?* Write *First* on the board in the sentence. Repeat the process with the second sentence and write *Next* on the board in the sentence. Ask students: *What kind of words are these?* Elicit *words to make the order clear.* If you wish, introduce the term *sequencing words.*

Answers
After that; Finally

b Answer the questions as a class. Check that students understand that *after that*, *next* and *then* mean the same in this context.

Answers
We can change *next* and *after that* with *then*.
We use a comma after these phrases.

📖 **LANGUAGE NOTES**

There are many ways to indicate sequence in a written text (e.g., the past simple and the past perfect, connectors like *when/while*), but at this level students need some words to use as 'flags' in their writing. For this reason, basic sequencing words are presented in the simplest possible way. *First* is used for the first item; *after that*, *next* and *then* are presented as synonyms for the next items; and *finally* is used for the last item. Most of the verbs in the model texts are imperatives, which also helps to keep the text as grammatically simple as possible and will allow students to focus their attention on the sequencing words.

c Individually, students read the sentences and put them in the correct order. Students then check in pairs. Check answers as a class.

Answers
2 Leave the beans ...
3 Put lemon and oil ...
4 Add salt and pepper ...

d Read the example sentence with the students. Check that they understand that more than one answer may be possible for each sentence. Students then add the words to the sentences in 3c. Check answers as a class and clarify that in sentences 2–4, the sequencing words can be used in any order.

Answers
1 First, cook the beans in hot water with a little salt.
2 After that / Next / Then, leave the beans until they are warm.
3 After that / Next / Then, put lemon and oil on the warm beans – not too much.
4 After that / Next / Then, add salt and pepper and mix everything together.
5 Finally, place the bean salad in a nice bowl and serve to your guests.

♀ **FAST FINISHERS**

Ask fast finishers to write simple instructions for another recipe using the five sequencing words.

---

4 WRITING

a Read the questions with the class. Students work individually to plan their blogs. Monitor and help with vocabulary and give students ideas if necessary.

b Students write their blogs, working individually. Remind students to use sequencing words to make the order clear. If you're short of time, this exercise can be completed for homework. Students could then bring their blogs to the next lesson.

c In pairs, students swap blogs and check their partner's work. Tell them to check that their partners have used the sequencing words correctly. They then give each other feedback. If they've made any mistakes with the sequencing words or in other areas, they prepare a second draft of their blogs before giving them to you for correction.

⊕ **ADDITIONAL MATERIALS**

Workbook 4D

UNIT 4
Review and extension

1 GRAMMAR

a Individually, students read the text and correct the words that are wrong. Check answers and spelling as a class by asking students to write the correct answers on the board.

> **Answers**
> 1 ✓
> 2 vegetable~~s~~
> 3 ~~fruits~~ fruit
> 4 potato~~es~~
> 5 ✓
> 6 ~~butters~~ butter
> 7 ✓
> 8 egg~~s~~
> 9 ~~fishes~~ fish
> 10 ✓

b Students underline the correct words to complete the questions. Check answers as a class and drill the questions.

> **Answers**
> 1 any
> 2 much
> 3 many
> 4 some
> 5 any
> 6 much

c Check that students understand that only one of the three options is possible. They then choose the correct answers, working individually. Check answers as a class.

> **Answers**
> 1 c   2 b   3 b   4 a

2 VOCABULARY

a Students match the words with the categories and then add one more word to each group. They compare in pairs. Check answers and students' suggested words as a class.

> **Answers**
> 1 chicken, lamb
> 2 potato, carrot
> 3 pear, grape
> 4 cheese, yoghurt
> 5 grilled, boiled

b Individually, students read the list and decide if the items are normal or unusual (or impossible). Check answers by drawing a tick and a cross on the board and asking individual students to come up and write the word on the board under the correct heading.

> **Answers**
> 3 ✓
> 4 ✗
> 5 ✓
> 6 ✗
> 7 ✓
> 8 ✓
> 9 ✓

> 💡 **FAST FINISHERS**
>
> Ask fast finishers to write down all the other normal combinations they can think of with *baked*, *boiled*, *fried*, *grilled* and *roast*.

3 WORDPOWER *like*

a Books closed. Ask more confident students the following questions: *Do you like cooking?*; *I have a tablet in my bag. Would you like to see it?*; *Do you have a favourite café? What's it like?* Don't worry if they have problems answering, but notice if students can understand the questions. Then, write the three questions with *like* on the board, leaving a gap in place of *like*. Point to the gaps and ask: *What's this word?* Elicit *like* and write it in a circle above the questions. Students open their books and match the conversation with the picture. Check the answer as a class.

> **Answer**
> Conversation 2

b Students read the questions and match them with the questions in 3a. Check answers as a class.

> **Answers**
> 1 What vegetables would you like?   3 What kind of fruit do you like?
> 2 Would you like to join us?

c Students read the sentences and match them with the questions in 3b. Check answers as a class.

> **Answers**
> a 1   b 3   c 2

d Individually, students match the words in bold with the meanings. Check answers as a class.

> **Answers**
> 1 b   2 d   3 c   4 a

e As an example, elicit a question with *like* for the first situation from the class. Students work individually for the other situations. Monitor and point out errors for students to self-correct. They then compare ideas in pairs. Elicit possible questions and write them on the board.

> **Possible answers**
> 1 Would you like to come to the cinema on Friday?
> 2 I'd like some apples, please.
> 3 Would you like cream and sugar with that?
> 4 What would you like for lunch/dinner?
> 5 What's New York like?

f Put students into pairs to ask and answer the questions from 3e. As you monitor, don't interrupt fluency, but note down mistakes with *like* and the auxiliaries *would* and *do*. After the activity, write these on the board and ask students to correct them.

> 💡 **EXTRA ACTIVITY**
>
> Ask students questions with *like* and talk about them as a class, e.g., *Would you like to try Japanese/Russian/Mexican food? Why / Why not?*; *What food from your country do you like? What food from your country don't you like? Why?*; *Are you like your parents? Are your children like you? In what ways?*; *What's it like to study in this class?*

 Photocopiable activities: Wordpower 4

> 🔄 **LOA TIP ELICITING**
>
> Students look back through the unit, think about what they've studied and decide how well they did. Students work on weak areas by using the appropriate sections of the Workbook and the Photocopiable activities.

UNIT 5
PLACES

At the end of this unit, students will be able to:

- understand information, texts and conversations about towns and cities, homes and furniture and neighbourhoods
- ask for and give information about places in a town or city
- describe their home and talk about their furniture
- understand conversations in which people give directions and ask for and give directions themselves
- use simple phrases to check what other people say
- write a description of their neighbourhood

UNIT CONTENTS

G GRAMMAR
- *there is / there are*
- Possessive pronouns and possessive *'s*

V VOCABULARY
- Places in a city: *bridge, building, café, centre, concert hall, flat, hotel, metro station, park, police station, post office, restaurant, river, sports centre, square, stadium, street, theatre*
- Furniture: *armchair, bedside table, bookcase, chest of drawers, cooker, cupboard, curtains, lamp, mirror, sink, wardrobe, washing machine*
- Linking ideas with *and, but* and *so*
- Wordpower: Prepositions of place: *at the end of, behind, between, in, in front of, next to, on, on the corner of, opposite*

P PRONUNCIATION
- Words that end in /s/ and /z/
- Sound and spelling: /b/ and /p/
- Sound and spelling: vowels before *r*
- Sentence stress

C COMMUNICATION SKILLS
- Talking about where you live and the things you like in your town or city
- Asking and answering questions about what there is in a town or city
- Describing the furniture in the different rooms in your home
- Using appropriate phrases to check what other people say
- Asking for and giving directions
- Asking and answering questions about your neighbourhood
- Writing a description of your neighbourhood

GETTING STARTED

♀ OPTIONAL LEAD-IN

Books closed. Write these questions on the board: *What's your home like? Is it big or small? Who do you live with? Where's your home? Do you like it? Why / Why not? Would you like to live somewhere else? Where?* Put students into pairs or small groups to discuss the questions. Monitor and praise students who are able to express their ideas, even if their English isn't perfect.

Students may show each other pictures of their homes on their mobile phones if they have them. Ask students to open their books and look at the picture. Ask: *Would you like to live here?* Elicit a short reaction from the class.

a 💬 Give students one minute to read the ideas and decide which they think are true before talking about the picture as a class.

🌎 CULTURE NOTES

This picture shows an abandoned cabin in Colorado in the USA.

b 💬 Read the questions and the ideas with the students, and check that they understand the vocabulary. Put students into pairs to discuss reasons why this is a good or bad place for a home. Ask students for their ideas about what a 'good home' is and to share any other ideas they have. Help with vocabulary and pronunciation, but don't interrupt fluency.

💡 EXTRA ACTIVITY

Ask students to discuss the good and bad aspects of some specific homes in the area where you're teaching. Give them three contrasting real locations, giving the names of a place or street if possible, e.g., a big house in a small town up in the mountains, a small flat in the town/city near your school, a beach house on the coast. Put students into pairs or small groups to discuss their ideas. Take feedback as a class.

Exercises a and b can be prepared as homework before this lesson to give students time to look up unfamiliar vocabulary. Ask students to look at the picture and to prepare their answers to the questions as homework to talk about in the next lesson.

5A | THERE AREN'T ANY PARKS OR SQUARES

At the end of this lesson, students will be able to:
- read and understand a text about a town
- use a lexical set of places in a city correctly
- use positive, negative, question and short answer forms of *there is / there are*
- ask for and give information about places in a town or city

💡 OPTIONAL LEAD-IN

Give students the chance to learn something more about you. Put students into pairs or small groups to brainstorm things they would like to ask you about where you come from, e.g., *Where do you come from? Is it a good place for a home? Why / Why not? Does your town/city have a lot of cafés / a sports centre / a theatre? What are the bad things about where you live?* Monitor and point out errors for students to self-correct.

Students take turns asking you their questions. Encourage them to ask additional questions if they wish.

1 READING

a 💬 Discuss the question as a class and write students' ideas on the board. If you used the optional lead-in, you might like to ask students which picture they think is most like the place where you come from. Don't check answers at this point.

📖 VOCABULARY SUPPORT

unusual (A2) – different in a way that is surprising or interesting

roof (A2) – the covering over the top of a building

tunnel (B1) – a long passage under or through the ground

b Students read the text quickly and check their answers to 1a. Check the answer as a class. If you wish, give students information from Culture Notes below.

> **Answer**
> Everything is in one building. You get there through a tunnel.

🌍 CULTURE NOTES

Whittier is a very remote town; it can only be reached by sea or by a one-lane tunnel that is closed at night and in which traffic can run in only one direction. Around 80% of the town's residents live in one building, and the building houses services such as a supermarket and even a bed and breakfast. All tenants also have access to small storage areas under the main building to store the things they can't fit in their flats.

c Tell students to read the text again in detail. Individually, students answer the questions. Encourage students to guess the meaning of any new words from the context. Check answers as a class.

> **Answers**
> 1 No
> 2 No
> 3 Yes
> 4 Yes
> 5 Yes
> 6 No

💡 EXTRA ACTIVITY

Ask students to read the text again and answer Questions 1–5: *1 Do people live in other places in the town?* (Yes, they do.) *2 Do people work in the main building* (Yes, they do.) *3 How long is the tunnel to Whittier?* (3 km) *4 How often do cars pass through the tunnel?* (once every hour) *5 What happens if you want to leave Whittier at 11 pm?* (You can't leave. You have to wait until the next morning.)

d 💬 In pairs, students talk about if they would like to visit or live in Whittier. Ask all students to share their ideas. Encourage students to justify their answers as much as possible.

2 VOCABULARY Places in a city

a Elicit the first two or three examples with the class. Students then underline the places in the text and identify the ones they can see in the pictures. Check answers as a class. Drill each word.

> **Possible answers**
> 1
> shop, building, church, police station, hospital, flat, office, college, university, school, café
> 2
> street, park, square (*also* street café)

b ⟫ ▶ 05.01–05.02 Students complete the exercises in Vocabulary Focus 5A on SB p. 164. Play the recording for students to check their answers to Exercise a and complete the Pronunciation activity. Monitor Exercise d and check other answers as a class. Tell students to go back to SB p. 51.

> **Answers (Vocabulary Focus 5A SB p. 164)**
> **a** 1 concert hall   3 post office   5 police station
>   2 stadium   4 sports centre   6 theatre
> **b** a stadium   d bridge   g square
>   b park   e theatre   h concert hall
>   c post office   f police station i sports centre
> **c** *building* and *bridge* are strong; *park* and *post office* are weak.

c 💬 Students work in small groups, brainstorming more places in a city. Check answers by drawing three columns on the board and asking individual students to come up and write their words on the board. Drill each word.

> **Answers**
> Students' own answers

d 💬 In pairs, students tell each other about three places they like in their town or city. Monitor, but don't interrupt fluency unless students make mistakes with the vocabulary for places in a city. Ask some students to tell the class about the places they chose.

💡 FAST FINISHERS

Ask fast finishers to talk about places that they don't like in their towns or cities and to justify their answers as much as possible.

3 GRAMMAR *there is / there are*

a Books closed. Write on the board: *Positive or negative? Singular or plural?* Read the complete first sentence to the class (*There aren't any parks or squares.*) and point to the two questions on the board to elicit that it's negative and plural. Students open their books. Individually, they complete the sentences in the book. Check answers as a class.

Answers
1 There aren't   2 There's   3 There isn't   4 There are

b Point to the first column in the table and say *positive,* then point to the second column and elicit *negative.* Point to the first row and say *singular,* then point to the second row and elicit *plural.* Students complete the table. They then compare answers in pairs. Check answers as a class.

Answers

+	–
There<u>'s</u> a police station.	There <u>isn't</u> a normal road.
There <u>are</u> a few shops.	There <u>aren't</u> any street cafés.

c Students match the questions with the answers. They compare in pairs. Check answers as a class.

Answers
1 b   2 c   3 d   4 a

d Individually, students complete the table. They compare answers in pairs. Check answers as a class. Ask students: *When do we use 'there is'?* (positive, singular) and *When do we use 'there are'?* (positive, plural) Repeat with the negative forms. Then ask: *How is the word order of questions with 'there is' and 'there are' different from the word order of positive or negative sentences with 'there is' and 'there are'?* (We put 'is' or 'are' first.)

Answers

Yes/No questions	Short answers	
<u>Is there</u> a good hotel in the town?	Yes, there <u>is</u>.	No, there <u>isn't</u>.
<u>Are there</u> any good restaurants?	Yes, <u>there are</u>.	No, <u>there aren't</u>.

⊙ CAREFUL!

There are several common student mistakes with *there is / there are.* As students work through the Grammar Focus, make sure they understand that the verb and the noun must always agree, e.g., ~~There isn't many buildings~~ (Correct form = *There **aren't** many buildings*). Mistakes with agreement are particularly common before uncountable nouns like *information,* e.g., ~~There are more informations ...~~ (Correct form = *There **'s** more information ...*) and with lists. Point out that we use a singular verb before a list if the first item is singular, e.g., ~~There are a river, a town square ...~~ (Correct form = *There **is** a river, a town square, and a lot of cafés*).

e ⊙ 05.03 Students read the information in Grammar Focus 5A on SB p. 146. Play the recording where indicated and ask students to listen and repeat. Students then complete the exercises. Check answers as a class, making sure students are using contractions where appropriate, ordering the words correctly and distinguishing between singular and plural. Tell students to go back to SB p. 51.

Answers (Grammar Focus 5A SB p. 147)

a 2 There are six cafés.
   3 There isn't a stadium.
   4 There are a lot of shops.
   5 There are four parks.
   6 There aren't many schools.
   7 There's a/one river.
   8 There are two bridges.

b 2 How many cafés are there in the town? There are six (cafés).
   3 Is there a stadium in the town? No, there isn't.
   4 Are there any shops in the town? Yes, there are a lot (of shops).
   5 How many parks are there in the town? There are four (parks).
   6 Are there any schools in the town? Yes, there are.
   7 Is there a river in the town? Yes, there is.
   8 How many bridges are there in the town? There are two (bridges).

c Students' own answers

ⓦ FAST FINISHERS

Ask fast finishers to write additional sentences about other things in their towns using *there is/isn't/are/aren't.*

f ⊙ 05.04 **Pronunciation** Play the recording for students to answer the questions. Check they understand that the contracted form *there's* is only used in positive sentences.

Answers
1 c
2 a

g ⟫ Divide the class into pairs and assign A and B roles. Student As read the instructions and look at the picture on SB p. 131 and Student Bs read the instructions and look at the picture on SB p. 132. Students then ask and answer questions to find the six differences. Tell students to go back to SB p. 51.

4 SPEAKING

a ⊙ 05.05 Point to the picture and ask students: *Is Vienna a good place to visit? Why / Why not?* Individually, students complete the conversation. Play the recording for students to listen and check. Check answers as a class.

Answers
1 There are   4 there are   7 Is there
2 there are   5 Are there   8 there isn't
3 Are there   6 there are   9 there are

⟳ LOA TIP DRILLING

- Practise the conversation in 4a as a split-class choral drill. Divide the class in half down the middle and tell the group on your left that they are 'Tom' and the group on your right that they are 'Sofia'. Drill Tom's first question with the group on the left and Sofia's response with the group on the right. Then, put the two pieces together with the groups asking and answering the first question all together. Repeat the process until students can perform the whole conversation without you having to model the lines for them.

- Pay particular attention to the pronunciation of *there is / there are* and the vocabulary for places in a city.

b 💬 Put students into pairs and then put pairs together to make groups of four. Assign Pair A and Pair B roles. Ask each group to choose a town or city and to follow the instructions. Monitor and help as necessary.

c 💬 In their groups of four, students role play the conversation. Monitor, but don't interrupt fluency unless students make mistakes with the content of this lesson. Students may swap roles and repeat the activity with a different town or city.

💡 EXTRA ACTIVITY

To consolidate work on places in a city and *there is / there are*, ask students to produce a written conversation between two people about a famous tourist city in their country using the conversation in 4a as a model. They can use their ideas from 4b and 4c or choose a different town or city.

If you and your students have the technology available, students could work in pairs and record their conversations. Then, instead of giving you a written script, they can give you an audio recording to correct.

⊕ ADDITIONAL MATERIAL

Workbook 5A

Photocopiable activities: Grammar 5A, Vocabulary 5A, Pronunciation 5A

Documentary video Unit 5 *Places*

Video worksheet Unit 5 *Places*

5B | WHOSE WARDROBE IS THAT?

At the end of this lesson, students will be able to:

- use a lexical set of furniture correctly
- understand a conversation in which people talk about the furniture in their home
- use possessive pronouns and possessive *'s*
- describe their home and talk about their furniture

💡 OPTIONAL LEAD-IN

Books closed. Draw a simple floor plan of your home on the board or of a fictional house/flat if you prefer. Draw a bed in the bedroom(s), a television in the living room, a shower in the bathroom and a cooker in the kitchen, leaving room to draw other items of furniture in each room as taught in 1c below. Point to the different rooms on the floor plan and ask students: *What room is this?* Elicit and label the rooms. If you wish, tell students a bit more about your home as you elicit the name of each room, e.g., *I cook our meals here. It's really nice because there's a park outside and I can hear the birds.*

1 VOCABULARY Furniture

a 💬 Students discuss the questions in pairs or small groups. Invite students to share their ideas with the class.

b Students read the advertisement quickly and find out who the shop is for. You may wish to pre-teach the words in the Vocabulary Support box. Check the answer as a class and ask students: *Do you know any shops like this?*

Answer

b people who don't want to spend too much money on furniture

📖 VOCABULARY SUPPORT

classic (B2) – describing something that people like and that doesn't change over time

crazy (A2) – different, strange or unusual; in this context, in a positive way

quality (B1) – the way something is made; it can be good or bad

c Individually, students match the words with the pictures. Check answers as a class. Drill each word. If you used the optional lead-in, you could now go back and add the furniture in your home to the floor plan on the board with labels. Use *there is / there are* and tell students what you're drawing as you go along, e.g., *In the living room, there's a sofa here and there are two armchairs there. In the kitchen, there's a sink here.*

Answers

1	armchair	7	washing machine
2	cooker	8	wardrobe
3	bedside table	9	sink
4	curtains	10	lamp
5	bookcase	11	sofa
6	mirror	12	chest of drawers

💡 FAST FINISHERS

Ask fast finishers to brainstorm other things that you typically find in a house, e.g., *bath, carpet, dishwasher.*

d ▶ 05.06 **Pronunciation** Play the recording for students to listen and decide if the letters in bold have long or short sounds. Check answers as a class.

Answers
1	short	4	long
2	long	5	short
3	long	6	short

e Answer the questions as a class. Drill the words in 1d and *far*, *her* and *door*.

Answers
1 the letter *r*
2 no
3 f**ar** - **ar**mchair; h**er** - c**ur**tains; d**oor** - w**a**rdrobe

> **💡 EXTRA ACTIVITY**
>
> Write these words on the board: *Argentina, bar, burger, farmer, jar, more, park, poor, sports centre, Turkey.*
>
> Ask students to classify them into three groups: those that have /ɑː/ like *far* and *armchair* (Argentina, bar, farmer, jar, park); those that have /ɜː/ like *her* and *curtains* (burger, Turkey); and those which have /ɔː/ like *door* and *wardrobe* (more, poor, sports centre).

f Give students a few minutes to prepare and write notes about the furniture in the room they're in now. Monitor and help as necessary.

g 💬🗣 In pairs, students compare their lists. Monitor and check they're using *there is / there are* and the vocabulary from this lesson correctly.

2 LISTENING

a 💬🗣 Discuss the questions as a class. Encourage students to justify their ideas as much as possible, e.g., *My favourite room is my living room because there's a comfortable sofa and I have a big TV there.*

b ▶ 05.07 Play the recording for students to listen for general meaning and identify which rooms Jim shows Ruth. Check answers as a class.

Answers
b the living room   d the bedroom

Audioscript

JIM So, what do you think of this room?

RUTH Mmm … Nice and big. I love that armchair.

J Yes, it's … interesting.

R Is it yours?

J No, it's David's. He's my flatmate.

R I love it. That mirror over there. Is that Mum and Dad's?

J Well, yes, but really it's mine now.

R Well, no it isn't. It comes from my old room. It's really mine.

J Are you sure? I don't remember it in your room. Well, it's Mum and Dad's, not ours.

R But it comes from my old room at their place.

J Yes, well, anyway – let's take a look at another room. … So, this is my favourite room, of course.

R Lovely – it's nice and light and clean.

J And it's a good size.

R Whose wardrobe is that? Is it Mum and Dad's?

J Yeah, it's theirs. It's from home. They said I can use it.

R But that's from their bedroom.

J They've got a new one.

R So it's all our parents' furniture in here?

J Well … I guess … some of it. The bed's mine.

R Are you sure?

c ▶ 05.07 Students listen to the recording again for specific details and write down the furniture they talk about in each room. Students compare in pairs. Check answers as a class.

Answers
Room 1: armchair, mirror
Room 2: wardrobe, bed

d Elicit the answer to the question from the entire class.

Answer
She thinks most of it isn't Jim's.

3 GRAMMAR
Possessive pronouns and possessive *'s*

a ▶ 05.08 Books closed. Show the students your book and say: *This is my book.* Borrow a pen from a student, point to him/her and say to the class: *This is his/her pen.* Finally, point to a backpack and ask the student nearest to it: *Is this your backpack?* Write the three sentences on the board and circle the possessive adjectives. Ask students: *What are the other possessive adjectives?* Elicit *its, our, their.* Students open their books. Explain that this section is about other ways to talk about possession. Students then look at the conversation and complete it with words from the box. Play the recording for students to listen and check. Check answers as a class.

Answers
1 yours
2 David's
3 Mum and Dad's
4 mine

b Individually, students decide which sentences are correct. Check answers as a class.

Answers
3 ✓ It's Jim's flat.
6 ✓ It's my parents' flat.

> **🔄 LOA TIP CONCEPT CHECKING**
>
> • After looking at the sentences in 3b, check that students fully understand the various different uses of *'s* in English. Write sentences 1–3 on the board: *1 It's a very old cooker. 2 That is my dad's armchair. 3 His parents' flat is in the centre of town.* Then, write uses a–c on the board and ask students to match them to the sentences: *a possessive 's with a singular noun; b possessive s' with a plural noun; c contraction of 'is'* (Answers: *1 c, 2 a, 3 b*). Ask students: *Which sentences have a possessive 's or s'?* (sentences 2 and 3).

c Students look at the question and the example answers. Then, answer the questions as a class.

Answers
1 No, we don't.
2 b is better.

d Elicit the first answer from the class. Students then complete the sentences with the words in the box. Check answers as a class. Ask students: *Which possessive adjective in sentences 1–5 (my, your, etc.) is the same as the possessive pronoun in the answers?* (his).

Answers
1 mine
2 yours
3 hers
4 theirs
5 his

👁 CAREFUL!

Emphasise for students the importance of using possessive adjectives (especially *my, your*) and possessive pronouns (especially *mine, yours*) correctly, e.g., ~~This is mine house.~~ (Correct form = This is **my** house.); ~~Is this yours bedroom?~~ (Correct form = Is this **your** bedroom?); ~~It's my!~~ (Correct form = *Don't take that book. It's **mine**!*).

Highlight that the possessive *'s* can cause problems even for native speakers when writing. Make sure students avoid using the possessive *'s* where it shouldn't be used, e.g., ~~I always go to the sport's centre …~~ (Correct form = *I always go to the **sports** centre on Saturdays*). Make sure they don't use it instead of plurals, e.g., ~~There are a lot of café's and restaurant's …~~ (Correct form = *There are a lot of **cafés** and **restaurants** here*).

e ≫ ▶05.09–05.11 Students read the information in Grammar Focus 5B on SB p. 146. Play the recording where indicated and ask students to listen and repeat. Students then complete the exercises. Check answers as a class, making sure students put apostrophes in the correct position and distinguish between possessive adjectives and possessive pronouns. After students complete the Grammar Focus activities, ask them: *Is talking about possession easy or difficult?* Elicit an indication of their confidence level. Tell students to go back to SB p. 53.

Answers (Grammar Focus 5B SB p. 147)
a 2 hers   3 theirs   4 his   5 ours   6 yours
b 2 It's   4 parents'   6 Whose   8 your
   3 Our   5 mine   7 Anita's
c What's (C – What is) brother's (P); he's (C – he is); Paul's sister (P);
   That's (C – that is);
   Paul's got (C – Paul has got); name's (C – name is);
   What's (C – what is); It's (C – it is)

💡 FAST FINISHERS

Ask fast finishers to look around the classroom at other objects and write sentences about them similar to the sentences in Exercise a, e.g., *It's that man's bag.*, *They're her boots.*

f ▶05.12 Individually, students complete the text about Jean-Paul's flat with the words in the box. Play the recording for students to listen and check. Check answers as a class.

Answers
1 mine   5 mine
2 parents'   6 mother's
3 sister's   7 yours
4 hers   8 mine

💡 EXTRA ACTIVITY

Play a memory game (see p. 154) with students. Ask each student to choose one personal object from their bag that they don't mind sharing with the class and lending you for a few minutes. They then take turns giving you their objects. Say clearly what each person is giving you, e.g., *This is Sara's pencil*, *This is Pablo's notebook*, and show it to the class before putting each object out of sight, either in a bag or a box, or simply behind your desk. Don't allow students to take notes at this point.

When you have collected one object from each student, put students into pairs and give them three minutes to write down the objects you have, e.g., *Sara's pencil*, *Pablo's notebook*. Get answers by asking students: *What objects have I got?* or *What objects are in the bag/box?* Elicit answers with *You've got …* or *There's … .* As you take each object out and return it to its owner, confirm whose it is by asking: *Is this yours?* If there are any objects students are unsure about, ask the class questions like *Is it his or is it hers?* or *Whose is this?* Pairs win one point for every object they remembered correctly. The pair with the most points wins.

4 SPEAKING

a Give students a few minutes to write their sentences, using Jean-Paul's words in 3f to help them. Point out errors for students to self-correct.

b 💬 Students work in pairs, reading their sentences to each other and trying to remember the information. Don't allow students to make notes.

c 💬 Students try to remember what their partner said about their home. Monitor, but don't interrupt fluency unless students make mistakes with possessive adjectives, possessive pronouns, or *'s*.

⊕ ADDITIONAL MATERIAL

Workbook 5B

Photocopiable activities: Grammar 5B, Vocabulary 5B

5C EVERYDAY ENGLISH

Is there a bank near here?

At the end of this lesson, students will be able to:

- understand conversations in which people talk about where things are and give directions
- use appropriate phrases to check what other people say
- use appropriate phrases to ask for and give directions
- identify the stressed words when we give directions
- maintain a conversation in which they ask for and give a friend directions

OPTIONAL LEAD-IN

Look at the pictures of Dan and Leo with the class. Write: *Leo never goes to the gym after work.* and *Dan likes sugar in his tea.* on the board. Ask students: *Which sentence is false?* (The first sentence is false. Leo sometimes goes to the gym after work.)

Divide the class in half. Tell one half to write True/False statements about Leo and the other half to write True/False statements about Dan. Students can work in pairs or small groups to write their sentences. Monitor and point out errors for students to self-correct.

Put students into pairs, so that one student has sentences about Leo and one has sentences about Dan. They read their sentences to each other and decide if they are true or false.

1 LISTENING

a Read through the questions and look at pictures a and b with the class. Elicit ideas from students and write them on the board.

b ▶ 05.13 Play Part 1 of the video or the audio recording for students to check their answers to 1a. Check answers as a class.

> **Answers**
> 1 c a meeting
> 2 The map on Leo's phone shows a different street from the one they are on.

Video/Audioscript (Part 1)

DAN Come on, Leo. This meeting's really important. We can't be late.
LEO OK. I don't understand.
D What?
L This says 'Bedford Street', but on my phone it says 'Park Road'.
D Are you sure it's here?
L I think so.

D What street do we want?
L Park Road.
D Are you certain?
L Yes, South Street is off Park Road.
D I don't want to be late for this meeting. Can I have a look at your phone?

c ▶ 05.13 Students watch or listen again for specific details. Play Part 1 of the video or the audio recording again for students to choose the correct answers. Check answers as a class.

> **Answers**
> 1 b   2 a   3 b

2 CONVERSATION SKILLS
Checking what other people say

▶ 05.14 Individually, students read the sentences and answer the questions. They check in pairs. Check answers as a class. Drill the questions as they appear in the Student's Book and then drill them again reversing *sure* and *certain*.

> **Answers**
> a Yes
> b He wants to check something with Leo.

3 LISTENING

a Individually, students read the ideas and choose what they usually do when they are lost. Don't check answers at this point.

b ▶ 05.15 Play Part 2 of the video or the audio recording for students to check their answer to 3a. Check the answer as a class.

> **Answer**
> Students' own answers (Dan and Leo ask someone for help to find the correct street.)

Video/Audioscript (Part 2)

DAN This map shows there's a bank on the corner of Park Road and South Street. … Excuse me, sorry. Is there a bank near here?

MAN A bank? Yes. There's a bank down there. It's about 50 metres away.
D Thanks very much. Let's go.

c ▶ 05.15 Students watch or listen again for specific details. Play Part 2 of the video or the audio recording again for students to decide if the sentences are true or false. When checking answers, ask students to correct the false sentence.

> **Answers**
> 1 T
> 2 F (The man on the street says there's a bank about 50 metres away.)

d In pairs, students look at picture c and guess what the problem is. Elicit ideas from students and check they understand that Dan and Leo still can't find the bank.

e ▶ 05.16 Play Part 3 of the video or the audio recording for students to answer the questions. Check answers as a class.

> **Answers**
> 1 No   2 Yes

Video/Audioscript (Part 3)

LEO Are you sure this is the right bank?
DAN I don't know … this is Henrietta Street, not South Street.
L So, where's South Street?
D Sometimes these maps aren't very clear.
L Excuse me.
WOMAN Yes?
L Can you tell us how to get to South Street?
W South Street. Yes, sure. Go straight on, turn right at the corner.

L Into King Street?
W That's right. Then go along King Street until you come to Park Road.
L Ah! So Park Road is further along?
W That's right, about 100 metres. Turn right into Park Road, go straight on and South Street is on your left.
D So, we turn right and then right again and it's on the left?
W That's it.
D Great, thanks. Let's run!

f ▶ `05.16` Students watch or listen again for specific details. Play Part 3 of the video or the audio recording again for students to follow the woman's directions and write *South Street* on the map. Check the answer as a class.

Answer

4 USEFUL LANGUAGE
Asking for and giving directions

a Individually, students complete the questions with the words in the box. They then compare in pairs. Check answers as a class.

Answers
1 there	3 How
2 tell	4 Where

b Students change the words in bold. Check they understand that the meaning may change when they change the words in bold for words in the box that fit the sentences. Check answers as a class. Ask students: *Which sentence has the same meaning when you change the word?* (sentence 1).

Answers
1 Go straight <u>on</u>.
2 The bank is on your <u>left</u>.
3 Go straight on until you come to <u>a supermarket</u>.

c Complete the exercise as a class. Ask students: *When do we use 'at'?* (with a specific place) and *When do we use 'into'?* (with the name of a road or street).

Answers
1 b   2 a

d ▶ `05.17` Individually, students complete the conversation. They then check in pairs. Play the recording for students to listen and check. Check answers as a class.

Answers
1 can	5 go
2 get	6 come
3 go	7 turn
4 turn	8 go

e 💬📢 In pairs, students practise the conversation, taking turns being A and B. Monitor and correct students' pronunciation as appropriate.

♀ FAST FINISHERS

Ask fast finishers to change the place, the street names and the distance in the conversation and practise it again.

---

5 PRONUNCIATION Sentence stress

a ▶ `05.18` Play the recording and highlight the stressed words for students.

b Answer the question as a class.

Answer
2 the words for direction and place

♀ EXTRA ACTIVITY

Give students some additional practice in identifying stressed words in directions. Write sentences 1–5 on the board (without the underlining) and ask students to decide which words are stressed: *1 <u>Go</u> <u>right</u> at the <u>metro</u> <u>station</u>. 2 Then <u>turn</u> <u>left</u> into <u>Park</u> <u>Road</u>. 3 <u>Go</u> <u>straight</u> <u>on</u> until you come to the <u>supermarket</u>. 4 The <u>centre</u> of the <u>town</u> is about a <u>hundred</u> <u>metres</u> away. 5 <u>Go</u> <u>along</u> <u>South</u> <u>Street</u> and the <u>café</u> is on your <u>right</u>.*

Check answers by asking individual students to come up and underline the stressed words on the board.

c 💬📢 In pairs, students ask for and give directions using the conversation in 4d as a model, the phrases from 4 and the map in 3f.

⟳ LOA TIP MONITORING

- Monitor 5c and note down mistakes students make with the phrases for asking for and giving directions. Also note down any pronunciation problems students are having. After the activity, write the mistakes on the board for students to correct and provide additional help with difficult pronunciation. Remind students that they should avoid repeating the same mistakes in the next exercise.

- In 6a, monitor, but don't interrupt fluency. However, if students repeat mistakes that you drew their attention to after 5c, try to catch their eye discreetly so that they can correct their mistake.

---

6 SPEAKING

a ⟫ Divide the class into pairs and assign A and B roles. Student As read the first card on SB p. 131 and Student Bs read the first card on SB p. 132. Students then role play the conversation. Students then read the second card and role play the second situation.

♀ FAST FINISHERS

Ask fast finishers to use the map on SB p. 55, invent additional situations like those on the cards and practise them together.

⊕ ADDITIONAL MATERIAL

Workbook 5C

Photocopiable activities: Pronunciation 5C

Unit Progress Test

5D

SKILLS FOR WRITING It isn't very exciting, but it's a nice place to live

At the end of this lesson, students will be able to:

- understand people talking about what makes a good neighbourhood
- understand a website in which people describe their neighbourhood
- link their ideas with *and*, *but* and *so*
- write a description of their neighbourhood

💡 OPTIONAL LEAD-IN

Books closed. Write *In this neighbourhood …* on the board and explain that *neighbourhood* means the area of a town or city where people live or work. Draw two columns underneath headed *there is/are* and *there isn't/aren't*. Put students into pairs or small groups to think of as many complete sentences beginning with *there is/are* or *there isn't/aren't* as possible, e.g., *There's a very big sports centre*, *There aren't any cafés or restaurants*. Monitor and point out any errors in spelling for students to self-correct. Check that students are only giving facts in their sentences and aren't giving opinions about what makes a good or bad neighbourhood. Ask students to share their ideas with the class and collate them on the board.

1 SPEAKING AND LISTENING

a Individually, students tick four things they think make a good neighbourhood.

b 💬 In pairs or small groups, students compare their ideas in 1a. If you used the optional lead-in, students could also discuss if they think any of the things on the board are essential to a good neighbourhood. Take feedback as a class and ask students to share any other ideas they have for what makes a good neighbourhood.

c ▶ 05.19 Play the recording for students to listen for general meaning and answer the questions. Check answers as a class.

> **Answers**
> 1 a Jia b Antonella c Keith
> 2 Students' own answers

Audioscript

ANTONELLA For me, it's very important for a neighbourhood to have lots of cafés and restaurants. I like an exciting neighbourhood. I like going out and meeting my friends a lot. I like a neighbourhood with lots of people in it. My neighbourhood is quite exciting. There's also a museum near my house, so I'm really lucky.

KEITH I think a good neighbourhood is a quiet one. So, for example, no clubs or restaurants – nothing like that – only houses. My neighbourhood isn't like that – there are lots of shops and restaurants. And there's a cinema close to my house – I really don't like that.

JIA I think a good neighbourhood is a new one – new houses and shops. I also like a neighbourhood that is close to a shopping mall. It's good to have lots of new shops near you – it's interesting. In my neighbourhood, there aren't any shops – there's only a park. It's a little bit boring.

d ▶ 05.19 Students listen to the recording again for specific details and write the places in the box next to the people. They compare in pairs. Check answers as a class.

> **Answers**
> 1 Antonella – cafés, restaurants, museum
> 2 Keith – clubs, restaurants, houses, shops, cinema
> 3 Jia – houses, shops, shopping mall, park
>
> Antonella likes her neighbourhood. Keith and Jia don't like their neighbourhoods.

e 💬 In pairs, students ask and answer questions about their neighbourhoods. Monitor, but don't interrupt fluency.

💡 FAST FINISHERS

Ask fast finishers to talk about the best neighbourhoods in their town/city and discuss anything that those neighbourhoods have that their own doesn't.

2 READING

a Tell students they should read only *Around the World Online*. They then work individually, answering the questions. Check answers as a class.

> **Answers**
> 1 You can read about different neighbourhoods from around the world.
> 2 It wants you to write about your neighbourhood.

b Tell students to read *In My Neighbourhood* on SB p. 57. Check the answer as a class.

> **Answer**
> No, they don't.

c Individually, students decide if the sentences are about Anita or Blanca. They compare in pairs. Check answers as a class. When checking answers, elicit which words or sentences in the texts helped students decide.

> **Answers**
> 1 Anita
> 2 Blanca
> 3 Anita
> 4 Anita
> 5 Blanca

💡 EXTRA ACTIVITY

Ask students to read the complete text again and decide if sentences 1–5 are true or false:

1 *The places on the website are all popular with tourists.* (F – They are places tourists never go.)
2 *It's very difficult for Blanca to get to the city centre.* (F – It's easy because there's a metro station near her house.)
3 *Blanca is happy in her neighbourhood.* (T)
4 *Anita often goes to the city centre.* (F – She doesn't go to the city centre very often.)
5 *Anita lives in a modern part of the city.* (F – There are some beautiful old buildings there.)

3 WRITING SKILLS
Linking ideas with *and*, *but* and *so*

a Books closed. Write sentences 1–3 on the board and give students one minute to decide which word in each sentence connects two ideas. Check answers as a class. Ask students: *What kind of words are these?* Elicit *words to connect ideas*. Introduce the term *linking words*.

> **Answers**
> 1 and   2 but   3 so

b Complete the rules as a class. Show students how *and* adds an extra idea by pointing to the first part of the first sentence on the board and saying *one idea* and then pointing to the second part and saying *an extra idea*. Repeat the process with *but* (first part: *one idea*; second part: *a different idea*) and *so* (first part: *one idea*; second part: *the result of the idea*).

> **Answers**
> 1 *and*   2 *but*   3 *so*

> 📖 **VOCABULARY SUPPORT**
>
> Linking words don't generally cause students any serious problems. However, some students might not be clear about the difference between *so* and *because*.
>
> *So* is used to introduce a result, whereas *because* is used to introduce a cause. Most sentences with *so* can be rewritten with *because* and vice versa, e.g., *There aren't any restaurants or bars in the area, <u>so</u> it's nice and quiet.* / *It's nice and quiet <u>because</u> there aren't any restaurants or bars in the area.*

c Students read *In My Neighbourhood* again and underline examples of *and*, *but* and *so*. They then compare answers in pairs. Check answers by eliciting the number of examples of each word in the text (*and* 4, *but* 3, *so* 5).

> **Answers**
> … city centre, <u>but</u> everything I need …
> … in my neighbourhood, <u>so</u> I don't go …
> … the City museum <u>and</u> there are some …
> … old buildings here, <u>so</u> it's an interesting part …
> … restaurants in my neighbourhood <u>and</u> my flat's …
> … their food <u>and</u> it's cheap, <u>so</u> I eat …
> … from the city centre, <u>but</u> there's a …
> … near my house, <u>so</u> it's easy …
> … in the area, <u>so</u> it's nice …
> … park <u>and</u> a sports centre
> … isn't very exciting, <u>but</u> it's a nice …

> 💡 **EXTRA ACTIVITY**
>
> Write incomplete sentences 1–6 on the board and ask students to complete them with *and*, *but* and *so*: *1 There's a café … a restaurant on our street.* (and) *2 It's very expensive here, … a lot of houses are empty.* (so) *3 There's a river in my town, … there is only one bridge.* (but) *4 My office is close to my flat, … I can walk to work.* (so) *5 There are two cinemas here, … there isn't a concert hall.* (but) *6 We have everything here – a post office, a supermarket, … a sports centre.* (and).

d Students work individually, putting the linking words in the correct place in each sentence. They then check in pairs. Check answers as a class.

64

> **Answers**
> 1 My neighbourhood's in the centre of town <u>and</u> there are lots of different shops near my house.
> 2 I live near the university, <u>so</u> there are lots of interesting shops in my neighbourhood.
> 3 My neighbourhood's quite busy during the day, <u>but</u> it's nice and quiet at night.
> 4 My house is near a park <u>and</u> there's a small river with a bridge in the park.
> 5 My neighbourhood is very friendly, <u>so</u> it's a nice place to live, <u>but</u> sometimes it's noisy in the evening.
> 6 There's a popular café in my neighbourhood, <u>but</u> I don't like coffee, <u>so</u> I never go there.

> 💡 **FAST FINISHERS**
>
> Ask fast finishers to look for sentences that contain the linking words in the conversation in 4a on SB p. 51.

4 WRITING

a Students work individually to plan their descriptions. Monitor and help with vocabulary and give students ideas if necessary.

> 🔄 **LOA TIP ELICITING**
>
> • If students need more support or ideas, collate words and phrases for the four categories in 4a on the board after students have had a few minutes to start making notes. They will then be able to borrow ideas from each other and use a wider range of vocabulary in their writing. As you monitor 4a, notice if students think of interesting words or phrases. Then, during a class brainstorming stage, say things like: *Jo has a very good word meaning 'very big' – can you guess what it is?* Elicit ideas from the class before asking the student to share the word he/she originally thought of.
>
> • Take some of the ideas from the brainstorming stage and ask students to connect them with *and*, *but* and *so*. For example, point to *city centre* and *expensive* on the board and ask students to connect them, e.g., *Tina lives in the city centre, so it's expensive.*

b Students write about their neighbourhoods, working individually. Remind students to use *and*, *but* and *so* to link their ideas. If you're short of time, this exercise can be completed for homework. Students could then bring their descriptions to the next lesson.

c In pairs, students swap descriptions and check their partner's work. Tell them to check that their partner has used linking words correctly. They then give each other feedback. If they've made any mistakes with the linking words or mistakes in other areas, they prepare a second draft of their description before giving it to you for correction.

d After correcting students' work, ask them to make a final version to share with other students. Display the descriptions around the classroom for other students to read and decide which neighbourhood is the most different from their own. Alternatively, if you and your students have the technology available, set up a class blog where students can post their written work and comment on each other's texts.

> ⊕ **ADDITIONAL MATERIAL**
>
> Workbook 5D

UNIT 5
Review and extension

1 GRAMMAR

a Individually, students complete the conversation. Check answers as a class and check that students are using contractions where appropriate. Drill the conversation.

Answers

1 There is / There's	5 is there
2 Is there	6 there is / there's
3 there isn't	7 are there
4 there is / there's	8 There are

b Highlight the example and complete the second item with the class. Check that students understand that they can use possessive pronouns or possessive *'s*. Monitor and help as necessary. Point out errors for students to self-correct. Check answers as a class.

Answers

2 mine 3 ours 4 hers 5 his 6 his 7 mine 8 yours

2 VOCABULARY

a Students underline the correct words in each sentence. Check answers as a class.

Answers

1 flat	4 park
2 hotel	5 bridge
3 restaurants; square	6 station

b Students complete the sentences, working individually. Check answers and spelling as a class by asking students to write the correct answers on the board.

Answers

1 mirror	5 washing machine
2 sink	6 cooker
3 chest of drawers	7 bedside table
4 sofa	

> ♀ **FAST FINISHERS**
>
> Ask fast finishers to write similar sentences about things you find in a room with the other vocabulary from Lesson 5B, e.g., *armchair*, *bookcase*, *curtains* and *lamp*.

3 WORDPOWER Prepositions of place

a Tell students to close their books. Ask a student to come to the front of the class and help you. Stand immediately behind your student and ask the class: *Where am I?* Elicit: *You're behind (student's name)*. Then, to elicit *in front of*, change places with the student and ask: *Now where am I?* To elicit *behind* again, stay in the same position and ask: *Where's (student's name)?* To elicit *next to*, stand alongside the student and ask: *Where am I now?* Thank the student and ask him/her to sit down. Say *behind, in front of* and *next to* and ask: *What kind of words are these?* Elicit *prepositions of place*. Students then look at the map in their book and find the cafés. Check answers as a class.

Answers

1 d 2 f 3 a 4 e 5 b 6 c

b Highlight the underlined examples in 3a. Then, to elicit *behind*, point behind you and ask: *What was this preposition?* Repeat the process with *in front of* and *next to*. Students underline the other prepositions of place in 3a. Check answers as a class.

Answers

2 On the corner of Newton Street and Green Street.
3 … just in front of the train station.
4 … on Green Street, between the market and the library.
5 At the end of Newton Street, opposite the station.
6 It's on a small street behind the Rex Cinema.

c Individually, students add one word to each sentence to make them correct. They then check in pairs. Check answers as a class.

Answers

1 … next to the supermarket.
2 … cash machine at the end of …
3 … in front of the bank …
4 … bookshop on the corner of …

> ◉ **CAREFUL!**
>
> Students often confuse the prepositions of place *in* and *on* with the prepositions of movement *into* and *onto*. Check that students understand that when we use a preposition with a verb indicating movement, we usually use a preposition of movement, e.g., *Turn right onto King Street*. However, when the verb doesn't indicate movement, we usually use a preposition of place, e.g., *The café is on Park Road*. In 3d, students are not being asked to describe movement, only position, and should therefore only be using prepositions of place.

d 💬 Describe one of the places yourself as an example before students work in pairs to describe and guess a place. Monitor and listen for correct use of the prepositions of place. Point out errors for students to self-correct.

> ♀ **EXTRA ACTIVITY**
>
> Ask students to work in pairs and assign A and B roles. Student A is a tourist in the city centre. Student B lives in the city and knows it well. Ask them to decide exactly where the conversation takes place before they start. Student A stops Student B and asks for directions to a common tourist destination, e.g., a museum. Student B then gives directions. Students then change roles and role play a second conversation.

≫ Photocopiable activities: Wordpower 5

> 🔄 **LOA REVIEW YOUR PROGRESS**
>
> Students look back through the unit, think about what they've studied and decide how well they did. Students work on weak areas by using the appropriate sections of the Workbook and the Photocopiable activities.

UNIT 6

FAMILY

⟳ UNIT OBJECTIVES

At the end of this unit, students will be able to:

- understand information, texts and conversations and exchange information about family, family relationships, life events and childhood hobbies
- talk about their family tree
- leave a voicemail message
- make a phone call and use appropriate phrases to ask for someone and ask someone to wait
- write the life story of someone in their family

UNIT CONTENTS

G GRAMMAR
- Past simple: *be*
- Past simple: positive

V VOCABULARY
- Family: *aunt, brother, cousin, grandchildren, granddaughter, grandfather, grandmother, grandparents, grandson, parents, sister, uncle*
- Years and dates
- Past simple irregular verbs: *ate, became, bought, brought, came, cost, cut, did, found, gave, got, lost, made, read, sold, spent, thought, told, went, won*
- Linking ideas in the past: *in, when, later*
- Wordpower: *go – go by (bus/train), go home, go out, go shopping, go to (a party / the cinema)*

P PRONUNCIATION
- /ʌ/ in family words: *cou*sin, grandm*o*ther, grands*o*n, *u*ncle
- *was* and *were* in statements, questions and short answers
- Past simple *-ed* endings
- Sound and spelling: a (/æ/, /ɔː/, /ɪ/, /eɪ/)

C COMMUNICATION SKILLS
- Talking about families and asking and answering questions about a family tree
- Talking about your hobbies when you were young
- Leaving a voicemail message and making a phone call
- Using appropriate phrases when asking someone to wait
- Writing the life story of someone in your family

GETTING STARTED

♀ OPTIONAL LEAD-IN

Use a 'live listening' to review the basic family words that students will need in Getting Started, i.e., *grandfather, grandmother, grandparents, mother, father, parents, brother, sister, son, daughter* and *children*. Be careful not to include other family words as these will be introduced in Lesson 6A. Tell students about your immediate family, e.g., *My family all live in the same neighbourhood in Melbourne. My mother is a dentist and my father is a photographer, and they live in a small house in the city centre. I've got one brother and one sister. My sister lives in a flat near my parents, and my brother lives with Mum and Dad. They haven't got any children, but I have. I've got two sons and a daughter.* Students listen and note down any information about you that they didn't know before. They then open their books and compare your family with the family in the picture.

a 💬🗩 Give students one minute to think about their answers to the questions before talking about the picture as a class.

b 💬🗩 Read the questions and check that students understand that they should talk about a family they know well, but not their own family. In pairs, they ask and answer the questions. Ask students to share their ideas. You may also tell the class about a family you know.

♀ EXTRA ACTIVITY

Put students into pairs or small groups to prepare a description of a famous family. Check that each pair/group writes about a different family and monitor and help with vocabulary if necessary. Finally, ask pairs/groups to read their descriptions to the class, but to say *beep* instead of the people's names. Their classmates listen and identify the missing names of the famous people.

Exercises a and b can be prepared as homework before this lesson to give students time to look up unfamiliar vocabulary. Ask students to look at the picture and to prepare their answers to the questions as homework to talk about in the next lesson.

6A | THEY WERE MARRIED IN 1968

At the end of this lesson, students will be able to:

- use a lexical set of family words correctly
- understand a conversation in which people talk about family and life events
- use the positive and negative past simple forms of *be*
- talk about years and dates correctly
- ask and answer questions about their family tree

♀ OPTIONAL LEAD-IN

Revise possessive *'s* by writing *your father's mother* on the board. If students are still having problems with the possessive *'s*, write *the mother of your father* in brackets after it. Ask: *Who is your father's mother?* Elicit *your grandmother.* Dictate phrases 1–6 and ask students to write them down, paying attention to the possessive *'s*. Point out that they don't need to write the answers, only the phrase itself: *1 your mother's sister 2 your daughter's son 3 your sister's mother and father 4 your parents' parents 5 your father's brother 6 your mother's brother's son.* Check the phrases by writing them on the board. Don't elicit the answers to phrases 1–6 until 1b below (*1 aunt 2 grandson 3 parents 4 grandparents 5 uncle 6 cousin*).

1 VOCABULARY Family

a 💬📢 Give students a few minutes to prepare and make notes about their parents, brothers and sisters. Put students into pairs or small groups to talk about the people in their families.

b ▶06.01 If you used the optional lead-in, ask students to match the definitions on the board with the family words before you start this exercise. Point to the illustration and ask students: *What's this in English?* Elicit/Teach *family tree.* Ask *Where's Greg?* for students to find him on the family tree. You may also wish to pre-teach the phrase *be born* (come out of a mother's body and start to live). Play the recording for students to listen for general meaning and check the people Greg talks about. Check answers as a class.

> **Answers**
> Greg mentions all of the people except *granddaughter* and *grandson.*

Audioscript

FRIEND What's this, Greg?

GREG Oh, it's my family tree. You can download a special program to make it.

F That's really good. So are these your grandparents?

G Yes. Sally, she's my grandmother and that's my grandfather, Nathan. They're my mother's parents. They've got two children – a son and a daughter. Michael's their son, he's my uncle, and they have a daughter, Mary – that's my mother.

F And so Alessio's your father?

G That's right, yeah. They've got three children – there's me,

there's my brother Rick and my sister Ella – that's her there.

F Alessio's an Italian name, right?

G Yeah, it is, yeah. His parents, Lucia and Matteo, are from Italy, but Dad was born here in London. And his brother Simone was born here, too – so Simone's my other uncle.

F Right. So, he's married, too.

G Yes, you can see here – he's married to my aunt Alice. And they've got two children, Hugo and Olivia. They're my cousins.

F So your grandparents in Italy have got five grandchildren?

G Yes, they're very happy about it!

c Individually, students choose words from 1b to complete the family tree. They compare in pairs. Don't check answers at this point.

d ▶06.01 Students listen to the recording again for specific details. They check their answers to 1c and identify which people in the family were born in Italy. Check answers as a class.

> **Answers**
> **1c** Matteo: grandfather; Lucia: grandmother; Nathan: grandfather; Sally: grandmother; Alice: aunt; Simone: uncle; Michael: uncle; Hugo: cousin; Olivia: cousin; Ella: sister; Rick: brother
> **1d** Alessio and Simone's parents were born in Italy.

e ▶06.02 **Pronunciation** Play the recording for students to tick the family words that have the same sound as *but* /ʌ/. Check answers as a class and drill each word.

> **Answers**
> ✓ cousin, ✓ uncle, ✓ grandmother, ✓ grandson

f Look at the example as a class and check that students understand that Greg, Ella and Rick could all say the sentence. Individually, students identify who can say the other sentences. They then check in pairs. Check answers as a class.

> **Answers**
> 2 Greg, Ella, Rick
> 3 Matteo, Lucia, Nathan, Sally
> 4 Hugo, Olivia
> 5 Sally, Nathan

♀ EXTRA ACTIVITY

Tell the class about your extended family, using the vocabulary from this section. If you used the optional lead-in on the Getting Started page, elicit information about your immediate family that students already know. Draw that part of your family tree on the board and write each person's name. Then, continue talking about your extended family. If you didn't use the optional lead-in, start by describing your immediate family before talking about your more extended family. Name the people and talk about their relationships to you and to other people in your family, e.g., *My mum's name's Jennifer and she's Barbara and Frank's daughter, so they are my grandparents.* Complete your family tree on the board, write the names of the people and elicit their relationships to you and to other people from the class as you go along.

g 💬📢 Individually, students draw their family trees. Monitor and help with any other vocabulary students might need to talk about their families, e.g., *stepmother/ father/brother/sister, half brother/sister, only child.*

Then, put students into pairs to show each other their family trees and talk about their families. Monitor and point out errors for students to self-correct.

2 LISTENING

a ▶06.03 Look at the timeline with students and show them how it runs from left to right. Play the recording for students to listen for general meaning. Students then listen to the recording again for specific details and complete the timeline. Check answers as a class.

Answers

1943 2 (grandfather was born)
1945 5 (grandmother was born)
1968 1 (got married)
1969 4 (photographer took the picture)
2010 3 (grandmother retired from her job)

📖 VOCABULARY SUPPORT

alive (B1) – something that is living and not dead

romantic (B1) – relating to love or a close loving relationship

Audioscript

FRIEND So, your grandparents are all still alive?

GREG Yes, they are. But we don't see my grandparents in Italy very much.

F Your grandmother, Sally – she looks nice and friendly.

G She's lovely, yes, but she's very old now, of course. Look – here's a photo of her with my grandfather. I think this is from about 1969, yeah, you can see that she was a very beautiful woman.

F Oh, yes. She really was. So, when was she born?

G Um, she was born in 1945, I think, I'm not sure. But I know her birthday's the 16th of July. And my grandfather was born two years before her.

F Mmm … interesting.

G Yes, my grandmother's a really interesting woman. She was a doctor at the university hospital

in London for about 40 years, I think, until she was 65. So, until 2010.

F Until 2010? Wow, that's a long time. What about your grandfather? Was he a doctor, too?

G Yes, he was. And they were at the same school together.

F Really? Were they in the same class?

G No, they weren't. They weren't even friends at school. But then when they went to university, they met again and of course then things were very different ….

F Ah, right.

G Yes, in fact they got married in 1968. They were still students.

F Oh, so in this photo she was … 24 and just married?

G Yes, that's right.

F Ah, that's so romantic.

3 GRAMMAR Past simple: *be*

a Books closed. Write on the board: *Greg's grandfather … born in 1943 and his grandmother … born in 1945.* Point to the gaps and ask students: *What's this word?* Elicit *was* and say: *This is called the past simple. What's the verb?* Elicit *be*. Students then open their books and underline the correct word in each sentence. Check answers as a class.

Answers

1 are   2 isn't   3 was   4 were   5 weren't

b Complete the rules as a class. Then, ask students to circle all the examples of *n't* in 3a and tell them that the position of the apostrophe is important.

Answers

1 b the past
2 b *n't*

c Individually, students complete the table. Check answers by copying the table onto the board and asking individual students to come up and complete the sentences.

Answers

(+)	(−)
I was ill. She <u>was</u> a doctor.	I wasn't ill. He <u>wasn't</u> a teacher. He was a doctor.
We were at school together. They <u>were</u> friends at university.	No, we <u>weren't</u> in the same class. In 1960, they <u>weren't</u> married.

⟳ LOA TIP CONCEPT CHECKING

- Write the pronouns *I, you, he, she, it, we* and *they* on the board and ask students: *With the present simple of 'be', which forms are the same?* (the *you, we* and *they* forms – they are all *are*). Ask: *What are the 'I' and the 'he/she/it' forms?* (*am* and *is*). Remind students of the positive contracted forms by showing them two fingers representing *I* and *am* and closing them up to illustrate *I'm*. Repeat the process with the other present simple forms.

- Repeat the process with the past simple by asking: *With the past simple of 'be', which forms are the same?* (the *you, we* and *they* forms – they are all *were*). Elicit that the *I* and the *he/she/it* forms are also the same: *was*. Ask students: *Do we contract the past simple positive of the verb 'be'?* (no) *What about negatives?* (yes). Show students three fingers representing *I, was* and *not* and close up the second and third fingers to illustrate *I wasn't*. Repeat the process with the other negative past simple forms.

d ▶06.04 Play the recording for students to complete the conversation. Check answers as a class. Make sure students understand that the verb is repeated in the question and the answer, although positive turns to negative in a negative answer.

Answers

1 Was   4 weren't
2 was   5 was
3 Were   6 was
The subject pronouns are repeated.

👁 CAREFUL!

Since *be* has more forms than other verbs and uses different grammar, students are likely to make mistakes. Highlight the following typical errors: tense – this type of error may be obvious, e.g., ~~I am …~~ (Correct form = *I **was** there yesterday*), but may sometimes cause misunderstandings, e.g., ~~My grandmother is …~~ (Correct form = *My grandmother **was** very friendly.* Past simple = the grandmother is no longer alive); word order in questions, e.g., ~~Your whole family was …~~ (Correct form = ***Were** your whole family at the party?*); subject/verb agreement, e.g., ~~My parents wasn't …~~ (Correct form = *My parents **weren't** at home last night*); auxiliary verbs – students may incorrectly use *didn't* to form negatives, e.g., ~~It didn't expensive~~ (Correct form = *It **wasn't** expensive*).

e ⟫ ▶**06.05** Students read the information in Grammar Focus 6A on SB p. 148. Play the recording where indicated and ask students to listen and repeat. Students then complete the exercises. Check answers as a class. After students complete the Grammar Focus activities, ask them: *Is the past simple with 'be' easy or difficult?* Elicit an indication of their confidence level. Tell students to go back to SB p. 61.

Answers (Grammar Focus 6A SB p. 149)

a 2 were   4 wasn't   6 were   8 were
    3 Weren't   5 were   7 Was

b 2 They weren't friends.
    3 **A** Was your grandfather rich? **B** No, he wasn't.
    4 We were at school together.
    5 It was a beautiful day.
    6 My teacher's name was Miss Smith.
    7 She wasn't at home.
    8 There were 20 people in my class.
    9 I wasn't tired.
   10 **A** Were you happy? **B** Yes, I was.

c 2 Was the film good?
    3 Were there a lot of people at the party?
    4 What was your grandmother's name?
    5 Were you at school yesterday?
    6 Was there a pool at your hotel?

FAST FINISHERS

Ask fast finishers to look at the questions in Grammar Focus 6A Exercise c on p. 149 and to write short answers to the questions.

f ▶**06.06** **Pronunciation** Play the recording for students to underline *was/were* when they are stressed. Check answers as a class.

Answers

4 Was she a doctor? Yes, she <u>was</u>.

g Complete the rules as a class. Drill the sentences in 3f.

Answers

1 aren't
2 are

h Individually, students complete the questions. Check answers as a class. Drill the questions before students ask and answer them in 3i.

Answers

1 were   2 was   3 was   4 Was

i 💬 In pairs, students ask and answer the questions. Monitor and correct students' pronunciation as appropriate.

4 VOCABULARY Years and dates

a ▶**06.07** Play the recording for students to listen and answer the questions about years and dates. Check answers as a class. Ask students: *What's the date today?* and elicit the date, including the year, in the correct format.

Answers

1 b nineteen forty-five
2 c both a and b are correct
3 We add -*th* to 16.

b ▶**06.08** Play the recording for students to listen and tick the years they hear. Check answers as a class.

Answers

✓ 2012   ✓ 1930   ✓ 1989   ✓ 2001

EXTRA ACTIVITY

Play bingo (see p. 152) with the class. Write 25 different years on the board in numerals. Ask students to draw a bingo grid with four columns and two rows. Tell them to complete it with eight years from the board. Read out the years on the board in random order, making a note of the ones you read out. The first student to complete his/her card calls out 'Bingo!'. After you have checked that his/her card is correct, that student is the winner.

c ⟫ ▶**06.09–06.10** Students complete the exercises in Vocabulary Focus 6A on SB p. 165. Play the recording for students to check their answers to Exercises a and b and to repeat the months in Exercise a. Monitor Exercise e and check other answers as a class. Tell students to go back to SB p. 61.

Answers (Vocabulary Focus 6A SB p. 165)

a January, February, March, April, May, June, July, August, September, October, November, December
b 1 in   2 on   3 in
c 2 the twenty-first of February (21 February)
    3 two thousand and seven (2007)
    4 the seventh of July (7 July)
    5 nineteen ninety-eight (1998)
    6 the second of December (2 December)

5 SPEAKING

a Students write more detailed notes about the people in their family trees from 1g. Give students any jobs that they don't know how to say in English.

b 💬 In pairs, students ask and answer questions about their family trees. Monitor and listen for correct use of family vocabulary, years, dates and *be*.

FAST FINISHERS

Ask fast finishers to cover their family trees. They work in pairs and take turns trying to draw each other's family tree as their partner says each person's name and their relationship to other people in the family tree.

⊕ ADDITIONAL MATERIAL

Workbook 6A

Photocopiable activities: Grammar 6A, Vocabulary 6A, Pronunciation 6A

Documentary video Unit 6 *Family*

Video worksheet Unit 6 *Family*

6B | I PLAYED ANYTHING AND EVERYTHING

At the end of this lesson, students will be able to:

- read and understand a text about the life of Steve Jobs
- use the past simple positive form of regular verbs
- understand people talking about childhood hobbies
- use a lexical set of past simple irregular verbs correctly
- talk about a childhood hobby in some detail

◊ OPTIONAL LEAD-IN

Books closed. Put students into pairs. On the board, draw a simple complete outline of an apple with a short stem sticking out the top. Ask students: *What's the first thing you think of when you see this … ?* Tell pairs to discuss their ideas. Don't ask them to share their ideas at this point. Write these years on the board: *1666, 1968, 2007.* Ask students: *How are these years connected with apples?* Students discuss the question in their pairs. Invite students to share their ideas with the class. (*1666 – an apple falls on Isaac Newton's head and he understands gravity; 1968 – The Beatles start Apple Records; 2007 – Apple Inc. sells the first iPhone.*) Find out how many students in the class first thought of the fruit when they saw the apple and ask students if any of them thought of anything else, e.g., *Adam and Eve, Snow White, Johnny Appleseed.*

1 READING

a 💬 Look at the pictures and discuss the answers to the questions as a class. You may give students information from Culture Notes below. Ask students: *Have you got any Apple products?*

🌐 CULTURE NOTES

Steve Jobs (1955–2011) is remembered as one of the great visionaries of the digital age. In fact, it was his friend Steve Wozniak who designed the first Apple computers, but it was Jobs who had an innate ability to know what people wanted to buy before they even knew it themselves, and he was one of the first people to see the enormous potential of home computing.

Jobs was fired from Apple in 1985 and used his fortune to take over Pixar Animation Studios, where he helped produce *Toy Story.* In his absence, Apple went from bad to worse, and in 1997 he returned to the company. In the following years, he is credited with creating some of the most innovative products in the history of personal computing, including the iMac, iPod, iPhone and iPad. He was diagnosed with pancreatic cancer in 2003 and died in 2011. At the time of his death, his personal fortune was estimated at over $7 billion.

b 💬 Pre-teach the word *secret* (not known to many people, very private). In pairs, students talk about the ideas and choose one. Don't check the answer at this point.

c Pre-teach the phrase *be adopted* in the Vocabulary Support box (you may wish to wait until Exercise 1d to pre-teach the other words). Students read the text quickly and check their answer to 1b. Check the answer as a class.

Answer

2 He had a secret sister.

📖 VOCABULARY SUPPORT

be adopted (B2) – be legally taken as a child by people who are not your biological parents, but who make you part of their family

be worth (B1) – have a specific value in money

close (adj) (A2) – with a very good relationship and who know each other well

electronics (B2) – small pieces of technological equipment used inside things like computers and phones.

d Students read the text again in detail. Individually, students put the events in the correct order. Encourage students to guess the meaning of any new words from the context. Check answers as a class.

Answers

1 d (Steve's real parents couldn't keep him.)
2 f (Clara and Paul Jobs became Steve's parents.)
3 b (His sister Mona was born.)
4 a (Steve started a new hobby: electronics.)
5 c (Steve became friends with Steve Wozniak.)
6 h (Apple Computers began.)
7 g (The two Steves became very rich.)
8 e (Steve met his sister.)

◊ EXTRA ACTIVITY

Ask students to read the text again and decide if sentences 1–5 are true or false: *1 Most people don't know who Steve Jobs is.* (F – We all think we know Steve Jobs's story.) *2 Steve Jobs's real parents were born in 1955.* (F – Steve Jobs was born in 1955. His parents were college students at that time.) *3 There are lots of big technology companies near Mountain View in California.* (T) *4 In 1980, Apple Computers was worth $1.2 billion.* (T) *5 Steve's real mother, Mona, is now a famous writer.* (F – His sister, Mona, is now a famous writer.).

2 GRAMMAR Past simple: positive

a Tell students to close their books. Write sentences 1–5 on the board (not the verbs in brackets): *1 Steve's real parents … not to keep their son.* (decided) *2 The Jobs family … in California.* (lived) *3 The two Steves both … electronics.* (loved) *4 In 1976, they … Apple Computers.* (started) *5 They … hard.* (worked). Ask students: *Are the sentences about the past, present or future?* (past). Then ask: *Can you remember the verbs?* Put students into pairs or small groups to try and remember. Elicit the answers (in brackets) from the class, making sure you pronounce the words correctly. Don't write the past simple forms on the board. Students open their books, look at the verbs and find the past simple forms in the text. Check answers as a class.

Answers

1 worked   4 decided
2 started   5 loved
3 lived

b Ask students to look at the past simple forms of the verbs in 2a. Complete the rule as a class.

> **Answer**
> *-ed* or *-d*

c ▶ **06.11** **Pronunciation** Play the recording for students to listen and identify which two verbs have an extra syllable. Check answers as a class.

> **Answers**
> started; decided

d Say the two verbs from 2c that have an extra syllable, i.e., *start − started*, *decide − decided*, and complete the rule as a class.

> **Answer**
> /t/, /d/

e ▶ **06.12** 💬 Students work individually or in pairs and identify the past simple forms that have an extra syllable. Play the recording for students to listen and check. Check answers as a class. Drill the infinitive and past simple forms of each verb.

> **Answers**
> hated; waited; wanted; needed

f Students look at the verbs and find the past simple forms in the text. Check answers as a class. Ask students: *Where can you find a list of irregular verbs in this book?* (on SB p. 129).

> **Answers**
> 1 had   2 found   3 made   4 became
> These verbs are irregular.

⊙ CAREFUL!

When using the past simple form of verbs other than *be*, students often use the infinitive where they should use the past simple, e.g., ~~Steve Jobs love ...~~ (Correct form = *Steve Jobs* **loved** *his sister, Mona*) and may also use the past simple where they should use the present, e.g., ~~We can watched ...~~ (Correct form = *We can* **watch** *the film tomorrow*). They also often confuse specific verbs, particularly *had* and *got*, e.g., ~~I had ...~~ (Correct form = *I* **got** *my first job in 2001*) and *did* and *had*, e.g., ~~I did ...~~ *(Correct form = I* **had** *a great time*). Students may also make mistakes with word order in more complex sentences, e.g., ~~They started in 1976 Apple Computers~~ (Correct form = *They started* **Apple Computers in 1976**), or ~~To live with the Jobs family went Steve~~ (Correct form = **Steve went to live** *with the Jobs family*).

---

g ≫ ▶ **06.13** Students read the information in Grammar Focus 6B on SB p. 148. Play the recording where indicated and ask students to listen and repeat. Students then complete the exercises. Check answers as a class, making sure students refer to the Irregular Verbs list on SB p. 129 if necessary. Tell students to go back to SB p. 63.

> **Answers (Grammar Focus 6B SB p. 149)**
> **a** 1 R   3 I   5 R   7 R   9 R 11 I   13 R   15 I 17 R 19 R
>   2 I   4 I   6 R 8 I   10 I 12 R 14 R   16 I 18 I 20 I
> **b** 2 cooked   4 enjoyed   6 liked   8 played 10 worked
>   3 decided 5 finished 7 planned 9 tried
> **c** 2 became   4 told   6 wrote   8 went
>   3 found   5 won   7 bought   9 got
> **d** 2 ~~buyed~~ bought   4 ~~eated~~ ate   6 ~~dicide~~ decided
>   3 ~~liket~~ liked   5 ~~gotten~~ got

♀ FAST FINISHERS

Ask fast finishers to test themselves on the irregular past simple verbs by covering the past simple columns in the verbs list on SB p. 129 and trying to remember the past simple forms and correct spelling.

---

3 LISTENING

a Individually, students tick the hobbies they had as children. Take feedback as a class. Elicit other common hobbies and write them on the board. You may then wish to teach the word *childhood* (the part of your life when you're a child, not an adult).

b ▶ **06.14** Play the recording for students to listen for general meaning and identify what Hannah's and Charlie's childhood hobbies were. Check answers as a class.

> **Answers**
> Hannah: sports
> Charlie: baking

Audioscript

HANNAH My childhood hobby was sports. I loved it. I played anything and everything: basketball, tennis, swimming, football. But I think my favourite was tennis – I played every summer. Every day of the week, I went to some kind of sports activity or game. My parents, poor things, spent all the time driving me to different activities and games and things like that. I never got a train or bus. I think it was really difficult for them! I don't play sports very much now – I don't have the time.

CHARLIE My hobby when I was a child was a bit unusual, I think. I really loved sweet things – cakes, biscuits – food like that. So, my hobby was baking. After school and at the weekend, I made cakes and biscuits and my friends came to my place and ate them. My parents bought all the things I needed. They told me it cost a lot, but they were always happy to eat the things I made. I still bake biscuits and cakes now. My wife loves it because she never needs to bake anything.

c ▶ **06.14** Students listen to the recording again and complete the notes. They compare in pairs. Check answers as a class.

> **Answers**
>
> | | Hannah | Charlie |
> |---|---|---|
> | hobby details | basketball, tennis, swimming, football | cakes, biscuits |
> | parents' problem | They spent all their time driving her to activities and games. | It was expensive because they bought all the things he needed. |
> | now | She doesn't have time to play sports. | He still bakes and his wife loves it because she doesn't have to bake. |

4 VOCABULARY
Past simple: irregular verbs

a Individually, students match the past simple forms in the box with the infinitives. They check their answers by looking at the Irregular Verbs list on SB p. 129.

Answers
1 bought
2 ate
3 told
4 went
5 cost
6 spent
7 made
8 got
9 came

b ≫ ▶ 06.15–06.17 Students complete the exercises in Vocabulary Focus 6B on SB p. 165. Play the recording for students to check their answers to Exercises a and c and complete the Pronunciation activity. Monitor Exercise d. Tell students to go back to SB p. 63.

Answers (Vocabulary Focus 6B SB p. 165)
a
1 did	4 thought	7 lost	10 cut
2 read	5 brought	8 found	11 sold
3 gave	6 won	9 became	

b They sound different. The present **read** is pronounced /riːd/. The past **read** is pronounced /red/.
c
| 1 won | 3 bought | 5 gave | 7 found out | 9 thought |
| 2 did | 4 sold | 6 read | 8 became | 10 cut |

💡 EXTRA ACTIVITY

Reinforce simple regular and irregular forms by playing a game of 'tennis' (see p. 154). Demonstrate the activity by asking a stronger student to help you. Say the infinitive of a verb from this lesson, e.g., *spend*, and ask the student to respond with the past simple form, i.e., *spent*. The student continues with a different infinitive and you respond with the past simple. For example: **A** *spend*; **B** *spent – become*; **A** *became – remember*; **B** *remembered*, etc. Check that students understand the game before playing in pairs. Tell them they should continue for as long as possible. If they make a mistake or pause for more than three seconds, they lose the game and start again.

c 💬🗨 Put students into pairs or small groups to talk about the topics. Monitor, but don't interrupt fluency unless students make mistakes with the past simple forms.

5 SPEAKING

a ▶ 06.18 Individually, students complete the text. They then compare in pairs. Play the recording for students to listen and check. Check answers as a class.

Answers
1 liked
2 bought
3 started
4 had
5 listened
6 played

b Students make notes about hobbies they had when they were children.

🔄 LOA TIP MONITORING

- Effective preparation in 5b is essential for effective task completion in 5c, so monitor the note-taking stage intensively. Make sure students aren't writing full sentences and check that they know how to pronounce any difficult words. Students may also need specific words to talk about their hobbies, so be prepared to give them these and to model the correct pronunciation before the speaking stage.

- During the speaking stage, monitor for correct usage of any specific language you gave students during 5b. If students make mistakes with this, try to catch their eyes discreetly so that they can correct their mistakes. Also, note down any mistakes with the past simple. After the activity, write these on the board and ask students to correct them.

c 💬🗨 In pairs, students talk about their hobbies. Encourage them to ask each other questions to keep the conversation going.

💡 FAST FINISHERS

Ask fast finishers to talk about the hobbies of other people in their families or any other people they know who have particularly unusual hobbies.

⊕ ADDITIONAL MATERIAL

Workbook 6B

Photocopiable activities: Grammar 6B, Vocabulary 6B, Pronunciation 6B

Documentary video Unit 6 *Family*

Video worksheet Unit 6 *Family*

6C EVERYDAY ENGLISH

Can you call me back?

At the end of this lesson, students will be able to:

- understand voicemail messages and phone calls
- use appropriate phrases when leaving a voicemail message and asking for someone on the phone
- use appropriate phrases for asking someone to wait
- relate the letter *a* to the sounds /æ/, /ɔː/, /ɪ/, and /eɪ/
- make an informal phone call

💡 OPTIONAL LEAD-IN

When all students are in the classroom, glance quickly at your mobile phone and say: *Oh sorry! I've got a message.* Gesture for students to wait with an apologetic expression as you listen to the 'message'. As you listen, look bewildered and then when you hang up say: *Sorry. It was my mum. I need to phone her – one minute.*

Simulate making a phone call, gesture to students that they should listen and pause at each '…' as if your mother was saying something to you, e.g., *Hi, Mum – it's me. … No, I'm at work. … Well, yes, but I'm a bit busy at the moment. … OK, quickly. … What? … A penguin? … There's a penguin in your kitchen? … It's in the sink?* [roll your eyes as if your mother was completely insane] *… Well, I don't know how it got there. … No, Mum, I don't know what penguins eat! … Have you got any fish? … Look, I need to go. I've got class now. … Speak later!*

Check students understood the gist of the conversation by asking: *Who was the message from?* (your mother) and *What is the problem at home?* (There's a penguin in the sink in the kitchen!).

1 LISTENING

a 💬 Individually, students read the ideas and choose what they usually do when there's no answer. They then compare in pairs.

b ▶ 06.19 Play Part 1 of the video or the audio recording for students to find out which two people leave messages. Check the answer as a class.

> **Answer**
> Annie and Dan leave messages.

Video/Audioscript (Part 1)

MESSAGE 1

DAN Hello, this is Dan Morton. I can't answer your call at the moment. Please leave a message after the tone.

ANNIE Hi, Dan – it's Annie. Can you call me back? You can call me on my work number or my mobile. Thanks.

MESSAGE 2

A Hi! It's Annie. I'm not here right now. You know what to do after the tone. Have a nice day!

D Hi, Annie. I got your message. I'm here at my desk now. Could you call me back? Bye.

c ▶ 06.19 Students watch or listen again for specific details. Play Part 1 of the video or the audio recording again for students to decide if the sentences are true or false. When checking answers, ask students to correct the false sentence.

> **Answers**
> 1 F (She tells Dan to call her on her work number or her mobile.)
> 2 T

2 USEFUL LANGUAGE

Leaving a voicemail message

a Complete the first item as an example with the class. Individually, students read the sentences and decide who says them. Don't check answers at this point.

b ▶ 06.19 Play Part 1 of the video or the audio recording again for students to check their answers to 2a. Check answers as a class.

> **Answers**
> 1 V
> 2 A
> 3 D
> 4 A
> 5 V
> 6 A

c ▶ 06.20 Individually, students complete the messages. Play the recording for students to listen and check. Check answers as a class.

> **Answers**
> 1 this
> 2 here
> 3 message
> 4 it's
> 5 back
> 6 call

📖 LANGUAGE NOTES

When answering the phone, some students may use *I'm (name).*, because using *This is* or *It's* to introduce themselves may seem very unnatural. In English, until a caller has been clearly identified, we tend to speak in the third person on the phone, e.g., *Who's calling?* not *Who are you?* If students have problems understanding this, tell them that what we are really saying when we start a phone call is *This (voice that you can hear now) is Lisa('s voice).* or *It's Lisa('s voice that you can hear now).*

🔄 LOA TIP DRILLING

- Drill the voicemail message and the caller's message before students work in pairs in 2d. Work on the messages in small chunks, e.g., *Hello, this is Alex. | Sorry, | I'm not here just now. | Please leave a message | and I'll call you later.* Repeat the chunks as many times as necessary and make sure students can repeat each chunk correctly before putting them together.

- Pay particular attention to the intonation in the messages. To make them sound friendly, students should use a wide pitch range and be careful not to sound too flat. As you drill the messages, consider showing students the up and down movements, using hand gestures to give them a visual reference.

d 💬 Tell students that they can now practise leaving a voicemail message. Check students understand the dialogue map before they start. In pairs, students take turns to give their voicemail message and leave a message for their partner. Monitor and praise students with a smile or a nod when they use the language from this section correctly.

> ### 💡 EXTRA ACTIVITY
>
> If you and your students have the technology available, ask them to make an audio recording of their voicemail messages to give to you to evaluate their pronunciation. Students could use their smartphones to do this, or any other recording device they have available, and then email you the recording.

3 LISTENING

a ▶️ 06.21 Read through the events with the class. Students then work individually and put them in a logical order. Play Part 2 of the video or the audio recording for students to listen and check. Check answers as a class.

> **Answers**
> 2 c (Leo answers the phone.)
> 3 a (Annie chats to Leo.)
> 4 d (Dan brings some coffee.)
> 5 e (Dan talks to Annie.)

Video/Audioscript (Part 2)

DAN Would you like a coffee?	**A** Oh, great – just great.
LEO Yeah, that'd be great. Thanks, Dan. … Hello. Dan's phone.	**L** Oh, good. That's, erm … great.
ANNIE Oh. Hello. Is Dan there?	**A** Yeah.
L Sorry, he's not here just now. He went to get coffee.	**L** He's back. … It's Annie.
	D Oh, good. Just a minute.
A Oh. It's his sister, Annie. Can he call me back?	**L** He's got coffee for us.
L Hi, Annie. It's Leo.	**A** Lucky you!
A Leo? Oh … Leo. Hi!	**D** There you are.
L Can you wait a minute? He'll be back soon.	**L** Bye, Annie.
	A Bye.
A Sure … So … Leo. How are you?	**D** Thanks. Hi, Annie. It's me.
L I'm … I'm really well. What about you?	**D** Dan – finally!
	D You left a message.
	A Yes, that's right. I need your help with something …

b Individually, students answer the questions. If necessary, play Part 2 of the video or the audio recording again. Check answers as a class and elicit students' ideas for question 2.

> **Answers**
> 1 a how they are
> 2 Suggested answers: shy, nervous, embarrassed

4 USEFUL LANGUAGE
Asking for someone on the phone

a ▶️ 06.21 Students look at Annie's questions and Leo's answers and underline the correct words. Check answers by playing the beginning of Part 2 again and pausing each time Annie and Leo say one of the sentences. Drill the questions and answers.

> **Answers**
> 1 there
> 2 here
> 3 back
> 4 back

b 💬🔊 Check students understand the dialogue map before they start. Put them into pairs to practise making phone calls, each time asking for someone and then asking him/her to call them back. Monitor and correct students' pronunciation as appropriate.

5 CONVERSATION SKILLS
Asking someone to wait

a Individually, students complete the conversation. They then check in pairs. Check answers as a class.

> **Answers**
> 1 wait
> 2 minute
> 3 Just
> 4 minute

b Answer the question as a class.

> **Answer**
> b 'a short time'

c 💬🔊 If possible, put students into new pairs so they aren't working with the same partner as in 4b. Students practise making phone calls again, but this time asking the person to wait a short time until the other person is free.

> ### 💡 FAST FINISHERS
>
> Ask fast finishers to invent different contexts for the call, e.g., *She went to get tea.*, *He's on the phone / his mobile.* Also tell them to make polite conversation with the other caller while they wait, e.g., by talking about the weather.

6 PRONUNCIATION
Sound and spelling: *a*

a ▶️ 06.22 Play the recording and highlight the four possible sounds for the letter *a*.

> ### 📖 LANGUAGE NOTES
>
> This section introduces some of the most frequent sounds which correspond to the letter *a*: /æ/, /ɔː/, /ɪ/ and /eɪ/. Don't ask students to look for other examples of words with *a*, as they may well find words which contain the letter *a* but aren't pronounced with the four sounds being worked on.

b ▶️ 06.23 Students classify the words into four groups. Play the recording for students to listen and check. Check answers as a class. Ask students to repeat the words after the recording and practise the pronunciation.

> **Answers**
>
> | Sound 1 (/æ/) | Sound 2 (/ɔː/) | Sound 3 (/ɪ/) | Sound 4 (/eɪ/) |
> |---|---|---|---|
> | b**a**ck | t**a**lk | vill**a**ge | w**ai**t |
> | bl**a**ck | t**a**ll | lugg**a**ge | voicem**ai**l |
> | | sm**a**ll | | s**a**me |
> | | | | t**a**ble |

c 💬📱 In pairs, students test each other on words which have the same sound. Monitor and correct students' pronunciation as appropriate.

> ### 💡 EXTRA ACTIVITY
>
> Write these words with the underlining on the board: _actor, amazing, April, became, Canada, had, hall, manager, packet, stadium, wall_. Ask students to classify the sound of the underlined _letter a_ into four groups: /æ/ like _thanks_ (actor, Canada, had, packet); /ɔː/ like _call_ (hall, wall); /ɪ/ like _message_ (manager); /eɪ/ like _later_ (amazing, April, became, stadium).

7 SPEAKING

a ▶️ 06.24 Play the recording for students to listen and complete the phone conversation. Check answers as a class. Ask students: _Is this a formal or an informal conversation?_ (informal, particularly the second part).

> **Answers**
> 1 It's   5 call
> 2 here   6 minute
> 3 message   7 It's
> 4 back   8 phoned

b ≫ Divide the class into groups of three and assign A, B and C roles. Student As read the first card on SB p. 131, Student Bs read the first card on SB p. 132 and Student Cs read the first card on SB p. 130. Students then role play the conversation. Monitor, but don't interrupt fluency unless students make mistakes with the content of this lesson. Students then read the second card and role play the second situation, and then finally the third.

> ### ⊕ ADDITIONAL MATERIAL
>
> Workbook 6C
>
> Unit Progress Test

6D SKILLS FOR WRITING
Five months later, we got married

At the end of this lesson, students will be able to:

- understand someone talking about important events in their life
- understand a series of life events and put them in a logical order
- link ideas in the past using _in_, _when_ and _later_
- write the life story of a person in their family

> ### 💡 OPTIONAL LEAD-IN
>
> Books closed. Model the activity in 1a and 1b to give students a clear idea of what is expected. Write two important years in your life on the board. Point to both years and ask students: _How do you say this year?_ Tell the class the two years are both important in your life and explain briefly what happened in each. As you talk about the years, try to limit your language to the past simple of _be_ and positive past simple verbs. Avoid using the negative of verbs other than _be_ at this point and aim to recycle some of the language from this unit as much as possible.

1 LISTENING AND SPEAKING

a Individually, students write down two important years in their lives and make notes about what happened in each. Monitor and help with vocabulary and give students ideas if necessary. Point out that as students are going to tell a partner what happened in those years, they should choose something they are happy to share.

b 💬📱 In pairs, students talk about their two important years. You may allow time for students to share their answers and ask students to tell the class about one of the important years in their lives.

c ▶️ 06.25 Point to the picture of Eva on SB p. 66 and say: _This is Eva. She's from Sicily._ Then, point to the list of events and years and tell students to match the phrases with the years in a logical order for Eva. Play the recording for students to listen for general meaning and check. Check answers as a class.

> **Answers**
> 1 2014
> 2 2005
> 3 2019
> 4 1992
> 5 2017

Audioscript

EVA OK, well, 1992 was a very important year for me. I was born in that year! I was born in a small town in the south of Sicily. My whole family lived there – my parents, my grandparents, uncles, aunts, cousins, everyone. It's a very nice place, historic, very hot. I really loved it.

And then 2005 was a very important year. Everything changed. My parents moved to England, my father got a job in Cambridge, so we went to live in the UK and I went to school there. I learned English quite quickly.

In 2014, I got my first job. I was a school teacher. I taught small kids, six to ten years old. It was great.

Then in 2017, I met Niko – he's my husband. He's German, but we met in the UK, and then in 2019 I moved to Germany to be near him, and we got married last year. And then I found a job. I teach English to business people, so here I am today.

d ▶06.25 Students listen to the recording again for specific details and underline the correct answers. They compare in pairs. If necessary, play the recording again. Check answers as a class.

Answers
1 small
2 with her parents
3 young children
4 to be near Niko

e 💬 Students work individually and write two more important years. Put students into pairs and tell them to try to guess what happened in the years their partner chose.

💡 FAST FINISHERS

Ask fast finishers to close their books. They write down everything they can remember about Eva from 1c and 1d before referring back to the Student's Book to check.

2 READING

a Point to the picture of Okan on SB p. 67 and explain that the timeline across the top of the page represents his life. Tell students to cover sentences a–f. In pairs, they look at the timeline, say the years and talk about what they can see in the pictures. They then look at the sentences and put them in the correct order. Check answers as a class.

Answers
2 a (When I was 11, we moved to Istanbul and I went to school there.
3 f (I left school in 2009 and I got a job in a bank.)
4 c (A year later, I went to university in Istanbul and studied engineering.)
5 e (After university, I met Carolina and we got married a few months later.)
6 b (Then in 2016, I got a job as an engineer in the UK.)

💡 FAST FINISHERS

Ask fast finishers to circle the verbs in sentences a–f, decide if they are regular or irregular and then write the infinitive of each verb.

3 WRITING SKILLS
Linking ideas in the past

a Books closed. Write the first sentence on the board, leaving a gap in place of *and*. Point to the gap and ask students: *What's this word?* Elicit *and* and ask: *What other words can we use to link ideas?* Elicit *but* and *so* from the previous unit. Students then open their books and complete the second sentence. Check the answer as a class.

Answer
2 When

b Individually, students complete the three sentences. They then compare in pairs. Check answers and answer the final question as a class.

Answers
1 when
2 In
3 When
a *in*
b *when*

🔄 LOA TIP ELICITING

- Before students complete 3c, write possible endings to the seven sentences in random order on the board, but without including *in* or *when*, e.g., *1991, I was 19, I was a student*. Include three distractors that don't correspond to any of the sentences, to make a total of ten endings. Read the first sentence *I started school …* and point to the board. Elicit a sentence from the class using the ending and *in* or *when*.

- As students complete each sentence orally, ask them to change the linking word so that they transform sentences with *in* to sentences with *when* and vice versa.

c As an example, complete the first sentence so that it's true for you. Students then work individually, completing the sentences. Monitor and check that students are completing the sentences with *in* or *when* and point out errors for students to self-correct. Ask each student to tell the class one or two of their sentences.

Answers
Students' own answers

d Read sentence 1 and then elicit ideas from students to complete sentence 2 as a class.

Answer
2 later

e Write the sentences from 3d on the board and circle the phrases *In 2010* and *A year later* to highlight how students should change the sentences. Students work individually, rewriting the underlined expressions with a time expression and *later*. Check answers as a class.

Answers
1 A year later / One year later
2 Five months later
3 Three years later

f Check that students understand that they should write two sentences, one with *in* and one with *later*. Monitor and point out errors for students to self-correct.

g 💬📣 In pairs, students take turns reading out their sentences with *later*, stopping after *later* to see if their partner can guess how the sentence ends.

💡 **EXTRA ACTIVITY**

Consolidate the work on linking words from Units 5 and 6 by writing *and*, *but*, *so*, *in*, *when* and *later* on the board. Read out sentences 1–6, saying *beep* where indicated:

1 *My parents were both born [beep] 1973.* (in)
2 *I've got two aunts [beep] four uncles.* (and)
3 *[beep] he was 25, Steve Jobs became a billionaire.* (When)
4 *He wasn't in the office, [beep] I left a message.* (so)
5 *She hasn't got any brothers, [beep] she's got ten sisters.* (but)
6 *My parents met when they were 15 and three years [beep], they got married.* (later)

Students listen and write down the linking word that they think completes each sentence correctly. Check answers as a class.

---

4 WRITING AND SPEAKING

a Students work individually to draw a timeline about someone in their family and add notes. Monitor and help with vocabulary and give students ideas if necessary.

b Individually, students write the life story of their person using their notes. Check that students understand that they shouldn't include their relationship to the person or the person's name in the life story. Remind them to use linking words to connect their ideas. If you're short of time, this exercise can be completed for homework. Students could then bring their life stories to the next lesson.

📖 **VOCABULARY SUPPORT**

relationship (B2) – how two people are connected, e.g., brother, sister, cousin, friends, colleagues

---

c 💬📣 In pairs, students swap their life stories and try to guess who the people are.

d Ask students to read each other's life stories again and check that their partner has used linking words correctly. They then give each other feedback. If they've made any mistakes with the linking words or in any other areas, they prepare a second draft of the life story before giving it to you for correction.

⊕ **ADDITIONAL MATERIAL**

Workbook 6D

UNIT 6
Review and extension

1 GRAMMAR

a Individually, students complete the conversation. Check answers as a class and check that students are using contractions where appropriate. Drill the conversation.

> **Answers**
>
> | | | |
> |---|---|---|
> | 1 are | 6 Was |
> | 2 'm | 7 wasn't |
> | 3 Were | 8 was |
> | 4 was | 9 Is |
> | 5 wasn't | 10 's |

b Individually, students complete the text. They then check in pairs. Check answers as a class.

> **Answers**
>
> | | |
> |---|---|
> | 1 was | 5 was |
> | 2 wanted | 6 decided |
> | 3 loved | 7 studied |
> | 4 had | 8 found |

c Complete the first gap as an example with the class. Check that students understand that they can use the present simple or the past simple, so they need to think carefully about the meaning. Check answers as a class.

> **Answers**
>
> 1 stayed; cooked
> 2 went; had
> 3 plays; gets; got
> 4 spent; were; see

2 VOCABULARY

a Students complete the text with the correct family words. Check answers as a class and then ask students to draw the family tree for the text to check that they have understood the meaning.

> **Answers**
>
> | | |
> |---|---|
> | 1 grandparents | 4 aunt |
> | 2 grandmother | 5 uncle |
> | 3 grandfather | 6 cousins |

b Read the example with the students. They then write the dates in words. Check answers by asking individual students to come up and write them on the board.

> **Answers**
>
> 1 the nineteenth of October two thousand and fourteen / twenty fourteen
> 2 the twelfth of June nineteen eighty-five
> 3 the third of September nineteen ninety
> 4 the twenty-second of April two thousand and eight
> 5 the thirty-first of August twenty twenty
> 6 the ninth of January two thousand and twelve / twenty twelve

> ### ♀ FAST FINISHERS
>
> Ask fast finishers to write down dates, first in numbers and then in words, when important things happened to them. Next to the dates, they write a short note of why they're important.

3 WORDPOWER *go*

a Books closed. In a column on the board, write: *home, by bus, shopping, swimming, out to a restaurant*. Ask students: *What word can I write before all of these?* Elicit *go*. Students open their books, look at the conversation and answer the questions. Check answers as a class.

> **Answers**
>
> 1 Viv
> 2 to go for a swim and go out to a restaurant

b Students match the phrases with *go* with the meanings. Students check in pairs. Check answers as a class.

> **Answers**
>
> | | |
> |---|---|
> | a 2 go by | d 5 go out |
> | b 1 go home | e 4 go for |
> | c 3 go shopping | |

c Individually, students match the verbs and the nouns to make more phrases with *go*. Check answers as a class and elicit alternative nouns for each phrase from the class, e.g., *go to a café / friend's house, go by car/taxi*.

> **Answers**
>
> 1 c 2 e 3 d 4 b 5 a

d Students read the sentences and, working individually, find and correct the mistakes. Check answers as a class.

> **Answers**
>
> 1 They want to go ~~to~~ home now.
> 2 I need to go ~~for~~ shopping in town this afternoon.
> 3 I'd like to go <u>to</u> the cinema this evening.
> 4 He usually goes to work <u>by</u> bus.
> 5 Would you like to go <u>for</u> a coffee?

e As an additional example, change the example sentence so that it's true for you. Students then write sentences about their lives using the prompts. Monitor and point out errors for students to self-correct.

> **Answers**
>
> Students' own answers

f ⚲ In pairs, students tell each other their sentences and decide how similar they are. Ask students to share their ideas with the class and ask pairs to justify why they think they are similar or different, e.g., *Antoni goes home at 6:00 pm every day, but I go home two and a half hours later at 8:30 pm.*

> ### ♀ EXTRA ACTIVITY
>
> Play a drawing game with students. Choose one of the phrases with *go* and start drawing a simple picture on the board. When students think they know what it is, they raise their hands. Continue the game either as a whole class, with the first student who guesses correctly being the next to draw on the board, or in pairs or small groups. The student who guesses the most phrases correctly wins.

≫ Photocopiable activities: Wordpower 6

> ### ◁▷ LOA TIP REVIEW YOUR PROGRESS
>
> Students look back through the unit, think about what they've studied and decide how well they did. Students work on weak areas by using the appropriate sections of the Workbook and the Photocopiable activities.

↻ UNIT OBJECTIVES

At the end of this unit, students will be able to:

- understand information, texts and conversations about travel and transport
- exchange information and express opinions about travel and transport
- get someone's attention, apologise and show interest in the other participants in a conversation
- introduce themselves using personal emails

UNIT CONTENTS

G GRAMMAR

- Past simple: negative and questions
- *love / like / don't mind / hate* + verb + *-ing*

V VOCABULARY

- Transport: *aeroplane (plane), bike, bus, cruise ship, ferry, helicopter, motorcycle, scooter, speedboat, train*
- Transport collocations: *catch (the train), change (trains), get off (the train), get on (the train), miss (the train), take (the train)*
- Transport adjectives: *cheap – expensive, clean – dirty, comfortable – uncomfortable, empty – crowded/full, fast – slow, safe – dangerous*
- Linking ideas with *after, when* and *while*
- Wordpower: *get* meaning *arrive, become, bring, receive, take, travel on*

P PRONUNCIATION

- Past simple questions: *did you* /ˈdɪdʒə/
- Stress in adjectives
- Intonation for saying *excuse me*
- Emphasising what we say

C COMMUNICATION SKILLS

- Talking about different trips
- Evaluating different forms of transport
- Saying *excuse me* and *I'm sorry*
- Showing interest
- Discussing English-speaking countries you'd like to visit
- Writing an email about yourself

GETTING STARTED

♀ OPTIONAL LEAD-IN

Books closed. Write the following wordsnake on the board:

tbusrtaxiiboatpcars

Tell students to find four kinds of transport in the wordsnake. Tell them that there are five extra letters, which form a word connected with transport. Students work individually, finding the kinds of transport and the word connected with transport. They compare in pairs. Check answers by asking individual students to circle the kinds of transport in the wordsnake on the board and to open their books and look at the title of the unit. (Answers: *bus, taxi, boat, car*. *The other letters spell 'trips'.*)

a 💬 Give students one minute to think about their answers to the questions before talking about the picture as a class.

🌏 CULTURE NOTES

This picture shows three tourists riding their bikes through Alentejo. Alentejo is a region in south central and southern Portugal. Although it's not very popular among tourists, Alentejo is known for its beautiful scenery and Roman history.

b 💬 Read the questions with students and then put them into pairs to discuss their imaginary travel plans. Help with vocabulary and pronunciation, but don't interrupt fluency.

♀ EXTRA ACTIVITY

Individually, students draw the routes they want to take on the trips they discussed in Exercise b and then check in their pairs. Tell them to mark the places they would like to visit and the sights they would like to see. Make sure they know how to say the names of these places in English.

Divide up the pairs students worked in for Exercise b and put students into new small groups, if possible, so that each student in the group has a different country. Students take turns to talk about their trip. Students in each group then decide which trip they think is best and why.

Exercises a and b can be prepared as homework before this lesson to give students time to look up unfamiliar vocabulary. Ask students to look at the picture and to prepare their answers to the questions as homework to talk about in the next lesson.

7A THE FERRY DIDN'T ARRIVE

At the end of this lesson, students will be able to:
- read and understand blog posts about travel
- use a lexical set of transport words and transport collocations correctly
- use the negative and question forms of the past simple
- understand a conversation about a long trip
- ask and answer questions about trips

⚙ OPTIONAL LEAD-IN

Draw a rough world map on the board and elicit the names of the different parts of the world from Vocabulary Focus 1A by pointing to the different geographical areas and asking: *What part of the world is this?* (Africa, Asia, Central and South America, Europe, North America, Oceania)

Drill the pronunciation of each part of the world and ask students: *Where's the stress?* Underline the stressed syllable in each.

Tell students you're going to read out three famous tourist attractions for each part of the world. They listen and write down the part of the world. *1 the Leaning Tower of Pisa, the Eiffel Tower, Big Ben* (Europe) *2 Victoria Falls, the Pyramids, Serengeti National Park* (Africa) *3 Machu Picchu, Sugarloaf Mountain, Panama Canal* (Central and South America) *4 Uluru / Ayers Rock, Botany Bay National Park, Milford Sound* (Oceania) *5 the Golden Gate Bridge, the Rockies, Yellowstone National Park* (North America) *6 Mount Everest, the Taj Mahal, the Forbidden City* (Asia). Students compare in pairs. Check answers as a class.

1 READING

a 💬🔖 If you used the optional lead-in, before students open their books, mark the three trip destinations on the map on the board and elicit the countries by asking students: *Where does this trip start/finish?* In pairs, students open their books, look at the trips and discuss which one they would like to go on and why. Ask some students to tell the class their ideas and justify their decisions as much as possible.

b Students work individually, answering the questions. Check answers as a class. Ask students if they know about any of the three places mentioned in the blog posts. If you wish, give students information from Culture Notes below about Valdez Glacier.

Answers
a = Ethan
b = Kayla
c = Jessica

🌍 CULTURE NOTES

Valdez Glacier is located in Valdez, Alaska, the snowiest place in the United States. In the late 1800s, many people used the Valdez Glacier to enter Alaska and look for gold.

The best way to see the glacier is by kayak, but it can be very dangerous to get close to the glacier. As the ice melts, large portions of ice break off, which can change the water levels a lot in a very short time.

c Students read the blog quickly and match the sentences with the people. Check answers as a class and ask students: *Which words helped you find the answers?*

Answers
1 E 2 K 3 J 4 E 5 J 6 K

📖 VOCABULARY SUPPORT

selfie stick – a long tool you can attach to your mobile phone and use for taking a selfie (a photograph of yourself)

kayak – a light, narrow canoe that is covered over the top

fly(-ies) – a small insect with two wings

mosquito – a small, flying insect that bites people and animals and sucks their blood

make-up – coloured powder and liquid used on your face to change or improve its look

⚙ FAST FINISHERS

Ask fast finishers to write more sentences that they think Jessica, Ethan or Kayla might say about their trips.

⚙ EXTRA ACTIVITY

Ask students to read all three texts again and answer questions 1–5:

1 How long did it take Jessica to get from Pattaya to Koh Larn on the speedboat? (15 minutes)

2 Who travelled on the water? (Jessica and Ethan)

3 Who made a new friend? (Jessica)

4 Who do you think travelled the furthest? (probably Kayla)

5 Whose trip do you think was most expensive? (probably Ethan's)

d 💬🔖 Tell students that in this activity, the emphasis is on communication and not on perfect English. In pairs, students talk about the questions.

🔄 LOA TIP MONITORING

- Asking students who perform well on a task to share what they said can provide a realistic and achievable model for students. If you use yourself as a model, this can sometimes set up an unrealistic expectation and a sense of 'Of course I can't do it as well as the teacher'.

- Monitor 1d intensively and identify students who give good, clear arguments for why they think Jessica's, Ethan's or Kayla's trip was best. Allow time so students can share their ideas with the class. Ask the other students: *Who do you agree with most? Why?*

2 VOCABULARY Transport

a Ask students to cover the words in the box and see how many of the kinds of transport in the pictures they already know. Individually, students then match the words with the pictures. Monitor for any problems and clarify these as you check answers as a class. Check that students understand that *aeroplane* is the more formal word, but *plane* is more common in everyday English. Explain that *speedboat* and *cruise ship* are two forms of water transport, but a *speedboat* is very fast and for a small number of people, while a *cruise ship* is a lot bigger, goes more slowly and can hold many more people. Drill the vocabulary.

> **Answers**
> 1 cruise ship   6 ferry
> 2 train   7 helicopter
> 3 bus   8 scooter
> 4 aeroplane (plane)   9 tram
> 5 speedboat   10 coach

b 💬🔊 Read the questions with the students and check that they understand the task. Give them one minute to think about answers for the questions before they work in pairs. Monitor, but don't interrupt fluency. Check ideas with the class.

> 💡 **FAST FINISHERS**
> Ask fast finishers to brainstorm other kinds of transport.

c ≫ ▶ **07.01–07.03** Students complete the exercises in the Vocabulary Focus 7A on SB p. 167. Play the recordings as necessary and monitor students as they speak. Check other answers as a class. Tell students to go back to SB p. 71.

> **Answers (Vocabulary Focus 7A SB p. 167)**
> **a** 1 d 2 e 3 f 4 a 5 b 6 c
> **b** 1 take 2 miss 3 get off 4 caught 5 took 6 on
> **c** 1 bought, saw 2 long

3 GRAMMAR Past simple: negative

a Read the two sentences and complete them as a class.

> **Answers**
> 1 didn't
> 2 buy

b Students check in pairs. Elicit the rule and concept-check the position of the auxiliary verb in relation to the infinitive by asking students: *Which comes first in negative sentences, 'didn't' or the main verb?*

> **Answer**
> *didn't*

c Individually, students look at Jessica's and Kayla's blog posts again to find more examples of the past simple negative forms.

> **Answer**
> Jessica's blog post: *didn't arrive*
> Kayla's blog post: *didn't use, didn't know, didn't wear*

4 LISTENING

a ▶ **07.04** Students listen to the conversation for general meaning and answer the questions. Check the answers as a class.

> **Answers**
> 1 Kayla's story
> 2 Carly
> 3 food

> **Audioscript**
>
> **SCOTT** Which story did you like most?
> **CARLY** Kayla's – it was very funny.
> **S** Yes, it really was.
> **C** Lipstick on a scooter – you don't think of things like that.
> **S** What about your holidays? Any stories to tell?
> **C** Um … well … nothing like that – nothing funny.
> **S** But?
> **C** Well, when I went to Mexico with two of my best friends …
> **S** Did you go last year?
> **C** That's right.
> **S** How did you travel there?
> **C** By plane. We went to Mexico City.
> **S** Right.
> **C** … and we tried to order food from this place – it was a very simple restaurant.
> **S** What did you choose?
> **C** Well, that was the problem. We didn't speak Spanish and we didn't understand the words on the menu.
> **S** Oh, dear. What did you do?
> **C** Well, we started to use the dictionaries on our mobile phones.
> **S** A long, slow process.
> **C** It was. But then this Mexican man saw us and he offered to help. He told us what things were and then he ordered the food for us.
> **S** Wow! What a nice guy!
> **C** Exactly – we said 'thank you' about a hundred times! And then he went away. But that's not all.
> **S** Oh?
> **C** Yeah, we went to pay for the meal and the man – he paid for our meals before he left!
> **S** Unbelievable! That's incredible.
> **C** Yeah – just so kind.

b ▶ **07.04** Students listen to the conversation again for specific details and underline the correct answers. Tell them that for some items, they may need to underline more than one word. Students compare in pairs. Check answers as a class.

> **Answers**
> 1 Mexico City
> 2 two friends
> 3 menu
> 4 mobile phone
> 5 food
> 6 paid then left

c 💬🔊 Discuss the question briefly as a class. If possible, share a simple personal story of your own. In pairs, students answer the question.

5 GRAMMAR Past simple: questions

a ▶️ **07.05** Write the positive sentence: *Carly went to Mexico City.* (+) on the board. Then, write *Carly / go / Mexico City* (–) on the board and elicit the negative sentence: *Carly didn't go to Mexico City.* Finally, write *Carly / go / Mexico City* (?) on the board and see if students can form the question: *Did Carly go to Mexico City?* Tell the class that now they are going to look at past simple questions. Individually, students complete the questions in the book. Play the recording for students to listen and check. Check answers as a class.

> **Answers**
> 1 Did   2 did   3 did

b Students check in pairs. Write the following jumbled question on the board: *you / visit / Mexico / did ?* Ask students: *What's the correct order?* (Did you visit Mexico?) and elicit the rule (*did* + subject + infinitive).

> **Answer**
> *did*

c ▶️ **07.05** **Pronunciation** Play the recording and ask students to listen to the pronunciation of *did you*. Elicit that you can't hear both words clearly and that *did you* is pronounced as one word /ˈdɪdʒə/. Play the recording again for students to listen and repeat. Then, drill the questions. Ask students to give themselves a mark for their pronunciation: *3 Good, people can understand me – no problem!, 2 OK, but I need to practise this more!, 1 This is very difficult for me!*

> **Answer**
> No, you can't

d ≫ ▶️ **07.06** Students read the information in Grammar Focus 7A on SB p. 150. Play the recording where indicated and ask students to listen and repeat. Students then complete the exercises. Check answers as a class, making sure students are using the auxiliary verb correctly. Tell students to go back to SB p. 71.

> **Answers (Grammar Focus 7A SB p. 151)**
> **a** 2 didn't take   4 didn't answer   6 didn't see
>   3 didn't want   5 didn't like   7 didn't get
> **b** 2 We didn't travel across the country.
>   3 We didn't have a good time.
>   4 The tickets didn't cost a lot of money.
>   5 She didn't visit China.
>   6 They didn't stay in hotels.
>   7 The people didn't speak English, so I didn't understand them.
> **c** 2 Did, spend, didn't
>   3 Did, start, didn't
>   4 Did, travel, did
> **d** 2 How much did the trip cost?
>   3 How many countries did you visit?
>   4 Where did you stay?
>   5 When did you arrive home?

e ▶️ **07.07** Tell students that this is a friendly, informal conversation. Individually, students complete the conversation. They then check in pairs. Play the recording for students to listen and check. Check answers as a class.

> **Answers**
> 1 was
> 2 was
> 3 did (you) visit
> 4 went
> 5 did (you) travel
> 6 took
> 7 hired
> 8 did (you) enjoy
> 9 loved

6 SPEAKING

a Tell students that now they can practise using all the language from the lesson with a partner. Read the instructions with the students and check that they understand the task. Give them one minute to write notes and help with vocabulary if necessary.

b 💬 In pairs, students ask and answer each other's questions about their trips. Tell them to use questions similar to those in 5e, such as: *How was your trip to __?; How did you travel around __?; What did you enjoy most?* Monitor, but don't interrupt fluency unless students make mistakes with the past simple.

c 💬 In groups, students share their partners' stories. Don't interrupt fluency unless students make mistakes with the past simple.

> ⊕ **ADDITIONAL MATERIAL**
>
> Workbook 7A
>
> Photocopiable activities: Grammar 7A, Vocabulary 7A, Pronunciation 7A
>
> Documentary video Unit 7 *Trips*
>
> Video worksheet Unit 7 *Trips*

7B | I LIKE THE STATIONS

At the end of this lesson, students will be able to:

- read and understand a website with information and reviews
- use a lexical set of transport adjectives correctly
- understand a conversation in which people talk about trips and give their opinions
- use *love / like / don't mind / hate* + verb + *-ing*
- talk about the types of transport they use

♀ OPTIONAL LEAD-IN

Books closed. Tell students not to look at their books or their notes. Ask students: *What were the ten kinds of transport we learnt last lesson?* Elicit the ten words from Lesson 7A orally, but don't let students write anything down. Drill the kinds of transport, but don't check the spelling.

Then, draw this puzzle on the board:

In pairs, students complete the puzzle with five kinds of transport from Lesson 7A. Explain that the vertical box is another word for a kind of transport. Check answers as a class by asking students to complete the puzzle on the board or spell the answers out to you. (Answers: *1 scooter 2 ferry 3 speedboat 4 cruise ship 5 aeroplane. The vertical word is 'train'.*)

1 READING

a 💬🗩 In pairs, students talk about the question. Brainstorm as a class cities that have metros and/or express buses.

b Students read the text quickly and match the cities with the pictures. Tell students they should only read the text *Fast City Transport Around the World*, not *From the locals*. You may wish to pre-teach the words in the Vocabulary Support box. Check answers as a class.

Answers
a Cape Town
b Moscow
c London

📖 VOCABULARY SUPPORT

above ground – above the level of the streets and roads

bridge (A2) – a structure built over a river, road or railway to allow people and vehicles to cross

deep (A2) – a long way down into the earth

palace (B1) – a large house that is the official home of a king, queen or other important person

platform (A2) – a flat raised area or structure

statue (B1) – a model usually made of stone or metal and often of a person

steps (B1) – the individual blocks which, when joined together, form 'stairs'

system (B1) – a set of connected things that operate together

c Tell students to read the text again in detail. Individually, students answer the questions. Students compare in pairs. Check answers as a class and ask students to read the sections of the text that helped them answer the questions.

Answers
1 London
2 Cape Town
3 Cape Town
4 Moscow
5 Cape Town
6 Students' own answers

d Individually, students look at the text again and underline two things that surprise them. They then compare their ideas in pairs. Ask pairs to share their answers with the class to find out what surprised students most.

e Ask students: *What do you think people say about the metro and express buses in Cape Town / Moscow / London?* and elicit ideas, e.g., *It's new/expensive/slow.* If students have visited any of the cities, ask about their experiences. Tell students to read the opinions of people that use the different forms of transport in *From the locals* and answer the questions. Check answers as a class.

Possible answers
Sergei – Moscow: stations like palaces
Antonia – Cape Town: express buses, roads are busy
Joanna – London: trains are full, over 300 steps

f 💬🗩 In pairs, students answer the questions. Take feedback as a class.

♀ EXTRA ACTIVITY

Write sentences 1–5 on the board for students to decide if they are true or false. When checking answers, ask students to correct the false sentences.

1 *The London Underground isn't a popular way to travel.*
   (F – The trains are often full.)

2 *Traffic is a problem for the express bus system in Cape Town.*
   (F – Traffic isn't a problem – the buses have their own lanes.)

3 *The Moscow Metro is very dangerous at night.* (F – There are police at the stations, so it's very safe.)

4 *In Cape Town, you pay for the bus with a card.* (T)

5 *The London Underground is a very cheap way to travel.*
   (F – The London Underground is expensive.)

2 VOCABULARY Transport adjectives

a Ask students to cover the texts and see if they know any of the words to complete the table. Individually, students then look at the texts and find the opposite adjectives. Don't check answers at this point.

b ▶ **07.08** **Pronunciation** Play the recording for students to check their answers. Play the recording again for students to listen and repeat.

> **Answers**
> | | |
> |---|---|
> | fast | slow |
> | safe | dangerous |
> | empty | crowded/full |
> | comfortable | uncomfortable |
> | cheap | expensive |
> | clean | dirty |

c Tell students to classify the adjectives in the table as positive or negative. Complete the first two items (positive: *fast*; negative: *slow*) as an example. Individually, students decide if the other words are positive or negative. Check answers as a class by asking students to write the correct answers in two groups on the board.

> **Answers**
> Positive: fast, safe, empty, comfortable, cheap, clean
> Negative: slow, dangerous, crowded/full, uncomfortable, expensive, dirty

d ▶ **07.09** **Pronunciation** Play the recording for students to underline the stressed syllable in each word. Check answers as a class. Model the pronunciation for students to listen and repeat.

> **Answers**
> <u>com</u>fortable
> <u>dan</u>gerous
> ex<u>pen</u>sive

e 💬 Divide the class into pairs and ask one pair to read the example. In a speech bubble on the board, write: *I don't agree*. Ask: *What other expressions do you know to say 'I don't agree'?* Elicit ideas, e.g., *I disagree, I'm not sure*, and write them on the board. Students work in pairs, making sentences and responding, and taking turns to be A and B. Monitor, but don't interrupt fluency unless students make mistakes with the transport adjectives.

> **💡 EXTRA ACTIVITY**
>
> Work as a class to build up a paragraph on the board for the website citytripper.com about the metro or bus system in the students' own area. Tell students to look for phrases and sentences in the texts on SB p. 72 that they can use and adapt for their own city. Tell students that when they do their written work, it is fine to use and adapt phrases from the model texts. Elicit sentences from the class, e.g., *The Rome Metro <u>is unusual because it's</u> in a capital city, but it has only two underground lines. <u>There are</u> very old buildings above and below the ground everywhere in Rome, <u>so it's very</u> difficult to build metro lines in the city centre.*

3 GRAMMAR AND LISTENING
Love / like / don't mind / hate + verb + -ing

a 💬 Tell the class how you usually travel when you go to meet a friend, e.g., *I always use public transport because it's fast and cheap*. Discuss the question as a class. Encourage students to justify their decisions using transport adjectives from the previous section.

b ▶ **07.10** Students listen to the conversation for general meaning and complete the table. Check answers as a class. You may wish to pre-teach the word *traffic* (n.) (a lot of cars, buses, etc. on the road at the same time).

> **Answers**
> | | She came by … | The journey took … |
> |---|---|---|
> | Svetlana | metro | half an hour |
> | Alex | car | one hour |

> **Audioscript**
>
> **ALEX** Hi, Svetlana. Sorry I'm late. It was the traffic. So how did you get here?
> **S** On the metro, of course.
> **A** Really? Do you use the metro?
> **S** Yes, I love going on the metro; it's so quick. It only took half an hour. Don't you use the metro?
> **A** No, I don't like using the metro; it's so crowded. And it isn't always very clean in the trains. And the stations, they're terrible. So many people.
> **S** Oh, I love the stations. I think they're beautiful. So did you come by car?
> **A** Yes, of course, I go everywhere by car. I like driving in Moscow.
> **S** You like it? But it's always so slow. How long did it take you to get here?
> **A** About an hour, maybe. The traffic was bad.
> **S** But it's always bad. I hate sitting in traffic. It's so boring.
> **A** Oh, I don't mind it; it's not too bad. You can listen to the radio, you can chat to people.
> **S** Well, you must have a very nice car.
> **A** It is quite a nice car, yes. It's very comfortable and big inside.
> **S** Ah.

c ▶ **07.10** Tell students that now they need to listen for Svetlana's and Alex's specific opinions on the different kinds of transport. Play the recording again for students to complete the table. Students compare in pairs. Check answers as a class.

> **Answers**
> | | Svetlana thinks | Alex thinks |
> |---|---|---|
> | the metro is … | quick | crowded, dirty |
> | the stations are … | beautiful | terrible |
> | driving is … | slow | not too bad |
> | Alex's / Her car is … | very nice | nice, comfortable, big |

d ▶ `07.11` Tell students to close their books. Write on the board: *I … going on the metro.* Ask students: *Can you remember what Svetlana said?* (love) Then ask students: *What's the opposite of 'love'?* (hate) Tell students that they are going to look at verbs of preference in detail. Students look at the sentences in their books and try to complete them. Play the recording for students to listen and check. Check answers as a class.

Answers
1 love
2 don't like
3 love
4 like
5 hate
6 don't mind

e Students then match the verbs in 3d with the meanings. Check answers as a class.

Answers
1 love
2 hate
3 don't mind

🔵 LOA TIP CONCEPT CHECKING

- Draw emoticons on the board and ask students to write the five answers to 3d next to them to check that they understand the meaning:

  ☺☺☺   (love)
  ☺   (like)
  😐   (don't mind)
  ☹   (don't like)
  ☹☹☹   (hate)

- Ask students: *What kinds of word can come after 'love', 'like', 'don't mind' and 'hate'?* Students look at the examples in 3d and elicit the possibilities: *the -ing form or a noun/pronoun.*

⊙ CAREFUL!

When verbs of preference are followed by a verb, students are likely to use the wrong form for the second verb. They may use the infinitive of the verb, e.g., ~~I hate use …~~ (Correct form = *I hate* **using** *public transport*), or they may use *to* + infinitive, e.g., ~~I love to go …~~ (Correct form = *I love* **going** *by car*). Note that the *to* + infinitive form is in fact acceptable and used by native speakers in certain circumstances. However, at this level, students should always use the *-ing* form as the difference in meaning between the verb followed by the *-ing* form or by the *to* + infinitive is complicated.

Some students may add the *-ing* form to the verb of preference when it isn't followed by another verb, e.g., ~~Hoving cars~~ (Correct form = *I* **love** *cars*).

Students may also start to overuse *like* and use it instead of *would like*, e.g., ~~I like travelling …~~ (Correct form = *I* **would like to travel** *to the Valdez Glacier*).

---

f ⟫ ▶ `07.12` Students read the information in Grammar Focus 7B on SB p. 150. Play the recording where indicated and ask students to listen and repeat. Students then complete the exercises. Check answers as a class, making sure students are using *-ing* forms after the verbs where necessary and spelling them correctly. Tell students to go back to SB p. 73.

Answers (Grammar Focus 7B SB p. 151)
a 2 driving   5 flying   8 having   11 standing 14 trying
   3 walking 6 relaxing   9 speaking   12 staying   15 using
   4 getting   7 being   10 sitting   13 running   16 agreeing
b 1 He doesn't mind cooking or getting pizza. He loves trying new food.
   2 Lisa likes eating in restaurants. She hates cooking. She doesn't like getting pizza. She loves trying new food.

---

4 SPEAKING

a Individually, students tick three kinds of transport from the list.

b Read the instructions with the students and check that they understand the task. Give them one minute to write notes and help with vocabulary if necessary.

c 💬 In pairs, students tell each other their ideas and find out how similar they are. As you monitor, don't interrupt fluency, but note down any problems with pronunciation and write down any mistakes with *love / like / don't mind / hate* + verb + *-ing*. After the activity, write these on the board and ask students to correct them.

💡 FAST FINISHERS

Ask fast finishers to work together in their pairs and complete the sentence: *I …, but (my partner) … .* in as many ways as possible using information they learnt about their partner in 4c, e.g., *I don't like taking a plane, but Sophia loves it!*

⊕ ADDITIONAL MATERIAL

Workbook 7B

Photocopiable activities: Grammar 7B, Vocabulary 7B, Pronunciation 7B

EVERYDAY ENGLISH

Excuse me, please

At the end of this lesson, students will be able to:

- understand informal conversations in which people say *excuse me* and *I'm sorry* and talk about where they are travelling to
- use appropriate phrases to say *excuse me* and *I'm sorry*
- emphasise what they say appropriately
- use appropriate phrases to show interest during a conversation
- maintain an informal conversation in which they apologise about something and show interest

◊ OPTIONAL LEAD-IN

Books closed. Write *going away for the weekend* in the centre of the board. Ask students: *What does 'going away' mean?* (go and stay in a place away from your home). Create a word map on the board by drawing a circle around *going away for the weekend* and adding three lines. At the end of the lines write: *places, activities* and *people*. Elicit places to go, e.g., *the beach, a spa, a big city*; typical activities, e.g., *swimming in the sea, visiting museums, sleeping late*; people to go with, e.g., *friends, family, partner,* and add them to the word map.

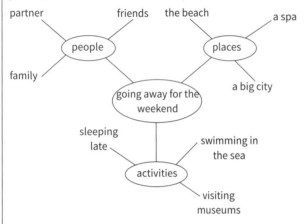

In pairs, students add more vocabulary to the word map. Take feedback as a class and add their ideas to the word map on the board. Leave the word map on the board for students to refer to in 1a.

1 LISTENING

a ⬚ Discuss the questions as a class. If you used the Optional lead-in, remind students that they can use the vocabulary on the board.

b ⬚ Tell students to look at picture 1 and ask them what they can see. They then work in pairs, answering the questions. Ask some students to tell the class their ideas, but don't tell them if they are right or wrong.

c ▶ **07.13** Play Part 1 of the video or the audio recording for students to listen and check their answers to 1b. Check answers as a class.

Answers

1 Annie is at the train station.
2 She runs into the woman.
3 a Annie says 'I'm so sorry!'
  b The woman says 'Watch out!'

Video/Audioscript (Part 1)

ANNOUNCEMENT The train at platform 3 is the 11.50 for Bristol.
ANNIE Oh no!

PASSENGER Watch out!
A I'm so sorry.
P That's all right.

d ⬚ Tell students to look at picture 2 and read through the questions as a class. They then work in pairs, answering the questions. Ask some students to tell the class their ideas, but don't tell them if they are right or wrong.

e ▶ **07.14** Play Part 2 of the video or the audio recording for students to listen and check their answers to 1d. Check answers as a class.

Answers

1 They are on a train.
2 Students' own answers
3 b

Video/Audioscript (Part 2)

LEO Excuse me. Excuse me, please. … Excuse me, but I think this is my seat. I booked it online.
ANNIE Oh. I'm very sorry.
L Annie!
A Leo! I'm sorry I took your seat. I just sat down. I didn't check. I'm really sorry.
L No problem!

A Um. Your seat.
L No, no, you have the seat.
A But you booked it.
L It doesn't matter. It's yours now.
A Thank you.
L I can sit here.

f ▶ **07.14** Students watch or listen again for specific details. Play Part 2 of the video or the audio recording again for students to underline the correct answers. Check answers as a class.

Answers

1 Leo
2 Annie
3 Leo

2 USEFUL LANGUAGE
Saying *excuse me* and *I'm sorry*

◊ EXTRA ACTIVITY

Write *Excuse me, please.* and *I'm sorry!* in two speech bubbles on the board. Walk around the class and mime accidentally bumping into a student with your elbow. Look horrified, point to your mouth and to the two phrases on the board to elicit which you should use (*I'm sorry!*). Then try to reach a part of the classroom that you can't get to because a student is in the way. Look frustrated, gesture for the student to move and point to the phrases again to elicit which one you should use (*Excuse me, please.*). Tell students that now they're going to look at how to say *excuse me* and *I'm sorry*.

a Individually, students match the phrases with the meanings. Check answers as a class.

Answers

1 b
2 a

b ▶ **07.15** **Pronunciation** Play the recording and highlight the intonation for students.

c Discuss the questions as a class and check students are clear about the two different uses of *Excuse me*. Drill the phrases, completing the first one appropriately, e.g., *Excuse me, but I don't understand.*

> **Answers**
> a Excuse me, but … b Excuse me, please.

d Elicit the rule as a class. Make sure students understand the position of *very*, *really* and *so* in the expression by writing: *I'm very/really/so sorry.* on the board with *very/really/so* underlined, circled or in a different colour.

> **Answer**
> You put *very*, *really* and *so* before *sorry*, e.g., *I'm very/really/so sorry.*

e ▶07.16 Students match the pairs of sentences. Play the recording for students to listen and check. Check answers as a class. Ask students to underline *very*, *really* and *so* in the sentences to help them remember the position.

> **Answers**
> 1 e 2 c 3 b 4 a 5 d

f If you used the Extra activity earlier, once again mime accidentally bumping into a student with your elbow. Say *I'm sorry!* and gesture to elicit a response from the student. Students then think about which replies are correct to use when someone apologises. Check answers as a class.

> **Answers**
> 1 ✓ That's all right.   5 ✓ It doesn't matter.
> 2 ✓ That's OK.   6 ✓ Don't worry.
> 3 ✓ No problem.

g ▶07.17 Tell students to work individually and order the sentences to make two short, separate conversations. Play the recording for students to listen and check. Check answers as a class.

> **Answers and audioscript**
> **Conversation 1**
> b **A** Excuse me, but I think that's my coat.
> c **B** Is it? I'm so sorry. I took the wrong one.
> a **A** No problem. They all look the same.
>
> **Conversation 2**
> f **A** Excuse me, but I think this is my seat.
> e **B** Oh dear. I'm very sorry. I thought this was number 35.
> d **A** Don't worry. The seat numbers are hard to read.

h 💬🔊 In pairs, students practise the conversations. Monitor and correct students' pronunciation as appropriate. Then elicit an indication of students' confidence level for saying *excuse me* and *I'm sorry*.

3 PRONUNCIATION
Emphasising what we say

a ▶07.18 Play the recording and highlight the stress for students.

b Individually, students choose the best answer. Check the answer as a class.

> **Answer**
> 2 We want to sound more sorry.

c 💬🔊 Students work in pairs, practising saying the sentences in 3a. Monitor and correct students' pronunciation as appropriate.

> **⟳ LOA TIP DRILLING**
>
> * Before students work together in 3c, drill the sentences in 3a to check they are emphasising *very/really/so* and *sorry* and giving the other underlined words enough stress.
> * Model the very weak pronunciation of *I'm* /əm/ in isolation and make sure students don't start to over-emphasise it once they start to practise at sentence level. This is particularly important for students whose L1 is a syllable-timed language (e.g., French, Chinese, Spanish), as they are more likely to try and give each syllable equal weight. In contrast, students whose L1 is a stress-timed language (e.g., Portuguese, Russian, Arabic) will probably have fewer problems with the pronunciation.

4 CONVERSATION SKILLS
Showing interest

a ▶07.19 Read through the sentences as a class. Then play Part 3 of the video or the audio recording for students to decide if they are true or false. When checking answers, ask students to correct the false sentences.

> **Answers**
> 1 F (Annie is on her way to Bristol and Leo is on his way to Reading.)
> 2 F (Annie is visiting her mum in Bristol.)
> 3 T

> **Video/Audioscript (Part 3)**
> **ANNIE** Are you on your way to Bristol?
> **LEO** No, Reading. I went to university there.
> **A** Really?
> **L** You?
> **A** Bristol. For the weekend.
> **L** To see … a friend?
> **A** A friend? No, no, my mum lives there. I go to see her every month.
> **L** Great!

b ▶07.19 In pairs, students look at the two extracts and try to remember which two words aren't correct. Check all students have the correct answers by playing the video or the audio recording again and asking students to shout *Stop!* when they hear the different words.

> **Answers**
> **ANNIE** ~~Right.~~ Really?
> **LEO** ~~Oh.~~ Great!

c Discuss the question as a class. Remind students that an important part of communication is showing that we are interested in what other people are saying.

> **Answer**
> 2 to show they are interested

> **📖 LANGUAGE NOTES**
>
> Some students may feel uncomfortable using what seems to them to be exaggerated intonation patterns for interjections such as *Great!* and *Really?*.
>
> To help students understand the importance of showing interest, drill the conversations in 4b with flat, bored intonation and use *Oh.*, rather than *Great!* and *Really?*. Ask students how they would feel if someone talked to them in that way. Then drill the conversation again, this time with *Great!* and *Really?* and the intonation patterns in 2b. Ask students which conversation they would prefer to be part of.

d ▶ 07.20 **Pronunciation** Play the recording and highlight the vowel sounds for students. Check answers as a class.

> **Answers**
> 1 No, they don't.
> 2 The sounds are short: Gr*eat!* /eɪ/, R*eally?* /ɪə/.

5 SPEAKING

a 💬 Tell students that they can now practise using all the language from the lesson with a partner. Check students understand the dialogue map before they start. In pairs, students take turns to be A and B. Monitor and correct students' pronunciation as appropriate and listen for correct usage of the target language from this lesson.

b 💬 In pairs, students practise new conversations using different reasons for being late. Remind students to be careful to use the correct intonation and to use the

phrases for emphasising and showing interest. Nominate a few pairs to perform their conversations for the class.

> ### ♀ FAST FINISHERS
>
> Ask fast finishers to practise additional conversations based on their own ideas, e.g., *someone waiting at an airport to meet a friend*, *a work colleague apologising for arriving late at a meeting.*

> ### ⊕ ADDITIONAL MATERIAL
>
> Workbook 7C
>
> Unit Progress Test

7D | SKILLS FOR WRITING
It really is hard to choose

At the end of this lesson, students will be able to:

- understand a person discussing with a friend which homestay family he would prefer to stay with
- understand an email in which someone introduces himself/herself
- link ideas using *after*, *when* and *while*
- write an email introducing themselves to a homestay family

> ### ♀ OPTIONAL LEAD-IN
>
> Books closed. Write the following question on the board: *What makes a house a home?* Give students a few ideas, e.g., *a cat or a dog*; *a comfortable sofa and a big TV; a nice garden*. Students work in small groups to think of ideas. Ask groups to share their answers with the class and write their ideas on the board.
>
> Ask students: *Do you stay in other people's houses? When? Why?* Elicit some answers, e.g., *at a friend's after a night out.* Pre-teach *stay with a homestay family* (be with a family in their house while a person studies or works) and find out if any students are staying or have ever stayed with a homestay family. If they are/have, ask them to tell the class about their experiences.
>
> Tell students that they can use the ideas and useful language from this activity to help them with their writing later in the lesson. Give them time to note down any new words or expressions. Alternatively, if you have an interactive whiteboard, save the vocabulary brainstorm for students to refer back to later in the lesson.

1 SPEAKING AND LISTENING

a 💬 Individually, students tick three ideas from the list. They then compare their ideas in pairs.

b 💬 Students work in pairs, read the profiles and answer the questions. Monitor, but don't interrupt fluency. Ask pairs to share their answers with the class and find out which family is more popular and why.

> ### ♀ EXTRA ACTIVITY
>
> Students work individually using the profiles in 1b to create a homestay family profile for their own family. When students have completed their profiles, collect them. Divide the class into small groups and give each group an equal number of profiles. Students discuss which of the profiles would be the most attractive for a foreign student coming to their country to study. If students are not comfortable talking about their own family situation in class, tell them to invent the information in their profile.

c ▶ 07.21 Students listen to the conversation for general meaning and answer the question. Play the recording and check the answer as a class.

> **Answer**
> No, he doesn't.

Audioscript

AHMED So here are the photos and the profiles of the families I can choose from.

FINN Hmm – OK so two very different kinds of families.

A Yes, it's difficult to decide.

F Well, both families look very friendly.

A Yes, they do.

F And the Conways look very kind.

A But maybe a bit quiet?

F Mm maybe. Look, the Philips like doing sport – swimming, surfing – that kind of thing.

A Yes, but I don't like going to the beach much. I like playing football.

F You mean soccer. In Australia, we say soccer, not football.

A Oh, of course, I forgot.

F And, I have to say, in Australia soccer isn't so popular. Everyone loves rugby.

A But the Conways like watching any sport, so maybe I can watch soccer with them. That'd be nice.

F Yeah, that's true. But you like listening to music, don't you?

A Yes, I do.

F And the Philips like listening to music, too.

A I'm not sure about children.

F Children are fun.

A Yes, but maybe not so quiet!

F No, not if you want to study.

A And I really want to study a lot.

F You also need to think about transport. It's quite expensive in Sydney.

A So I can save money if I stay at the Conways?

F Yeah, you probably can.

A It really is hard to choose.

F It sure is. But you are the only person who can decide!

d ▶**07.21** Students listen to the recording again for specific details and tick the true phrases. They compare in pairs. Check answers as a class.

> **Answers**
> 2 ✓ likes watching sport
> 3 ✓ likes listening to music
> 6 ✓ wants to study a lot
> 7 ✓ likes playing football

e 💬 Students work in pairs, talking about which family is good for Ahmed and why. Monitor, but don't interrupt fluency. Ask some students to share their ideas with the class. Encourage students to justify their decisions as much as possible.

> 💡 **FAST FINISHERS**
>
> Ask fast finishers to list all the personal information they know about Ahmed, e.g., *Ahmed likes playing football / listening to music.* When they finish 2b, they check what extra information in the email isn't on their lists.

2 READING

a Tell students that Ahmed thinks it would be a good idea to send an email to the Conways. Students read the email quickly and check the main reason he writes to them. Check the answer.

> **Answer**
> 3 ✓ to tell them about himself

b Tell students to read the email again in detail. Individually, students number the information in the order they find it. Encourage students to guess the meaning of any new words from the context. Check answers as a class.

> **Answers**
> 1 his home town   3 his hobbies
> 2 his family's jobs   4 his future plans

3 WRITING SKILLS
Linking ideas with *after*, *when* and *while*

a Ask students to identify the word in each sentence that is different from Ahmed's email. They then check their own answers by looking back at the email. Check answers as a class.

> **Answers**
> 1 while
> 2 when
> 3 after
> 4 When

b Individually, students complete the rules. Check answers as a class.

> **Answers**
> 1 *while*
> 2 *after*
> 3 beginning

> **CAREFUL!**
>
> A common learner error is to use *will* after *after/when/while*. Although students have not yet studied the future form in this course, it is something they may have learnt in the past and may transfer to this structure, e.g., ~~When I will be …~~ (Correct form = *When I'm in Sydney, I want to …*), ~~I want to be a teacher after I will finish …~~ (Correct form = *I want to be a teacher after I finish university*). When students are writing their emails, monitor to make sure they don't make this mistake.

c Students read the sentences and underline the correct words. Students compare in pairs. Check answers as a class.

> **Answers**
> 1 After, When
> 2 when, while
> 3 after, when
> 4 After, When
> 5 when, while

4 SPEAKING AND WRITING

> 🔄 **LOA TIP ELICITING**
>
> - Elicit some English-speaking countries as a class, e.g., Australia, Canada, New Zealand, the UK, the USA, by projecting the countries' flags one after the other onto the board.
> - Alternatively, draw a rough world map on the board. Point to the different countries and ask: *What country is this?* and *How do you spell that?*

a Use the LOA Tip to elicit some English-speaking countries as a class. Alternatively, ask students to work in pairs and brainstorm English-speaking countries. Ask pairs to share their answers with the class and collate students' ideas on the board. You may also give students information from Culture Notes on the next page.

🌍 **CULTURE NOTES**

In answer to 4a, students may suggest countries that might not exactly be considered English-speaking, but that, nevertheless, have English either as an official language or have a very large number of English speakers. The USA has more people who speak English as a first language than any other country. India is the second country although the majority of people speak English as a second language. Other countries with a significant number of English speakers include Pakistan, Nigeria and the Philippines. English is now an official language in nearly 100 countries.

b 💬 Give students one minute to think about which country they would like to visit and why. In pairs, students discuss the countries in 4a. Ask some students to share their ideas with the class. Encourage them to justify their decisions as much as possible.

c Students plan their emails, working individually. Tell them to use the ideas from the lesson and the linking words *after*, *when* and *while*. Monitor and help with vocabulary and suggest more ideas if necessary. If you're short of time, 4c–d can be completed for homework. Students could then bring their emails to the next lesson.

d Read the checklist with students before they start writing their emails. Tell them to make sure they tick each box in the checklist. Students write a first draft of their emails.

e 💬 Remind students of the importance of checking their work carefully before handing it in. In pairs, students swap emails and check that their partner has included all the ideas in 4d. They then give each other feedback. If they have missed any of the points, they prepare a second draft of their emails and make sure all areas are covered.

⊕ **ADDITIONAL MATERIAL**

Workbook 7D

UNIT 7
Review and extension

1 GRAMMAR

a Individually, students complete the text. They then check in pairs. Check answers and spelling as a class by asking individual students to write the correct answers on the board.

Answers
1	called	6	was
2	didn't come	7	landed
3	took	8	arrived
4	was	9	asked
5	waited	10	didn't have

b Students look at the example and then complete the questions. Check answers as a class and drill the questions.

Answers
2	How did you get there?	5	How long did you stay?
3	Did you have a good time?	6	Was it hot?
4	Where did you stay?		

c 💬🗨 Give students one minute to choose a place they've visited and think about the answers to the questions in 1b. In pairs, students take turns asking and answering the questions.

d Students complete the sentences, working individually. Check answers as a class.

Answers
2 Clare hates listening to Mozart.
3 Clare doesn't mind taking the metro.
4 Clare doesn't like watching football.
5 Clare likes speaking French.

💡 EXTRA ACTIVITY
Give students a spelling test using regular and irregular past simple forms and -ing forms. Test students on words that you've noticed they often have problems with. Alternatively, give each student a small slip of paper and ask them to write down one past simple or -ing form that they find difficult to spell. Collect the papers and use these words for the test. Check answers by asking individual students to write the words on the board.

2 VOCABULARY

a Individually, students complete the words. They then compare in pairs. Check answers as a class.

Answers
2	train	5	ferry
3	ship	6	scooter
4	helicopter		

b Students correct the sentences. Check answers and spelling as a class by asking individual students to write the correct answers on the board.

Answers
2	dirty	5	dangerous
3	uncomfortable	6	expensive
4	fast		

3 WORDPOWER *get*

a Tell students to close their books. On the left of the board, in a vertical column, write *arrive, become, bring, receive, take* and *travel on*. Draw an = sign in the middle of the board and ask students: *Which word can mean all of these?* Elicit *get*. Write *get* in a circle on the right of the board. Students open their books and match the questions and answers. Check answers as a class.

Answers
1 d   2 e   3 a   4 b   5 c

b Students read the verbs and match them with the answers with *get* in 3a. They then check in pairs. Check answers as a class.

Answers
1 d   2 c   3 e   4 a   5 b

c Individually, students read the story and think about what happened next. Ask some students to share their ideas with the class. They then identify the meanings of *get* in the story. Check answers as a class.

Answers
1 Students' own answers
2 a 2 receive   b 5 take or bring   c 3 travel on   d 4 arrive   e 1 become

d Tell students to classify the phrases in the box according to the meaning of *get*. Complete the first two items as an example. Ask: *What does 'get' mean in 'get angry'?* Elicit *become*. Then ask: *Which two phrases in the box can we use with 'become'?* Elicit *sad* and *better*. Individually, students match the phrases with 1–5. Check answers as a class and elicit the meanings of *get*.

Answers
1 get sad, get better
2 get a phone call, get an email
3 get a taxi, get the train
4 get to the airport, get to school
5 get a glass of water

e Before they write sentences about their lives, give students one or two examples about yourself using *get* and the phrases in 3d, e.g., *I never get angry with my students!* and *I got an email from my cousin in New Zealand yesterday.* Monitor and help as necessary. Point out errors for students to self-correct.

f 💬🗨 In pairs, students tell each other their sentences and find out how similar they are.

💡 FAST FINISHERS
Using information they learnt in 3f, ask fast finishers to complete the sentence: *We both …* in as many ways as possible, e.g., *We both get the train home in the evening.*

≫≫ Photocopiable activities: Wordpower 7

🔄 LOA TIP REVIEW YOUR PROGRESS
Students look back through the unit, think about what they've studied and decide how well they did. Students work on weak areas by using the appropriate sections of the Workbook and the Photocopiable activities.

🔁 **UNIT OBJECTIVES**

At the end of this unit, students will be able to:

- understand information, texts and conversations and exchange information about sport, sports personalities, events, free-time activities, doing exercise and getting fit
- ask for and give information about abilities
- talk about what is necessary and what isn't necessary when doing sports and free-time activities
- understand conversations in which people talk about health and how they feel
- use appropriate phrases to express sympathy
- write an article about a free-time activity

UNIT CONTENTS

G **GRAMMAR**
- can/can't, could/couldn't for ability
- have to / don't have to

V **VOCABULARY**
- Sports and exercise: *dance, do yoga, play badminton, ride a bike, skate, ski*
- Sports and exercise collocations: *do exercises / martial arts; go fishing/running/sailing/snowboarding; play football/ golf/hockey/volleyball*
- Parts of the body: *arm, back, finger, foot, hand, head, leg, neck, stomach, toe*
- Appearance: *attractive, curly/dark/blonde/long/short/straight hair, fit, good-looking, unfit*
- Linking ideas with *however*
- Adverbs of manner
- Wordpower: *tell/say*

P **PRONUNCIATION**
- *can, can't, could* and *couldn't*
- *have to*
- Stress in adjectives
- Connecting words

C **COMMUNICATION SKILLS**
- Talking about which free-time activities you could/couldn't do well as a child and which you can/can't do now
- Talking about what you have to do and have to have for different activities
- Talking about health and how you feel
- Expressing sympathy
- Writing an article about a free-time activity

GETTING STARTED

> ⚑ **OPTIONAL LEAD-IN**
>
> Write *Last week …* on the board and under it, write the following jumbled sentences and ask students to put them in order: *1 I / to the gym / five times / went*; *2 every morning / walked /to work / I*; *3 a lot of / and vegetables / I / salad, fruit, / ate*; *4 two litres / I / every day / drank / of water* (1 I went to the gym five times. 2 I walked to work every morning. 3 I ate a lot of salad, fruit and vegetables. 4 I drank two litres of water every day.)
>
> Write *I'm … and … !* on the board and ask for suggestions to complete it. Tell students to look at the title of Unit 8. Elicit the sentence: *I'm fit and healthy!*

a 💬📢 Give students one minute to think about their answers to the questions before talking about the picture as a class. You may give students information from Culture Notes below.

> 🌐 **CULTURE NOTES**
>
> This picture shows the sport sepak takraw, or kick volleyball. The sport began in Malaysia approximately 500 years ago, but it's played throughout Asia – in Cambodia, India, Indonesia, Singapore, Laos, Myanmar, Singapore, Thailand and Vietnam. Scoring is similar to volleyball, but unlike volleyball, players may not use their hands. They can only use their feet, knees, chest and head to touch the ball.

b Individually, students make a list of other sports and exercise the men in the picture would like. Help with vocabulary as necessary.

Exercises a and b can be prepared as homework before this lesson to give students time to look up unfamiliar vocabulary. Ask students to look at the picture and to prepare their answers to the questions as homework to talk about in the next lesson.

c 💬📢 Put students into pairs to share their lists and see if they thought of the same things. Ask pairs to share their answers with the class and find out how many different ideas the class had in total.

> ⚑ **EXTRA ACTIVITY**
>
> Extend the discussion and get students to talk more about the sports and exercise they thought of in Exercise b. Write the following questions on the board and put students into small groups to discuss them: *Which sports and exercise from Exercise b do you like? How often do you do them? Who do you do them with? Are you good at them? Which do you like watching? Do you watch them on TV, at a stadium or somewhere else? Which don't you like watching? Why?*

8A | THEY CAN DO THINGS MOST PEOPLE CAN'T

At the end of this lesson, students will be able to:

- read and understand a text about a sports personality
- use *can / can't*, *could / couldn't* correctly to talk about ability
- understand a podcast in which people talk about running marathons
- use a lexical set of sports and exercise words correctly
- ask for and give information about their abilities

♀ OPTIONAL LEAD-IN

Draw the Olympic rings on the board and ask students what they represent. Write sentences 1–5 under the rings and put students into pairs or small groups to try and complete them with a place or a person: *1 The first modern Olympic Games were in …* (Athens); *2 The person with the most Olympic medals is …* (Michael Phelps (at time of publication)); *3 The first Paralympic Games were in …* (Rome); *4 The Olympic torch always comes from …* (Olympia); *5 The first Olympic Games shown on television were in …* (Berlin). If students don't understand *medal* or *torch*, draw pictures on the board to clarify the meaning. Check answers as a class.

📖 VOCABULARY SUPPORT

artificial (B2) – something made by people, not a natural thing

athlete (B1) – a person who is good at physical activities like running, jumping, etc., and who is often in competitions

disabled (B1) – someone who has trouble doing things because of a physical or mental problem

meningitis – a very dangerous infection usually caused by bacteria, viruses or fungi in the brain and spine

surprised (A2) – the feeling when something happens that you didn't expect

1 READING

a 💬📱 Read the questions with the students and check that they understand that questions 3a–d refer to the picture of Jonnie Peacock (the man on SB p. 80). Put students into pairs to ask and answer the questions. Don't check answers at this point.

b Students read the text quickly and check their answers to 1a. Ask students what other things they wanted to know about Jonnie Peacock and see if the questions they wrote in 1a were answered in the text. If you wish, give students information from Culture Notes below.

Answers
3 a He runs / does track.
   b He's from Cambridge, England.
   c He's at the Paralympic Games.
   d Students' own questions

🌍 CULTURE NOTES

Jonnie Peacock (b. 1993) started competing in track and field competitions in 2009, but he didn't become a household name until the final of the 100 metres at the London 2012 Paralympic Games. At the age of 19, 14 years after spending four days in a coma and losing his right leg, he set a new Paralympic record with his winning time of 10.90 seconds. He was the youngest athlete competing in the final and his win was watched by over six million people. Peacock also won gold for the 100 metres at the IPC Athletics World Championships in Lyon, France, in 2013. He was awarded an MBE in 2013 for his services to track and field. Then, in 2016, he won a gold medal again at the 2016 Paralympic Games in Rio de Janeiro with an even faster time.

c Tell students to read the text again in detail. Individually, students answer the questions. Check answers as a class. You may wish to help students with words in the Vocabulary Support box.

Answers
1 He was like most boys. He loved to do sports.
2 He became very ill with meningitis. The doctors saved his life, but they couldn't save his right leg.
3 They were surprised because he could do so much only 18 months after he lost his leg.
4 Some of the Paralympic athletes can't walk and some can't see at all or very well. But in their sports, they can do things that most people can't.
5 Jonnie is famous because he won a gold medal in the 2012 and 2016 Paralympic Games. He also competed on a TV programme called *Strictly Come Dancing*.

♀ EXTRA ACTIVITY

Ask students to read the text again and decide if sentences 1–5 are true or false: *1 Jonnie nearly died because his parents didn't take him to hospital.* (F – His parents took him to hospital and he nearly died there.) *2 Running was always Jonnie's favourite sport.* (F – Football was his favourite sport when he was a child.) *3 Jonnie's parents gave him his artificial leg.* (F – The doctors gave him his artificial leg.) *4 One of the first activities Jonnie did with his new artificial leg was dancing.* (T) *5 Jonnie started to practise a lot a year before the London 2012 Paralympic Games.* (F – He started to practise a lot two years before the London 2012 Paralympic Games.)

d Individually, students underline the parts of the text that surprise them. They then tell a partner.

e 💬📱 Discuss the question as a class.

2 GRAMMAR
can / can't, *could / couldn't* for ability

a Books closed. On the board, write *I … speak English really well.* Point to yourself, show students a confident face and then point to the gap. Elicit the missing word (*can*) and write it in the sentence. Then, write on the board *I … speak Chinese at all.* (Change *Chinese* to a language you can't speak, if necessary.) Again, point to yourself, but this time show students a frustrated face. Elicit the missing word (*can't*) and write it on the board. Ask students: *Do we use 'can' to talk about something that's possible or something that's necessary?* Elicit *something that's possible*. Students open their books and complete the exercise. Check answers as a class.

Answers
1 couldn't
2 could
3 can't
4 can; can't
5 Can

93

b Give students one minute to read the rules and complete them. Check answers as a class.

> **Answers**
> present; past
> question

c Elicit the two correct answers as a class.

> **Answers**
> b and c

d ▶ **08.01** **Pronunciation** Play the recording for students to listen and answer the question. Check the answer as a class. Drill the sentences, making sure students are not pronouncing /l/ in *could/couldn't*.

> **Answer**
> 1 b
> 2 no

⊙ CAREFUL!

There are several common student mistakes with *can/can't*, *could/couldn't* for ability. Highlight the following typical errors:

- using the present in place of the past and vice versa – this type of error may be obvious, e.g., *... and can't believe it.* (Correct form = *His parents were very surprised and* **couldn't** *believe it*).

- using *to* + the infinitive of the verb after *can/can't/could/couldn't*, e.g., *I couldn't to swim ...* (Correct form = *I* **couldn't** *swim when I was a child*), or using *-ing*, e.g., *Later, we can playing football ...* (Correct form = *Later, we* **can play** *football in the park*).

e ≫ ▶ **08.02** Students read the information in Grammar Focus 8A on SB p. 152. Play the recording where indicated and ask students to listen and repeat. Students then complete the exercises. Check answers as a class, making sure students are not confusing past and present and are using the infinitive after *can/can't*, *could/couldn't*. Tell students to go to SB p. 81.

> **Answers (Grammar Focus 8A SB p. 153)**
> **a** 2 couldn't 4 can't 6 can
> 3 can 5 couldn't 7 could
> **b** 2 Rob couldn't cook a meal when he was a boy. He can cook a meal now.
> 3 Rob could ride a bike when he was a boy. He can't ride a bike now.
> 4 Rob couldn't run 25 km when he was a boy. He can run 25 km now.
> 5 Rob couldn't speak Spanish when he was a boy. He can speak Spanish now.
> **c** 2 She ~~cans~~ can speak ...
> 3 ... ~~you can swim~~ can you swim?
> 4 I could ~~ran~~ run ...
> 5 I ~~didn't could~~ couldn't understand ...
> 6 ~~Does he can~~ Can he cook?
> 7 Yes, he ~~did~~ could.

♀ FAST FINISHERS

Ask fast finishers to write sentences like those in Grammar Focus, Exercise b about themselves, e.g., *I couldn't speak English when I was a girl. I can speak English now.*

3 LISTENING

a 💬🔊 Give students one minute to read items 1–4. Ask students how they would form the questions to ask their classmates about items 1–4. Write on the board the correct forms: *Do you go running? Have you ever run in a marathon or half-marathon? How often do you exercise?* Students get up and ask and answer each other's questions to find someone who 1) often goes running, 2) never goes running, 3) once ran in a marathon or half-marathon and 4) exercises once a week or more. As you monitor, don't interrupt fluency. Once it appears that students have asked most or all of their classmates, ask them to share their findings in complete sentences.

b Give students one minute to read the question and form an opinion. Take feedback as a class and encourage students to justify their answers as much as possible.

c ▶ **08.03** Play the recording for students to listen for general meaning and answer the question. Check the answers as a class.

> **Answers**
> 1 running, exercise
> 2 running too much

Audioscript

HOST Hanna, welcome.
HANNA Thank you.
HO So, it's an interesting question. Running is very popular, lots of people train for marathons. But is it actually good for you?
HA Well, yes, running is good for you. It's good for your heart, it makes you feel good, it's fun ...
HO But it can be bad for you?
HA Sure. If you train over a long time or if you do too much, it can be bad for your heart. That's quite clear.
HO OK, someone wants to train for a marathon. What do you tell them? How can they stay safe?
HA Well, first I'd say, don't do a marathon; start with a half-marathon!
HO OK, half-marathon.
HA And then – basically follow three rules.
HO OK.
HA Number one: don't do too much. Don't go from nothing to two hours' running. Start with 20 minutes, then do a bit more, then a bit more.
HO So you build up slowly.
HA Exactly. Then number two: drink a lot of water, and I mean a lot. When you run, your body gets hot, so you need water. You see people in marathons sometimes – they seem just fine, then suddenly boom, they're down. They can't continue. Usually – I'd say, 70, 80 percent of the time – it's because they didn't drink enough water. Simple as that.
HO OK, so water. What's rule number three?
HA Listen to your body; that's really important. You feel tired ... stop. Your foot hurts ... stop. People often fight against it. They think, 'Yeah, I can do this', but that's how you have problems. And also – enjoy it. It's for fun, it's not your work.
HO OK, so that's rule number four!
HA I guess so, yeah.

d ▶ **08.03** Students listen to the recording again for specific details and answer the questions. They compare in pairs. Check answers as a class.

> **Answers**
> Rule No. 1: Don't <u>do too much.</u>
> At the start, run <u>for 20 minutes.</u>
> Rule No. 2: <u>Drink</u> a lot of <u>water.</u>
> When you run, you <u>need water.</u>
> Rule No. 3: Listen <u>to your body.</u>
> If you feel tired, <u>stop.</u>
> If your foot hurts, <u>stop.</u>
> Rule No. 4: <u>Enjoy it!</u>

e 💬🔊 Students work in small groups, discussing their ideas. Groups share their answers with the class.

4 VOCABULARY Sport and exercise

a Individually, students match the words with the pictures. Check answers as a class. Drill each word.

Answers
1	play badminton	4	ice-skate
2	do yoga	5	ride a bike
3	dance	6	ski

b ≫ ▶ 08.04–08.05 Students complete the exercises in Vocabulary Focus 8A on SB p. 167. Play the recording for students to complete the Pronunciation activities. Monitor Exercise f and check other answers as a class. Tell students to go back to SB p. 81.

Answers (Vocabulary Focus SB p. 167)

a
1	judo	5	rugby	9	snowboarding
2	fishing	6	volleyball	10	football
3	golf	7	running	11	exercises
4	tennis	8	sailing		

b

go	play	do
fishing	golf	judo
running	tennis	exercises
sailing	rugby	
snowboarding	volleyball	
	football	

c 1 *play* 2 *go* 3 *do*
d Football: short
   Judo: long
e 1 short 2 short 3 long 4 short 5 long 6 long
f Students' own answers

💡 FAST FINISHERS
Ask fast finishers to add more activities to the columns in Vocabulary Focus, Exercise b, e.g., *go climbing/surfing*, *play badminton/basketball*, *do aerobics*.

c Individually, students read the sentences and put them in order. They then check in pairs. Check answers as a class. Ask students which of the sentences is true for them.

Answers
1 c (I can play baseball really well.)
2 a (I can play baseball quite well.)
3 b (I can't play baseball very well.)
4 d (I can't play baseball at all.)

d 💬🔲 In pairs or small groups, students ask and answer questions about the activities. Monitor, but don't interrupt fluency unless students make mistakes with *can/can't*.

5 SPEAKING

a Give students a few minutes to prepare and write sentences for the four categories. Monitor and help as necessary.

💡 EXTRA ACTIVITY
Before students work together in 5b, drill some example statements and questions to check that students are stressing them correctly. Check that students understand that in positive sentences and questions, *can/can't/could/couldn't* isn't stressed, e.g., I can <u>dance</u> the <u>samba</u>. Can you <u>dance</u> the <u>samba</u>? However, in negative sentences, both *can't/couldn't* and the main verb are stressed, e.g., I <u>can't</u> <u>dance</u> the <u>samba</u>. The rhythm is very important as native speakers differentiate positive from negative primarily by the stress of the sentence, not by the /t/ on the end of *can't*, which, as in the example above (I can't dance …), is often omitted.

Students may also benefit from hearing you clap out the rhythm for them so that they can then apply the rhythm to the sentence, e.g, I can <u>dance</u> the <u>samba</u> would be 'clap clap CLAP clap CLAP clap'.

b 💬🔲 Students work in small groups, asking and answering each other's questions to find out if they can or could do the same things. As you monitor, don't interrupt fluency, but note down any mistakes with the content of this lesson. After 5c, write the mistakes on the board and ask students to correct them.

c 💬🔲 Read the examples with the class. Then, ask students to share the things they have in common.

🔄 LOA TIP REVIEW AND REFLECT
- Draw a scale on the board from 1 to 5. Under 1, write: *This is difficult for me.* Under 5, write: *This is easy for me.*
- Students put their hands behind their backs. Tell them that you will count down (3, 2, 1 …) and then you want them to show you between one and five fingers, depending on how confident they feel about the topics *can/can't* and then *could/couldn't*.

⊕ ADDITIONAL MATERIAL
Workbook 8A

Photocopiable activities: Grammar 8A, Vocabulary 8A, Pronunciation 8A

Documentary video Unit 8 *Fit and Healthy*

Video worksheet Unit 8 *Fit and Healthy*

8B HOW EASY IS IT TO GET FIT?

At the end of this lesson, students will be able to:

- read and understand a text about a new type of exercise
- use *have to / don't have to* correctly to talk about rules and things they need and don't need to do
- understand people talking about doing exercise
- use a lexical set of parts of the body correctly
- talk about what they have to do and have to have for different activities

◉ OPTIONAL LEAD-IN

Before students arrive, write a mini-questionnaire on the board:

Are you fit and healthy?
Can you …
– swim for 30 minutes?
– ride a bike 10 kilometres?
– run a half-marathon?
– do a lot of exercise and not feel tired?

Do you …
– eat healthy food?
– drink two litres of water every day?
– sleep eight hours every night?
– go to the gym every week?

As students arrive, put them into pairs or small groups to talk about the questions. Monitor and check that they are using the correct auxiliary verbs in the short answers. Invite students to share their answers with the class and find out if any students can answer yes to all the questions.

1 READING

a 💬 Pre-teach the phrase *get fit* (to become healthy and strong after a lot of exercise). Give students one minute to think about their answers to the questions. They then talk in pairs or small groups about getting fit and doing exercise. If you used the optional lead-in, students can also discuss which of the things in the mini-questionnaire they think are important for getting fit.

b Tell students they should read only the first paragraph of the article (*Only Five Minutes of Exercise a Day* …). They then work individually, answering the questions in that paragraph.

c 💬 Elicit from the class what they think the new type of exercise is. They then read the rest of the text for general meaning to find out if they were correct. You may then wish to teach the word *intensity* (the level you do something, usually high, medium or low).

> **Answer**
> The new type of exercise is High Intensity Interval Training (HIIT).

d Students read the text again in detail. Individually, they complete the fact sheet. Check answers as a class. You may wish to help students with words in the Vocabulary Support box.

> **Answers**
> warm up ➔ 20 to 30 seconds of intense exercise ➔ rest (repeat 2 times)
> How often? Time: a few minutes a day
> Good for: Getting fit, preventing diabetes and heart disease

📖 VOCABULARY SUPPORT

diabetes – a problem where the body can't control the quantity of sugar in the blood correctly

heart disease – a serious problem with the heart, often caused by bad diet and/or insufficient exercise

muscle (B2) – the parts of your body that are connected to bones and make them move

scientist (B1) – a person that works in science

e 💬 Discuss the questions as a class and find out if any students have tried an exercise routine like HIIT.

2 GRAMMAR *have to / don't have to*

a Books closed. Write incomplete sentences 1–3 on the board and ask students to complete them orally as a class. Don't complete the sentences on the board yet. Drill the sentences. Students open their books and complete the sentences. Check answers by completing the sentences on the board.

> **Answers**
> 1 have to
> 2 don't have to
> 3 have to

b Individually, students underline the correct answers. They compare in pairs. Check answers as a class.

> **Answers**
> a need to
> b don't need to
> c need to

🔄 LOA TIP CONCEPT CHECKING

- Check that students have fully understood the meaning of *have to / don't have to*. Write sentences 1–3 and meanings a–c on the board. Ask students to match 1–3 with a–c: *1 You don't have to bring a dictionary to class. 2 You have to be quiet during the exam. 3 You have to spend more time studying. a This is a rule. b This is something that is necessary. c This is something that isn't necessary.* (Answers: 1 c, 2 a, 3 b)

- Focus students' attention on the negative (*You don't have to bring a dictionary to class.*) and ask: *Is it necessary to bring a dictionary to class?* (no), *Is there a problem if you bring a dictionary to class?* (no), *Can you do it if you want?* (yes).

c ▶ 08.06 Pronunciation Play the recording for students to answer the questions. Check answers as a class. Drill the sentences.

> **Answers**
> 1 /f/   2 unstressed

CAREFUL!

At this level, students will probably use *have to* correctly. However, when they are not working on it in controlled exercises, they may inadvertently substitute *must* in contexts where it isn't appropriate, e.g., ~~*Why do I must practise?*~~ (Correct form = *Why do I **have to** practise?*). The most common error with the negative is the formation. Students may make the negative with *nothing*, e.g., ~~*You have to pay nothing!*~~ (Correct form = *You **don't** have to pay **anything**!*) or may omit the auxiliary *don't*, e.g., ~~*I have not to take the bus …*~~ (Correct form = *I **don't have to** take the bus to work. I can walk.*).

d ≫ ▶ 08.07 Students read the information in Grammar Focus 8B on SB p. 152. Play the recording where indicated and ask students to listen and repeat. Students then complete the exercises. Check answers as a class, making sure students are forming the negative sentences with the auxiliary *don't* correctly. Tell students to go back to SB p. 83.

Answers (Grammar Focus 8B SB p. 153)
a 2 f   3 g   4 h   5 c   6 b   7 a   8 e
b 2 A Do you have to buy; I do   6 I have to give; you don't
   3 I don't have to pay   7 does he have to be
   4 I have to wear   8 you have to walk
   5 do we have to do
c Students' own answers

FAST FINISHERS

Ask fast finishers to write sentences about things they *have to / don't have to* do in class, e.g., *We have to speak only in English.*, *We don't have to do homework every night.*

e Students work individually and write their sentences. Monitor and point out errors for students to self-correct.

f 💬📱 Read the example with the students. Then, put them into pairs to tell each other about things they have to do and ask each other follow-up questions. Monitor and listen for correct use of *have to / don't have to* and check that students are forming the questions correctly.

EXTRA ACTIVITY

Read out the following to students: *I'm a(n) … . I have to answer the phone, write emails and take messages. I usually have to make people coffee, too! I don't have to work at weekends, but sometimes I have to work late in the evening.* Ask students to write down what job they think you're describing. When all students have decided, tell them to say the job at the same time to find out if they are correct. Count down *3, 2, 1 …* and elicit the answer from the class. (*receptionist*)

Individually, students then prepare their own clues for a job. Monitor and help as necessary. Then, put students into small groups to read their sentences and try to guess the jobs they are describing.

3 LISTENING

a 💬📱 Tell students to look at pictures a and b. In pairs, students answer the questions. Check the answer to question 1 as a class.

Answers
1 yoga
2 Students' own answers

b ▶ 08.08 Play the recording for students to listen for general meaning and match the speakers and the pictures. Check answers as a class.

Answers
Stella – picture a; Mariana – picture b

Audioscript

STELLA Yoga is a great way to be fit, strong and healthy, and anyone can do it. My friends and I go to yoga classes every week. My favourite yoga position is quite difficult, but it looks really good. You put your arms on the floor, then you put your legs in the air and try to touch your head with your toes. It's not easy, but I love it. But, please don't try it at home! I needed years of practice to do that!

MARIANA I only started yoga three weeks ago. I'm very lazy, so I wanted to do some exercise that's easy. But, you know, it's not so simple! You need to think about how you move different parts of your body: your stomach, arms and legs … And sometimes you don't move at all – you just stand in one place for two or three minutes. But my favourite part is the end of the class. We all lie on the floor and relax for five minutes. Can I tell you something? Last class, I was so tired that I fell sleep on the floor in the middle of the studio!

c ▶ 08.08 Students listen to the recording again for specific details and decide if the sentences are true or false. They then check in pairs. When checking answers, ask students to correct the false sentences and, if possible, to justify their answers.

Answers
1 T
2 F (Her favourite yoga exercise is quite difficult to do.)
3 T
4 F (Mariana doesn't think beginner yoga is easy.)
5 T
6 F (The end of each yoga lesson is her favourite part of the class.)

4 VOCABULARY   Parts of the body

a Books closed. Pre-teach the vocabulary and correct pronunciation by pointing to parts of your body and eliciting the word if students know it, or saying it yourself if they don't. Drill each word. Don't allow students to write anything down. As you introduce new items, keep going back to revise items you've already taught by pointing at that part of your body again. Increase the pace as you go to increase the challenge for students. When you've taught all the words, students open their books and match the words in the box with the picture. Check answers as a class.

Answers
1 head   6 hand
2 back   7 finger
3 neck   8 leg
4 stomach   9 foot
5 arm   10 toe

b 💬📱 In pairs or small groups, students talk about the questions. Check answers as a class.

Possible answers
1 arm, back, finger, foot, hand, leg, neck, toe
2 back, head, neck, stomach

c ⟫ ▶ 08.09–08.10 Students complete the exercises in Vocabulary Focus 8B on SB p. 168. Play the recording for students to check their answers to Exercise c and complete the Pronunciation activity. Monitor Exercises e and h and check other answers as a class. Tell students to go back to SB p. 83.

> **Answers (Vocabulary Focus 8B SB p. 168)**
> **a** 1 f 2 h 3 d 4 a
> **b** short/long
> **c** b She's got short curly dark hair.
> c He's got short curly fair hair.
> e He's got long straight dark hair.
> g She's got long curly fair hair.
> **d** and **e** Students' own answers
> **f** 1 e 2 a 3 d 4 f 5 b 6 c
> **g** prett|y a|ttrac|tive good-look|ing

💡 **FAST FINISHERS**

Ask fast finishers to write sentences to describe people in their families using the vocabulary for appearance.

5 SPEAKING

a Give students a few minutes to choose one of the activities and make notes. Monitor and help as necessary.

b 💬🗩 Put students into pairs. Students then tell each other about what people have to do to get ready for the activity they have chosen and what they have to have. They try to guess each other's activity.

> ⊕ **ADDITIONAL MATERIAL**
>
> Workbook 8B
>
> Photocopiable activities: Grammar 8B, Vocabulary 8B

8C

EVERYDAY ENGLISH
I feel a bit tired

At the end of this lesson, students will be able to:

- understand informal conversations in which people talk about health and how they feel
- use appropriate phrases to talk about health and how they feel
- use appropriate phrases to express sympathy
- join words ending in /t/ and /d/ to the next word in a sentence
- talk about health and how they feel

💡 **OPTIONAL LEAD-IN**

Tell students you're going to give them four clues to guess a sport or free-time activity. Read the following clues: *1 You have to play this game in a team. 2 You can watch this game at a stadium. 3 You can't touch the ball with your hands. 4 You don't have to wear special clothes or shoes to play it.* (football) Repeat the process with: *1 You have to do this activity with a partner. 2 You can do it at a sports centre. 3 You can't wear shoes to do this activity. 4 You have to wear special white clothes.* (judo)

Put students into pairs to choose another sport or free-time activity and write four clues. If students use *can/could* and *have to / don't have to*, check they are using them correctly. However, don't insist that they use them in every sentence. Pairs then read their clues to the class for other students to guess.

1 LISTENING

a 💬🗩 Ask students: *Is Dan fit and healthy?* (no) *What about Leo?* (yes). Then check students remember where the characters work. Ask: *Where do Dan and Leo work?* (in an office) *What about Martina?* (at the gym). In pairs, students then look at the pictures and answer the questions. Elicit students' ideas, but don't check answers at this point.

b ▶ 08.11 Play Part 1 of the video or the audio recording for students to check their answers in 1a and find out what Martina tells Dan to do. Check answers as a class.

> **Answers**
> 1 at the gym
> 2 tired and ill
> 3 picture b
> 4 Students' own answers
> Martina tells Dan to sit down and drink some water.

> **Video/Audioscript (Part 1)**
> **LEO** Right, the running machine next!
> **MARTINA** Hey, are you OK? … Are you all right?
> **DAN** Um … , I think so.
> **M** Are you sure? You don't look well.
> **D** Yes, I feel a bit tired. Actually, I feel awful …
> **M** Oh dear. Come and sit down. I'll get you some water. … Here's some water.

c ▶ 08.12 Read through the questions with the class. Play Part 2 of the video or the audio recording for students to choose the correct answers. Check answers as a class.

> **Answers**
> 1 c
> 2 b

Video/Audioscript (Part 2)

MARTINA Here's some water.

DAN Thanks.

M You poor thing. What's the matter?

D I'm not sure. I don't feel well.

M Have you got a headache?

D No, I haven't.

M Does your back hurt?

D No, nothing like that.

M Your face looks red, but that's probably from the exercise. … I don't think you've got a temperature.

D No, I'm sure I haven't. I don't feel well, that's all.

LEO Are you OK, Dan?

D Yes, fine.

L Is he OK?

M Yeah, I'm sure he's fine. … Did you have lunch?

D No … I didn't have time for lunch. I had too much work to do.

M What about breakfast?

D Just a coffee – I was late for work, remember?

M Oh, yes. So nothing to eat all day?

D I … well … um … no. It was a busy day.

M Poor you. Well, I'm not surprised you don't feel well. You have to work so hard you don't have time to eat!

L That's right. Poor Dan. Are you OK?

D Yes, yes, I'm fine.

L Are you sure you're OK?

D Yes, really!

L Great! There's an aerobics class now. Let's go.

M Come on. I'll take you home.

2 USEFUL LANGUAGE
Talking about health and how you feel

a Individually, students complete the mini-conversations.

b ▶ 08.11–08.12 Play Parts 1 and 2 of the video or the audio recording again for students to check their answers in 2a. Check answers as a class.

> **Answers**
> 1 all right
> 2 look well
> 3 feel a bit tired
> 4 the matter
> 5 feel well

c Read through the words in the box and check students understand the meaning by asking them: *What's 'toothache'?* In monolingual classes, you could ask: *What's 'toothache' in (students' L1)?* Individually, students decide which words in the box they can use instead of the words in bold in the sentences. They then check in pairs. Check answers as a class.

> **Answers**
> I'm sick/hungry/ill.
> I've got a stomach ache / a cold / toothache / a temperature.
> My arm/foot hurts.

d 💬 In pairs, students take turns to invent health problems and ask each other about how they feel. Monitor and check students are using *feel*, *have got* and *hurts* for the correct problems.

> **💡 EXTRA ACTIVITY**
>
> Play a 'listing game' (see p. 154) with students. Mime having a sudden pain from your tooth and say *I've got …* to elicit *toothache*. Then mime a pain in your back and say *My back …* to elicit *hurts*. Point to your tooth and then at your back to elicit *I've got toothache and my back hurts*. Clutch your stomach and look ill to elicit *I feel sick.* and then point to all three things to elicit *I've got toothache, my back hurts and I feel sick*. Gesture for another student to continue and add another problem and elicit it from the class. They then nominate another student to continue and so on until the list is too long to remember. Students can then play in small groups.

3 CONVERSATION SKILLS
Expressing sympathy

a Suddenly hold your hand up to your head and groan loudly. Elicit an appropriate question from the class, e.g., *Are you all right?* or *What's the matter?* Say: *I'm not sure. I don't feel well. I've got a headache and I feel sick.* Gesture to elicit a response and see if students can remember an appropriate phrase from the video or audio, e.g., *Oh dear.*, *You poor thing.* or *Poor you.* Students look at the extracts from the video/audio and complete what Martina says. Check answers as a class.

> **Answers**
> 1 dear
> 2 thing
> 3 Poor

b Answer the question as a class.

> **Answer**
> 1 I feel sorry for you.

c ▶ 08.13 Play the recording for students to answer the questions. Check answers as a class. Drill the sentences.

> **Answers**
> 1 b the last word
> 2 The intonation goes down at the end.

d 💬 In pairs, students take turns saying the sentences and giving sympathy with appropriate phrases.

> **⟳ LOA TIP MONITORING**
>
> • As students practise telling each other the problems, monitor and check they are using correct sentence stress and falling intonation in the phrases for expressing sympathy. If necessary, clap out the rhythm of the sentences and phrases for them so that they can then apply the rhythm to the sentence, e.g., *You poor thing*. would be 'clap clap CLAP'. You could also show students the downward movement at the end of the phrases using hand gestures to give them a visual reference.

4 PRONUNCIATION Joining words

a ▶ 08.14 Play the recording for students to listen to sentences 1–4 and underline the correct words in the sentence. They then check in pairs. Check answers as a class.

> **Answers**
> joins; no

> **📖 LANGUAGE NOTES**
>
> Joining words can cause serious problems for students trying to understand English spoken by native speakers. The most common example of this is covered in 4a, when, in connected speech, a word which ends in /t/ and /d/ transfers this sound to the beginning of the following word, or even loses it completely. This type of exercise helps students understand that what they hear in spoken English may not correspond with breaks between words when the words are written down.

b 💬🔊 Students work in pairs, practising saying the sentences and giving replies. Monitor and correct students' pronunciation as appropriate.

5 SPEAKING

a–b ⟫ Divide the class into pairs and assign A and B roles. Student As read the first card on SB p. 85 and Student Bs read the first card on SB p. 134. Students then role play the conversation. Monitor, but don't interrupt fluency unless students make mistakes with the content of this lesson. Students then read the second card and role play the second situation.

💡 **FAST FINISHERS**

Ask fast finishers to close their books and invent a similar conversation without looking at the phrases in 2a or 3a to help them.

⊕ **ADDITIONAL MATERIAL**

Workbook 8C

Photocopiable activities: Pronunciation 8C

Unit Progress Test

8D SKILLS FOR WRITING

However, I improved quickly

At the end of this lesson, students will be able to:

- understand an informal conversation in which people talk about a free-time activity
- ask and answer questions about something they do in their free time
- understand an article about a free-time activity
- link ideas with *however*
- use adverbs of manner correctly
- write an article about a free-time activity

💡 **OPTIONAL LEAD-IN**

Write the following free-time activities on the board: *using social media, exercising, eating at restaurants, online shopping, watching TV*. Tell students that these are five of the most popular free-time activities in the UK. Put students into pairs or small groups and ask them to put them in order from 1 to 5 (with 1 being the favourite activity). Ask groups to share their answers with the class and tell students the correct order. (*1 watching TV, 2 using social media, 3 eating at restaurants, 4 online shopping, 5 exercising*) Ask students if they think the order would be similar or different in their country and ask them if they are surprised by any of the things that are or aren't on the list.

1 SPEAKING AND LISTENING

a 💬🔊 Read the questions with the students and, if necessary, check the meaning of the six items in 1 by referring students to the pictures. Students then work in pairs or small groups, asking and answering the questions. If you used the optional lead-in, students can also discuss the five extra activities on the board. Invite students to share their answers with the class and ask students what their favourite free-time activity is.

b Point to the picture of Gina and Andy next to the staff email and ask students: *Where do they work?* (in an office) and *What do you think they do?* (businessman/ businesswoman, manager, receptionist, etc.). Students then read the email and answer the questions. Check answers as a class.

> **Answers**
> 1 b It's a bit boring.
> 2 a information about their free time

c ▶ 08.15 Play the recording for students to listen for general meaning and answer the questions. Check answers as a class. If your students work, ask them: *Would you write an article for your company blog? Why / Why not?*

> **Answers**
> 1 cycling
> 2 No, he doesn't.

Audioscript

GINA Did you see the email about writing an article for the company blog?

ANDY Yes, I did.

G I suppose it's true. We don't know each other very well. I mean, I've got no idea if you have a hobby or not. You seem fit so … I don't know … maybe you do some kind of sport?

A Yeah, you're right. About a year ago, a friend of mine asked me to go cycling with him. I laughed and said, 'I can't do that – I don't have a bike.' 'No problem', he said. 'I can lend you one.' Well, I went and it was amazing. About two weeks later, I bought my own bike.

G That's great!

A Yeah, I go cycling all the time – almost every day after work. I love it because it's a way of keeping fit and being outdoors at the same time. I could never go to a gym!

G No, I hate gyms, too.

A Cycling can be a bit dangerous in the city, and you always have to be careful in the traffic. A couple of months ago, a car sort of hit me.

G Oh dear!

A I wasn't hurt badly – I just hurt my arm and my foot a bit. But I try to get out of the city into the country. For example, last weekend I went for a two-day ride in the hills. There was almost no one on the road. It was amazing – I couldn't believe it.

G Well, there's something I didn't know about. You could write an article about that.

A Me? Write an article? No, I couldn't do that. I haven't got time.

d ▶08.15 Students listen to the recording again for specific details and match the beginnings with the endings of the sentences. They then check in pairs. Check answers as a class.

Answers
1 f   4 d
2 a   5 c
3 b   6 e

💡 **EXTRA ACTIVITY**

Ask students to listen again and decide if sentences 1–5 are true or false: *1 Andy and Gina are good friends.* (F – They don't know each other very well.) *2 Gina thinks Andy looks healthy.* (T) *3 Andy's friend lent him a bike the first time he went cycling.* (T) *4 Gina and Andy both love the gym.* (F – They both hate gyms.) *5 Andy hurt his hand and his leg badly.* (F – Andy hurt his arm and his foot a bit.)

e Students work individually. They think about an activity and answer the questions. Tell students to make notes, but not write complete sentences. Monitor and help as necessary.

🔄 **LOA TIP ELICITING**

- When students have finished making their notes in 1e, give them an opportunity to revise question words and brainstorm useful questions before continuing. To elicit *what, where, when, who, which, whose,* etc., write a large *W* on the board and say: *Tell me question words!* Point out that some common questions start with *H* and elicit *how, how often, how much/many,* etc.

- Ask students to look at their notes from 1e and try to predict questions that their partner could ask them, e.g., *Why did you start doing it?, How much does it cost to do it?.* As students share their questions with the class, write the questions on the board for students to refer to in 1f. If students need more support, consider giving them prompts to help them formulate useful questions, e.g., *Why / start?, How much / cost / do?.*

f 💬 Tell students that in this activity the emphasis is on communication, not on perfect English. In pairs, students ask and answer questions about their activities.

💡 **FAST FINISHERS**

Ask fast finishers to write a short paragraph to summarise the information their partner told them.

2 READING

a Point to the picture of Dylan and the article and say: *This is Dylan. He works for the same company as Andy and Gina. He wrote this article for the company blog. What's his favourite free-time activity?* Elicit *hiking.* Students then read the article quickly and tick the things that are the same. Check answers as a class.

Answers
1 ✓ they do their free-time activities outdoors
3 ✓ they get fit doing their free-time activities

b Tell students to read the article again in detail and decide if the sentences are true or false and correct the false sentences. They then compare in pairs. Check answers as a class.

Answers
1 T
2 F (He didn't like the idea of hiking immediately because it didn't sound very interesting.)
3 T
4 T
5 F (It's easy to learn how to go hiking because you only have to know how to walk.)

3 WRITING SKILLS
Linking ideas with *however*; adverbs of manner

a Books closed. Write the example sentences on the board, leaving a gap in place of *However.* Point to the gap and ask students: *What's this word?* If students suggest *but,* point clearly at the full stop and tell them that we don't usually start a new sentence with *but.* Elicit *however.* Students then open their books and answer the question. Check the answer as a class.

Answer
Yes, it is.

b Students read Dylan's article again and underline three more examples of *however.* Check answers as a class.

Answers
However, I was quite unfit.
However, I improved quickly …
However, you have to buy special boots …
We use a comma after *however.*

c Students work individually, linking the sentences with *however.* Monitor and check that students are writing them as two sentences and putting a comma after *however.* Check answers as a class.

Answers
1 c I can only do very simple exercises. However, I feel really fit.
2 b I started doing yoga about six years ago. However, I can't do the difficult positions.
3 a I fell off my bike and hurt my leg. However, I didn't stop cycling.

d Read the example sentence and answer the question as a class.

Answer
It tells us how he did it.

e Individually, students look at the article in 2a again and find the adverbs that go with the verbs. Check answers as a class.

Answers
1 walk slowly; walk quite fast
2 improve quickly

f Read the rule with the class and elicit which adverb from the article is different.

Answer
Fast is different because it is irregular.

4 WRITING

a Students work individually to plan an article about a free-time activity. Suggest they write about the activity they talked about in 1f, but allow them to choose a different activity if they prefer. Monitor and help with vocabulary and suggest ideas if necessary.

b Remind students to use adverbs of manner when writing their articles. If you're short of time, this exercise can be completed for homework. Students could then bring their articles to the next lesson.

c In pairs, students swap articles and check their partner's work. They then give each other feedback.

♀ EXTRA ACTIVITY

If you normally use a code or abbreviations when correcting students' written work, e.g., *GR* for a grammar mistake, *WW* for a wrong word, *SP* for spelling, remind students of the system in place and ask them, in pencil, to mark mistakes in their partner's work. If you don't normally use a code or abbreviations, ask students to circle things in pencil which they think their partner should check. Monitor and help as necessary. If students have not included the items in 4c, or have made any other mistakes, they prepare a second draft of the article.

⊕ ADDITIONAL MATERIAL

Workbook 8D

UNIT 8
Review and extension

1 VOCABULARY

a Complete the first sentence as an example with the class. Students then complete the other sentences with the words in the box. Check answers as a class.

> **Answers**
> 1 baseball 2 ski 3 cycling 4 badminton 5 dance 6 yoga

b Students look at pictures 1–3 and then complete the words for the body. Check answers and spelling by asking individual students to write the correct answers on the board.

> **Answers**
> 1 head, neck 2 arm, hand, finger 3 leg, foot, toe

2 GRAMMAR

a Individually, students complete the text. They then check in pairs. Check answers as a class.

> **Answers**
> 1 can   4 can't
> 2 can   5 can
> 3 could   6 couldn't

b Students complete the sentences with the correct form of *have to*. Check answers as a class.

> **Answers**
> 1 have to   4 have to
> 2 don't have to   5 has to
> 3 Do (I) have to

3 WORDPOWER *tell / say*

a Books closed. Dictate sentences 1–3, saying *beep* instead of *told* and *say*. Students listen and write down the sentences. They then check in pairs and try to decide together the word they think can complete each sentence. Check that they understand that they don't have to use the same word in all three sentences. Students open their books, look at the sentences and check their answers. Finally, they match the sentences with the pictures. Check answers as a class.

> **Answers**
> 1 c   2 a   3 b

b Point to the bold words in 3a and elicit which word, *tell* or *say*, matches each group of phrases as a class.

> **Answers**
> 1 say   2 tell

> ### ◉ CAREFUL!
> Students often have problems with the constructions which follow *tell* and *say*. Most mistakes are usually connected with the indirect object and word order. Students may use *to* after *tell*, e.g., *I told to my little sister a story* (Correct form = I **told my little sister** a story), or they may not use *to* after *say*, e.g., *He said me hello quickly* (Correct form = He **said** hello **to me** quickly).
>
> Other problems relate to the specific collocations, e.g., *tell a story / the truth*, *say hello/sorry*. If students ask, tell them that they have to memorise these as there is no clear rule governing when to use *tell* and when to use *say*.

c Individually, students complete the sentences with *to* if possible. Check answers as a class and ask students: *Which verb do we use* to *with?* 'Say' *or* 'tell'? (say).

> **Answers**
> 1 –
> 2 to
> 3 –
> 4 to
> 5 –

d Students complete the sentences, working individually. They then check in pairs. Check answers as a class.

> **Answers**
> 1 story
> 2 me
> 3 truth
> 4 thanks
> 5 sorry
> 6 you

e As an example, complete one or two of the sentences so that they are true for you. Students then complete the sentences with their own ideas. Monitor and point out errors for students to self-correct.

f ☺️🗨️ In pairs, students tell each other their sentences. Encourage students to ask follow-up questions if possible.

> ### 💡 EXTRA ACTIVITY
> Write the following jumbled sentences on the board and ask students to put them in order:
> 1 never / she / to her brother / sorry / says
> 2 tell / can / a really funny joke / me / you ?
> 3 thank you / I / to them / for lunch / didn't say
> 4 a really strange story / me / told / my friend / yesterday
> 5 I / the truth / don't think / told / me / he
> Answers:
> 1 She never says sorry to her brother.
> 2 Can you tell me a really funny joke?
> 3 I didn't say thank you to them for lunch. / I didn't say thank you for lunch to them.
> 4 My friend told me a really strange story yesterday.
> 5 I don't think he told me the truth.

⟫ Photocopiable activities: Wordpower 8

> ### ⟳ LOA REVIEW YOUR PROGRESS
> Students look back through the unit, think about what they've studied and decide how well they did. Students work on weak areas by using the appropriate sections of the Workbook and the Photocopiable activities.

UNIT 9

CLOTHES AND SHOPPING

⟳ UNIT OBJECTIVES

At the end of this unit, students will be able to:

- understand information, texts and conversations about shopping and shopping malls, what people shop for and buying clothes and presents
- ask for and give information about where people are, what they are doing and what clothes they are wearing
- shop and pay for clothes
- use appropriate phrases when choosing and paying for clothes and when saying something nice
- distinguish between formal and informal emails
- write formal and informal thank-you emails

UNIT CONTENTS

G GRAMMAR
- Present continuous
- Present simple or present continuous

V VOCABULARY
- Shopping: *ATM, bookshop, bus stop, café, car park, cash machine, chemist, clothes shop, department store, entrance, fast food restaurant, information desk, stairs*
- Money and prices
- Clothes: *boots, dress, earrings, gloves, jeans, jewellery, jumper, necklace, raincoat, ring, scarf, shirt, shoes, shorts, skirt, socks, T-shirt, trainers, trousers, watch*
- Wordpower: *time*

P PRONUNCIATION
- Word stress in compound nouns
- Sentence stress with the present continuous
- Sound and spelling: *o* (/ɒ/, /uː/, /ʌ/ and /əʊ/)
- Silent letters
- Connecting words

C COMMUNICATION SKILLS
- Asking and answering questions about what people are doing
- Talking about festivals in your country and which festival you would like to go to
- Describing what a person is wearing
- Choosing clothes in a shop and paying for them
- Using appropriate phrases to say something nice
- Talking about who you give presents to and how you say thank you
- Writing formal and informal emails to say thank you for a present

GETTING STARTED

♡ OPTIONAL LEAD-IN

Books closed. Write these sentences on the board: *I love going shopping – it's my favourite thing to do. I hate buying clothes – I can never find what I want. I prefer shopping in small, local shops, not big shops in the city centre.* Put students into pairs or small groups to discuss the sentences and say if they agree or disagree and why. Monitor and praise students who are able to express their ideas, even if their English isn't perfect. Invite pairs or small groups to share their answers with the class. Encourage students to justify their ideas as much as possible. Ask students to open their books and look at the picture. Ask: *Did you like shopping when you were a child?* Elicit a short reaction from the class.

a 💬📢 Give students one minute to think about their answers to the questions before talking about the picture as a class.

b 💬📢 Read the question with students and then put them into pairs to discuss where the best places to shop are. Help with vocabulary and pronunciation, but don't interrupt fluency. Students share their ideas as a class.

♡ EXTRA ACTIVITY

Individually, students write down two sentences about their shopping habits, e.g., *I go to the shops every Saturday, but I never spend any money; I bought this watch for £10 near my house.* One sentence should be true and one false. Monitor and point out errors for students to self-correct. In pairs, they then read their sentences to each other and decide if they are true or false. Each student then chooses one of their sentences to read to the class for the other students to decide if it is true or false.

Exercises a and b can be prepared as homework before this lesson to give students time to look up unfamiliar vocabulary. Ask students to look at the picture and to prepare their answers to the questions as homework to talk about in the next lesson.

9A | WE AREN'T BUYING ANYTHING

At the end of this lesson, students will be able to:

- use a lexical set of shopping words correctly
- understand conversations in which people plan to meet at a shopping centre
- use the positive, negative and question forms of the present continuous
- ask and answer questions about what people are doing

⚘ OPTIONAL LEAD-IN

Books closed. Write the following questions on the board:

Where do you usually go to …

get a new book or magazine?

sit down and relax with a coffee?

have a burger, chips and cola?

choose some new clothes for a party?

look for the perfect present for someone?

buy something when you have a headache?

Give students one or two examples, e.g., *When I go to the city centre, I always go to my favourite bookstore, Waterstones. They sell thousands of books; My favourite place to sit down and relax with a coffee is Hot Numbers on my street;* to make it clear that you want them to discuss specific places in their area. Put students into pairs or small groups to talk about the questions. Invite pairs or small groups to share their answers with the class and find out which places are particularly popular.

1 VOCABULARY Shopping

a Individually, students look at pictures 1–6 and match them with the words in the box. They compare in pairs. Check answers as a class. If you used the optional lead-in, students can match the places they talked about with the words in the box, e.g., *Waterstones is a bookshop., Hot Numbers is a café.*

Answers	
1 a café	4 a clothes shop
2 a bookshop	5 a chemist
3 a fast food restaurant	6 a department store

b Point to the map of the shopping centre and ask students to match the words in the box with the letters on the map. Check answers as a class.

Answers	
a bus stop	d information desk
b entrance	e cash machine (*or* ATM)
c stairs	f car park

c ▶09.01 **Pronunciation** Play the recording for students to identify which word is stressed in each case. Check the answer as a class. Drill each word.

Answer
the first word

d Complete the first item as an example with the class. You may wish to pre-teach the word *aspirin* (medicine to stop a part of your body from hurting). Students work individually, deciding where the people can go in the shopping centre. They then check in pairs. Check answers as a class.

Answers	
1 clothes shop / department store	4 chemist
2 department store	5 car park
3 bookshop	6 fast food restaurant / café
	7 cash machine (*or* ATM)

⚘ FAST FINISHERS

Ask fast finishers to write sentences about some of the places not included in 1d (*bus stop, entrance, information desk, stairs*).

e ⟫ ▶09.02 Students complete the exercises in Vocabulary Focus 9A on p. 169. Play the recording for students to check their answers to Exercise a and repeat the prices. Monitor Exercise b and drill the prices. Tell students to go to SB p. 91.

Answers (Vocabulary Focus 9A SB p. 169)
a 1a 2b 3b 4b 5a 6b 7b 8a

⚘ EXTRA ACTIVITY

Play Bingo (see p. 153) with the class. Write 25 different prices on the board in numerals. Also include some pairs of numbers that you know often cause students problems, e.g., *£19 and £90* or *£76.99 and £67.99*. Students draw a Bingo grid and complete it with eight prices from the board. Play the game as a class.

2 LISTENING

a 💬 Students discuss the question in pairs or small groups. Invite pairs or small groups to share their answers with the class.

b Look at the map of the shopping centre and elicit suggestions for a good place for a group of friends to meet.

Answer
Students' own answers

c ▶09.03 Play the recording for students to listen and answer the questions. Check answers as a class.

Answers
Simon wants to meet Susie at the shopping mall. They might have problems finding each other.

Audioscript

CONVERSATION 1
SUSIE Hello?
SIMON Hey, Susie. It's Simon. Do you want to go and see a film tonight with Amy and Sandeep?
SU Yeah, great idea, I'd love to.

SI Let's meet at the shopping mall at around seven. OK?
SU Where? The mall's really big!
SI Oh, I don't know. I'll call you when we get there and we can find each other.
SU OK …

d ▶09.04 Tell students that they are going to listen to two more phone conversations. Play the recording for students to listen and underline the correct answers. Check answers as a class and ask students to show you where the four people are on the map of the mall.

Answers

1 in the bookshop   3 in the department store
2 at the bus stop   4 at the cash machine

Audioscript

CONVERSATION 2

SIMON Hello?

SUSIE Simon! Hi! Where are you? Are you having a coffee?

SI No, I'm just buying that new book I told you about. What are you doing?

SU I'm just getting off the bus. So where do you want to meet? It's nearly seven.

SI Let's meet at the entrance in five minutes.

SU All right.

SI And can you call Amy and Sandeep to tell them where to meet?

SU Yeah, sure, no problem. Hurry up!

CONVERSATION 3

SANDEEP Hello?

SUSIE Sandeep, it's Susie. Where are you?

SA Oh! Hi, Susie. I'm just getting some cash. Amy's looking at furniture.

SU Furniture? Are you buying furniture?

SA No, we aren't buying anything. She's just looking.

SU OK, well, can you meet Simon and me at the entrance to the cinema in five minutes?

SA Yeah, sure. See you there!

e 💬🔊 Point to the pictures of Simon and Susie on their phones. Put students into pairs to answer the questions.

f ▶09.05 Play the recording for students to listen and check. Check answers as a class.

Answers

1 Simon is looking at his watch because he thinks the others are late. He's waiting by the main entrance, but they're waiting by the cinema entrance.
2 Susie feels annoyed because Simon isn't at the cinema entrance on time.

Audioscript

CONVERSATION 4

SUSIE Hi, Amy! Hi, Sandeep! Great to see you!

SANDEEP/AMY Hi! Good to see you too!

SA Where's Simon?

SU I don't know. He told me to meet him here. Let me just call him.

SIMON Hello?

SU Simon, where are you waiting for us?

SI I'm standing by the entrance – you aren't here!

SU Yes, we are! We're waiting for you. I just bought our tickets.

SI What? ... Oh, no! I'm at the main entrance, not the cinema entrance.

SU What? Quick, run! The film is about to start!

3 GRAMMAR Present continuous

a ▶09.06 Books closed. Write the following four jumbled sentences on the board. Tell students they are about the information in 2d and ask them to put them in order: *1 a book / Simon / buying / is* (Simon is buying a book.); *2 getting off / Susie / is / the bus* (Susie is getting off the bus.); *3 is / Amy / at furniture / looking* (Amy is looking at furniture.); *4 Sandeep / some cash / is / getting* (Sandeep is getting some cash.). Ask: *What's similar about all four sentences?* Elicit that they all have the verb *be* and the *-ing* form of the verb. Tell students that this is called the present continuous. Students then match the questions and answers in the book. Play the recording for students to listen and check. Check answers as a class.

Answers

1 b 2 d 3 a 4 c

b Complete the rule as a class.

Answer

a now

c Individually, students complete the tables. Check answers by copying the tables onto the board and asking individual students to come up and complete the sentences.

Answers

Positive (+)		Negative (−)	
I'm We're He's/She's	reading a magazine. talking on the phone.	I'm not We aren't / We're not He isn't / He's not She isn't / She's not	drinking coffee. waiting at the entrance.

Yes/No questions (?)	
Are you Is he/she	parking the car?

d ▶09.07 **Pronunciation** Play the recording for students to listen and notice the stress.

Answer

b in negative sentences

👁 CAREFUL!

One of the most common student mistakes with the present continuous is with the spelling of the *-ing* forms. The spelling rules for *-ing* forms are highlighted in Grammar Focus 7B on SB p. 150. Highlight the correct spelling and the top five errors at this level: *writing* (NOT ~~writting~~), *coming* (NOT ~~comeing~~ or ~~comming~~), *studying* (NOT ~~studing~~) and *swimming* (NOT ~~swiming~~).

e ≫ ▶09.08 Students read the information in Grammar Focus 9A on SB p. 154. Play the recording where indicated and ask students to listen and repeat. Students then complete the exercises. Check answers as a class, making sure students are spelling the *-ing* forms correctly. Tell students to go back to SB p. 91.

Answers (Grammar Focus 9A SB p. 155)

a 2 They're talking.   5 She isn't wearing shoes.
3 He isn't riding a horse.   6 They're playing tennis.
4 I'm doing a grammar exercise.
b 2 is (she) smiling; 's feeling
3 Are (you) sleeping; 'm not
4 are (they) standing; aren't standing
5 Is (your brother) playing; isn't; 's playing
c 2 I'm shopping   5 I'm standing   8 we aren't stopping
3 We're looking   6 are you wearing
4 We're driving   7 I'm wearing

💡 FAST FINISHERS

Ask fast finishers to choose other pictures of people in the Student's Book and write sentences like those in Exercise a about what they are doing.

f Give students a few minutes to prepare and write three sentences. Monitor and check that they are spelling the *-ing* forms correctly and point out errors for them to self-correct.

g 💬🔊 Read the example with the students. Put students into pairs to tell their partner their sentences and try to guess where they are. Monitor, but don't interrupt fluency unless students make mistakes with the present continuous forms.

EXTRA ACTIVITY

Ask a student to come to the front of the class and stand looking at the other students with his/her back to the board. Tell the rest of the class that you're going to write an action on the board, e.g., *playing the piano*. The students can't say anything, but when you count down *3, 2, 1 …,* they all mime that action. The student at the front of the class has to guess what they are doing and ask a present continuous question, e.g., *Are you playing the piano?* The class replies *Yes, we are* or *No, we aren't.* Other possible actions include: *dancing, drinking coffee, listening to music, painting a picture, playing golf, reading a book, sleeping, swimming, writing a letter.*

If you wish, students can also play the game in small groups (see 'Backs to the board' on p. 154), choosing the actions themselves and using vocabulary from the course so far.

LOA TIP MONITORING

- Make sure students take full advantage of the two-minute note-writing stage in Exercise a. The idea is that they should be thinking about what words and phrases they will need to complete the task and the best way to express themselves before they start working in pairs in Exercise b. Check that students are making notes and answer any questions they have about vocabulary.

- As students ask and answer their questions, monitor and check that they are only stressing the auxiliary verb in the negative form of the present continuous. When students make mistakes with the pronunciation, try to catch their eyes discreetly so that they can correct their mistakes.

4 SPEAKING

a ⟫ Divide the class into pairs and assign A and B roles. Student As read the instructions and look at the picture on SB p. 134. Student Bs read the instructions and look at the picture on SB p.136. Students then ask and answer questions to find the five differences.

⊕ ADDITIONAL MATERIAL

Workbook 9A

Photocopiable activities: Grammar 9A, Vocabulary 9A, Pronunciation 9A

9B EVERYONE'S DANCING IN THE STREETS

At the end of this lesson, students will be able to:

- read and understand posts about people's shopping habits and local festivals
- talk about festivals in their country
- distinguish between the present simple for things we usually do and the present continuous for things happening at the time of speaking
- understand conversations in which people talk about what they are wearing
- describe what a person is wearing

⚲ OPTIONAL LEAD-IN

Tell students you're going to describe a picture from Units 1–8 in the Student's Book. Tell students to close their books and listen. Read the following sentence twice: *They're riding their bicycles.* Say: *OK. Open your books. Find the picture!* (SB p. 69) Repeat the process with: *She's talking on the phone.* (middle left, SB p. 64) *They're sitting at their desks in a big room. They're taking an exam.* (bottom left, SB p. 22) *He's looking at clothes in a clothes shop.* (middle left, SB p. 56) *They're in a restaurant and they're looking at the menu and talking.* (bottom, SB pp. 44–45) Put students into pairs and ask them to write two or three similar sentences about pictures in the Student's Book using the present continuous. Monitor and point out errors for students to self-correct. Put students into larger groups. Separate students from their original partners. Students read their sentences and find the pictures.

1 READING

a 💬 Give students one minute to think about their answers to the questions before talking as a class about when they go shopping.

b Point to the two posts and ask students: *What kind of website is this?* (It's a social media site.) You may want to pre-teach the word *mask* using the picture on SB p. 92. Students read the texts quickly and match the people with the things they write about. Check answers as a class.

Answers
a B   b D   c L   d L

c Tell students to read the texts again in detail. Individually, students decide if the sentences are true or false. When checking answers, ask students to correct the false sentences. If you wish, give students information from Culture Notes on the next page.

Answers
1 F (He speaks English at work because his colleagues all speak English.)
2 T
3 T
4 F (She loves Venice in the winter.)
5 T
6 F (It's Carnevale and the whole city is like one big party.)

💡 EXTRA ACTIVITY

Ask students to read the texts again and answer questions 1–6: *1 Is Lucas happy in Shanghai?* (Yes, he is.) *2 Does he like his colleagues?* (Yes, he does.) *3 Where is the New Year's party?* (It's in the street.) *4 Does Diana have a lot of time to relax?* (No, she doesn't.) *5 What does she do at weekends?* (She walks around and looks at the old buildings or goes to museums.) *6 Where is the Carnevale party?* (It's in a piazza / town square.)

🌐 CULTURE NOTES

Chinese New Year is usually celebrated in late January / early February, but the exact date changes each year. The celebrations last for two weeks. There are many different traditions associated with each day and these vary from region to region. On the first day, fireworks are very common. It is also traditional for married couples to give the younger members of the family red envelopes with money to give them luck for the year ahead. The most famous images are perhaps the huge street parties with lion and dragon dances, like the one in the picture on SB p. 92.

Carnevale in Venice is believed to have started around 1,000 years ago, although its exact origins are unclear. It usually takes place in late February / early March and ends on Shrove Tuesday, 40 days before Easter. Carnevale finally became an official festival during the Renaissance. At the end of the 18th century, it was prohibited, although it continued to be celebrated quietly in private houses. It was revived in the early 1980s with the aim of increasing tourism in the winter months. The festival is famous for its elaborate costumes and its masks. The masks are often beautifully decorated, like the traditional *volto* (or 'larva') mask in the picture on SB p. 92.

d Individually, students read the messages and decide which is Lucas's and which is Diana's. Check answers as a class. You may wish to teach the word *dragon* using the picture on SB p. 92.

Answers
left message – Lucas
right message – Diana

e 💬📱 Students discuss the questions in pairs or small groups. Invite pairs or small groups to share their answers with the class.

2 GRAMMAR
Present simple or present continuous

a Books closed. Write prompts 1 and 2 on the board and ask students to write the complete sentences that appear in Lucas's online post and message: *1 I / meet / friends / shopping centre* (I usually meet friends at a shopping centre.), *2 We / watch / dragon* (We're watching a big, beautiful dragon). Students check answers by looking at the complete sentences in the book. Students match the sentences with the correct meaning. Then, ask students to look at Lucas's post and message and find more examples of his normal routine, e.g., *In my free time, I sometimes study Mandarin and relax.*, and things happening now, e.g., *Everyone's wearing red.*

Answers
1 a   2 b

b Complete the rule as a class.

Answers
1 present simple
2 present continuous

🔄 LOA TIP CONCEPT CHECKING

- Check that students have fully understood the difference in meaning between the present simple and the present continuous by asking: *Is Lucas's post about his normal routine?* (Yes, it is.) *What about his message?* (No, it's about what's happening now.) Then ask: *What tense are most of the verbs in Lucas's post?* (present simple) and *What tense are most of the verbs in his message?* (present continuous).

- Write the following words and phrases on the board: *always, at the moment, every week, never, now, often, right now.* Ask students which ones we usually use with the present simple (*always, every week, never, often*) and which ones we usually use with the present continuous (*at the moment, now, right now*).

c Students read Diana's post and message again and underline more examples of the present simple and present continuous.

Answers
Present simple:
I <u>love</u> it here in Venice!
It'<u>s</u> so beautiful…
… but at the weekends I <u>get</u> some free time.
I usually <u>walk</u> around and <u>look</u> at the old buildings…
I <u>go</u> to museums.
There <u>are</u> so many interesting …
It'<u>s</u> very different …
This week it'<u>s</u> Carnevale and the whole city <u>is</u> like one big party.
It'<u>s</u> tonight…
Present continuous:
Everyone'<u>s dancing</u> in the streets and <u>having</u> a great time.
We'<u>re</u> all <u>wearing</u> amazing clothes – I'<u>m</u> even <u>wearing</u> a dress!

👁 CAREFUL!

Students will often confuse the two verb forms and use the present continuous where they should use the present simple, e.g., ~~All the masks are being really beautiful.~~ (Correct form = *All the masks* **are** *really beautiful.* – the masks are not only beautiful at the moment of speaking, they are always beautiful) and vice versa, e.g., ~~I stand in the middle …~~ (Correct form = *I'm standing in the middle of the piazza.* – the person is only standing in the middle of the piazza at the moment of speaking and isn't always standing there).

d ≫ Students read the information in Grammar Focus 9B on SB p. 154. Students then complete the exercises. Check answers as a class, making sure students understand why the present simple or present continuous is correct in each case. Tell students to go back to SB p. 93.

Answers (Grammar Focus 9B SB p. 155)
a 2 today   4 this morning   6 'm enjoying   8 often
   3 never   5 's dancing   7 at weekends
b 1 We're getting; I'm watching
   2 He's singing; he sings; They often play
   3 Are you playing; I'm trying; are you doing
c Students' own answers

💡 FAST FINISHERS

Ask fast finishers to write more sentences like the ones in Exercise c using their own ideas.

e ▶ **09.09** Students work individually, completing the conversation. Play the recording for students to listen and check. Check answers as a class.

> **Answers**
> 1 'm getting   2 don't go   3 are arriving

3 LISTENING AND VOCABULARY Clothes

a ▶ **09.10** Play the recording for students to listen for general meaning and answer the questions. Check answers as a class.

> **Answers**
> 1 b wearing red
> 2 c wearing dresses

Audioscript

Conversation 1

LUCAS Hello?
TINA Hi Lucas, it's Tina.
L Oh, Tina – hi!
T I just read your message. Sounds like you're having fun.
L Yeah, it's great here – I love it.
T I can't believe you're wearing red.
L I know, I know.
T You hate red.

L Yes, but it's Chinese New Year – everyone's wearing red – I'm even wearing red socks and a red belt. And someone also gave me a red scarf.
T I hope you're not wearing red shoes.
L No, no – I'm wearing black boots.

Conversation 2

DIANA Hello?
PETE Hi, Diana. It's Pete.
D Oh hi, Pete! Thanks for calling!
P Thanks for the message and the picture.
D No problem. I'm having such a brilliant time here.
P That doesn't look like you in the picture.
D Yeah, that's me.
P But you're wearing a dress. You never wear dresses! And gloves, too. You look so cool.

D Thanks. I wear dresses sometimes you know.
P Yeah, but I normally see you in jumpers and jeans. And you're wearing jewellery, too – those are lovely earrings.
D Well, this is special – it's *Carnevale*. I'm having so much fun.

b ▶ **09.10** Students listen to the recording again for specific details and tick the clothes words they hear. They compare in pairs. Check answers as a class.

> **Answers**
> Lucas: ✓ socks, ✓ scarf, ✓ shoes, ✓ boots
> Diana: ✓ gloves, ✓ dress, ✓ earrings, ✓ jeans, ✓ jumper

💡 EXTRA ACTIVITY

Play the recording again and ask students to write down what Lucas and Diana are wearing. Point out that they both use some clothes words but say that they are not wearing these items. Check answers as a class and make sure that students understand the meaning of *belt* by showing them your belt if you're wearing one or drawing a picture on the board. (*Lucas is wearing red socks, a red belt, a red scarf and black boots. Diana is wearing a dress, gloves and earrings.*)

c **Pronunciation** Model the four words and the four vowel sounds in the table. Elicit from students which column *shoe* should go in.

> **Answer**
> Sound 2 /uː/ – boot, shoe

📖 LANGUAGE NOTES

3c and 3d introduce some of the most frequent sounds which correspond to the letter *o*: /ɒ/, /uː/, /ʌ/ and /əʊ/. Don't ask students to look for other examples of words with *o*, as they may well find words which contain the letter *o* but are not pronounced with the four sounds being worked on.

d ▶ **09.11** Students match the words with the sounds. Play the recording for students to listen and check. Check answers as a class. Then, drill each word.

> **Answers and audioscript**
>
> | Sound 1 /ɒ/ | Sound 2 /uː/ | Sound 3 /ʌ/ | Sound 4 /əʊ/ |
> |---|---|---|---|
> | sock | boot | glove | coat |
> | coffee | shoe | come | know |
> | box | group | mother | phone |
> | | two | | |

e ≫ ▶ **09.12–09.14** Students complete the exercises in Vocabulary Focus 9B on SB p. 168. Play the recording for students to check their answers to Exercise a and complete the Pronunciation activities. Monitor Exercise d and correct students' pronunciation as appropriate. Tell students to go back to SB p. 93.

> **Answers (Vocabulary Focus 9B SB p. 168)**
> **a** 1 d (skirt)   3 a (T-shirt)   5 h (trainers)   7 b (watch)
>   2 g (necklace) 4 e (shorts)   6 c (jewellery) 8 f (ring)
> **b** jewellery (You don't hear the second or third *e*.)
> **c** 1 vegetable   3 chocolate   5 comfortable
>   2 interesting   4 camera

4 SPEAKING

a Individually, students think of someone that they saw before the lesson and make notes about what that person is wearing. Monitor and help with any other vocabulary students might need to talk about the people, e.g., *high heels*, *leggings*, *suit*, *tie*.

b 💬 In pairs, students talk about the people they chose. Monitor and listen for correct use of clothes vocabulary and the present continuous.

💡 FAST FINISHERS

Ask fast finishers to close their eyes and, from memory, describe what their partner is wearing in as much detail as possible.

⊕ ADDITIONAL MATERIAL

Workbook 9B

Photocopiable activities: Grammar 9B, Vocabulary 9B, Pronunciation 9B

Documentary video Unit 9 *Clothes and Shopping*

Video worksheet Unit 9 *Clothes and Shopping*

EVERYDAY ENGLISH

It looks really good on you

At the end of this lesson, students will be able to:

- understand conversations in which people choose clothes in a shop and pay for them
- use appropriate phrases for shopping in a clothes shop
- use appropriate phrases to say something is nice
- join words to the next word in the sentence by moving the final consonant sound
- ask for something in a clothes shop, ask to try it on and pay for it

♀ OPTIONAL LEAD-IN

Play 'Guess who?' (see p. 154) with students. Tell them that you're thinking of a person in the class and that they have to guess who it is by asking questions about what they are wearing. They are allowed to ask you five *Yes/No* questions with the present continuous to find out who it is, e.g., *Is this person wearing jeans?*, *Is this person wearing earrings?* Make sure you reply only with *yes* or *no* (NOT ~~Yes, he/she is.~~) in order not to give away if it is a man or a woman. Once you're sure students have understood what they have to do, they can continue playing the game in small groups. Monitor and check students form the present continuous correctly and pronounce the clothes words from Lesson 9B correctly.

1 LISTENING

a 💬 Put students into pairs to ask and answer the questions. Take feedback as a class.

b ▶09.15 Tell students to look at the picture at the bottom of the page and ask them where Dan and Annie are. Play Part 1 of the video or the audio recording for students to answer the question. Check the answer as a class.

| **Answer** |
| Dan |

Video/Audioscript (Part 1)

ANNIE Dan! Hi!

DAN Hi, Annie, how are things?

A Fine.

D Um, look. Are you free at lunchtime?

A Yes.

D Great. Could we meet? I need help to buy some clothes for this evening.

A Yeah, sure. But what about Martina? Can't she help?

D Well, I'm meeting her this evening for dinner. She always says I wear the same old clothes, so I want to get something new. I want to surprise her.

A OK, sure. I'm free at 12:30.

c ▶09.15 Students watch or listen again for specific details. Play Part 1 of the video or the audio recording again for students to identify the incorrect information in the text. When checking answers, ask students to correct the information.

| **Answers** |
| … ~~to go to a concert~~ for dinner |
| … meet Dan at ~~5 pm~~ 12:30. |
| She ~~isn't~~ is happy … |

d ▶09.16 Play Part 2 of the video or the audio recording for students to answer the questions. They then check in pairs. Check answers as a class.

| **Answers** |
| 1 a shirt and trousers |
| 2 trousers: probably 36; shirt: large |
| 3 No, he probably doesn't enjoy shopping. |

Video/Audioscript (Part 2)

ANNIE So what are you looking for?

DAN I don't know really. A shirt and trousers. Just something casual.

A OK. What size are you?

D In trousers? 32. … OK, 34.

A Or 36? And probably a large for the shirt?

D Yeah, I think so.

A What colour would you like?

D Oh, I don't know. Something dark?

A What about this? … Why don't you try them on?

D OK. Excuse me, where are the fitting rooms?

SHOP ASSISTANT The fitting rooms are just over there, sir.

D Thanks.

SA Thank you.

e 💬 Students ask and answer the questions in pairs or small groups. Take feedback as a class.

2 USEFUL LANGUAGE Choosing clothes

a Individually, students match the questions with the answers. Don't check answers at this point.

b ▶09.16 Play Part 2 of the video or the audio recording again for students to check their answers in 2a. Check answers as a class.

| **Answers** |
| 1 c |
| 2 a |
| 3 b |
| 4 d |

c 💬 Drill the questions and answers before students work in pairs. Monitor and correct students' pronunciation as appropriate.

d 💬 In pairs, students practise helping each other choose clothes. Monitor, but don't interrupt fluency unless students make mistakes with the questions.

♀ FAST FINISHERS

Ask fast finishers to close their books and ask and answer the questions in 2a from memory, using their own ideas for the answers and changing the clothes, colour and size.

3 LISTENING

a ▶09.17 Play Part 3 of the video or the audio recording for students to answer the questions. Check answers as a class.

| **Answers** |
| 1 No, she doesn't. |
| 2 She thinks they look great. |

DAN What do you think?

ANNIE No …

D This one?

A Ugh …

D And this?

A No. Try the next one.

D How about this one?

A No, Dan … That's it! That looks great.

D These are mine! This is what I came in!

A Well, it looks really good on you …

SHOP ASSISTANT Can I help you, sir?

D Hi. There's no price on these shoes. How much are they?

SA They're 49.99.

D Great. I'll take them.

SA OK.

A And these trousers and this shirt, please.

SA OK. Altogether that's £115.97, please.

D Can I pay by card?

SA Yes, of course. Just enter your PIN, please. … Shall I put the receipt in the bag?

D Yes – thanks.

SA There you go, sir.

D Thank you.

SA Thank you.

A Bye.

SA Take care now.

[VIDEO only]

MARTINA Wow! You look great!

D Thank you very much.

---

b ▶ **09.17** Play Part 3 of the video or the audio recording again for students to complete the receipt. Check answers by copying the receipt onto the board, and asking individual students to come up and complete the gaps.

Answers

Shoes	£49.99
Trousers	£39.99
Shirt	£25.99
Total	£115.97

♀ EXTRA ACTIVITY

Set students a mathematical challenge. Tell students: *I went to the clothes shop yesterday and I bought a shirt for £19.99, a pair of trousers for £24.49 and some boots for £66.75. How much was the total?* Allow students to use their mobile phones to work out the answer if they have them (£111.23). Repeat with: *I bought a lot of new clothes yesterday. I got some socks, they cost €9.99, two T-shirts, they were €24.99 each, and a pair of shorts for my holiday. I paid €94.96. How much were the shorts?* (€34.99)

Students then work individually to prepare their own mathematical challenge. Monitor and check students know the answer themselves. Put students into small groups to test each other.

---

4 USEFUL LANGUAGE Paying for clothes

a ▶ **09.18** Individually, students look at the sentences and try to find the mistakes. Play the recording for students to check their ideas. Check answers as a class.

Answers

1 I~'ll~ take them.
2 How much ~~they are~~ are they?
3 Can I pay ~~with~~ by card?

b Students complete the conversation, working individually. They then check in pairs. Check answers as a class.

Answers

1 help   2 much   3 take   4 card

🔁 LOA TIP DRILLING

- Drill the conversation in Exercise 4b before continuing. Try drilling the conversation chorally with you being the shop assistant (A) and the class being the customer (B). Work on the customer's sentences, building them up word by word, starting at the end of each sentence, e.g., *sunglasses – these sunglasses – are these sunglasses – much are these sunglasses – How much are these sunglasses?*, until the class can chorus it together with correct pronunciation. Then ask them the shop assistant's first question: *Can I help you?* and elicit the response from the class as a chorus. Repeat with the customer's second line and continue until you've built up the whole conversation.

- Provide appropriate models of joining words, but don't actively draw students' attention to them at this point as they will study these in detail in the Pronunciation section.

c 💬📋 Write on the board: **B** *Yes, how much* <u>*are these*</u> *(sunglasses)?* **A** *They're (£29.99).* **B** *OK, I'll take* <u>*them*</u>. Ask students: *Is 'sunglasses' singular or plural? What happens to the underlined words if we change 'sunglasses' to 'shirt'?* Check students understand that these words will change to *is this / It's / it* when they use a singular noun. In pairs, students practise the conversations. Monitor and point out errors for students to self-correct.

---

5 CONVERSATION SKILLS
Saying something nice

a Read the sentences together and elicit suggestions for how to complete the sentences from the class.

Answers

1 looks
2 looks

b Answer the questions as a class. Ask students: *Which words make it clear that the sentence is about something someone's wearing?* (on you).

Answers

a Sentence 1
b Sentence 2

c 💬📋 Demonstrate the activity by paying two or three students compliments using the language from this unit, e.g., *Silvi, I love your ring. It looks really good on you. Marc, I really like your trainers. They look fantastic!* Students then work in pairs, saying nice things about something their partner is wearing. Monitor and help with any vocabulary students need.

---

6 PRONUNCIATION Joining words

a ▶ **09.19** Play the recording for students to listen to sentences 1–5 and see if there is a pause between the words in bold. Check the answer as a class.

Answer

No, there isn't.

b Read through the explanations as a class. Drill each example.

> 📖 **LANGUAGE NOTES**
>
> This section develops the work on joining words started in Unit 8 and gives examples of two features common in connected speech. In sentences 1–4 students see how the consonant sound moves to the beginning of the second word when one word finishes with a consonant sound and the next word begins with a vowel sound. Sentence 5 gives an example of a linking /r/: when one word ends with a vowel sound and the next word begins with a vowel sound, we add an extra sound, which isn't written, to make it easier to join the two words smoothly. Other common linking sounds between vowels are: /j/ as in *I am* (individually /aɪ/ and /æm/, but together /aɪjæm/), and /w/ as in *go away* (individually /gəʊ/ and /əˈweɪ/, but together /gəʊwəˈweɪ/). One of the reasons students often have problems understanding spoken English is because they hear these sounds at the beginning of words and are therefore unable to recognise words in speech that they would normally recognise in writing.

c 💬🗩 Students work in pairs, practising saying the sentences and giving replies. Monitor and correct students' pronunciation as appropriate.

7 SPEAKING

a Tell students that they can now practise choosing and paying for clothes. Check students understand the dialogue map before they start. Give them a few minutes to make notes about what they want to say.

b 💬🗩 In pairs, students take turns to be the shop assistant and the customer. Monitor and praise students when they use the language from this lesson correctly.

c 💬🗩 Students work with a different partner and practise more conversations, but using different clothes.

> ⊕ **ADDITIONAL MATERIAL**
>
> Workbook 9C
>
> Unit Progress Test

SKILLS FOR WRITING

Thank you for the nice present

At the end of this lesson, students will be able to:

- understand people talking about who they give presents to and what they give
- talk about who they give presents to and how they say thank you
- understand emails saying thank you for a present
- distinguish between formal and informal emails
- write formal and informal emails to say thank you for a present

�💡 OPTIONAL LEAD-IN

Books closed. Draw a present with a ribbon around it on the board and write underneath it: *The perfect present for me is …*

Tell students: *The perfect present for me is something I can eat, with lots of sugar, and it certainly isn't healthy!* Elicit suggestions, e.g., *a box of chocolates*, *a really big cake*. Then give students another example, e.g., *The perfect present for my sister is expensive jewellery!* Again, elicit ideas, e.g., *earrings*, *a ring*, *a necklace*. Ask students to work individually and write two sentences like yours about perfect presents, one for themselves and one for someone else. In pairs or small groups, they then read each other their sentences and suggest appropriate presents.

1 LISTENING AND SPEAKING

� LOA TIP ELICITING

- Consider eliciting some of the vocabulary in 1a by miming rather than using the picture in the book. Books closed. Mime opening a present and showing a delighted face. Take the 'present', e.g., some earrings, out of the 'box' and 'put them on'. Point to them and ask students: *What are these?*

- As you elicit each word, drill it for correct pronunciation. Then, ask students *How do you spell '(word)'?* Gesture for them to write the word down. After eliciting all the vocabulary, check that students have spelt the words correctly by writing them on the board for them to check.

a 💬💭 Read the questions with students and then give them one minute to think about their answers. Discuss the questions as a class and find out which presents are popular and which aren't popular and why. If you used the optional lead-in, ask students if they think any of the presents mentioned are 'perfect' presents.

b ▶09.20 In pairs, students look at the people and discuss which presents they think the people give. Play the recording for them to listen for general meaning and check their ideas. Check answers as a class.

Audioscript

AXEL I always give my girlfriend an expensive birthday present. I don't give her flowers or chocolates. I often give her jewellery, maybe a necklace or earrings. Or maybe a beautiful dress. She loves expensive clothes. But clothes are difficult because I don't know what she likes. So she usually chooses them and then we buy them together.

BOB We don't buy presents. We give the children some cash and then they always buy their own presents. I think that's better because they know what they want. And then we do something fun together, maybe go out for a meal or go to the cinema.

FERNANDA We buy small birthday presents for the children – usually toys or clothes, something small, like a toy car or a T-shirt maybe. Some people buy things like a laptop or a bike, but I don't like giving expensive presents. I prefer to give small presents.

LEILA My husband doesn't think clothes or computers are important. He doesn't need many things – he doesn't like spending money on himself. But he reads lots of books and he likes music, – so for his birthday I usually buy him a book or a record. He's very easy!

c ▶09.20 Students listen to the recording again for specific details and decide who the sentences are about. They compare in pairs. Check answers as a class.

Answers

2 Leila's husband
3 Fernanda's children
4 Axel's girlfriend
5 Bob and his family

d 💬💭 Students talk about the questions in pairs or small groups. Monitor, but don't interrupt fluency.

💡 FAST FINISHERS

Ask fast finishers to talk about situations where it is typical to give presents in their countries, e.g., birthdays, Mother's/Father's Day, Valentine's Day, when people get married, and whether any specific presents are typical on those days.

2 READING

a Tell students it was Axel's 30th birthday last week and Molly gave him a present. Individually, students then complete the thank-you email. Check answers as a class.

Answers

1 d 2 a 3 c 4 e 5 b

b Students read the email in 2a again and answer the questions. Check that they understand that the answer to question 2 isn't included directly in the email, so they have to understand it from the context. Check answers as a class.

> **Answers**
> 1 a Axel's sister
> 2 He says 'Love' at the end of the email, which you use for someone you know very well.

c Students read Molly's email to Mr Lewis and answer the questions. Check answers as a class.

> **Answers**
> 1 a
> 2 b

d Discuss the question as a class and check that students understand the differences between the two emails. Ask them: *Which email is formal and which is informal?* Check that they are clear that Axel's email is informal while Molly's email is formal. Ask students: *Do you usually write formal or informal emails or both?*

> **Answers**
> 1 Molly's email is more formal than Axel's in 2a. She says 'Dear Mr Lewis', not 'Hi', 'I just want to say thank you', not 'Thanks very much'; and she finishes with 'Regards', not 'Love'.
> 2 It's different because they have a formal relationship – they aren't friends.

3 WRITING SKILLS
Writing formal and informal emails

a Read the example with the class. Students work individually, adding one word to each sentence. They then check in pairs. Check answers as a class.

> **Answers**
> 2 … to say thank you very <u>much</u> for the …
> 3 Thanks so <u>much</u> for the …
> 4 Thank you <u>for</u> the …

b Answer the question as a class. Ask students which phrase makes the sentence sound more formal (*I'd just like to say …*), and ask students to find a similar phrase in Molly's email in 2c (*I just want to say …*).

> **Answer**
> Sentence 2 is more formal.

c Individually, students classify the phrases as informal (1) or formal (2). Check answers as a class.

> **Answers**
>
> | Beginning | Ending |
> |---|---|
> | 2 Hello, Mrs Finch. | 1 Love, |
> | 1 Hi there! | 1 Thanks, |
> | 1 Hi Marie, | 2 Best wishes, |
> | 2 Dear Mr Parker, | 2 Regards, |
> | | 1 See you, |

💡 **EXTRA ACTIVITY**

Write sentences 1–5 on the board. Tell students they all come from a friendly email from Sara to her friend Juan. Students have to decide if they are appropriate for a friendly email and change the phrases that are too formal to more informal ones. *1 Dear Mr García,* (Hi there! / Hi Juan,) *2 I just want to say thank you very much for the earrings.* (Thank you for … / Thanks so much for …) *3 They're really beautiful!* (✓) *4 There's a party tomorrow night, so I can wear them then.* (✓) *5 Regards, Sara Lopez* (Love, Sara / Thanks, Sara / See you, Sara). Students compare in pairs. Then, check answers as a class.

4 WRITING

a To make sure all students receive a 'present', tell each student who they should choose a present for. Students then write their 'presents' on pieces of paper and exchange them. Encourage them to say thank you briefly, e.g., *Oh thank you, it's just what I always wanted!* If you used the optional lead-in, ask students to try to remember their partner's perfect present.

b Students work individually to plan their emails. Monitor and help with vocabulary and give them ideas if necessary.

c Students write their thank-you emails, working individually. Remind students to use the informal phrases in 3c for beginning and ending their emails. If you're short of time, this exercise can be completed for homework. Students could then bring their thank-you emails to the next lesson.

d 💬 In pairs, students swap emails and check their partner's work. Tell them to check that their partner has used appropriate informal phrases in their email. They then give each other feedback. If they have made any mistakes with the informal phrases, or mistakes in other areas, they prepare a second draft of their email before giving it to you for correction.

e Tell students to imagine that the present was from someone they don't know well. Ask them to write a second version of their thank-you email. Elicit from the class that they need to use more formal phrases for the beginning, the sentence saying thank you, and the ending.

⊕ **ADDITIONAL MATERIAL**
Workbook 9D

UNIT 9
Review and extension

1 GRAMMAR

a Highlight the example question and answer. Students then write questions and answers for the people in the picture. Monitor and help as necessary. Point out errors for students to self-correct. Check answers as a class.

> **Answers**
> 2 What's she doing? She's running.
> 3 What are they doing? They're doing yoga.
> 4 What's she doing? She's reading a newspaper.
> 5 What are they doing? They're playing football.
> 6 What's he doing? He's playing a guitar.

b Individually, students complete the conversation. Check answers as a class by asking individual students to write the correct answers on the board.

> **Answers**
> 1 are you doing
> 2 'm cooking
> 3 cook
> 4 'm making
> 5 make
> 6 put
> 7 'm adding
> 8 'm trying

2 VOCABULARY

a Read the first sentence and elicit the answer as an example. Students then read the sentences and identify the places. Check answers as a class.

> **Answers**
> 1 a chemist
> 2 a clothes shop / a department store
> 3 a fast food restaurant
> 4 a bookshop
> 5 a café
> 6 a department store

b Individually, students look at the pictures and write the correct clothes words. Check answers and spelling as a class.

> **Answers**
> 1 scarf
> 2 shoes
> 3 gloves
> 4 boots
> 5 dress
> 6 raincoat

> ### ♀ FAST FINISHERS
> Ask fast finishers to write down all the other clothes words they remember from the unit, making sure they spell them correctly.

3 WORDPOWER time

a Tell students to close their books. Write the five verbs *find, save, spend, take* and *waste* on the board and draw a large clock face next to the verbs. Ask students: *What word can go after all of these?* Elicit *time.* Students open their books, look at the sentences and match the phrases with the meanings. Check answers as a class.

> **Answers**
> 1 b
> 2 d
> 3 a
> 4 e
> 5 c

> ### ♀ EXTRA ACTIVITY
> Books closed. Write sentences 1–5 on the board underneath the five verbs from 3a. Ask students to complete the sentences with the correct form of the verbs: *1 She _____ a lot of time with her brothers and sisters.* (spends) *2 It _____ time to check the prices online first.* (takes) *3 I can't always _____ time to do my homework.* (find) *4 Don't _____ time – your exams are next week.* (waste) *5 You can _____ time by taking the bus and not walking.* (save)

b Individually, students read the mini-conversations and underline the adjectives. They then compare in pairs. Check answers as a class. Ask students to think of other adjectives that can be used with *time* as well as *nice* and *good,* e.g., *fantastic, great,* and also to think of negative adjectives, e.g., *awful, terrible.*

> **Answers**
> Have a <u>nice</u> (good) time.
> … like doing in your <u>free</u> (spare) time?

c As an example, complete one or two of the sentences so that they are true for you. Students then complete the sentences with their own ideas. Monitor and point out errors for students to self-correct.

d 💬 In pairs, students tell each other their sentences and find out how similar they are.

》》》 Photocopiable activities: Wordpower 9

> ### 🔄 LOA REVIEW YOUR PROGRESS
> Students look back through the unit, think about what they've studied and decide how well they did. Students work on weak areas by using the appropriate sections of the Workbook and the Photocopiable activities.

🔄 UNIT OBJECTIVES

At the end of this unit, students will be able to:
- understand information, texts and conversations about technology, languages and communication habits
- talk about and compare different kinds of technology
- ask and answer questions about their own and other languages and about their communication habits
- understand conversations in which people ask for help
- ask for help and check instructions
- write a post on an online discussion board about something that annoys them and an appropriate reply to another student's post

UNIT CONTENTS

G GRAMMAR
- Comparative adjectives
- Superlative adjectives

V VOCABULARY
- IT collocations: *charge a phone/computer, check my email, click on a link, download a document/file, log into a computer/ website, make calls, save a document/file, visit a website*
- High numbers
- Linking ideas with *also, too* and *as well*
- Wordpower: *most*

P PRONUNCIATION
- *than* with comparative adjectives
- Word stress in superlative adjectives
- Main stress and intonation

C COMMUNICATION SKILLS
- Talking about different kinds of technology
- Comparing two pieces of similar technology
- Asking and answering questions about languages and language learning
- Asking for help and responding appropriately
- Using appropriate phrases to check instructions
- Writing a post about something that annoys you and writing a reply to someone else's post

GETTING STARTED

💡 OPTIONAL LEAD-IN

Books closed. Write these beginnings of sentences and questions on the left side of the board: *1 Can you call; 2 He'll; 3 This is; 4 Just; 5 Can you wait; 6 Is; 7 Here's my; 8 He's not; 9 Can he; 10 What do you think of.* Write these endings on the right side of the board, leaving the area in the middle clear: *a location. Come and meet me! b a minute? c this picture? d Dan there? e me back? f be back soon. g here right now. h my new phone number. i a minute. j call me back?*

Ask students to match the sentence halves. Then, they compare in pairs. Check answers by asking individual students to draw lines joining the two sentence halves on the board (1 e, 2 f, 3 h, 4 i, 5 b, 6 d, 7 a, 8 g, 9 j, 10 c).

Ask students: *Where do we use all these phrases?* (on the phone or in text messages). Tell students that some of the phrases are from text messages and some are from phone calls. Put students into pairs and ask them to classify the phrases. Check answers as a class (text messages: *3, 7, 10*; phone calls: *1, 2, 4, 5, 6, 8, 9*).

a 💬 Give students one minute to think about their answers to the questions before talking about the picture as a class.

b 💬 Individually, students decide which sentences are true for them. They then compare in pairs. Take feedback as a class and ask students if they think mobile phones are good or bad when families are together.

💡 EXTRA ACTIVITY

Write other common kinds of communication on the board, e.g., *face-to-face, letters, emails, social media sites, instant messaging, blogs, video chats.* Ask students to write three sentences about how they use some of these forms of communication. Some of the sentences should be true and some false, e.g., *I sometimes write letters to my grandparents because they don't use the Internet; I usually talk to my friends over texts.* Monitor and point out errors for students to self-correct. In pairs or small groups, they then read their sentences to each other and decide if they are true or false.

Exercises a and b can be prepared as homework before this lesson to give students time to look up unfamiliar vocabulary. Ask students to look at the picture and to prepare their answers to the questions as homework to talk about in the next lesson.

10A

THEY'RE MORE COMFORTABLE THAN EARBUDS

At the end of this lesson, students will be able to:

- read and understand a text comparing earbuds with headphones
- use comparative adjectives correctly
- understand a casual conversation that compares mobile phones with landlines
- use a lexical set of IT collocations correctly
- compare two pieces of similar technology

⚲ OPTIONAL LEAD-IN

Books closed. Tell students they are going to have a test on technology words. Explain that you're going to read a definition for each word and they have to write down the word with the correct spelling. Read definitions 1–10: *1 You use this at a party so everyone can listen to music.* (speaker) *2 You use these to listen to music. You put them on your ears.* (headphones) *3 You use this small object on your arm to send messages and emails and use the Internet.* (smartwatch) *4 You can make phone calls, send messages and emails and use the Internet with this small object.* (smartphone) *5 Families usually have one of these at home for working or playing games.* (computer) *6 This object has numbers, symbols and all the letters of the alphabet on it. You use it to write an email on the computer.* (keyboard) *7 When you travel a lot on business, you need this so that you can work easily on the plane or train.* (laptop) *8 This is what photographers use to take pictures. They're sometimes very expensive.* (camera) *9 This is very useful when you need a copy of a document on paper.* (printer) *10 This is great for using the Internet or watching movies. It has quite a big screen and you touch it to control it.* (tablet)

Check answers as a class and give one point for the correct word and an additional point for spelling it correctly. The student with the highest score is the winner.

1 READING

a 💬 In pairs, students ask and answer the questions. Invite pairs to share their answers with the class.

b Students read the posts quickly and find out what they talk about. Check the answer as a class.

Answers
1 Kentaro, Emily, Alyssa   3 Alyssa, Pedro, Monica, Nils
2 Kentaro, Monica, Nils, Alyssa   4 Monica, Nils

c Tell students to read the posts again in detail. Individually, students find the people. They then check in pairs. When checking answers, ask students to read the sections of the text which helped them find the answers.

Answers
1 in her pocket   6 in its case
2 in his bag   7 They cover your ears.
3 He likes good sound.   8 He has small ears, so the
4 She loses things.   earbuds fall out.
5 in the gym

⚲ EXTRA ACTIVITY

Ask students to read the posts again and answer questions 1–4: *1 Why doesn't Monica like headphones?* (They're not comfortable if you're working out.) *2 Who thinks the sound is better with headphones but prefers earbuds?* (Monica) *3 Who prefers headphones?* (Kentaro, Nils, Pedro) *4 Who prefers earbuds?* (Alyssa, Emily, Monica)

d 💬 Discuss the question as a class. Encourage students to justify their answers as much as possible.

2 GRAMMAR Comparative adjectives

a Books closed. On the board, write: *Earbuds are ... than headphones.* Point to the gap and ask students to complete the sentence trying to remember the posts from the previous page (*better, smaller*). Help students if they can't remember. Then, write: *Headphones are ... than earbuds.* Ask students to complete the sentence using what they remember from the posts on the previous page (*bigger*). Say each adjective / comparative adjective pair, e.g., *small – smaller, big – bigger,* and say *These are comparative adjectives.* Wipe the board before students work individually, looking at the sentences and underlining the adjectives. They then circle the correct words to complete the rule. Check answers as a class.

Answers
1 better
2 bigger
3 more expensive
4 smaller, cheaper, easier
The adjectives tell us how earbuds and headphones are <u>different</u>.

b Individually, students underline the comparative adjectives in the posts. Check answers as a class.

Answers
Alyssa: better   Nils: more comfortable
Pedro: bigger   Monica: clearer
Kentaro: more expensive Nils: better
Emily: cheaper   Alyssa: smaller, cheaper, easier
Monica: smaller, lighter

c Give students a few minutes to complete the rules and the examples. They then check in pairs. Check answers as a class.

Answers
1 -er; harder   3 more; more interesting
2 i; -er; happier   4 better

⟳ LOA TIP DRILLING

- Check that students have fully understood why we use comparative adjectives by asking them: *When we use comparative adjectives, how many things are we usually talking about?* (two) *Are the things exactly the same?* (no)

- After checking students have understood the use of comparative adjectives, double-check they are clear about the form by asking: *Can I say 'my headphones are more big than my earbuds'?* (no) *Why not?* (Because 'big' is a short adjective – the comparative is 'bigger'.); *Can I say 'my laptop was expensiver than my tablet'?* (no) *Why not?* (Because 'expensive' is a long adjective – the comparative is 'more expensive'.); *Can I say 'my smartphone is gooder than my computer'?* (no) *Why not?* (Because 'good' is an irregular adjective – the comparative is 'better'.)

117

d ▶ **10.01** Students complete the sentences, working individually. Play the recording for students to listen and check. Check answers as a class.

> **Answers**
> 1 than
> 2 than

e ▶ **10.01** **Pronunciation** Play the recording again for students to listen to the pronunciation of *than*. Check the answer as a class. Drill the sentences.

> **Answer**
> not stressed

◉ CAREFUL!

One of the most common mistakes with comparative adjectives is with the spelling. The spelling rules for comparative adjectives are highlighted in Grammar Focus 10A on SB p. 156. At this level, the most common mistakes are with double letters. Students may either not double the final consonant in comparative adjectives, e.g., ~~biger~~ (Correct form = *bigger*), or double the final consonant where it isn't necessary, e.g., ~~cheapper~~ (Correct form = *cheaper*). Students may also use *more* with one-syllable adjectives, which should form the comparative with *-er*, e.g., ~~more hard~~ (Correct form = *harder*) and ~~more light~~ (Correct form = *lighter*). They may also use both *more* and *-er* at the same time, e.g., ~~more heavier~~ (Correct form = *heavier*) and ~~more smaller~~ (Correct form = *smaller*).

After studying *more* for comparatives, students may then start to overuse it in sentences which require *very*, e.g., ~~… they are more expensive~~ (Correct form = *I haven't got headphones because they are **very** expensive*).

f ≫ ▶ **10.02** Students read the information in Grammar Focus 10A on SB p. 156. Play the recording where indicated and ask students to listen and repeat. Students then complete the exercises. Check answers as a class, making sure students are forming and spelling the comparative adjectives correctly. Tell students to go back to SB p. 101.

> **Answers (Grammar Focus 10A SB p. 157)**
>
> **a** 2 worse   12 noisier
>   3 cleaner   13 older
>   4 colder   14 more popular
>   5 more comfortable   15 sadder
>   6 more crowded   16 stranger
>   7 faster   17 stronger
>   8 fatter   18 thinner
>   9 better   19 wetter
>   10 more interesting   20 wider
>   11 more modern
> **b** 2 The film is more interesting than the book.
>   3 Her children are noisier than my children.
>   4 She is a better cook than my dad.
>   5 Dubai is more modern than Dublin.
>   6 This hotel is more comfortable than the last hotel.
>   7 My friends are funnier than me / than I am.
> **c** 1 She's / is quicker   5 ~~weter~~ wetter
>   2 ~~good~~ better   6 ~~more big~~ bigger
>   3 ~~worser~~ worse   7 ~~most~~ more interesting
>   4 ~~prettyer~~ prettier   8 faster than mine

♀ EXTRA ACTIVITY

Draw two simple cars on the board, one a high-end, expensive car, e.g., a Ferrari, and one a smaller, cheaper car, e.g., a Honda. Label them with the makes. Put students into pairs and give them one minute to compare the two cars in as many ways as possible. If you wish, write some adjectives as prompts down the side of the board, e.g., *comfortable*, *big/small*, *expensive/cheap*, *fast/slow*. Ask some pairs to share their sentences with the class. Then, nominate a student to choose two things and to draw and label two simple pictures of them on the board, e.g., two stick people to represent two famous actors, two skylines to represent two cities. Students work in pairs to compare the two things. In pairs or small groups, students can then choose two things to compare and continue the activity.

g ≫ Divide the class into pairs and assign A and B roles. Student As read the instructions and look at the picture on SB p. 134. Student Bs read the instructions and look at the picture on SB p. 137. Check that they understand that they first should ask and answer questions about the smartphones and then they should compare them. Monitor, but don't interrupt fluency unless students make mistakes with comparative adjectives. Tell students to go back to SB p. 101.

♀ FAST FINISHERS

Ask fast finishers to write sentences to compare a piece of technology they have or use at home with a similar piece of technology in the classroom/school.

3 LISTENING

a ▶ **10.03** Play the recording for students to listen for general meaning and answer the questions. Check the answers as a class.

> **Answers**
> 1 He wants to give up his landline phone.
> 2 No, she doesn't.

Audioscript

GREG Your mum and I are thinking about giving up our landline.

RUBY Oh, OK.

G I don't really think I need a normal telephone any more.

R You never know …

G Well, I have a smartphone and I can do everything with it – go online, check my email – and, obviously, make calls.

R But what happens if … if, I don't know, there's an emergency or something?

G I still have my smartphone for that.

R But what if you forget to charge it or something?

G I always charge my phone! I keep it plugged in.

R Or what if the power goes off? There are times when a landline is really useful.

G I thought you'd be happy for me to give up the landline. You never call me on it – you just text me.

R Yeah, I know, but … but if something really bad happened – like a big storm – often smartphones don't work. But landlines do – they're much safer.

G So you want me to keep the landline?

R Well, that's not what I'm saying – I just think you should … well, think about it.

G Oh, I have. And I've found out that with no landline, I'll save £30 a month.

b ▶ **10.03** Students listen to the recording again for specific details and complete the chart. Check answers as a class.

	good	*bad*
Landline phones	3	1
Smartphones	4	2

c 💬🗨 Discuss the question as a class. Don't interrupt fluency, but write any mistakes with comparative adjectives on the board. After the class discussion, ask students to correct any mistakes on the board.

4 VOCABULARY IT collocations

a Individually, students complete the phrases. Check that they understand that the number of lines indicates the number of missing letters. Check answers as a class.

> **Answers**
> 1 go online
> 2 check my emails
> 3 make calls

b Students match the verbs with the nouns, working individually. Make sure students understand that there are two possibilities for some of the verbs. They then check in pairs. Check answers as a class and point out the verbs which have two possibilities (*download*, *log into*, *save* and *charge*). Drill all the possible collocations.

> **Answers**
> 1 b; c
> 2 e
> 3 a
> 4 a; f
> 5 b; c
> 6 d; f

c 💬🗨 Students work in pairs or small groups, asking and answering questions using IT collocations. Monitor and check that they are using the vocabulary from this section correctly.

5 SPEAKING

a Individually, students decide if they want to talk about idea 1 (something new versus something old) or idea 2 (two similar things that they use).

b Give students a few minutes to prepare and make notes about the two things. Monitor and help as necessary.

c 💬🗨 Students work in pairs, telling each other about the two things they chose and asking and answering each other's questions. As you monitor, don't interrupt fluency, but note down any mistakes with comparative adjectives or the IT collocations. After the activity, write the mistakes on the board and ask students to correct them.

> 💡 **FAST FINISHERS**
>
> Ask fast finishers to talk about two objects from the category in 5a that they didn't write notes about.

> ⊕ **ADDITIONAL MATERIAL**
>
> Workbook 10A
>
> Photocopiable activities: Grammar 10A, Vocabulary 10A, Pronunciation 10A

WHAT'S THE MOST BEAUTIFUL LANGUAGE IN THE WORLD?

At the end of this lesson, students will be able to:

- understand a radio programme in which an expert talks about languages
- use superlative adjectives correctly
- read and understand a text with unusual facts and figures about languages
- use high numbers correctly
- ask and answer questions about their own and other languages

♀ OPTIONAL LEAD-IN

Books closed. Organise a quiz to review some of the countries that students have seen in the class. Consider including some of the countries that students will need to complete question 3 in 1a and any additional countries that you know your students have problems spelling. To elicit the countries, either tell students the capital city (e.g., *Australia – Canberra, Canada – Ottawa, China – Beijing, France – Paris, Greece – Athens, Italy – Rome, Japan – Tokyo, Portugal – Lisbon, Saudi Arabia – Riyadh, Spain – Madrid, Switzerland – Bern*), or select a typical tourist picture for each country (e.g., the Sydney Opera House for Australia, the CN Tower for Canada) and show these to students. Students work in teams, writing down the names of each country without referring back to their books or their notes. Check answers as a class. Elicit the names of the countries and write them on the board for students to check their spelling. Give one point for identifying the country correctly and a bonus point for correct spelling. The team with the highest score is the winner.

1 LISTENING

a 💬🔊 Students ask and answer the questions in pairs or small groups. If you used the optional lead-in, tell students that they can use the countries on the board to help them with question 3. Invite pairs or small groups to share their answers with the class and give students some of the suggested answers below to question 3, if you wish.

Possible answers for 3

Greek – Greece, Cyprus; Italian – Italy, southern Switzerland; English – the UK, the USA, Canada, Australia, New Zealand, South Africa, Antigua and Barbuda, The Bahamas, Barbados, Belize, Dominica, Grenada, Guyana, Ireland, Jamaica, St Kitts and Nevis, St Lucia, St Vincent and the Grenadines, Trinidad and Tobago; French – France, Belgium, Canada, Switzerland, Benin, Burkina Faso, Burundi, Cameroon, Chad, the Ivory Coast, the Democratic Republic of the Congo, Djibouti, Equatorial Guinea, Haiti, Luxembourg, Madagascar, Mali, Monaco, Niger, Rwanda, Senegal, Seychelles, Togo and Vanuatu; Arabic – North Africa and the Middle East; Turkish – Turkey; Japanese – Japan; Mandarin Chinese – northern and southwestern China; Portuguese – Portugal, Brazil, Mozambique, Cape Verde, Guinea-Bissau, Mozambique, Angola and São Tomé and Príncipe, East Timor, Equatorial Guinea and Macau; Spanish – Spain, Central and South America (except Brazil)

b ▶️ 10.04 Play the recording for students to listen for general meaning and tick the languages that Professor Hunter talks about. You may wish to pre-teach the word *population* (the total number of people who live in a city, country, etc.). Check answers as a class.

Answers

Italian ✓, English ✓, Japanese ✓, Mandarin Chinese ✓, Basque ✓, Spanish ✓

Audioscript

HOST Good evening and welcome to the programme. Today, we're talking to Professor Ryan Hunter. The professor is well known for his love of languages and has a new book in the shops tomorrow. Professor, welcome!

PROFESSOR Thank you. It's great to be here!

H So let's start with my first question. Professor, in your opinion, what's the most beautiful language in the world?

P That's a very good question. Of course, there is no right or wrong answer here. I'm sure we all have our favourites. But for me, the answer is easy: Italian. It was the first language I learnt. I still remember my teacher, Signora Monti. Signora Monti was the best teacher at my school and she started my love of languages. Now I can speak more than 20 languages well, but Italian is the most musical language I know. It's the language of opera and love.

H OK, next question. What's the most difficult language in the world?

P Hmm. That's an interesting question, too. It partly depends on your first language. For example, for a speaker of English, Japanese is very difficult, but for a speaker of Mandarin Chinese, it's much easier. However, a few years ago, we did a project at my university and decided that the hardest language to learn is Basque, a language from parts of Spain and France. Last year, we did another project on the Internet to find the easiest language to learn. More than 3,000 people answered the question and the most popular answer was Spanish. So perhaps Spanish is the easiest language to learn. That's probably because it's not very different from many other European languages.

H And one final question, what's the most useful language to speak?

P That's easy – the language of the country where you live. But if you want to learn the most popular language in the world, then take lessons in Mandarin Chinese. More than 900 million people speak it. That's not a surprise, as China has the biggest population in the world. So with Mandarin Chinese, you can speak to about 14% of all the people in the world. That's pretty useful.

H That's very useful, indeed! Well, Professor Hunter, thanks for talking with us today. I'm sure our listeners enjoyed hearing your thoughts on language!

c ▶️ 10.04 Individually, students match the sentences with the languages. Play the recording for students to listen and check. Check answers as a class.

Answers

1 Italian
2 Japanese
3 Spanish
4 Mandarin Chinese

d ▶10.04 Students listen to the recording again for specific details and answer the questions. They compare in pairs. Check answers as a class.

Answers
1 Italian
2 more than 20
3 in parts of Spain and France
4 14%

e 💬 Individually, students choose one thing they found interesting and one thing they found surprising. They then compare in small groups or as a class.

2 GRAMMAR Superlative adjectives

a ▶10.05 Books closed. Copy the following table onto the board:

adjectives	_____ adjectives	_____ adjectives
big	bigger	_____
easy	easier	_____
good	better	_____
hard	harder	_____
musical	more musical	_____

Point to the first column. Say *adjectives*. Point to the second column. Elicit and write the heading *comparative (adjectives)*. Then, point to the last column. Elicit and write the heading *superlative (adjectives)*. If necessary, say *the biggest* as an example. Elicit the superlative adjectives, write them in the third column and drill them (*the biggest, the easiest, the best, the hardest, the most musical*). Students then open their books, look at the spelling of the superlative adjectives in the box and complete the sentences. Play the recording for students to listen and check. Check answers as a class.

Answers
1 best
2 musical
3 hardest
4 easiest
5 biggest

b Individually, students read the sentences and order the languages from very easy to very difficult. They then check in pairs. Check answers as a class.

Answers
1 Spanish
2 French
3 Japanese
4 Basque

c Discuss the question as a class. If you wish, extend the discussion by saying nationalities, e.g., *Thai, Japanese, German, Turkish*, and asking students if they think their language is easy or difficult for those particular nationalities to learn.

d Give students a few minutes to complete the rules and the examples. They then check in pairs. Check answers as a class.

Answers
1 *-est*; smallest
2 *most*; most
3 best

⊙ CAREFUL!

Student errors with superlative adjectives are generally similar to those with the comparative form. They may have problems with double letters, e.g., ~~bigest~~ (Correct form = *biggest*) and ~~cheappest~~ (Correct form = *cheapest*), or use *most* with one-syllable adjectives, e.g., ~~Basque is the most hard language …~~ (Correct form = *Basque is the **hardest** language to learn*). After studying both the comparative and superlative forms, students may then start to confuse the two forms, e.g., ~~This is the cheaper dictionary …~~ (Correct form = *This is the **cheapest** dictionary in the shop*) and ~~He's the more intelligent person …~~ (Correct form = *He's the **most intelligent** person I know*). They may also have problems with word order when using *most*, e.g., ~~This is the laptop most practical when …~~ (Correct form = *This is **the most practical** laptop when you're travelling*). Sometimes students may have problems with word order and also confuse *more* and *most*, e.g., ~~… I like more my smartphone~~ (Correct form = *I like my smartphone, my laptop and my tablet. But I like **my smartphone (the) most***).

e ≫ ▶10.06 Students read the information in Grammar Focus 10B on SB p. 156. Play the recording where indicated and ask students to listen and repeat. Students then complete the exercises. Check answers as a class, making sure students are forming and spelling the superlative adjectives correctly. Tell students to go back to SB p. 102.

Answers (Grammar Focus 10B SB p. 157)
a 2 the shortest 7 the friendliest 11 the safest
   3 the funniest 8 the best 12 the most exciting
   4 the driest 9 the biggest 13 the most tiring
   5 the prettiest 10 the nicest 14 the hottest
   6 the worst
b 2 The shortest 5 The fastest
   3 the most popular; 6 the most important
     the most interesting 7 the best
   4 The most useful 8 the worst

♀ FAST FINISHERS

Ask fast finishers to brainstorm other adjectives they know and write down the comparative and superlative forms of each one, e.g., *angry – angrier – the angriest*; *intelligent – more intelligent – the most intelligent*.

f ▶10.07 **Pronunciation** Play the recording for students to listen to how the words are stressed.

g ▶10.08 **Pronunciation** Students listen to the questions and identify the main stress. Drill each word in 2f and the questions in 2g.

Answer
on the adjective

h 💬 In pairs or small groups, students ask and answer the questions in 2g. Monitor, but don't interrupt fluency unless students make mistakes with the form or pronunciation of the superlative adjectives.

3 READING

a 💬 Students ask and answer the questions in pairs or small groups. Invite pairs or small groups to share their answers with the class, but don't check the answer to question 3 at this point.

b Students read the text quickly and find out if their guesses in 3a were correct. Check the answer as a class.

Answer
It has interesting facts about languages and learning languages.

c Individually, students complete the text with the superlative forms of the adjectives in the box. Check answers and spelling by asking students to write the correct answers on the board.

Answers
1 the best	6 the heaviest
2 the fastest	7 the shortest
3 the most popular	8 the longest
4 most expensive	9 the most difficult
5 the biggest	10 the most difficult

d Tell students to read the text again in detail. Individually, students identify who or what the people are talking about. They then check in pairs. Check answers as a class.

Answers
1 Harold Williams
2 Quechua
3 Khmer
4 the *Oxford English Dictionary*
5 Fran Capo
6 English

e 💬 Discuss the questions as a class. Encourage students to justify their answers to question 1 as much as possible.

4 VOCABULARY High numbers

> 💡 **EXTRA ACTIVITY**
>
> Revise numbers 1–100. Put students into small groups and tell them to stand in a circle and try to count from 1–100 around the circle. Tell them that if they make a mistake or pause for more than three seconds, they have to start again. If you want to give your students an additional challenge, ask them to repeat the activity counting down from 100 or to add the word *beep* after every two numbers, i.e., *one, two, beep, three, four, beep,* etc.

a Individually, students find the numbers and write down what they refer to. Check answers by copying the table onto the board and asking individual students to come up and complete it.

Answers
nine hundred million	people who speak Mandarin Chinese
six hundred and three	words Fran Capo can say in 54 seconds
six hundred thousand	words in the *Oxford English Dictionary*

b ≫ ▶ 10.09 Students complete the exercises in Vocabulary Focus 10B on p. 169. Check the answers to Exercise a as a class, play the recording for students to check their answers to Exercise b and monitor Exercises c and d. Tell students to go back to SB p. 103.

Answers (Vocabulary Focus 10B SB p. 169)
a 1 d 2 g 3 a 4 f 5 c 6 e 7 j 8 i 9 h 10 b
b 2 two thousand <u>and</u> two
  3 –
  4 three hundred <u>and</u> eighty-one thousand two hundred <u>and</u> forty-five
  5 two million six hundred <u>and</u> seventy
  6 fifteen million six hundred <u>and</u> eighty thousand four hundred <u>and</u> thirty

> 💡 **EXTRA ACTIVITY**
>
> Choose ten high numbers to say to the class for students to write down in numerals. Practise a variety of numbers, including examples with *hundred, thousand* and *million*, and focus particularly on any that students have problems with. Read each number twice, making sure you say *and* in the correct position. Students then compare in pairs. Check answers by asking individual students to come up and write the numbers in numerals on the board as you say them. Drill the numbers.

c 💬 Students take turns writing down a high number for their partner to say. Monitor and check that students are using *and* in the correct position.

5 SPEAKING

a Individually, students complete the questions. Check answers and spelling by asking students to write the correct answers on the board. Drill the questions.

Answers
1 the nicest
2 the most beautiful
3 the best
4 the longest
5 the hardest
6 the most difficult
7 the most interesting

b 💬 In pairs or small groups, students ask and answer the questions. Monitor, but don't interrupt fluency unless students make mistakes with the content of this lesson.

> 🔄 **LOA TIP** MONITORING
>
> - Give students a few minutes to think about their work in Lesson 10A on comparative adjectives and their work in Lesson 10B on superlative adjectives. Tell them to look back at the exercises and see where they made mistakes and where they did well. Ask them to identify one thing they were good at and one thing they need to improve.
>
> - Students take turns sharing the things they were good at and the things they need to improve with the class. Encourage them to explain why things were difficult for them, e.g., *It's difficult to remember when to use 'more' and when to use 'most'. It's the same word in my language.*

> ⊕ **ADDITIONAL MATERIAL**
>
> Workbook 10B
>
> Photocopiable activities: Grammar 10B, Vocabulary 10B
>
> Documentary video Unit 10 *Communication*
>
> Video worksheet Unit 10 *Communication*

EVERYDAY ENGLISH

There's something I don't know how to do

At the end of this lesson, students will be able to:

- understand informal conversations in which people ask for help, respond appropriately and check instructions
- use appropriate phrases for asking for help
- identify the main stress and intonation in questions asking for help
- use appropriate phrases to check they have understood instructions
- ask each other for help with a piece of new technology, respond appropriately and check they have understood the instructions

☞ OPTIONAL LEAD-IN

Books closed. Write sentences 1–5 on the board: *1 I get a new mobile phone every year. 2 I regularly use three or more social networking sites. 3 When I buy a new gadget, I never read the instructions. 4 I've got a laptop, a tablet and a smartphone. 5 My friends always phone me when they have problems with their gadgets.*

Put students into pairs or small groups to discuss how many of the sentences are true for them. Take feedback as a class and find out if all the sentences are true for any of the students. Tell students that these sentences are for people who use gadgets and technology a lot. Ask them to work in their pairs or small groups again and write five sentences for people who don't use gadgets and technology a lot, e.g., *I never check my email. In fact, I can't remember my email address.*, *I always get the simplest kind of mobile phone I can find*. Monitor and point out errors for students to self-correct. Ask students to share their sentences for people who hate technology with the class.

1 LISTENING

a 💬 Read through the questions with the class and give students one minute to think about their answers before they work in pairs. Monitor and allow time for class feedback.

b ▶10.10 Point to the picture of Annie and ask: *Do you think Annie knows how to use her tablet? Why / Why not?* Then play Part 1 of the video or the audio recording for students to answer the questions. Check answers as a class.

> **Answers**
> 1 Dan
> 2 Leo

Video/Audioscript (Part 1)

ANNIE Hi, Leo.
LEO Hi, Annie.
A Where is he?
L Sorry, Annie. I mean, Dan says sorry. He had to go to a meeting.
A What about our lunch?!
L He didn't know about the meeting. Someone called him about ten minutes ago.
A I wanted help with this.
L Oh? Right.
A Leo, could you help me?
L Erm …
A There's something I don't know how to do. Do you mind showing me?
L No, not at all – if I can.
A Great, thanks.
L Well, it is lunchtime. Would you like to have some lunch and …?
A … and you could help me with my tablet.
L Yes.
A That would be lovely.

c ▶10.10 Play Part 1 of the video or the audio recording again for students to answer the questions. They then check in pairs. Check answers as a class.

> **Answers**
> 1 He's in a meeting.
> 2 They decide to have lunch and Leo can help her with her tablet.

2 USEFUL LANGUAGE Asking for help

a ▶10.11 Individually, students look at the different ways to ask for help and try to remember which ones Annie uses. Play the recording for students to listen and check. Check answers as a class.

> **Answers**
> 1 Could you help me?
> 4 Do you mind showing me?

b ▶10.12 Tell students that some of the sentences have mistakes. They work individually to identify and correct the wrong sentences. Play the recording for students to listen and check. Check answers as a class.

> **Answers**
> 1 ✓
> 2 Would you mind ~~tell~~ telling me?
> 3 ✓
> 4 Could you ~~showing~~ show me?
> 5 ✓

c Check students understand that one answer matches both questions. Individually, students match the questions with the answers. Check answers as a class.

> **Answers**
> 1 a; b
> 2 a; c

3 PRONUNCIATION Main stress and intonation

a ▶10.11 Play the recording and highlight the main stress in question 4 for students.

b Answer the question as a class.

> **Answer**
> the main verb

c ▶10.11 Play the recording again for students to decide if the intonation goes up or down. Highlight the intonation movement by writing the questions on the board and drawing a falling arrow over the end of each.

> **Answer**
> The intonation goes down.

LOA TIP DRILLING

- Drill the four questions in 2a before students work in pairs in 3d. Try focusing on the main stress in each phrase first, before filling in the other words, e.g., *help – help me – Could – Could you – Could you help – help me – Could you help me?* If necessary, clap out the rhythm of the questions for them so that they can then apply the rhythm to the sentence, e.g., *Could you help me?* would be 'clap clap CLAP clap'.
- Show students the downward intonation movement at the end of the phrase using hand gestures to give them a visual reference.

d 💬🔊 Drill the questions in 2b and 3a. Students then work in pairs, practising saying the sentences. Monitor and correct students' pronunciation as appropriate.

e Individually, students think of a question to ask their partner for help with their studying, e.g., *Can you help me with the pronunciation of this word?* Monitor and point out errors for students to self-correct.

f 💬🔊 Remind students to stress the main verb in their questions and to make sure the intonation goes down. In pairs, they practise asking for help and agreeing to help each other. Monitor and praise students with a smile or a nod when they pronounce the questions correctly.

4 LISTENING

a ▶10.13 Play Part 2 of the video or the audio recording for students to answer the questions. They then check in pairs. Check answers as a class.

> **Answers**
> 1 She can't get into her email. 2 Yes, he does.

Video/Audioscript (Part 2)

LEO So … you wanted some help.
ANNIE Oh yes – I almost forgot. … Everything is fine – it's great. But I don't know how to get into my email. Can you have a look?
L Sure. OK – that's easy. You just need to change one small thing. … OK. So what you do is … touch this button here.
A OK.
L And a new screen opens.
A Oh yes.
L And now you just touch here where it says 'Yes'.
A Oh, that's easy. OK. So first I touch this button?
L That's right.

A And it takes me to a new screen – like this?
L Correct.
A And I touch 'Yes'. Is that right?
L Yeah. Now you can check your email.
A Great. Thanks, Leo. Thank you so much.
L You're welcome.
A Well, now I have to buy you another coffee.
L Mm, I think I have to get back to work. I've got a meeting with Dan in ten minutes.
A Dan? Oh, don't worry about him. Let's have another coffee!
L Well … OK!

b ▶10.13 Students watch or listen again for specific details. Play Part 2 of the video or the audio recording again for students to put the things in order. Check answers as a class.

> **Answers**
> 1 b 2 a 3 d 4 c

5 CONVERSATION SKILLS
Checking instructions

a Individually, students read the sentences and decide who says them. Check answers as a class.

> **Answers**
> Annie says all three sentences.

b Answer the question as a class. Ask students: *What would you say to ask someone to repeat instructions?* and elicit some ideas for option b, e.g., *Sorry, I didn't understand. Could you repeat that, please?* or *Sorry, I don't understand you. Can you say that again?*

> **Answer**
> a She wants to be sure she understands the instructions.

c Elicit the correct answer from the class.

> **Answer**
> Like this?

d Read through the instructions with the class. Students then work individually and put them in a logical order. Check answers as a class.

> **Answers**
> 1 c
> 2 a
> 3 b

e 💬🔊 Put students into pairs to practise giving the instructions in 5d and checking they understand them.

💡 **EXTRA ACTIVITY**

Ask students to work in pairs and use a piece of technology they have with them, e.g., a smartphone or a tablet, and write a script for a conversation similar to the one with Annie and Leo in the video/audio. They should choose just one area they have a problem with for their conversation and include appropriate phrases for asking for help and checking instructions. Monitor and help as necessary. When students have prepared their script, give them time to rehearse and check they are using correct stress and intonation. Correct students' pronunciation as appropriate. Pairs then take turns to perform their conversations for the class, using the piece of technology as a prop.

6 SPEAKING

a–b ≫ Divide the class into pairs and assign A and B roles. Student As read the first card on SB p. 105 and Student Bs read the first card on SB p. 136. Students then role play the conversation. Monitor, but don't interrupt fluency unless students make mistakes with the content of this lesson. Students then read the second card and role play the second situation.

💡 **FAST FINISHERS**

Ask fast finishers to choose another object which they don't know how to use and invent a similar conversation.

⊕ **ADDITIONAL MATERIAL**

Workbook 10C

Photocopiable activities: Pronunciation 10C

Unit Progress Test

10D SKILLS FOR WRITING
My friends send really funny texts

At the end of this lesson, students will be able to:

- understand text messages and people talking about what they use text messages for
- understand a post on an online discussion board and a series of responses agreeing and disagreeing
- link ideas using *also*, *too* and *as well*
- write a post about something that annoys them and an appropriate reply to another student's post

⚲ OPTIONAL LEAD-IN

Write on the board: *thx for the pic – LOL! pls send me + when u can xxx*.

Ask students: *Where do you sometimes see messages like these?* Elicit that they are used in text messages and instant messaging. Circle the abbreviations in the message, i.e., *thx*, *pic*, *LOL*, *pls*, *+*, *u*, *xxx*, and then put students into pairs to try and work out what the message means. Check answers as a class. (*Thanks* for the *picture* – (I was) *laughing out loud*! *Please* send me *more* when *you* can. *Kisses*.) Ask students if they know any other similar abbreviations, e.g., *PLZ* (please), *GR8* (great), *NP* (no problem), *TTYL* (talk to you later).

1 SPEAKING AND LISTENING

a 💬🎦 Read the questions with the students. Then, put them into pairs or small groups to ask and answer the questions together. Monitor and invite pairs to share their answers with the class.

b Individually, students match the texts with the pictures. They then compare in pairs and discuss where the people are and what they are doing. Check answers as a class. If you used the optional lead-in, ask students if the texts they send look more like the ones on the board or the ones in the Student's Book.

> **Answers**
> a 3 (She is at the airport and is texting her family to say she is going to be late.)
> b 2 (He is in Italy and is taking a picture of his meal.)
> c 4 (He is on a train and is texting someone to ask what is for dinner.)
> d 1 (They are waiting for someone and texting them.)

c ▶10.14 Play the recording for students to listen for general meaning and identify the texts. Check answers as a class.

> **Answers**
> Speaker 1 c
> Speaker 2 a
> Speaker 3 d

Audioscript

SPEAKER 1
I sometimes send text messages, usually to my parents to say when I'm coming home, but I usually chat online. It's easier if you're online anyway – and it's cheaper! I always have my phone with me so I can see what my friends are doing. It's really good to know what people are doing. I chat to everybody all the time and we send each other pictures.

SPEAKER 2
I only really send text messages when I'm travelling. I text my family to tell them when I arrive somewhere new or tell them when I'll be back. It's useful because I'm often away on business trips in other countries and of course it's cheaper than phoning. But usually I don't send text messages. I prefer to talk to people on the phone. It's easier and you can say more.

SPEAKER 3
I don't really like texting much. I think it's better to talk on the phone. It's friendlier. I sometimes send a text if I'm meeting a friend, but that's about all.

d ▶10.14 Students listen to the recording again for specific details and complete the table. They then compare in pairs. Check answers by copying the table onto the board and asking individual students to come up and complete it.

> **Answers**
>
> | | Sends texts to | Prefers to | Why? |
> |---|---|---|---|
> | Speaker 1 | parents | send texts; chat on social media apps | It's good to know what people are doing. |
> | Speaker 2 | family | talk on the phone | It's easier and you can say more on the phone. |
> | Speaker 3 | friends | talk on the phone | It's friendlier. |

e 💬🎦 Students talk about the questions in pairs, small groups or as a class. Invite students to share their answers with the class.

2 READING

a Individually, students read the posts on the discussion board quickly and tick the people who sometimes get annoyed. You may wish to pre-teach the word *laugh* (v.) (to make a noise when something is funny). Check answers as a class.

> **Answers**
> ✓ Genji, ✓ Meepe, ✓ MadMax, ✓ AdamB, ✓ Lars2

b Tell students to read the posts again in detail. Students identify who thinks the things. After checking answers, ask students: *Which person are you like?*

> **Answers**
> 1 Lars2
> 2 Rainbows
> 3 AdamB
> 4 Genji/Meepe/MadMax
> 5 MadMax

c Students read the posts again and underline the adjectives. They then check in pairs. Check answers as a class.

> **Answers**
> worst, annoying, rude, important, useful, funny
> Negative adjectives: worst, annoying, rude

d Tell students that they need to find short phrases/sentences, not just individual words. Check answers as a class.

> **Answers**
> 1 Yes, I agree; Yes, you're right.
> 2 I don't agree (with you, Genji).

> ♀ **FAST FINISHERS**
> Ask fast finishers to write their own short responses to Genji's original post.

3 WRITING SKILLS
Linking ideas with *also*, *too* and *as well*

a Tell students to close their books. Write the first sentence from 3a on the board, leaving a gap in place of *also*. Point to the gap and ask students: *What's this word?* Elicit *also* and write it in the sentence. Ask students: *What kind of word is this?* and elicit *a word to link ideas* (an adverb). Students open their books, look at the sentences with *also* and underline the correct answers. Check answers as a class.

> **Answers**
> 1 after
> 2 before
> 3 beginning

b Individually, students identify the words and phrases that mean the same as *also*. They then compare in pairs. Check answers as a class.

> **Answers**
> 1 too
> 2 as well
> They come at the end.

> ♀ **EXTRA ACTIVITY**
> Write sentences 1–4 on the board and ask students to decide if they are correct or not. Tell them to correct the wrong sentences. Tell them that there is more than one correct option to make correct sentences. *1 I can speak French and I can too speak German.* (✗ … I can (also) speak German (too / as well).) *2 Texting is really boring. Also, texts can be kind of confusing.* (✓) *3 I think Italian is the most beautiful language in the world, too.* (✓) *4 I've got a laptop and a tablet also.* (✗ … and (also) a tablet (too / as well).) Check answers as a class.

c Check that students understand that they can link the ideas in the sentences with *also*, *too* or *as well*, but tell them that they should use each linking word at least once. Students work individually, adding *also*, *too* or *as well* to the sentences. Monitor and check that students are putting the linking words in the correct position.

> **Answers**
> 1 … and I've <u>also</u> got a new laptop. / … and I have a new laptop <u>too</u> / <u>as well</u>.
> 2 … and we <u>also</u> took a street map. / … and we took a street map <u>too</u> / <u>as well</u>.
> 3 … and she <u>also</u> knows a lot about computers. / … and she knows a lot about computers <u>too</u> / <u>as well</u>.
> 4 … <u>Also</u>, they have a large screen, so they are easy to read. / … They have a large screen, so they are easy to read <u>too</u> / <u>as well</u>.

4 WRITING AND SPEAKING

> ↻ **LOA TIP** ELICITING
>
> • Monitor the Writing and Speaking section closely, making sure at all stages that students are completing the task correctly and are clear about what they have to do.
>
> • In 4a, monitor and help with vocabulary and give students ideas if necessary. If students complete 4b and 4c in class, then monitor and note down the kinds of mistakes they are making to see how well they have understood and can use the content of the unit. However, don't point out students' mistakes at this point as other students will do this in 4d. In the final speaking stage, listen for correct use of comparative and superlative adjectives, but don't interrupt fluency.

a Students work individually to plan a post about something that annoys them.

b If you're short of time, this exercise can be completed for homework. Students could then bring their posts to the next lesson.

c Students swap posts and write a comment agreeing or disagreeing with the original post and using *also*, *too* or *as well* if possible. Again, if you're short of time, this exercise can be completed for homework. They then pass the original post and their comment on to a third student.

> ♀ **FAST FINISHERS**
> Ask fast finishers to pass the original post and their comment on to another fast finisher, who can then write an additional response both to the post and the comment.

d Students read both the original post and the comment and check the other students' work. Tell them to check that the other students have used *also*, *too* or *as well* correctly. If there are any mistakes with the linking words or in other areas, students prepare a second draft of their original post/comments before giving it to you for correction.

e 💬👍 Put students into small groups to compare their posts and discuss which they think is the most interesting. After correcting students' work, ask them to make a final version to share with other students. You may display the posts and comments around the classroom for other students to read and comment on further. Alternatively, if you and your students have the technology available, set up a class discussion board where students can display their posts and comment on each other's texts.

> ⊕ **ADDITIONAL MATERIAL**
> Workbook 10D

UNIT 10
Review and extension

1 GRAMMAR

a Individually, students complete the conversation. Check answers as a class and check students are spelling the comparative adjectives correctly.

Answers
2 more powerful
3 bigger
4 more expensive
5 heavier
6 lighter
7 thinner
8 more practical
9 faster

b Check that students understand that they have to use one word from each box to complete the questions. Monitor and help as necessary. Point out errors for students to self-correct. Check answers as a class.

Answers
a the hottest place
b the longest river
c the most expensive hotel room
d the best footballer
e the biggest country

2 VOCABULARY

a Students underline the correct words in each sentence. Check answers as a class.

Answers
1 save
2 goes; website
3 log into; check
4 Click on; file

b Students write the numbers as words, working individually. Check answers and use of *and* as a class by asking students to write the correct answers on the board.

Answers
1 fifty million
2 two thousand and three
3 two hundred and fifty-six
4 one thousand five hundred
5 two hundred thousand
6 two thousand six hundred and fifty-five

3 WORDPOWER *most*

a Books closed. Ask students the following questions and discuss them as a class: *What language do most of the people in your country speak? Do most of them understand English? In your opinion, what's the most beautiful language in the world?* After discussing the questions, ask them: *What word is in all three questions?* Elicit *most* and write it in a circle on the board. Students open their books, read the text and answer the questions. Check answers as a class.

Answers
1 Spanish, German, English and Italian
2 writer – English – because she was at school in London and also because it's an international language and most people speak it; her mother – Spanish – she says it's the most beautiful language in the world

b Read the meanings with the students and discuss the first phrase (*Most of the people we know …* – meaning b) as an example. Students work individually, matching the phrases with *most* with the meanings. They then check in pairs. Check answers as a class.

Answers
a 4, 6   b 1, 2, 3, 5

c Check that students understand that this question is referring to items 1 and 5 from the text in 3a. Answer the questions as a class.

Answers
a most people   b most of the people

d Individually, students complete the sentences with the words in the box. Check answers as a class.

Answers
1 of the evening   2 people   3 of the way   4 of my friends

> ### ♀ EXTRA ACTIVITY
>
> Write sentence beginnings 1–4 and endings a–d on the board and ask students to match the sentence halves: *1 I do my homework most of; 2 I get up early most; 3 I think most of; 4 I love all my gadgets, but most of; a my friends speak English better than me.; b all, I love my smartphone.; c the time, but sometimes I forget.; d days, but not at the weekend.*
>
> Check answers as a class (1 c, 2 d, 3 a, 4 b). Tell students to use these as examples of the kind of sentences they should write in 3e.

e As an example, make sentences about your life using two of the phrases, e.g., *Most days I get up very early, but at weekends, I stay in bed until very late.* Students then write sentences about their lives. Monitor and point out errors for students to self-correct.

f 💬🗨 In pairs, students tell each other their sentences and find out how similar they are. Encourage students to ask follow-up questions if possible.

≫ Photocopiable activities: Wordpower 10

> ### ⟳ LOA TIP MONITORING
>
> Students look back through the unit, think about what they've studied and decide how well they did. Students work on weak areas by using the appropriate sections of the Workbook and the Photocopiable activities.

UNIT 11
ENTERTAINMENT

⟳ UNIT OBJECTIVES

At the end of this unit, students will be able to:

- understand information, texts and conversations about actors, music and films
- ask for and give information about films, TV programmes, books and music
- discuss things they've seen and places they've been to in their town or city
- understand conversations in which people express their opinions and agree or disagree
- use appropriate phrases to ask for, express and respond to opinions
- write a review of a film they've seen and structure it correctly

UNIT CONTENTS

G GRAMMAR
- Present perfect: positive
- Present perfect: negative and questions
- Present perfect or past simple

V VOCABULARY
- Irregular past participles: *been, bought, broken, caught, eaten, fallen, flown, forgotten, grown, had, heard, read* /red/, *seen, written*
- Music: *a band, classical, a DJ, a festival, folk, jazz, a musician, opera, an orchestra, pop, rock, a singer*
- Wordpower: Multi-word verbs: *call back, come over, fill out, grow up, lie down, try on*

P PRONUNCIATION
- Main stress in the present perfect
- Word stress in music words
- Main stress and intonation

C COMMUNICATION SKILLS
- Talking about actors, films, TV programmes, books and music
- Talking about things you have and haven't seen and places you have and haven't been to in your town or city
- Using appropriate phrases to ask for and express opinions
- Responding to opinions with short phrases and questions
- Discussing films that you've seen and enjoyed and films you would like to see
- Writing a review of a film you've seen

GETTING STARTED

♀ OPTIONAL LEAD-IN

Books closed. Write these jumbled phrases on the board and tell students they are all kinds of entertainment: *achwngti a limf* (watching a film), *inogg ot a cerntco* (going to a concert), *gnsiee a yapl ta het heatert* (seeing a play at the theatre). In pairs, students work out what the phrases are. Give students one minute to think of other common forms of entertainment, e.g., *watching a dance show, seeing a musical*. Invite pairs to share their answers with the class and add their ideas to the board. Ask students: *Which of these are most popular in your country? Choose the top three.* Students work individually. Take feedback as a class.

a 💬 Give students one minute to think about their answers to the questions before talking about the picture as a class. If you wish, ask students additional questions, e.g., *How old do you think the people are?* and *When and where do you think they took this photo?*

b 💬 In pairs or small groups, students talk about what films and TV programmes they enjoyed when they were children. If you have a class with a variety of ages, try to mix older and younger students together, as it will give them more to talk about. Help with vocabulary and pronunciation, but don't interrupt fluency. Invite pairs to share their answers with the class and ask students to share the thing they enjoyed most.

♀ EXTRA ACTIVITY

Extend the discussion and get students to talk more about what other entertainment they enjoy with their friends. Write the following questions on the board and put students into small groups to discuss them: *Do you and your friends play any games when you're together? What is your favourite indoor game? And outdoors? What music do you enjoy listening to with your friends? Do you think your parents enjoy the same kinds of entertainment as you do? Why / Why not? What about your grandparents?*

Exercises a and b can be prepared as homework before this lesson to give students time to look up unfamiliar vocabulary. Ask students to look at the picture and to prepare their answers to the questions as homework to talk about in the next lesson.

11A | I'VE HEARD SHE'S A GOOD ACTOR

At the end of this lesson, students will be able to:

- read and understand a text about three actors
- use the present perfect to talk about experience
- understand a conversation about actors and the films they are in
- use a lexical set of irregular past participles correctly
- ask for and give information about popular films, TV programmes and books

☉ OPTIONAL LEAD-IN

Write sentence beginnings 1–4 on the board: *1 Hugh Jackman and Nicole Kidman both lived …; 2 Robert Downey Jr. and Sean Penn both went …; 3 Ashton Kutcher and Charlize Theron were both …; 4 Leslie Mann and Milla Jovovich are both … .* Put students into pairs or small groups and ask them to discuss possible ways to complete the sentences. Then, ask students to match sentence endings a–d to the actors: *a models before they became actors.; b in Australia.; c married to film directors.; d to the same school.* Check answers as a class (1b Jackman was born in Australia. Kidman was born in Hawaii to Australian parents, but the family returned to Australia when Kidman was four years old. 2d They both went to Santa Monica High School in California, though at different times. 3a Kutcher modelled for Calvin Klein and Abercrombie & Fitch, and Theron was a model in Milan. 4c Mann is married to Judd Apatow and Jovovich is married to Paul W. S. Anderson.)

1 READING

a 💬🗨 Look at the pictures as a class. In pairs, students then decide what they think the three actors have in common.

📖 VOCABULARY SUPPORT

film director (B1) – the person who tells the actors what to do in a film

have something in common (B1) – to be the same for two or more people or things

b Tell students they should only read the fact files directly below each picture. Check the answer to 1a as a class.

> **Answer**
> b They all lived in Australia.

c 💬🗨 Put students into pairs to guess the answers to the questions. You may wish to pre-teach the word *ice-skate* (v.) (to move across ice using special shoes) and *trapeze* (n.) (a short bar that hangs high in the air from two ropes that is used in a circus).

d Tell students to read the main part of the article *Film International* and check their answers to the questions in the quiz. Check answers as a class. Ask students: *Do you know any other films that these actors are in?* If you wish, give students information from Culture Notes in the next column. You may wish to help students with words in the Vocabulary Support box.

> **Answers**
> 1 Rose
> 2 Mia
> 3 Mia
> 4 Margot
> 5 Rose
> 6 Margot

📖 VOCABULARY SUPPORT

act (B1) – to perform in a film or a play

award (B2) – a prize someone is given for something special they have done

soap opera (B1) – a TV programme with a story that continues for a very long time and is always about the same group of people

UNICEF – the United Nations Children's Fund, a charity that helps children in difficult situations around the world

🌍 CULTURE NOTES

Margot Robbie (b. 1990) starred in the 2019 film *Once Upon a Time in Hollywood* and has appeared in many other films, including *Bombshell* and *Focus*. In 2019, she was ranked among the world's highest paid actors.

Rose Byrne (b. 1979) started making films at the age of 15 when she appeared in *Dallas Doll*. Since then, she has made many films, including *Insidious*, *Bridesmaids*, *X-Men: Apocalypse*, *Neighbors*, *Neighbors 2: Sorority Rising* and *Instant Family*. She also co-starred alongside Glenn Close in all 59 episodes of the television series *Damages* from 2007 to 2012.

Mia Wasikowska (b. 1989) acted in the television drama *All Saints* in 2004 when she was 14. She became famous when she starred in Tim Burton's *Alice in Wonderland* in 2010. She has also starred in *The Kids Are All Right*, *Albert Nobbs*, *Stoker*, the 2011 film version of *Jane Eyre*, the 2014 film version of *Madame Bovary*, *Alice Through the Looking Glass* and *Blackbird*.

☉ EXTRA ACTIVITY

Ask students to read the fact files and the article again and decide if sentences 1–4 are true or false: *1 Mia has never acted in the USA.* (F – All three actors work in Hollywood in the USA.) *2 Mia is younger than Margot.* (F – Margot is the youngest of the three.) *3 Rose has acted in television.* (T) *4 Mia has won prizes for both acting and photography.* (T)

e 💬🗨 Students talk about the questions in pairs or small groups.

2 GRAMMAR Present perfect: positive

a Books closed. Write on the board: *Marilyn Monroe … (make) her first film in 1947.* Ask students to complete the sentence (*made*). Then, write on the board: *Sofia Coppola … (make) a new film right now.* Again, ask students to complete the sentence (*is making*). Finally, write: *Meryl Streep … (make) a lot of fantastic films.* Ask students to try to complete the sentence. They may suggest using *makes* (present simple), but tell them that a native speaker would use *has made*. Then, to elicit the three tenses (past simple, present continuous and present perfect), point to each verb one after the other and ask: *What tense is this?* Students then open their books and complete the sentences. Check answers as a class.

> **Answers**
> 1 They <u>have acted</u> in some very popular films.
> 2 Rose <u>has worked</u> for UNICEF in Australia.
> 3 Mia <u>has directed</u> some short films.

b Discuss the question as a class.

> **Answer**
> No, we don't.

c Individually, students complete the rule. Check answers as a class. Ask students: *How do we form the past participle of regular verbs?* (by adding *-ed* to the infinitive).

> **Answers**
> have
> has

3 LISTENING

a ▶ 11.01 Students listen to the conversation for general meaning and tick the films Maggie and Stephen talk about. Check answers as a class.

> **Answers**
> 1 No, they didn't. (Maggie got 1 and 5 wrong; Stephen got 2 and 4 wrong.)
> 2 All except a *Bridesmaids*

> **Audioscript**
>
> **STEPHEN** How many quiz answers did you get right?
>
> **MAGGIE** All of them except for numbers one and five.
>
> **S** I got question two and four wrong. How did you know Margot Robbie learnt to go on a circus trapeze?
>
> **M** I remembered she was in *The Legend of Tarzan*, but I haven't seen the film. I've only seen her in *I, Tonya*. Which of the films in the list have you seen?
>
> **S** I've seen *Mary Queen of Scots*. She's really good in it. I've never seen any of Mia Wasikowska's movies.
>
> **M** Really? Try *Jane Eyre* – she's great in that.
>
> **S** OK. I read the book in college, but I haven't seen the film. What about Rose Byrne? Have you seen any of her films?
>
> **M** No, I haven't, but I've heard she's a good actor.
>
> **S** Yeah, she's really good. I've seen her in a couple of *X-Men* films. She plays a CIA agent – she's great.

b ▶ 11.01 Students listen to the recording again for specific details and complete the table. They then check in pairs. Check answers as a class.

> **Answers**
>
> | | Rose Byrne | Mia Wasikowska | Margot Robbie |
> |---|---|---|---|
> | Maggie | | ✓ e | ✓ b |
> | Stephen | ✓ d | | ✓ c |

c Students try to remember what Maggie and Stephen thought about the actors. Play the recording again if necessary. Check the answer as a class.

> **Answer**
> They thought they were good.

4 VOCABULARY Irregular past participles

a ▶ 11.02 Individually, students complete the sentences with the words in the box. Play the recording for students to listen and check. Check answers as a class. Ask students: *How are these past participles different from the examples in 2c?* (They are irregular so they don't end in *-ed.*)

> **Answers**
> 1 seen
> 2 heard
> 3 read, seen
> No, they don't.

b ≫ ▶ 11.03–11.04 Students complete the exercises in Vocabulary Focus 11A on SB p. 170. Play the recording for students to check their answers to Exercise a and complete the Pronunciation activity. Check answers to Exercise b as a class and monitor Exercise d. Tell students to go back to SB p. 111.

> **Answers (Vocabulary Focus 11A SB p. 170)**
> **a** broken – break; read (/**red**/) – read (/**ri:d**/); been – be; caught – catch; written – write; seen – see; had – have; eaten – eat; bought – buy; heard – hear; flown – fly; forgotten – forget; fallen – fall; grown – grow
> **b** 1 caught 5 been 9 seen 13 fallen
>   2 written 6 bought 10 heard 14 grown
>   3 eaten 7 forgotten 11 broken
>   4 flown 8 read 12 had / eaten
> **c** 2 girl, learn, nurse, German, work

> 💡 **FAST FINISHERS**
>
> Ask fast finishers to use the irregular verbs list on SB p. 129 and take turns testing each other on the past participle forms.

5 GRAMMAR
Present perfect: negative and questions

a ▶ 11.05 Students complete the sentences with the words in the box. Play the recording for students to listen and check. Check answers as a class.

> **Answers**
> 1 seen 2 never 3 ever

b Ask students to look at the position of *not*, *ever* and *never* in the examples in 5a. Complete the rules as a class.

> **Answers**
> 1 after 2 before

c ▶ 11.05 **Pronunciation** Play the recording for students to listen again to the sentences in 5a. Check the answer by writing the sentences on the board and underlining the three past participles to indicate the main stress. Drill the sentences.

> **Answer**
> the past participle

⊙ CAREFUL!

There are several common student mistakes with the present perfect. Students may simply avoid using the present perfect altogether and use the present simple instead, e.g., ~~I see all of …~~ (Correct form = *I've seen* all of Brad Pitt's films), or they may use the incorrect auxiliary verb, using *has/hasn't* instead of *have/haven't* or vice versa, e.g., ~~I hasn't been …~~ (Correct form = *I **haven't been** to the USA.*).

When using *ever* and *never*, students are also likely to make mistakes. They may try and use both words in the same sentence, e.g., ~~… I never ever see~~ (Correct form = *It is the best film I **have ever seen***), or they may omit the auxiliary verb, e.g., ~~I never see a film …~~ (Correct form = *I**'ve** never seen a film with Rose Byrne*). When forming a negative with *never*, they often include a negative auxiliary verb, e.g., ~~I never don't see a city …~~ (Correct form = *I**'ve never seen** a city like it.*).

d ≫ ▶**11.06** Students read the information in Grammar Focus 11A on SB p. 158. Play the recording where indicated and ask students to listen and repeat. Students then complete the exercises. Check answers as a class, making sure students are forming the present perfect and positioning *ever* and *never* correctly. Tell students to go back to SB p. 111.

Answers (Grammar Focus 11A SB p. 159)

a 2 written   5 brought   7 driven   9 run
3 swum   6 done   8 ridden   10 been
4 had
b 2 've visited / have visited
3 hasn't borrowed
4 've never eaten / have never eaten
5 've walked / have walked
6 has played
7 haven't done
8 has had
c 1 I've seen; I've never seen
2 Have you ever met; I've met / I have met; Has he visited; he has been

◑ LOA TIP DRILLING

- Drill the two conversations in Exercise c in Grammar Focus 11A on SB p. 159 before continuing. Divide the class in half down the middle and tell the group on your left that they are A and the group on your right that they are B. Drill A's first question with the left-hand group and B's response with the right-hand group. Then, put the two lines together with the left-hand group asking and the right-hand group answering the first question all together. Repeat the process until students can perform the first conversation without you having to model the lines for them. Tell the groups to swap A and B roles before you work on the second conversation.

e ▶**11.07** Students work individually, completing the conversation. Play the recording for students to listen and check. Check answers as a class. If you wish, give students information from Culture Notes in the next column.

Answers

1 Have you seen   4 Have you read
2 I've read   5 I've heard
3 haven't seen   6 Have they made

🌍 CULTURE NOTES

The film *Crazy Rich Asians* is based on Kevin Kwan's 2013 best-selling novel. It's based on the writer's childhood in Singapore in a very rich family where they had their own cruise ships and private planes.

The film also got a lot of attention because there are so many Asian American and British Asian actors in it. There haven't been many opportunities in Hollywood for Asian actors, and many people saw this film as an opportunity for that to change.

6 SPEAKING

a Individually, students think of some popular films, TV programmes and books and write six questions about them. Monitor and help with any vocabulary students might need and the titles in English if necessary. Point out any errors in the students' questions for them to self-correct before they start on the groupwork stage in 6b.

b 💬 Put students into small groups to ask and answer each other's questions. As you monitor, don't interrupt fluency, but note down any mistakes with the present perfect. After the activity, write them on the board and ask students to correct them.

♡ EXTRA ACTIVITY

Ask each student to write down the other students' answers as they ask and answer the questions in 6b. They then summarise what they found out for the class. Demonstrate the activity by asking five students an example question, e.g., *Have you read all three of the* Crazy Rich Asians *books?* and pretending to write down their answers. Then, give the class a summary of what you learnt, e.g., *There are five people in my group. Two of them have read all of the* Crazy Rich Asians *books.* Students then work individually and write summary statements for each of the six questions they asked in 6a. Monitor and point out errors for students to self-correct. Ask each student to read two or three of their summary statements to the class.

⊕ ADDITIONAL MATERIAL

Workbook 11A

Photocopiable activities: Grammar 11A, Vocabulary 11A, Pronunciation 11A

11B | I BET YOU'VE NEVER BEEN TO THE OPERA

At the end of this lesson, students will be able to:
- read and understand a text about music in Budapest
- use a lexical set of music words correctly
- understand a conversation in which people talk about places they've been to
- distinguish between the past simple to say when something happened and the present perfect to talk about past experiences
- talk about things they have and haven't seen and places they have and haven't been to in their town or city

♀ OPTIONAL LEAD-IN

Write the names of a number of famous sights in the city/country where you're teaching on the board, e.g., in Mexico City – *the Zócalo, the Frida Kahlo Museum, the Chapultepec Castle, the Palace of Fine Arts*. Try to include two or three places connected with music and performing arts in the list. Write *Have you ever … ?* on the board and put students into pairs to think of questions they would like to ask you about the places, e.g., *Have you ever visited the Chapultepec Castle? Have you ever seen an opera at the Palace of Fine Arts?* Monitor and point out errors for students to self-correct.

As a class, students take turns to ask you their questions. Reply with *Yes, I have. / No, I haven't.* and then, if appropriate, give students a little bit of extra information using the past simple, e.g., *Have you ever visited the Frida Kahlo Museum? / Yes, I have. I went a few years ago. It's beautiful.* Don't draw students' attention to the use of the past simple or allow them to ask you additional follow-up questions at this point as they are likely to make mistakes with the tenses.

1 READING

a 💬🔊 Discuss the question as a class and elicit that the pictures show classical music, rock and pop and local, traditional Hungarian music. Ask the students: *Which city is this?* Elicit *Budapest.* Then ask students: *Have you ever been to Budapest?* If any students answer *yes*, then ask them one or two follow-up questions using the past simple, e.g., *When did you go? Did you hear any of these types of music?* Monitor to see if they use the correct tenses in their answers. Don't, however, correct any grammatical mistakes at this point.

b Individually, students guess what they think the text is about. They then read the text quickly and find out if they were correct. Check the answer as a class.

> **Answer**
> 2 places to hear music

c Tell students to read the text again in detail and answer the questions. They then compare in pairs. Check answers as a class. You may wish to help students with words in the Vocabulary Support box.

> **Answers**
> a Sziget Festival d Óbuda
> b National Concert Hall e the A38 Ship
> c Szimpla Kert

📖 VOCABULARY SUPPORT

basement (B2) – part of a house or a building that is under the level of the street
district (B1) – a specific area of a town, city or country
live /laɪv/ (B1) – not recorded in advance, something you watch or listen to while it is happening
season (B1) – a series of concerts, plays, etc. that all happen in the same place in a specific period of time

♀ EXTRA ACTIVITY

Write sentences 1–5 on the board. Ask students to read the text again and complete them with the names of the places.
1 In …, you can have a meal as you listen to Hungarian folk music. (Óbuda)
2 At …, you can hear top orchestras play. (National Concert Hall)
3 Guests at … can eat in a garden and listen to local bands. (Szimpla Kert)
4 Enjoy live rock and pop at this island festival. (Sziget Festival)
5 This place has concerts on the water. (A38 Ship)

d Tell students to read the text again in detail and answer the questions. They then compare in pairs. Check answers as a class.

> **Answers**
> 1 Szimpla Kert, small streets of Óbuda
> 2 Sziget Festival
> 3 National Concert Hall
> 4 A38 Ship, National Concert Hall

e 💬🔊 Discuss the places students would and wouldn't like to go to as a class. Encourage students to justify their answers as much as possible.

2 VOCABULARY Music

a ▶11.08 Students read the text again and underline more examples of kinds of music, people who play music and places where you can hear music. Play the recording for students to listen and check. Check answers as a class.

> **Answers**
> 1 classical music, jazz, opera, rock, pop, folk, dance, world music, live music
> 2 an orchestra, a musician, a band, a DJ, a singer, a rock star
> 3 A concert hall, a club, a music venue, a theatre, a festival

b ▶11.09 **Pronunciation** Look at the example with the class and then play the recording for students to circle the number of syllables and underline the stressed syllable. Check answers as a class. Drill each word.

> **Answers**
> 1 <u>sing</u>er 2 2 mu<u>si</u>cian 3 3 <u>clas</u>sical 3 4 <u>or</u>chestra 3 5 <u>fes</u>tival 3

c ▶11.10 Play the recording for students to listen to the pieces of music and match them with words from 2a. Check answers as a class.

> **Answers**
> 1 classical 2 rock 3 jazz 4 pop 5 opera

d 💬🔊 In pairs or small groups, students discuss the questions. Invite pairs to share their answers with the class. Find out which kinds of music are the most/least popular.

132

3 LISTENING

a ▶**11.11** Play the recording for students to listen for general meaning and list the places Max and Alana talk about. Check answers as a class.

> **Answers**
> Szimpla Kert, A38 Ship, National Concert Hall
> Alana has been to all three places; Max hasn't been to any of them.

Audioscript

MAX Hey, Alana, have you seen this article? It says Budapest is one of the world's top cities for music. I didn't know that.

ALANA You didn't? There's so much good music here in Budapest, Max!

M I haven't been to any of these places and I've lived here for over a year. You've lived here since you were 13, right? Have you ever been to these places?

A What places do you mean?

M Like Szimpla Kert. The article says it's a famous place to hear music, but I've never heard of it. Have you ever been to Szimpla Kert?

A Yes, I went there two weeks ago. They had a really good band.

M Oh right, and what about the A38 Ship?

A Well that's the ship on the river. You must know that!

M Sure, I know it, but I've never been inside. Have you been there?

A Yes, of course I have. We all went there for Zoltan's birthday. We had a fantastic time. Didn't you come?

M Zoltan's birthday…? Oh I remember, I had exams, I couldn't go. OK, well I bet you've never been to a concert at the National Concert Hall. I've heard it's really expensive.

A Yes, I have actually. I went there last year. It was my Dad's 50th birthday, we went to the opera.

M Really? What did you see?

A I don't remember, something by Mozart. I didn't like it much.

M You've been everywhere.

A Yeah, well you should go out more, you spend too much time studying. Look, it's a nice evening, why don't we go down to the A38 Ship and sit outside. I love going there. We can watch the sun go down.

M Mm, well I'd love to, I always wanted to go there. But I have this essay to write …

b ▶**11.11** Students listen to the recording again for specific details and complete the table. Check answers by copying the table onto the board and asking individual students to come up and complete it.

> **Answers**
>
> | Where? | When? | Did she like it? |
> |---|---|---|
> | 1 Szimpla Kert | two weeks ago | yes |
> | 2 A38 Ship | Zoltan's birthday | yes |
> | 3 National Concert Hall | father's 50th birthday | no |

4 GRAMMAR
Present perfect or past simple

a ▶**11.12** Individually, students match the questions with the answers. Play the recording for students to listen and check. Check answers as a class.

> **Answers**
> 1 b   2 c   3 a

b Give students a few minutes to answer the questions. Check answers as a class.

> **Answers**
> 1 b, d
> 2 a present perfect   b past simple
> 3 a present perfect   b past simple

◆ LOA TIP CONCEPT CHECKING

- Check that students fully understand when we use the present perfect and when we use the past simple by asking them: *When we use the present perfect, which is more important – when the action happened or the experience?* (the experience) *Which words do we often use with the present perfect to mean 'at any time in my life' and 'at no time in my life'?* (*ever* and *never*) *Which tense do we use when we want to ask for more details about an experience?* (past simple).

- After checking that students have understood the uses of the present perfect and past simple, double-check they are clear about the form by asking them: *Which auxiliary do we use in past simple negatives, questions and short answers?* (*did/didn't*) *What about with the present perfect?* (*have/haven't*).

◉ CAREFUL!

As well as the common student mistakes with the present perfect outlined in Lesson 11A, students are also likely to confuse the present perfect and past simple forms. They may use the past simple instead of the present perfect, e.g., ~~I didn't buy new clothes~~ … (Correct form = *I **haven't bought** new clothes this month for my holiday in Budapest!*) or the present perfect instead of the past simple, e.g., ~~Last year I've been to~~ … (Correct form = *Last year, I **went** to the National Concert Hall for my birthday.*).

c ▶**11.13** Students read the information in Grammar Focus 11B on SB p. 158. Play the recording where indicated and ask students to listen and repeat. Students then complete the exercises. Check answers as a class, making sure students are not confusing the present perfect or past simple forms and are using the correct auxiliary verbs. Tell students to go back to SB p. 113.

> **Answers (Grammar Focus 11B SB p. 159)**
> **a** 2 I've never seen   5 she's never won   7 I've never eaten
>   3 We went   6 We visited   8 Did he win
>   4 Have you ever danced
> **b** 2 c   3 e   4 h   5 a   6 d   7 f   8 b
> **c** 2 have   6 I went   10 was   14 Did you go
>   3 I've gone   7 Did you like   11 was   15 didn't
>   4 I've gone   8 did   12 I've seen   16 I wanted
>   5 I've gone   9 It was   13 she played   17 I finished

◌ FAST FINISHERS

Ask fast finishers to look at all the verbs in Exercises a–c and check that they know the infinitive, past simple and past participle forms of each one. They can use the irregular verbs list on SB p. 129 to check their answers.

d ▶**11.14** Tell students to work individually and order the sentences to make a conversation. Play the recording for students to listen and check. Check answers as a class.

Answers and audioscript

A 1 Have you ever been to a music festival?

B 2 Yes, I have. I went to one last summer.

A 3 Where was it?

B 4 It was in Novi Sad, in Serbia – the EXIT festival.

A 5 Who did you go with?

B 6 I went with a group of friends from university.

A 7 Did you enjoy it?

B 8 Yes, we all had a great time.

e 💬 In pairs, students practise the conversation in 4d. Monitor and correct students' pronunciation as appropriate.

5 SPEAKING

a Individually, students think of two things they've seen or places they've been to in their town or city. Give them a few minutes to make notes. Monitor and help as necessary.

b Students think of two things they haven't seen or places they haven't been to and make notes.

c 💬 Students work in pairs or small groups talking about the things and places they made notes about. Listen carefully to check that students are using the present perfect and the past simple forms correctly. When students make a mistake with the forms, try to catch their eye discreetly so that they can correct their mistake.

💡 FAST FINISHERS

Ask fast finishers to talk about things or places from the categories in 5a that they didn't make notes about, i.e., if they wrote notes about a concert and a play, they could talk about a music event, a movie, a club, etc.

⊕ ADDITIONAL MATERIAL

Workbook 11B

Photocopiable activities: Grammar 11B, Vocabulary 11B

Documentary video Unit 11 *Entertainment*

Video worksheet Unit 11 *Entertainment*

11C

EVERYDAY ENGLISH
I thought they were quite good

At the end of this lesson, students will be able to:

- understand informal conversations in which people ask for and express opinions and agree or disagree with one another
- use appropriate phrases to ask for and express opinions
- respond to opinions with short phrases and questions
- identify the main stress and intonation in short phrases and questions used to respond to opinions
- ask for, express and respond to opinions about a concert and a restaurant

💡 OPTIONAL LEAD-IN

Books closed. Write these questions on the board: *When was the last time you went out in the evening? Where did you go? What did you do? Who did you go with? Did you have a good time? Why / Why not? How did you get home? How did you feel when you got home? Was it a typical night out for you? What is your idea of a perfect night out?* Put students into pairs or small groups to discuss the questions. Monitor and praise students who are able to express what they want to say, even if their English isn't perfect. Take feedback as a class and discuss the last question to find out what students think would be a perfect night out.

1 LISTENING

a 💬 Students talk about the questions in pairs. Take feedback as a class and find out what the most popular kind of transport is.

b 💬 Tell students to look at pictures 1 and 2 and ask them to write down what they think Dan is saying.

c ▶11.15 Play Part 1 of the video or the audio recording for students to check their answers in 1b. Students then choose the correct answers. Check answers as a class.

Answers

In picture 1, Dan is saying 'Taxi!'.
In picture 2, Dan is saying their address, 'Windsor Road – number 15, please.'
1 on their way home
2 15 Windsor Road

Video/Audioscript (Part 1)

DAN Taxi! … Windsor Road – number 15, please.

DRIVER 15 Windsor Road.

MARTINA That's better.

D Tired?

M Yeah, a bit. It's nearly 12. Work tomorrow.

d ▶11.16 Tell students that Dan and Martina are now in the taxi. Play Part 2 of the video or the audio recording for students to answer the questions. Check answers as a class.

Answers

1 to a concert
2 No, they don't.

Video/Audioscript (Part 2)

DAN So, what did you think of it? Did you enjoy it?

MARTINA Yeah, it was a good concert. I really liked it. How about you?

D Yeah, me too.

M But I didn't like all the bands.

D No, me neither. I didn't like the first band very much.

M Really? Oh, I thought they were quite good.

D Did you? But all their songs were the same. They really only had one song.

M Yeah, but the singer was so good. She's got an amazing voice.

D Yeah, maybe. But I just thought they were a bit boring. And I don't really like that kind of pop music.

M Well, they aren't really pop, they're sort of folk rock. Anyway, I really liked them.

D But the last band – Atlantis – I thought they were really good. Really great music.

M Do you think so? I didn't really like them. They were too loud.

D Yeah, maybe.

e ▶ **11.16** Individually, students read the sentences and decide who they correspond to. They then watch or listen again for specific details. Play Part 2 of the video or the audio recording again for students to listen and check. Check answers as a class.

> **Answers**
> 1 B 2 B 3 M 4 D 5 M

2 USEFUL LANGUAGE
Asking for and expressing opinions

a ▶ **11.17** Students put the conversation in the correct order. Play the recording for students to listen and check. Check answers as a class.

> **Answers**
> 1 d So, what did you think of it?
> 2 a Did you enjoy it?
> 3 e Yeah, it was a good concert.
> 4 c I really liked it.
> 5 b How about you?

b 💬 In pairs, students practise the mini-conversation in 2a. Monitor and correct students' pronunciation as appropriate.

c Students match the opinions with the reasons, working individually. Check answers as a class.

> **Answers**
> 1 b 2 c 3 a

> ### 💡 EXTRA ACTIVITY
>
> Books closed. Write these prompts on the board:
> **A** What / you / think / it?
> **B** I / really / like. / you?
> **A** I / really / like / first band.
> **B** Yeah / I / think / singer / great.
> Ask students to work in pairs and write the complete conversation. Remind them to think carefully about which tenses to use. Students then open their books, look at the Useful Language section and check for any mistakes in their conversation. Check answers by eliciting a full version of the conversation and writing it on the board. Make sure students understand that more than one answer is possible. (Possible answer: **A** What did you think of it? **B** I really liked it. How about you? **A** I really liked the first band. **B** Yeah, me too. I thought the singer was great.)

3 LISTENING

a ▶ **11.18** Point to picture 3 and elicit ideas from the class about what is happening. Play Part 3 of the video or the audio recording for students to listen and check. Check the answer as a class.

> **Answer**
> Martina is listening to some music on Dan's phone. She doesn't like it.

Video/Audioscript (Part 3)

DAN I've got some of their music on my phone. Here, listen. This is one of their tracks. … What do you think?

MARTINA No, thanks. I've heard enough of them already.

4 CONVERSATION SKILLS
Responding to an opinion

a Ask students: *Do you think Martina and Dan like the same kind of music?* and encourage students to justify their ideas as far as possible. Point to the mini-conversations and ask students to decide if the replies mean the other person agrees or doesn't really agree. Check answers as a class.

> **Answers**
> 1 a
> 2 a
> 3 b
> 4 b
> 5 a

b Complete the table as a class. Check students have fully understood the use of the auxiliary verbs by writing these questions on the board and asking students to choose the correct answers: *Which auxiliary verbs do we use to respond to an opinion: 'do/did' or 'have/had'?* (do/did) *Do we use the same tense as the original sentence or a different one?* (the same tense).

> **Answers**
> 1 Did
> 2 Do

c 💬 Drill the mini-conversations in 4a. Students then work in pairs, practising saying them. Monitor and correct students' pronunciation as appropriate.

> ### 💡 FAST FINISHERS
>
> Ask fast finishers to close their books and invent similar mini-conversations without looking at the mini-conversations in 4a or the table in 4b to help them.

5 PRONUNCIATION Main stress and intonation

a ▶ **11.19** Play the recording and highlight that both words are stressed in each reply.

b ▶ **11.19** Play the recording again for students to answer the questions. They then check in pairs. Check answers as a class.

Answers

1 up: 1, 2; down: 3, 4
2 b surprised

c ▶ **11.19** Play the recording again for students to listen and repeat. Drill each reply.

d 💬🔊 Put students into pairs to practise responding to the opinions. Monitor and check students are using the correct stress and intonation.

6 LISTENING

a 💬🔊 In pairs, students look at picture d and answer the questions.

b ▶ **11.20** Play Part 4 of the video or the audio recording for students to check their answers in 6a. Check answers as a class.

Answers

1 They are at home.
2 'How about some music?'

Video/Audioscript (Part 4)

MARTINA Home at last. I'm tired.
DAN How about some music?
M OK, but not Atlantis.
D OK, not Atlantis. Promise! …

---

7 SPEAKING

a ≫ Divide the class into pairs and assign A and B roles. Student As read the first card on SB p. 134 and Student Bs read the first card on SB p. 136. Students then role play the conversation. Students then read the second card and role play the second situation.

🔄 LOA TIP MONITORING

- Monitor both the preparation stage and the speaking stage of the Speaking section closely. During the preparation stage, encourage students to think carefully about what they want to say before they start speaking so that they don't have to pause and ask you for vocabulary once they have started.

- During the speaking stage, monitor and check students are forming the short phrases and questions for responding to an opinion correctly and using the correct stress and intonation. When students make a mistake with the phrases or the pronunciation, try to catch their eye discreetly so that they can correct their mistake.

- If students continue to form the phrases and questions incorrectly, and aren't using correct stress and intonation, you may wish to check this again or ask them to do the activity in Workbook 11C.

💡 EXTRA ACTIVITY

Ask students to work in pairs and give them one minute to think of as many things as they can that they have both seen and done, e.g., seen the opera *Tosca*, been to a comedy club. Check they understand that they should just make a list at this point, not discuss the things in any detail. When students have finished preparing their list, tell them that now they should discuss each item in turn using the useful language for asking for, expressing and responding to opinions, e.g.,
A *We've both seen the opera* Tosca. *What did you think of it?*
B *I didn't like it very much.* **A** *Me neither. I thought the singers were great, but I didn't like the story.* Monitor and praise students with a smile or a nod when they use the language from this lesson correctly and use appropriate stress and tone in their replies.

⊕ ADDITIONAL MATERIAL

Workbook 11C

Photocopiable activities: Pronunciation 11C

Unit Progress Test

SKILLS FOR WRITING

It was an interesting film

At the end of this lesson, students will be able to:

- understand a conversation in which people discuss a film they've both seen
- understand positive and negative reviews of a film
- structure a review correctly and avoid repetition
- write a review of a film they've seen and structure it correctly

💡 OPTIONAL LEAD-IN

Before students arrive, write these questions on the board:

How many of these people in the photos do you know?

What do you know about them?

What are they famous for?

What films have they been in or directed?

Have you seen any of their films?

As students arrive, put them into pairs or small groups to look at the photographs on p 117 and answer the questions. Invite students to share their answers with the class and give students information from Culture Notes below, if you wish.

1 SPEAKING AND LISTENING

a 💬📢 Discuss the questions as a class and find out if they have ever watched a film more than once. If you didn't use the optional lead-in, give students information from Culture Notes below.

🌍 CULTURE NOTES

(Photos on p 117 clockwise from top left) Ryan Gosling and Emma Stone, who co-starred in *La La Land*, an award-winning romantic musical from 2016. Ryan Gosling, a Canadian actor, director and musician, has starred in many films, including *Crazy, Stupid, Love*, *Blade Runner 2049* and *First Man*. Emma Stone is an Oscar-winning actor from Arizona, USA. She began acting at the age of 11 when she appeared in a theatre production of *The Wind in the Willows*. She became widely known following her roles in *Crazy, Stupid, Love* and *The Amazing Spider-Man*. In the sports film *Battle of the Sexes*, she portrayed the tennis legend Billie Jean King, and she starred in the comedy *Zombieland*.

Lupita Nyong'o is an award-winning Kenyan-Mexican actor. Born in Mexico City, she grew up in Kenya. In 2013, she appeared in *12 Years a Slave*, her first major film, for which she won an Oscar. She became internationally famous following her roles in the *Star Wars* sequels and *Black Panther*, a Marvel superhero film. She has written a best-selling children's book, called *Sulwe*.

Chris Hemsworth is a leading actor from Melbourne, Australia. One of the highest paid actors in the world, he has starred in many films, including the Marvel film series *Thor* and *Avengers*, as well as *Star Trek* and *Extraction*. Although best known as an action film hero, he has also starred in comedies, such as *The Cabin in the Woods*, and he portrayed the British Formula 1 racing driver James Hunt in the film *Rush*.

Kevin Hart is an American actor, producer and comedian. Making his debut in the film *Paper Soldiers* in 2002, he has starred in many comedy films, including *Ride Along*, *Grudge Match*, *Central Intelligence* and *Jumanji*. In 2017, he founded the production company Laugh Out Loud to promote comedians from all around the world.

Bon Joon-ho is a South Korean film producer and director. His debut as a film director came in 2000 with the critically acclaimed black comedy *Barking Dogs Never Bite*. He achieved international fame with the release of the science fiction film *Snowpiercer*, his first English-language film, and in 2019, he directed the black comedy thriller *Parasite*, which won four Oscars, including Best Picture.

b ▶ **11.21** Tell students that they are going to listen to Melissa and John talking, but that they are not talking about any of the films on SB pp. 116–117. Play the recording for students to listen for general meaning and answer the questions. Check answers as a class.

Answers

1 *A James Bond film*
2 *yes; no.*

Audioscript

MELISSA Have you seen the new James Bond film

JOHN Yes, have you?

M Yes, I've seen it, yeah. Not very good, is it?

J Oh, I don't agree. I really enjoyed it.

M Well, I thought it was boring. James Bond films are always the same. James Bond is cool, he goes to some beautiful country and he meets a beautiful girl. The bad guys all die at the end. You always know what's going to happen. Of course the special effects were great, but that's about all.

J Well, it's not meant to be too serious, you know. I thought it was fun. I liked it.

M Did you really?

J Yes, I did. I thought it was exciting. It was great to watch, the actors were great and James Bond was fantastic. I'm going to see it again this weekend. Do you want to come?

M What, again? No thanks, once was enough. I'm going to see the new Tarantino film.

c ▶ **11.21** Students listen to the recording again for specific details and decide who the sentences correspond to. They then check in pairs. Check answers as a class.

Answers

1 M 2 J 3 M 4 J

d Individually, students choose two films, one they've seen and one they haven't seen, and make notes. Monitor and help with vocabulary if necessary.

💡 EXTRA ACTIVITY

Write jumbled questions/responses 1–6 on the board. Ask students to put them in order:

1 *you / so / do / think ?* (Do you think so?)
2 *enjoy / it / you / did ?* (Did you enjoy it?)
3 *agree / really / don't / I* (I don't really agree.)
4 *very much / like / it / I / didn't* (I didn't like it very much.)
5 *a / director / fantastic / he's / think / I* (I think he's a fantastic director.)
6 *story / thought the / I / good, / was pretty / actors were / awful / but the* (I thought the story was pretty good, but the actors were awful.)

Check answers as a class. Remind students to use appropriate phrases for asking for, expressing and responding to opinions in their discussion in the next exercise.

e 💬🗨 In small groups, students discuss the questions. Monitor and check that students are using the language for expressing opinions correctly.

2 READING

a Point to the photo of Ashley on SB p. 116 and tell students that they are going to read her review of *Roma*. Individually, students read the review quickly and find out if it's positive or negative. Check the answer as a class.

> **Answer**
> positive

b Tell students to read the review again in detail and answer the questions. They then check in pairs. Check answers as a class.

> **Answers**
> 1 twice
> 2 *Possible answers:* He's a Mexican film director; he directed *Roma*; he grew up in Mexico City.
> 3 *Possible answers:* She was the best; she's a great actor; she was unknown; she plays the role of a maid.

c Point to the photo of Oscar on SB p. 117 and his review. Students read it quickly to find out if it's positive or negative. Check the answer as a class.

> **Answer**
> negative

d Students read Oscar's review again in detail and answer the questions. They then check in pairs. Check answers as a class.

> **Answers**
> 1 A friend recommended it.
> 2 Good: the acting
> Bad: the story is boring; nothing exciting happens.

e Point to the photo of Anna on SB p. 117 and her review. Students read it quickly to find out if it's positive or negative. Check the answer as a class.

> **Answer**
> mainly positive

f Students read Anna's review again in detail and answer the questions. After checking answers, ask any students who have seen Roma if they agree with Ashley's, Oscar's or Anna's opinion.

> **Answers**
> 1 at a friend's house
> 2 *Possible answers:* It's a sad film; it's in black and white; the maid comes from a village.

3 WRITING SKILLS Structuring a review

a Look at the two reviews with the class and check that students understand that the numbers 1–6 appear in both Ashley's and Oscar's reviews. Read the example and show students how this question is answered in sentence 4 of both reviews. Students then work individually, identifying the sentences. Check answers as a class.

> **Answers**
> a 4 b 1 c 2 d 6 e 3 f 5

b Individually, students look at Anna's review again and compare it to Ashley's and Oscar's reviews. Check the answer as a class.

> **Answer**
> No. She talks about the film (f) and then about the actors (a).

c Read the first comment and elicit the answer as an example. Individually, students match the other comments with the questions in 3a. They then check in pairs. Check answers as a class.

> **Answers**
> 1 c   5 e
> 2 b   6 d
> 3 c   7 f
> 4 a

d Individually, students read the sentences and compare them with the ones in the reviews. Check answers as a class.

> **Answers**
> 1 The review uses *it*.
> 2 The review uses *she* and *her*.
> 3 The review uses *it*.

e 💬🗨 In pairs, students discuss the questions. Invite pairs to share their answers with the class and ask students: *Why do the reviews use 'it', 'this film', and 'the film'?* Check that students understand that it isn't good style to keep repeating words and names in English.

> **Answers**
> 1 Once, at the beginning.
> 2 *it, the film, this film.*

> 💡 **FAST FINISHERS**
>
> Ask fast finishers to read the three reviews again and find *good* and its comparative and superlative forms. They then underline all the other adjectives in the reviews and list their comparative and superlative forms.

---

4 WRITING AND SPEAKING

> 🔄 **LOA TIP** **CONCEPT CHECKING**
>
> - If students need more support, demonstrate 4a and 4b (making notes and the review) by eliciting notes and writing them onto the board for questions a–f in 3a. Then, work as a class to build the notes into a model review so that students fully understand the process.
>
> - Use questions a–f in 3a to write short notes down the left-hand side of the board. For example, choose a film together and ask the class: *When did you see the film?* Suggest that you saw it together as a class last week (note down: *last week, as a class*). Then ask: *Did you like it?* (e.g., *teacher – great, student – terrible!*). Continue with the other questions.
>
> - Elicit complete sentences from the class, helping the students by using the notes on the board, the comments in 3b and Ashley's, Oscar's and Anna's reviews in 2a, 2c and 2e. Write the review on the right-hand side of the board, e.g., *I went to see* The Call of the Wild *last week with my class. The teacher told us it was great, but I thought it was boring!* …. Tell students to use exactly the same process to prepare their reviews.

a Students work individually to plan a review of a film they've seen. Monitor and help with vocabulary and give students ideas if necessary. Check that students know the English title of the film they have chosen.

b If you're short of time, this exercise can be completed for homework. Students could then bring their reviews to the next lesson.

c In pairs, students swap reviews and check their partner's work. Tell them to check their partner has answered all six questions in 3a and has not repeated the name of the film or the names of the actors too often. They then give each other feedback. If they have made any mistakes with the structure or in other areas, they prepare a second draft of their review before giving it to you for correction.

d 💬📢 Put students into small groups to read each other's reviews and discuss which films they would like to see. If you and your students have the technology available, you could set up a class blog where students can post their reviews and respond to each other's opinions.

⊕ **ADDITIONAL MATERIAL**

Workbook 11D

UNIT 11
Review and extension

1 VOCABULARY

a Students underline the correct word in each sentence. Check answers as a class.

Answers

1 classical	4 pop
2 rock	5 musician
3 orchestra	6 opera

b Students write the past participle of each verb. They check their answers by looking at the irregular verbs list on SB p. 129.

Answers

1 been	5 read (/**red**/)
2 done	6 seen
3 gone	7 won
4 heard	8 written

> ### ◌ FAST FINISHERS
>
> Ask fast finishers to look at the verbs in 1b again and check the ones that have the same form for the past simple and the past participle. For the ones that are different, students write down the past simple form, too.

2 GRAMMAR

a Students write the statements and questions. Check answers as a class by asking individual students to write the correct answers on the board.

Answers

1 I have been … / I've been …
2 She has met … / She's met …
3 Have you seen …
4 He hasn't worked …
5 We've never won … / We have never won …
6 Have they read …
7 I haven't heard …

b Individually, students read the sentences, tick the correct sentences and correct the verb form in the ones that are wrong. Check answers as a class.

Answers

1 ✓		5 ✓
2 ~~He's read~~ He read		6 ✓
3 ~~I never saw~~ I've never seen		7 ~~I didn't read~~ I've never read
4 ~~They've won~~ They won		

c Complete the first item as an example with the class. Check that students understand that they can use the present perfect or the past simple and so need to think carefully about the meaning. Check answers as a class. Drill the conversation.

Answers

1 Have you been	4 went	7 did
2 've been	5 did you stay	8 was
3 've never been	6 wasn't	9 Have you ever tried

3 WORDPOWER Multi-word verbs

a Tell students to close their books. Write the following incomplete sentences 1–3 on the board: *1 I come … Brazil. 2 She sometimes wakes … very late. 3 We went … to a restaurant for dinner last night.* Point to the three gaps and ask students about each missing word. Write *from, up* and *out* on the board in each sentence. Then, circle the multi-word verb in each sentence (*come from, wakes up, went out*) and ask students: *What kind of words are these?* Elicit/Teach *multi-word verbs.* (You could also point out the alternative term, *phrasal verbs*, which students may already know.) Students open their books, look at the sentences and match them to make conversations. Check answers as a class.

Answers

1 c   2 e   3 b   4 f   5 a   6 d

b Individually, students match the multi-word verbs with the meanings. They then check in pairs. Check answers as a class.

Answers

1 c   2 f   3 e   4 a   5 d   6 b

c Students complete the sentences with the correct form of a multi-word verb from 3a. Check answers as a class.

Answers

1 try (things) on
2 fill (it) out
3 grew up
4 called (me) back
5 lie down
6 came over

> ### ◌ EXTRA ACTIVITY
>
> Write example answers a–f below to questions 1–6 in 3d on the board. Ask students to match them to the questions and complete the answers before they ask and answer the questions in pairs: *a No. I always _____ people _____ when they leave a message. (2 call … back) b Yes, I often _____ _____ after lunch and sleep for twenty minutes. (6 lie down) c I _____ _____ a form last week because I need a new passport. (5 filled out) d They never _____ _____ – they live far away! (1 come over) e No, I can't _____ them _____ because I buy everything on the Internet. (4 try … on) f I _____ _____ in a little town in the mountains in Colorado. (3 grew up)*

d 💬 In pairs, students ask and answer the questions. Monitor, but don't interrupt fluency unless students make mistakes with the phrasal verbs.

≫ Photocopiable activities: Wordpower 11

> ### ↻ LOA REVIEW YOUR PROGRESS
>
> Students look back through the unit, think about what they've studied and decide how well they did. Students work on weak areas by using the appropriate sections of the Workbook and the Photocopiable activities.

UNIT 12 TRAVEL

🔄 UNIT OBJECTIVES

At the end of this unit, students will be able to:

- understand information, texts and conversations about travel and holiday plans
- ask for and give information about holidays
- give each other advice about what to do on holiday
- use appropriate phrases to show surprise
- check into a hotel and ask for tourist information
- write an informal email giving information and advice about their home town and use appropriate paragraphs

UNIT CONTENTS

G GRAMMAR
- *be going to*
- *should / shouldn't*

V VOCABULARY
- Geography: *beach, coast, countryside, desert, field, forest, glacier, hill, island, jungle, lake, mountain, rainforest, river, waterfall, woods*
- Travel collocations: *book a hotel, change plans, go back home, live abroad, make plans, pack a bag, plan a holiday, stay home, stay in a hotel, take a holiday, travel abroad, unpack a bag*
- Linking words: *first, secondly, finally*
- Wordpower: *take*

P PRONUNCIATION
- Word stress in geography words
- Main stress in *be going to*
- *should / shouldn't*
- Rising intonation to show surprise
- Consonant clusters with /t/: *ts, st, ghts, xt, ft,* etc.

C COMMUNICATION SKILLS
- Talking about places you've been to and places you would like to go to on holiday
- Asking and answering questions about a working holiday
- Giving advice about what to do on holiday
- Using appropriate phrases to show surprise
- Checking in at a hotel
- Asking for tourist information
- Writing an informal email giving information and advice about your home town

GETTING STARTED

💡 OPTIONAL LEAD-IN

Use a 'live listening' to introduce the topic of travel. Choose a picture with friends or family on holiday to show the class. Find out about the people and holiday in the picture or make up your own ideas, e.g., *These are my friends Sarah and Russell. They are in Iceland.* Alternatively, use a picture of yourself on holiday. Write questions 1–3 on the board: *1 Where are the people? 2 Who are they? 3 What did they do while they were on holiday?* Project your picture on the board or print it out to show the class and tell students about it. Students listen, answer the questions on the board and note down any other information you give. They then check in pairs and ask you to confirm any information they are not sure about.

a 💬🗣 Give students one minute to think about their answers to the questions before talking about the picture as a class. If you wish, give students information from Culture Notes below and ask students if they would like to go on holiday to Egypt.

🌍 CULTURE NOTES

This picture shows the Giza pyramid complex in Egypt, also called the Giza Necropolis. All the pyramids were built in the Fourth Dynasty of the Old Kingdom of Ancient Egypt. The Great Pyramid (the largest in the photo) is the oldest of the Seven Wonders of the World and the only one still in existence. It's 147 metres high and made up of an estimated 2.3 million stone blocks, each weighing approximately 2.5 to 15 tons.

These pyramids are located approximately nine kilometres west of the Nile River in the city of Giza and about 13 kilometres southwest of Cairo.

b 💬🗣 Read the questions with students before they ask and answer them. If they wish, they can show each other pictures of friends and family, holidays, etc. on their phones if they have them. Invite students to share their answers with the class and find out what students do with their photographs after they've taken them, e.g., make albums, share them on social media.

💡 EXTRA ACTIVITY

Give students time for a 'long turn' at this point (see the extra activity after 3d on p. 32.). Ask students to choose a picture they have taken that is special to them and that they are happy to share with the class. If you used the optional lead-in, tell students that you want them to talk about their picture in the same way. If students don't have a suitable picture on their phone, ask them to prepare their notes for homework and bring the picture to the next class. Tell students to make notes about it, but not to write complete sentences. Monitor and help students make their notes if necessary. Ask students to speak to the class in turn about their picture and show it to the class. Remind students not to look at their notes too much while they are speaking. After each long turn, allow two or three students to ask the speaker questions based on their talk.

Exercises a and b can be prepared as homework before this lesson to give students time to look up unfamiliar vocabulary. Ask students to look at the picture and to prepare their answers to the questions as homework to talk about in the next lesson.

12A WHAT ARE YOU GOING TO DO?

At the end of this lesson, students will be able to:

- use a lexical set of geography words correctly
- read and understand a text about working holidays
- understand a conversation in which people talk about their holiday plans
- use *be going to* to describe future plans
- ask for and give information about a working holiday

♀ OPTIONAL LEAD-IN

Write *Holidays* on the board and underneath, write question beginnings 1–4 and endings a–d: *1 Where do you like 2 What time of year 3 Where do you 4 Who do you usually*; *a do you like going away? b go on holiday with? c going on holiday? d like staying?* Leave a small space, then write question beginnings 5–8 and endings e–h: *5 Where and when 6 How long did 7 What did 8 Was it a typical*; *e you stay? f holiday for you? g you do? h was your last holiday?*

Check that students understand that 1–4 match with a–d and 5–8 match with e–h. Individually, they match the beginnings and endings. Check answers as a class (1c, 2a, 3d, 4b, 5h, 6e, 7g, 8f).

Put students into pairs to ask and answer the questions. Finally, point to questions 1–4 and ask: *Are these questions about the past, present or future?* Elicit that they use the present simple to talk about general preferences. Then, point to questions 5–8 and repeat the question. Elicit that they use the past simple to ask about a specific holiday in the past. Tell students that Lesson 12A is about the future.

1 VOCABULARY Geography

a Ask students to cover the words and see how many of the things in the pictures they know. Individually, students then match the words with the pictures.

b ▶ **12.01** **Pronunciation** Play the recording for students to listen and check their answers to 1a. Then, read the questions with the class and, if necessary, play the recording again. Check answers as a class. Drill each word.

Answers
a 1 d 2 g 3 b 4 j 5 f 6 a 7 e 8 h 9 i 10 c
b 1 lake; beach 2 the first syllable

♀ EXTRA ACTIVITY

Put students into pairs. Explain that you're going to say ten places in the world and students have to write which part of the world they are in. Teach/Elicit *Antarctica*, if necessary. Allow students to refer to SB p. 162 if necessary.

1 Mount Everest – the world's highest mountain (Asia) *2 the Nile River – the world's longest river* (Africa) *3 the Amazon Rainforest – the world's biggest rainforest* (South America) *4 the Sahara Desert – the world's biggest sand desert* (Africa) *5 Lake Superior – the world's biggest lake* (North America) *6 Praia do Cassino Beach – the world's longest beach* (South America) *7 the Lambert Glacier –the world's biggest glacier* (Antarctica) *8 Angel Falls – the world's highest waterfall* (South America) *9 Greenland – the world's biggest island* (geographically North America, politically Europe) *10 the Taiga forest – the world's biggest forest* (North America, Europe and Asia).

Check answers as a class and award one point for each correct answer. The pair with the highest score is the winner.

c 💬🔊 In pairs, students ask and answer the questions. Monitor, but don't interrupt fluency unless students make mistakes with the pronunciation of the geography words.

d ≫ ▶ **12.02** Students complete the exercises in Vocabulary Focus 12A on SB p. 170. Play the recording for students to complete the Pronunciation activity. Monitor Exercise d and check other answers as a class. Tell students to go back to SB p. 120.

Answers (Vocabulary Focus 12A SB p. 170)
a a coast b jungle c hill d countryside e woods f fields
b jungle; countryside
c 1 field (It's not water.)
  2 hill (It's not trees.)
  3 mountain (It's not connected to the sea.)

♀ FAST FINISHERS

Ask fast finishers to write sentences about the geography of the place where they live, using the emails in Vocabulary Focus 12A, Exercise a as a model.

2 READING

a 💬🔊 Read the question and the ideas with students and check that they understand the vocabulary. In pairs, they discuss what's important for them when they're on holiday. Ask pairs to share their answers with the class.

b Students read the web page quickly and find out which ideas from 2a it mentions. Check answers as a class.

Answers
- meet new people
- do a lot of sightseeing
- understand a new culture
- try a new sport
- eat local food

c Tell students to read the web page again in detail. Individually, students identify which jobs would be appropriate for the different profiles. Encourage students to guess the meaning of any new words from the context. However, you may wish to help students with words in the Vocabulary Support box. Check answers as a class.

Answers
- job 2
- job 3
- job 1

📖 VOCABULARY SUPPORT

accommodation (B1) – the place where you live or sleep

kayaking – an activity using a small, narrow boat usually for only one person

local (B1) – from or in the area near you

scenery (B1) – views, especially beautiful, of the countryside

d 💬🔊 In pairs, students talk about whether they would like to do any of these jobs and decide which would be the most and least hard work. Ask students to share their answers with the class. Encourage them to justify their answers as much as possible.

3 LISTENING

a ▶**12.03** Play the recording for students to listen for general meaning and answer the question. Check the answers as a class.

> **Answer**
> Emily – holiday 3
> Chloe – holiday 2

Audioscript

CONVERSATION 1

ZOE So, about next year – what are you going to do?

EMILY I finally decided yesterday.

Z And?

E Well, I don't really want to continue studying. I'd like to do some travelling. So, I'm not going to go to university next year.

Z Go travelling? Nice idea – but that costs a lot of money.

E I've saved a bit of money. But you don't need a lot. Look. I found this website: Work Around the World.

Z OK …

E Well, you can go places and get free food and accommodation – you just have to do a bit of work.

Z I don't know … I heard you work really hard on those things.

E But look at this one. I'm going to email and ask about it. It looks so beautiful there close to the mountains and I love drawing and things, so it's perfect.

Z But what about … what about all our friends? I mean, university starts next year.

E I know. Sorry. It starts for everyone, but not for me.

CONVERSATION 2

CHLOE I want to do something different for a while. I'm going to leave this job.

FRANK Get a new one?

C No, I want to go away and have some fun.

F Ah, so a holiday.

C Yes, a very long holiday. Look at this website …

F Work Around the World holidays …

C There are some interesting things on it.

F … free accommodation and food … But no pay.

C No, but it doesn't matter. Look at this job I read about. I'm going to find out more about it. It's in such an amazing place. I can go to the beach every day.

F It says you have to spend a lot of time with children. Do you even like children?

C Yeah – I love them.

F And do you know how to teach?

C I'm sure I can learn.

b ▶**12.03** Students listen to the recording again for specific details and answer the questions. They then compare in pairs. Check answers as a class.

> **Answers**
>
> **Conversation 1**
> 1 Because she doesn't really want to continue studying and she'd like to do some travelling.
> 2 She likes the free food and accommodation. It's close to the mountains and she can draw.
> 3 Because she wants Emily to go to university at the same time as her and their friends.
>
> **Conversation 2**
> 1 Because she wants to do something different for a while.
> 2 It's in an amazing place and she can go to the beach every day.
> 3 He doesn't think it's a good job for Chloe because she doesn't know how to teach.

> 💡 **EXTRA ACTIVITY**
>
> Play the recording again for students to decide if sentences 1–6 are true or false: *1 Emily isn't sure if she wants to go on a Work Around the World holiday.* (F – She decided yesterday.) *2 She has a lot of money to take with her.* (F – She's saved a bit of money, but she doesn't need a lot.) *3 Zoe thinks you have to do a lot of work on these holidays.* (T) *4 Chloe only wants to go away for a couple of weeks.* (F – She wants a very long holiday.) *5 She's sure she wants to go to Mexico.* (F – She wants to find out more about it.) *6 Frank doesn't like the idea that there isn't any pay.* (T)

c 💬🗨 Students work in pairs or small groups, answering the questions. Invite students to share their answers with the class.

4 GRAMMAR *be going to*

a ▶**12.04** Books closed. Write the incomplete sentences on the board and ask students to complete them as a class. Students open their books. Play the recording for students to listen and check. Check answers as a class. Drill the sentences.

> **Answers**
> 1 going
> 2 going

b Ask students to look at the examples of *be going to* in 4a. They then underline the correct words to complete the rule. Check the answer as a class.

> **Answer**
> a future plan

c ▶**12.05** Individually, students complete the sentences with the positive, negative and question forms of *be going to*. Play the recording for students to listen and check. Check answers as a class by asking individual students to write the correct answers on the board.

> **Answers**
> + 'm going to find out
> – 'm not going to go
> ? are you going to do

d ▶**12.05** **Pronunciation** Play the recording for students to answer the questions. Check the answers as a class. Drill the sentences.

> **Answer**
> the main verb

> 👁 **CAREFUL!**
>
> There are several common student mistakes with *be going to*. They may omit part of the construction, possibly *going*, e.g., ~~How are you to get to the airport?~~ (Correct form = *How are you **going to get** to the airport?*) or possibly the auxiliary *is/are*, e.g., ~~We going to go to the beach~~ (Correct form = *We **are going** to go to the beach on the train*).
>
> Students may also make mistakes with the infinitive and use *to* + verb + *-ing*, e.g., ~~I'm going to wearing my …~~ (Correct form = *I'm **going to wear** my new shorts tomorrow*). Sometimes students will use *go to* instead of *be going to*, e.g., ~~I'm happy that I go to Finland~~ (Correct form = *I'm happy that **I'm going** to Finland*) or use *will go* in places where *be going to* is required, e.g., ~~I bought new boots because I will go hiking on holiday~~ (Correct form = *… I bought new boots because I'**m going to** go hiking on holiday*).

e ▶12.06 Students read the information in Grammar Focus 12A on SB p. 160. Play the recording where indicated and ask students to listen and repeat. Students then complete the exercises. Check answers as a class, making sure students are forming the sentences with *be going to* correctly. Tell students to go back to SB p. 121.

Answers (Grammar Focus 12A SB p. 161)
a 2 h 3 g 4 b 5 c 6 d 7 a 8 f
b 2 is/'s going to get   6 am/'m going to go
    3 are/'re going to do   7 isn't going to go
    4 aren't going to stay   8 aren't going to visit
    5 are going to buy   9 are/'re going to stay

💡 **FAST FINISHERS**

Ask fast finishers to rewrite the positive sentences in Grammar Focus 12A, Exercise b in the negative and vice versa, e.g., *1 I'm not going to travel to South America.*

---

f ▶12.07 Students work individually, completing the conversation. Play the recording for students to listen and check. Check answers as a class.

Answers
1 am/'m going to spend
2 going to go
3 am/'m going to travel
4 are you going to do
5 am/'m not going to do
6 am/'m going to look

5 SPEAKING

🔄 **LOA TIP** ELICITING

- If you think students need more support before completing the Communication activity, elicit a second model conversation from the class like the one in 4f. Write the following notes on the board in the same style as the ones on SB pp. 135 and 137.

Notes ⊕

Where: Africa
Why: see the desert and the Nile River
How long: seven weeks
Possible jobs: teaching in a local school, building basic houses
Before trip: buy a new camera
After trip: write a blog and share pictures

- Tell students: *I'm going to spend seven weeks travelling and working this summer.* Point to the word *Where* in the notes and elicit the question: *Where are you going to go?* Answer the question and then point to *Why* to elicit the next question and so on until you've elicited all the questions that students will need to complete the task.

a 💬 In pairs, students answer the question. Ask students to share their answers with the class and find out which of the three holidays is most popular.

b ≫ Tell students that they can now practise using all the language from the lesson with a partner. Divide the class into pairs and assign A and B roles (Student As go to SB p. 135 and Student Bs go to SB p. 137). Students read the information about their working holidays and write questions they can ask their partner. Monitor and point out errors in the questions for students to self-correct before they work in pairs, asking each other about their holidays. Monitor, but don't interrupt fluency unless students make mistakes with the content of this lesson. Tell students to go back to SB p. 121.

⊕ **ADDITIONAL MATERIAL**

Workbook 12A

Photocopiable activities: Grammar 12A, Vocabulary 12A

Documentary video Unit 12 *Travel*

Video worksheet Unit 12 *Travel*

12B | YOU SHOULD LIVE LIKE THE LOCAL PEOPLE

At the end of this lesson, students will be able to:

- read and understand a text about living in a different country
- use a lexical set of travel collocations correctly
- use *should / shouldn't* to give advice
- understand people talking about where and how they like spending time
- give people advice about what to do on holiday

💡 OPTIONAL LEAD-IN

Organise a 'grammar auction' (see p. 153) to study areas of grammar that you know students find problematic. Prepare 15 sentences containing items of grammar and/or vocabulary from the course. Some of them should be correct, e.g., *That was the best holiday I have ever had!*, and some of them incorrect, e.g., *I haven't never been to Egypt, but I really want to.* Write the sentences on the board. Put students into small groups, tell them they have £100, and explain that they need to buy the correct sentences. Students work in their groups, discussing which sentences they want to buy. Don't help and don't allow students to look at their notes or the Student's Book.

Run the auction, selling each sentence to the group that offers the most money. After all the sentences have been sold, reveal which are correct and which are incorrect and ask students to correct the mistakes. The winning group is the one with the most correct sentences.

1 READING

a 💬🗩 In pairs, students ask and answer the questions. Ask students to share their answers with the class and find out some of the places where students would like to live.

b Students read the texts quickly and match the people with the pictures. Check answers as a class.

> **Answers**
> 1 Tom
> 2 Kirsten
> 3 Liona
> 4 Maya

c Tell students to read the texts again in detail. Students identify who wrote each sentence. When checking answers, ask students to read the section of the text which helped them to find the answer.

> **Answers**
> 1 M 2 OK 3 T 4 M 5 OK

💡 EXTRA ACTIVITY

Ask students to read the texts again and answer questions 1–6:
1 How old was Tom when he moved to Portugal? (He was 39.)
2 How many jobs does Tom have? (two – He's an English teacher and a DJ.) *3 How many different countries did Oliver and Kirsten visit before they arrived in Egypt?* (They visited seven countries.)
4 Which other countries do they want to live in? (They want to live in Ecuador and South Africa.) *5 When did Maya start her very long holiday?* (She started after she finished university.) *6 When did she decide to do a course to become a diving teacher?* (when she was in Australia)

d 💬🗩 Discuss the question as a class. Encourage students to justify their answers as much as possible.

2 VOCABULARY Travel collocations

a Books closed. Write *do y_ _ _* and *c_ _ _ _ on a link* on the board. Point to the first missing word and mime a yoga pose. Ask students what the word is (*yoga*). Repeat the process by miming looking at a computer screen and clicking the mouse to elicit *click*. Remind students that *do yoga* is from the set of Sport and exercise collocations in Lesson 8A and *click on a link* is from the set of IT collocations in Lesson 10A. Explain to students that a collocation is two or more words which we often use together. Tell them that now they are going to see a set of travel collocations. Individually, students match the pairs of verbs with the words/phrases in the box, using the texts for help. Check answers as a class.

> **Answers**
> 1 plans   4 a holiday
> 2 abroad   5 a hotel
> 3 home   6 a bag

b ▶12.08 Students complete the sentences, working individually. Play the recording for students to listen and check. Check answers as a class.

> **Answers**
> 1 plan   4 pack
> 2 travel   5 go back
> 3 book   6 make

c 💬🗩 In pairs or small groups, students talk about which speakers they agree with. Encourage them to change the sentences that they don't agree with so that they are true for them, e.g., *I never plan my holidays carefully. I like to find things out when I'm there.*

3 GRAMMAR should / shouldn't

a Books closed. On the board, write: *You should try to make friends with people from the country.* Ask students: *Who said this?* (Kirsten). Then, draw ≠ on the board and write *You shouldn't try to make friends with people from the country.* Next, ask students which sentence they agree with. Ask: *Are these sentences giving advice or giving information?* (giving advice). *Which words tell us that this is advice? (should/shouldn't).* Circle *should/shouldn't* on the board and tell students to underline the correct words in the sentences in the Student's Book. Check answers as a class.

> **Answers**
> 1 should   2 shouldn't   3 should

b Complete the rules as a class.

> **Answers**
> b it's a good idea
> b infinitive

c ▶️**12.09** **Pronunciation** Play the recording for students to listen and answer the questions. Check that they understand that the letter *l* is an example of a silent letter, like the ones they saw in Lesson 9B. Drill the sentences.

| **Answers**
| 1 no 2 short

◉ CAREFUL!

Students often make mistakes with *should* and may use *do*, *can* or *may* instead, e.g., ~~What do I pack to go on holiday?~~ (Correct form = *What **should** I pack to go on holiday?*) or ~~You may take a course to learn to dive~~ (Correct form = *You **should** take a course to learn to dive*). They may also use *should* in contexts where it's not correct, most commonly confusing it with *would*, e.g., ~~It should be nice to travel abroad~~ (Correct form = *It **would** be nice to travel abroad*).

There are also several mistakes that students make with the negative form, *shouldn't*. Students often confuse the meaning of *don't have to* (= you don't need to do it, but you can do it if you want) with *shouldn't* (= I think it's a bad idea), e.g., ~~You don't have to stay in that hotel; it's horrible~~ (Correct form = *You **shouldn't** stay in that hotel; it's horrible*), or ~~You shouldn't know how to dive…~~ (Correct form = *You **don't have to** know how to dive; it's a beginners' course*). Students may also forget that *shouldn't* is negative and may make mistakes with *some/any/no* and similar words, e.g., ~~You shouldn't tell no one about the party~~ (Correct form = *You shouldn't tell **anyone** about the party*).

d ⟫ ▶️**12.10** Students read the information in Grammar Focus 12B on SB p. 160. Play the recording where indicated and ask students to listen and repeat. Students then complete the exercises. Check answers as a class, making sure students are using the infinitive after *should/shouldn't*. After students complete the Grammar Focus activities, ask them: *Is 'should/shouldn't' easy or difficult?* Elicit an indication of their confidence level. Tell students to go back to SB p. 123.

Answers (Grammar Focus 12B SB p. 161)
a 2 should drink 4 shouldn't drive 6 should come 8 should say
   3 shouldn't bring 5 should take 7 shouldn't pay
b 2 Should we go to a museum? 6 What time should we arrive?
   3 What clothes should I wear? 7 Where should we stay?
   4 Should I come back later? 8 Who should we ask for advice?
   5 Should we eat the local food?
c/d You ~~don't should~~ shouldn't book before you go.
   ~~I should go~~ Should I go to Bangkok?
   You should ~~to~~ go to Bangkok for a few days, …
   What ~~do I should do~~ should I do on an island?
   You ~~should not to~~ shouldn't worry about money on holiday!

e Students work individually, adding *should* or *shouldn't* and changing the verbs in blue as necessary. They then check in pairs. Check answers as a class.

Answers
1 You should go out and meet people.
2 You should try to visit a new place every weekend. You shouldn't wait until the last few weeks of your stay.
3 You should read about the country before you go there.
4 You shouldn't get angry when things go wrong.
5 You should remember that things work differently in other countries.

♀ FAST FINISHERS

Ask fast finishers to invent more sentences with *should* or *shouldn't* to add to the advice about living abroad in 3e.

4 LISTENING AND SPEAKING

a 💬🗨 Give students one minute to read the comments and think what the people mean. They then discuss in pairs or small groups whether they are the same. Discuss the questions as a class and find out what kind of people your students are.

b 💬🗨 Individually, students read the texts again quickly and decide which things they think Tom and Maya like. They then compare in pairs.

c ▶️**12.11** Play the recording for students to listen and check their answers in 4b. Then, check answers as a class.

Answers
T = big cities, cafés, shopping, noise, dancing, music
M = sports, the countryside, the sea, beaches

Audioscript

TOM I grew up in London and I've always lived in big cities. I love cities – I like going to cafés and I love shopping. Every city's different. I've been to Rome, Paris, Tokyo, Buenos Aires, Lisbon … and I love them all. I'm never very happy in the countryside. There's nothing to do there. I like people and noise.
In my free time, I listen to music a lot – mainly dance music, but I like rock music, too. I don't do much sport; I've never really liked sport, … well, I like dancing, but that's not really a sport, is it?

MAYA I think I've always been a sporty person. I loved sport at school. And I love water sports of all kinds. I go swimming, surfing, I love being in the water. I spend a lot of time on beaches; it's great to be by the sea. I'm not really a 'city person'. I don't really like big cities and I'm not interested in shopping. I only go shopping if I need to buy something, not for fun. And I never go to museums or concerts. I feel happier in the countryside … or on a beach by the sea somewhere. I live in Crete now and that's fine because it's got beautiful beaches.

♀ EXTRA ACTIVITY

Use one of the monologues in 4c as the basis of a dictation activity. Ask students which person they found easier to understand and then tell them that they are going to write down exactly what that person said. Remind them that Tom/Maya speak pretty quickly, so they aren't going to have time to write everything down the first time, but they should listen carefully and write down the most important words they hear, e.g., with Tom, they might write down *grew up, London, always lived, cities* for the first line. Play the recording twice without stopping. Then, put students into small groups and ask them to compare the words they wrote down and put them together to make the full text. Play the recording as many times as necessary, but don't break it down into sentences. Each time, students compare their ideas in their groups and try to put together a bit more of the text. Remind them to use the vocabulary and grammar they already know to help them. Check answers by asking students to come up and write the text on the board one sentence at a time. Play the recording after students write each sentence to correct any mistakes on the board.

d 💬🗨 In pairs or small groups, students talk about where Tom and Maya should and shouldn't go and what they should and shouldn't do in their countries and give reasons, e.g., *Tom should spend some time in Madrid. It's a really exciting city.*

LOA TIP MONITORING

- Monitor both the controlled practice in 4d and the freer practice in 4e and 4f closely, but adjust the way you give feedback in the two stages. During the more controlled practice in 4d, you could choose not to interrupt fluency, but write down any mistakes with *should/shouldn't* and then, after the activity, write these on the board and ask students to correct them. This method of monitoring and correction is best suited to hesitant speakers, who may become even more hesitant if they are constantly interrupted. Alternatively, if your students are more confident speakers, you may prefer to gently interrupt them as they are speaking so that they can self-correct.

- During 4e and 4f, allow students to focus more on fluency, so don't interrupt them – note down mistakes for later correction. However, monitor the activity closely and be available to help students if necessary. When students make a mistake with the content of this lesson, i.e., *should/shouldn't*, try to catch their eyes discreetly so that they can correct their mistakes.

e 💬 Regroup students and put them into pairs, preferably with a student they don't know very well. They then find out what their partner likes and doesn't like doing on holiday.

f 💬 Students use the information they learned in 4e to give their partner advice about what they should and shouldn't do in a city they know.

⊕ ADDITIONAL MATERIAL

Workbook 12B

Photocopiable activities: Grammar 12B, Vocabulary 12B

Documentary video Unit 12 *Travel*

Video worksheet Unit 12 *Travel*

12C EVERYDAY ENGLISH
Is breakfast included?

At the end of this lesson, students will be able to:

- understand informal conversations in which people show surprise, and use appropriate phrases for showing surprise themselves
- understand conversations in which people check in at a hotel and ask for tourist information
- pronounce consonant clusters with /t/ correctly
- use appropriate phrases for checking in at a hotel and asking for tourist information
- maintain a polite conversation with a hotel receptionist

💡 OPTIONAL LEAD-IN

Ask students to look at picture a of Annie, Leo, Martina and Dan on SB pp. 44–45, or project the picture on the board. Put students into pairs and give them three minutes to make a note of everything they can remember about the people. Don't allow them to refer to the Student's Book.

Test how much students can remember by asking them some specific questions, e.g., *What's Leo's surname?* (Seymour) *What TV programme do Martina, Annie and Dan all like?* (Top Cook) *Where does Annie's mum live?* (Bristol).

Tell pairs to look at their notes and write one question to test the rest of the class. They should make the question as difficult as possible. Monitor and point out errors for students to self-correct. Students then take turns asking the class their questions and seeing if the other students know the answer.

1 LISTENING

a 💬 Students talk about the questions in pairs. Take feedback as a class and find out where most students prefer to stay. Encourage students to justify their answers as far as possible.

b ▶12.12 Play Part 1 of the video or the audio recording for students to answer the questions. Check answers as a class.

Answers
1 Martina
2 No, they can't.

Video/Audioscript (Part 1)

MARTINA Wow!

DAN What?

M I've won a competition!

D Have you? Fantastic! What's the prize?

M A weekend for two in Bath. Train travel, hotel, museum tickets …

D Really? That's great.

M But we have to use it the weekend after next.

D So, that's Saturday the 20th?

M Yeah.

D We have to go to John and Charlotte's wedding – remember?

M Oh, no! I forgot about that. Oh what a pity.

D OK, so who do we know who could use the prize?

c ▶12.12 Students watch or listen again for specific details. Play Part 1 of the video or the audio recording again for students to complete the email. Check answers as a class.

Answers
1 Martina
2 two
3 Bath
4 Saturday
5 20

2 CONVERSATION SKILLS
Showing surprise

a Ask students to read the conversation and underline the two ways that Dan shows surprise. Check answers as a class.

> **Answers**
> Have you?
> Really?

b Answer the question as a class. Check students understand that *Really?* can be used to reply to any news.

> **Answer**
> Really?

c ▶ **12.13** Write: *A I love studying English. B Do you?* on the board. Ask students: *What's the subject in the sentence?* (I) and *What's the subject in the question?* (you). Then ask: *How do we form the short question to show surprise?* Elicit that we change *I* to *you* and use the same auxiliary we would use to form a normal question. Individually, students match the sentences with the questions. Play the recording for students to listen and check. Check answers as a class.

> **Answers**
> 1 c
> 2 a
> 3 d
> 4 b

d ▶ **12.13** **Pronunciation** Repeat the recording for students to listen to the intonation movement in the questions. Check the answer as a class.

> **Answer**
> The intonation goes up a lot.

e Individually, students think of two surprising things to tell a partner. Check they understand that they can invent things if they wish.

f 💬 Students work in pairs, taking turns to tell each other their surprising things and respond appropriately. Monitor and make sure students are not only using *Really?* but are also using the more complex short question forms.

> 💡 **FAST FINISHERS**
>
> Ask fast finishers to make sentences about other people and change the short questions in 2c as necessary, e.g., *A Our teacher is going to leave his job next month and travel around the world. B Is he?*

3 LISTENING

a ▶ **12.14** Point to the picture at the bottom of the page and ask students: *Where is this?* (a hotel reception). Elicit ideas for who they think Dan and Martina gave the prize to. Play Part 2 of the video or the audio recording for students to listen to the conversation for general meaning and check their ideas. Check the answer as a class.

> **Answer**
> Annie

> **Video/Audioscript (Part 2)**
>
> **RECEPTIONIST** OK. So here's your keycard. That's room 312 – a single room on the third floor. Turn left as you come out of the lift.
> **ANNIE** Is breakfast included?
> **R** Yes, it's from 7:00 am until 10:00 am in the dining room – just over there.
> **A** Great – thank you. And what time is checkout?
> **R** Checkout is at 11:00 am.
> **A** Thanks.

b ▶ **12.14** Students watch or listen again for specific details. Play Part 2 of the video or the audio recording again for students to complete the guest information card. Check answers as a class by asking individual students to write the correct answers on the board.

> **Answers**
> 1 312
> 2 7:00 am
> 3 10:00 am
> 4 11:00 am

4 USEFUL LANGUAGE
Checking in at a hotel

a Individually, students read the useful expressions and try to remember which two expressions Annie used. If necessary, play Part 2 of the video or the audio recording again. Check answers as a class.

> **Answers**
> 3 Is breakfast included?
> 5 What time is checkout?

b Answer the question as a class.

> **Answers**
> 2 Is there a car park?
> 3 Is breakfast included?
> 4 Is there wi-fi in the room?
> 6 Is there a safe in the room?

c ▶ **12.15** Individually, students complete the conversation. They then check in pairs. Play the recording for students to listen and check. Check answers as a class.

> **Answers**
> 1 've got a reservation for a double room for two nights
> 2 breakfast included
> 3 there wi-fi in the room
> 4 time is checkout

⚙ **LOA TIP DRILLING**

- Drill the conversation in 4c before continuing. Try drilling the conversation chorally with you taking the part of the receptionist and the class taking the part of the guest. Work on the guest's sentences, building them up using any of the techniques you've previously used, e.g., backward drilling (see notes to Lesson 2C, p. 26), drilling in small chunks (see notes to Lesson 6C, p. 73), focusing on the main stress (see notes to Lesson 10C, p. 124).
- Remind students of the importance of both stress and intonation. If necessary, clap out the rhythm of the guest's sentences so that they can then copy it themselves. You can also show students the intonation movement in the conversation using hand gestures to give them a visual reference.

5 PRONUNCIATION Consonant clusters

a ▶**12.16** Play the recording and highlight the consonant clusters with /t/ for students.

b ▶**12.17** Students listen to the sentences and underline the consonant groups with /t/. They check in pairs. Then check answers as a class. Drill the consonant groups.

> **Answers**
> 1 next
> 2 tourist
> 3 left
> 4 tickets

c 💬 In pairs, students practise conversations at a hotel reception. Monitor and correct students' pronunciation as appropriate.

6 LISTENING

a ▶**12.18** Tell students that Annie wants to go on a bus tour. Students watch or listen to Part 3 for specific details. Play the video or the audio recording for students to complete the information. Check answers as a class.

> **Answers**
> 1 outside the hotel
> 2 £15
> 3 (the hotel) reception
> 4 (by credit) card

Video/Audioscript (Part 3)

RECEPTIONIST Good morning.

ANNIE Good morning. Can you help me? Is there a city bus tour I can go on?

R Yes, there is. It leaves from just outside the hotel.

A Great. And how much is it for a ticket?

R It's £15.

A Can I buy a ticket here?

R Yes, you can.

A And can I pay by card?

R No problem.

A OK. I'll have a ticket then, please.

b 💬 Discuss the question as a class.

c ▶**12.19** Play Part 4 of the video or the audio recording for students to check their answer to 6b and answer the questions. Check answers as a class. Ask students: *Do you think Annie and Leo are happy to be in Bath together?*

> **Answers**
> 1 No, they didn't.
> 2 Students' own answers

Video/Audioscript (Part 4)

LEO Annie?

ANNIE Leo?! I don't believe it!

L What are you doing here?

A Well, Martina won this prize – two nights in a hotel. She gave it to me.

L Oh, really? That's interesting. Dan won a prize – a return train ticket. He gave it to me.

A And she also gave me a ticket to the museum tour at ten o'clock.

L Hmm, Dan also gave me a free ticket for the museum tour at ten o'clock.

A Right. So … here we are.

L Yes … here we are. Shall we go in then?

A Why not?

7 USEFUL LANGUAGE
Asking for tourist information

a ▶**12.20** Individually, students match the beginnings with the endings of the questions. Play the recording for students to listen and check. Check answers as a class. Drill the questions.

> **Answers**
> 1 c (Can you help me?)
> 2 d (Is there a city bus tour I can go on?)
> 3 a (How much is it for a ticket?)
> 4 e (Can I buy tickets here?)
> 5 b (I'll have a ticket, please.)

b Students answer the questions, working individually. Check answers as a class and elicit possible alternative questions for 2d.

> **Answers**
> 1 no
> 2 You have to change 2d.
> 3 Is there a museum tour I can go on? / Is there a museum I can visit?

💡 **EXTRA ACTIVITY**

Before students practise the conversation in 7c, put them into pairs to brainstorm other questions that could be useful at a Tourist Information Office, e.g., *Have you got a map of the city centre, please? Can you recommend a good restaurant near here? What time does the museum open/close? Are there any other interesting things to see and do here?* Point out errors for students to self-correct. Take feedback as a class and write students' questions on the board.

c 💬 In pairs, students practise conversations at a Tourist Information Office. Monitor and check students are using the questions in 7a correctly.

8 SPEAKING

a ≫ Divide the class into pairs and assign A and B roles. Student As read the first card on SB p. 135 and Student Bs read the first card on SB p. 137. Students then role play the conversation. Students then read the second card and role play the second conversation. Monitor, but don't interrupt fluency unless students make mistakes with the content of this lesson.

⊕ **ADDITIONAL MATERIAL**

Workbook 12C

Photocopiable activities: Pronunciation (x2) 12C

Unit Progress Test

SKILLS FOR WRITING

You should explore the River Douro

At the end of this lesson, students will be able to:

- understand people talking about their holiday plans
- understand an informal email about places to visit while on holiday
- use appropriate paragraphs and linking words to organise an email
- write a friendly email giving information and advice

♀ OPTIONAL LEAD-IN

Books closed. On the board, write: *Visiting (city)? Take our advice!* Use the name of the city where you're teaching. Give students some examples of things people should do and things they shouldn't do when visiting the city, e.g., *You should go and have coffee at the Hotel Villa Magna – it's beautiful inside. You shouldn't walk down streets late at night because it can be dangerous.* Put students into pairs and give them a few minutes to write as many sentences with *should/shouldn't* as possible. Monitor and point out errors for students to self-correct, and make sure they are using the infinitive of the verb after *should/ shouldn't.* Put pairs together to make groups of four and ask students to share their ideas.

Ask students: *When you travel to a city, how do you usually get information about the place?* Elicit ideas, e.g., from a guidebook, online, by talking to friends, by going to a Tourist Information Office.

1 SPEAKING AND LISTENING

a 💬 Individually, students choose an answer to the question. They then discuss in pairs and explain why. Ask pairs to share their answers with the class.

b 💬 Discuss the questions as a class and find out if any students have visited Porto. Elicit students' ideas about what they can see in the pictures, but don't tell them if they are correct.

♀ EXTRA ACTIVITY

▶ **12.21** Books closed. Before students listen for specific details in 1c, write questions 1–3 on the board: *1 What's the relationship between the two speakers?* (They are colleagues.) *2 Why is the man happy?* (He's decided to go on holiday.) *3 Where's he going to go?* (He's going to go to Porto in Portugal.) Play the recording for students to listen for general meaning and answer the gist questions. Check answers as a class.

c ▶ **12.21** Play the recording for students to listen for specific details and underline the correct answers. They then compare in pairs. Check answers as a class.

Answers
1 online
2 week
3 hostel
4 next
5 Louise

Audioscript

FRED Hey, Louise! Here's your coffee.

LOUISE Thanks, Fred. When's our next meeting?

F In half an hour.

L Good – time to take a break. You're looking happy today.

F Well, yeah, I feel happy.

L Oh – good news?

F Well, yeah, I just booked my next holiday. There was a sale online.

L Exciting! Where are you going to go?

F To Porto – for a week with my brother.

L Oh, great. Is it your first time in Portugal?

F Yes, it is – can't wait to go! We're going to stay in Porto, but we also plan to visit places in the countryside.

L Oh, yeah, I've heard it's really beautiful.

F I found tickets online at a really good price.

L Lucky you!

F Yes, and we're going to stay in this nice hostel with free wi-fi, a kitchen and these incredible sleeping pods – very private. And it's not expensive at all.

L So when are you going to go?

F At the end of next month.

L Early autumn? OK, I think the weather is still good then.

F That's right.

L I actually have a friend, Fabiana, who lives in Porto. You can email her for information so you can plan your holiday. She won't mind helping you. I'll send you her email address.

F Thanks!

d 💬 Put students into pairs to brainstorm questions to ask Fabiana. Ask students to share their questions with the class and write them on the board.

2 READING

a Students read the email quickly and identify the topic that Fabiana doesn't talk about. Check the answer as a class. Ask students to look at their questions from 1d again and ask: *Which of your questions did Fabiana answer?*

Answer
b the hostel

b Tell students to read the email again in detail. Individually, students complete the table. Check answers by copying the table onto the board and asking individual students to come up and complete it.

Answers
1 amazing
2 cafés
3 walks
4 sides
5 culture

♀ FAST FINISHERS

Ask fast finishers to read Fabiana's email again and try to work out exactly what Fred said to her in his email, e.g., *I'm going to spend some time in your home town. Can you help me plan my holiday? What are the top three tourist things to do in Porto?*

3 WRITING SKILLS Paragraph writing

a Look at the email from Fabiana again and check that students understand they need to use the numbers 1–17 to indicate which sentences go in each paragraph. Students then work individually, dividing the email into four paragraphs. Check answers as a class.

> **Answers**
> Paragraph 1: sentences 1 to 3
> Paragraph 2: sentences 4 to 12
> Paragraph 3: sentences 13 to 15
> Paragraph 4: sentences 16 to 17

b Individually, students look at Paragraph 2 and underline the linking words. They then check in pairs. Check answers as a class.

> **Answers**
> First, And secondly, Finally

☼ EXTRA ACTIVITY

Write jumbled sentences 1–3 on the board. Ask students to put them in order and identify the city (Rome):

1 visit / Piazza Navona / should / you / first (First, you should visit Piazza Navona.)
2 the Vatican Museums / to / should / second / go / you (Secondly, you should go to the Vatican Museums.)
3 should / see / you / the Colosseum / finally (Finally, you should see the Colosseum.)

Individually, students then choose another city and write three similar sentences about that city using *first*, *secondly* and *finally*. Monitor and point out errors for students to self-correct. Put students into pairs or small groups to read each other their sentences and guess the cities.

c Students read Alice's email for general meaning and answer the questions. Check answers as a class.

> **Answers**
> 1 She's going to visit your home town.
> 2 She wants to know some interesting things to see and some interesting sporty activities to do.

d Students look at the email again and divide it into three paragraphs. When checking answers, ask students what each paragraph is about (*Paragraph 1: Alice introduces herself and explains why she is writing; Paragraph 2: Alice asks about things to see and do; Paragraph 3: Alice finishes her email*).

> **Answers**
> Paragraph 1: sentences 1 and 2
> Paragraph 2: sentences 3 to 6
> Paragraph 3: sentence 7

✪ LOA TIP REVIEW AND REFLECT

- Before students start on the writing task, ask them to look back through the eleven pieces of writing they've done and note down any mistakes they have made more than once. These might be grammar, vocabulary or spelling errors. Monitor and take the opportunity to point out to students any mistakes you know that they often make in their writing.

- Ask: *How many emails have you written in the D lessons in the Student's Book?* (three – an email invitation in Lesson 3D; an email to a homestay family in Lesson 7D; an email to say thank you in Lesson 9D). Then ask: *How well did you do them? Do you feel confident writing friendly, informal emails?* Elicit an indication of their confidence level.

- Remind students that this is the last piece of writing they are going to do in the class, so it is an excellent opportunity to show how much they have learnt. When correcting students' emails in 4c, you might like to write a comment on them to highlight how much students have progressed and improved during the course, e.g., *In Lesson 3D, you could only use the present tense in your email, but now you can use the past and the future. Good progress!*

4 WRITING

a Students plan their emails, working individually. Monitor and help with vocabulary and give students ideas if necessary. Read the checklist with students before they start writing their emails.

b Individually, students write their emails. If you're short of time, this exercise can be completed for homework. Students could then bring their emails to the next lesson.

c Remind students of the importance of checking their work carefully before handing it in. In pairs, students swap emails and check that their partners can answer 'yes' to all three questions. They then give each other feedback. If they have made any mistakes with the paragraphs or the linking words, or mistakes in any other areas, they prepare a second draft of their emails before giving them to you for correction.

⊕ ADDITIONAL MATERIAL

Workbook 12D

UNIT 12
Review and extension

1 GRAMMAR

a Students complete the sentences with the correct form of *be going to* and a verb from the box. Check answers as a class.

> **Answers**
> 1 's going to have
> 2 're going to move
> 3 'm going to wear
> 4 's going to travel

b Highlight the example question. Students then complete the conversation. Check answers as a class.

> **Answers**
> 2 I'm going to go to New York.
> 3 What are you going to do there?
> 4 Are you going to stay with him?
> 5 he's going to find me a job.
> 6 How long are you going to stay?
> 7 I'm not going to book my flight back.

c Individually, students complete the text. They then check in pairs. Check answers as a class.

> **Answers**
> 1 you shouldn't
> 2 you should
> 3 You should
> 4 you shouldn't
> 5 you should

2 VOCABULARY

a Students underline the correct word in each sentence. Check answers as a class.

> **Answers**
> 1 island; beach
> 2 Desert
> 3 rainforest
> 4 waterfalls
> 5 mountains; glacier

b Individually, students put the words in the correct order to make questions. Check answers as a class. Drill the questions.

> **Answers**
> 1 Have you ever lived abroad?
> 2 Have you planned your next holiday?
> 3 When did you last stay in a hotel?
> 4 Do you always pack your own bags for a holiday?
> 5 Are you staying home this weekend?

c 💬 Students ask and answer the questions in 2b in pairs or small groups.

3 WORDPOWER *take*

a Tell students to close their books. Create a blank word map on the board by drawing a small circle in the middle and adding six lines. At the end of the lines, write: *the number 23, care, five minutes, the first left, your suitcase for you* and *one three times a day before meals*. Ask students: *What word can go before all of these?* Elicit *take* and write it in the circle. Students open their books, look at the phrases in context, and match them with the pictures. Check answers as a class and elicit what the people are talking about.

> **Answers**
> 1 d 2 a 3 f 4 c 5 b 6 e

b ▶ 12.22 Individually, students match the sentences with the uses of *take*. Play the recording for students to listen and check. Check answers as a class.

> **Answers**
> a 4 b 3 c 2 d 1 e 6 f 5

> **Audioscript**
>
> **CONVERSATION 1**
> **MAN 1** Excuse me. How can I get to the railway station?
> **MAN 2** The best way is by bus. You can take the number 23. It's just over there.
> **M1** Oh, OK, thank you.
>
> **CONVERSATION 2**
> **BOY** OK, I'm off on my bike. See you in a bit.
> **WOMAN 1** OK. Don't go on the main road. And please take care!
> **B** Don't worry. … Look, Mum. No hands!
>
> **CONVERSATION 3**
> **WOMAN 2** Excuse me, could I ask you a few questions? It will only take five minutes.
> **MAN 3** Um, I don't really have time.
> **W2** Just five minutes.
> **M3** Well, OK, if it's really just a few questions …
>
> **CONVERSATION 4**
> **MAN 4** Excuse me, is there a cash machine near here?
>
> **WOMAN 3** Er, yes. Go down this road. Then you take the first left. There's a bank on the next corner.
> **M4** So down here, then left.
> **W3** That's right.
> **M4** Thanks.
>
> **CONVERSATION 5**
> **MAN 5** Mrs Green?
> **WOMAN 4** Yes, hello.
> **M5** Hello. I'm Mark Thompson. Very nice to meet you. Let me take your suitcase for you.
> **W4** Oh, thank you.
> **M5** The car's right over there. I hope you had a good flight?
> **W4** Yes, thank you, it was fine …
>
> **CONVERSATION 6**
> **WOMAN 5** OK, here you are, this is for the tablets. Take one three times a day before meals.
> **WOMAN 6** Thank you.
> **W5** And if you aren't better in a week, come and see me again.

c Students complete the sentences, working individually. Check answers as a class.

> **Answers**
> 1 take hours
> 2 take a taxi
> 3 take care
> 4 take the first left
> 5 take my laptop
> 6 take my medicine

> 💡 **EXTRA ACTIVITY**
>
> Ask students to copy and extend the word map on the board, adding in the new expressions in 3c, i.e., *hours* (next to *five minutes*), *a taxi* (next to *the number 23*), *my laptop* (next to *suitcase for you*) and *my medicine* (next to *one three times a day*). Then, ask them to add to the word map any other expressions with *take* they can think of, e.g., *take a moment, take an aspirin, take the train*.

d Put students into pairs to choose two of the uses of *take* and write a conversation. Monitor and point out errors for students to self-correct.

e 💬 In pairs, students practise their conversations. Monitor and correct students' pronunciation as appropriate. Pairs then take turns performing their conversations for the class.

≫ Photocopiable activities: Wordpower 12

> 🔄 **LOA REVIEW YOUR PROGRESS**
>
> Students look back through the unit, think about what they've studied and decide how well they did. Students work on weak areas by using the appropriate sections of the Workbook and the Photocopiable activities.

Ideas for pre-teaching vocabulary

Before reading and listening tasks, it's often necessary to make sure students understand a few key words. This is called 'pre-teaching'. There are a number of ways to do this. Here are some ideas:

Give a definition: Use a short sentence to explain the meaning of a word. You could use the definitions given in the Vocabulary Support boxes throughout the Teacher's Notes. You could also use a learner dictionary to find on-level definitions, e.g., *dive – to swim underwater, usually with breathing equipment* (from *Cambridge Essential English Dictionary*, Second Edition).

Draw/Show a picture or object: One of the easiest ways to teach students new words is to draw a picture on the board or show a picture on an interactive whiteboard, computer or tablet. Using (or drawing) funny and/or interesting pictures is a good way to ensure students remember the new words; e.g., to teach the word *dive*, you could find a picture of a diver with a big shark behind him.

Act it out: With lower-level students, it can be useful to show the word by acting it out, rather than giving definitions which may use above-level vocabulary.

Elicit it: Elicitation allows you to check which words students may already know. Don't tell them the word you want to teach. Elicit it by asking questions or saying open-ended sentences, e.g., *What is the activity when we swim under the ocean and look at fish?* or *When we swim underwater and look at fish, we … ?* (dive).

Fill in the gaps: It's useful for students to see the word in a sentence to understand the context. Write a sentence with a gap on the board (this can be one from the text), e.g., *Cristina _____ in the sea every summer. She loves to see the beautiful fish under the water* (dives). Allow students to guess what word goes in the gap, but don't confirm if they're right or wrong. After they read the text, they can guess again. Then, confirm their answer.

Discussion questions: With more confident students, you can write discussion questions containing the new words on the board. Then, give students one or two example answers to these questions. Students try to guess the meaning. Give more example answers, if necessary. You may then wish to allow students to ask and answer these questions for themselves.

Pre-teaching for listening: You can use any of the above ideas or others you may have to teach new words before students listen. It may also be useful to model the pronunciation of the words so students are used to hearing how they sound. This is particularly useful when a word has an unfamiliar spelling rule. If you don't want to model the word, it can be useful to write the word in IPA on the board (you can find this in all dictionaries).

Extra activities – how to …

Bingo

Use: to revise numbers, times, prices, years, etc.
Dynamic: whole class
Procedure:

- Decide what kind of numbers you want to revise, e.g., *times*, and write 25 of these numbers on the board in numerals, e.g., 10:20, 11:30, 4:55.
- Ask students to draw a bingo grid with four columns and two rows. Tell them to complete it with eight times from the board.
- Play the game as a class. Read out the numbers on the board in random order, taking note of the ones you read aloud.
- Students cross out the numbers on their grid as they hear them. The first student to cross out all their numbers calls out 'Bingo!' Check that the numbers they crossed out were ones you read out, then announce that they're the winner.
- Depending on the kind of numbers you have chosen to revise, you may wish to adjust the difficulty of the activity. For example, if you are working with numbers 1–100, include some pairs of numbers that you know often cause students problems, e.g., 14 and 40 or 16 and 17. With times, you can get students to write out the numbers, e.g., ten twenty, half past eleven, or with *o'clock*, e.g., twenty past ten, a quarter to eleven, five to five.

Spelling competition

Use: to revise general vocabulary and reinforce the alphabet
Dynamic: whole class
Procedure:

- Ask all the students to stand. Nominate a student and give them a word to spell aloud by asking: *How do you spell '(word)'?* Nominate students in turn and ask each one to spell a word, e.g., *hello, book, open*. Choose students at random to prevent students from feeling stressed as they see their turn approaching.
- When a student makes a mistake, they are eliminated and have to sit down. Move on to the next student with the same word until someone spells it correctly.
- Gradually increase the length and difficulty of the words, e.g., *yellow, question, police officer*, leaving words you know students often have problems spelling until later in the activity.
- Eliminated students listen to the words and try to write them down before the nominated student completes the word. They then check their own spelling by listening to the student. The winner of the game is the last student standing.

Grammar auction

Use: to revise a specific grammar area or general grammar
Dynamic: whole class (in teams)
Procedure:

- Prepare 10 to 15 sentences containing either items of grammar from the unit you're currently working on or areas of grammar you know students find problematic. Some of them should be correct and some incorrect.
- Write the sentences on the board and explain what an auction is (when you sell something to the person who offers the most money).

- Put students into small groups and tell them they have £100 and need to buy the correct sentences. In their groups, students discuss which sentences they think are correct and decide which to buy and how much they are prepared to pay for each. Don't help or allow students to look at their notes or the Student's Book.
- Take the role of auctioneer and sell each sentence to the group that offers the most money. Keep track of how much each group has spent. Remind students that once they have spent all their money, they can't buy any more sentences, so they shouldn't spend too much too soon.
- After all the sentences have been sold, go through them one at a time, revealing which are correct and which are incorrect. Ask students to correct the mistakes. The winning group is the one that has bought the most correct sentences. If it's a draw, then the group with the most money left wins.

Guess who?

Use: to practise question forms: present simple, present continuous, past simple, etc.
Dynamic: whole class (with optional group/pair extension)
Procedure:
- Tell students that you are thinking of a person and that they have to guess who it is by asking *yes/no* questions. If you wish to practise a specific grammar area, you might tell students that this person is living (for present tenses), dead (for past tenses), etc. Alternatively, you can use this activity to practise question forms in general by not specifying anything about the person.
- Put students into pairs or small groups to brainstorm possible questions. Specify a total number of questions, between five and ten, for the class to try to guess who you're thinking of. Students then take turns asking you some of the questions they thought of. Make sure you reply only with *yes* or *no* (NOT *Yes, he/she is*) in order not to give away if the person is a man or a woman.
- Students win if they guess the person within the specified number of questions. The teacher wins if students can't guess the person.
- Continue the game either as a class, by asking a student to choose a person and take over for you at the front of the class, or by putting students into pairs or small groups to play.

Memory game

Use: to revise a specific lexical set, e.g., common objects, clothes, food
Dynamic: whole class
Procedure:
- Before the class, decide which lexical set you want to test students on and collect ten objects to take into class, e.g., for *clothes*, some earrings, a raincoat, a scarf, etc. Alternatively, source pictures of these items if you do not have the objects themselves readily available.
- Show each object to the class and elicit the word for it before putting it out of sight, either in a bag or a box or simply behind your desk. Don't allow students to make notes at this point.
- When you've shown students all the objects, put them into pairs and give them three minutes to write down as many of the ten objects as they can remember. Ask them to do so by using the grammar you'd like students to use in their replies, e.g., *What objects have I got?* (to elicit answers with *have got*), *What objects are there in the box?* (*there is / there are*), *What objects did I show you?* (past simple).
- Check answers as a class. Pairs win one point for every object they remember correctly. The pair with the most points wins.

Listing game

Use: to revise a specific lexical set, e.g., food, common objects.
Dynamic: groups
Procedure:
- Before the class, decide which lexical set you're going to test students on and decide the best sentence to lead in to this. If, for example, you want to revise food, you can say: *I went to the shops and I bought … .* However, if students haven't seen the past simple yet, you could adapt the game to revise common objects: *In my bag, I've got …*, etc.
- Demonstrate the activity with the lead-in sentence and then the first item, e.g., *In my bag, I've got a pen.* Gesture to a student to repeat your sentence and add an item, e.g., *In my bag, I've got a pen and a notebook.* They nominate the next student who repeats the sentence and adds another item, and so on until the list is too long to remember.
- Put students into groups of three to five to play together. Depending on your students, you may wish to adjust the difficulty of the activity. For example, ask students to include the number of each item, e.g., *… three textbooks, a notebook and five pens.* Or if students have studied quantifiers, you can suggest they use these in their answers, e.g., *… some textbooks, a notebook and a lot of pens.*

Backs to the board

Use: to revise a specific lexical set or general vocabulary
Dynamic: whole class (in teams)
Procedure:
- Put students into small groups of four to five. If possible, mix more and less confident students so no group is noticeably stronger or weaker than another.
- Tell students in each group to sit close together, leaving space between the groups so they can't easily hear one another. Tell one student in each group to sit with their back to the board and the others to sit so that they can see the board.
- Explain that you're going to write a word or phrase on the board and that the students who can see the board have to communicate the meaning to the student who can't. They can use any method to do this, such as drawing pictures, miming, using synonyms and providing simple explanations. However, use of a language other than English will mean they are disqualified.
- When the student(s) with their back(s) to the board think they know the word, they raise their hand(s). Ask the first student to raise their hand for the word and if they're correct, award their group a point. If they aren't, the other teams continue. Any student who shouts out the answer is also disqualified.
- The winning group is the one who has the most points at the end of the game.

Tennis

Use: to revise specific word pairs, e.g., opposite adjectives, past simple / past participle forms, collocations
Dynamic: pairs
Procedure:
- Explain which lexical set you're going to work on, e.g., *adjectives.* Demonstrate the activity by asking a confident student to help you. Say an adjective, e.g., *old,* and ask the student to respond with the opposite, i.e., *new.* The student continues with a different adjective and you respond with its opposite.
- Tell students that just like in a real game of tennis, it's important not to pause for a long time. If one of the students pauses too long between items, they lose that round, e.g., in *A old B new – good A bad – big B ummm ahhh … small,* **B** would lose.
- Put students into pairs to play together. Tell them they should continue for as long as possible. If one student loses the round, they start again.

Acknowledgements

The authors and publishers acknowledge the following sources of copyright material and are grateful for the permissions granted. While every effort has been made, it has not always been possible to identify the sources of all the material used, or to trace all copyright holders. If any omissions are brought to our notice, we will be happy to include the appropriate acknowledgements on reprinting and in the next update to the digital edition, as applicable.

Screenshots are taken from the Student's Book and Documentary videos.

Typeset by QBS Learning.

Corpus
Development of this publication has made use of the Cambridge English Corpus (CEC). The CEC is a computer database of contemporary spoken and written English, which currently stands at over one billion words. It includes British English, American English and other varieties of English. It also includes the Cambridge Learner Corpus, developed in collaboration with the University of Cambridge ESOL Examinations. Cambridge University Press has built up the CEC to provide evidence about language use that helps us to produce better language teaching materials.

English Profile
This product is informed by English Vocabulary Profile, built as part of English Profile, a collaborative programme designed to enhance the learning, teaching and assessment of English worldwide. Its main funding partners are Cambridge University Press and Cambridge Assessment English and its aim is to create a "profile" for English, linked to the Common European Framework of Reference for Languages (CEFR). English Profile outcomes, such as the English Vocabulary Profile, will provide detailed information about the language that learners can be expected to demonstrate at each CEFR level, offering a clear benchmark for learners' proficiency. For more information, please visit www.englishprofile.org.

CALD
The Cambridge Advanced Learner's Dictionary is the world's most widely used dictionary for learners of English. Including all the words and phrases that learners are likely to come across, it also has easy-to-understand definitions and example sentences to show how the word is used in context. The Cambridge Advanced Learner's Dictionary is available online at dictionary.cambridge.org.

This page is intentionally left blank.

This page is intentionally left blank.

This page is intentionally left blank.

This page is intentionally left blank.

This page is intentionally left blank.